PENGUIN CLASSICS

NOTES ON THE STATE OF VIRGINIA

Thomas Jefferson, the third president of the United States, was born in Shadwell, Virginia, on April 13, 1743. A member of the landed Virginia gentry, Jefferson studied liberal arts at the College of William and Mary before studying parliamentary law. He was admitted to the bar in 1767. Jefferson served in the Virginia House of Burgesses from 1769 until 1775, when he joined the revolutionary Continental Congress. That same year he authored one of the great political documents in history, the Declaration of Independence. In 1783 he also drafted the constitution for the state of Virginia. Jefferson was a key figure in the early years of the United States government. He was appointed George Washington's first secretary of state in 1790 and served as vice president under John Adams from 1797 until 1801. He began his two terms as president in early 1801. Throughout his life, Jefferson continued to study parliamentary law. His great work on the topic, *A Manual of Parliamentary Practice*, was published in 1801. He also showed great interest in the studies of science, philosophy, and architecture and designed several buildings, including his home, Monticello, near Charlottesville, Virginia. In a final tribute to higher education, Jefferson began to outline the creation of the University of Virginia in 1815. Jefferson married Martha Wayles Skeleton in 1772, and together they had four daughters: Martha (b. 1772), Jane Randolph (b. 1774), Mary (b. 1778), and Lucy Elizabeth (b. 1781). He died on July 4, 1826.

Frank Shuffelton is a professor of English and American literature at the University of Rochester. His other publications include *Thomas Hooker, 1586–1647* (1977); *Thomas Jefferson: A Comprehensive Annotated Bibliography of Writings About Him, 1826–1980* (1983); *Thomas Jefferson, 1981–1990: An Annotated Bibliography* (1992); ed., *A Mixed Race: Ethnicity in Early America* (1993); and ed., *The American Enlightenment* (1993).

NOTES ON THE STATE OF VIRGINIA

THOMAS JEFFERSON

EDITED WITH AN
INTRODUCTION AND NOTES BY
FRANK SHUFFELTON

PENGUIN BOOKS

PENGUIN BOOKS
Published by the Penguin Group
Penguin Putnam Inc., 375 Hudson Street,
New York, New York 10014, U.S.A.
Penguin Books Ltd, 27 Wrights Lane,
London W8 5TZ, England
Penguin Books Australia Ltd, Ringwood,
Victoria, Australia
Penguin Books Canada Ltd, 10 Alcorn Avenue,
Toronto, Ontario, Canada M4V 3B2
Penguin Books (N.Z.) Ltd, 182–190 Wairau Road,
Auckland 10, New Zealand
Penguin India, 210 Chiranjiv Tower, 43 Nehru Place,
New Delhi 11009, India

Penguin Books Ltd, Registered Offices:
Harmondsworth, Middlesex, England

First published in France 1785
This edition with an introduction and notes by Frank C. Shuffelton
published in Penguin Books 1999

3 5 7 9 10 8 6 4

LIBRARY OF CONGRESS CATALOGING IN PUBLICATION DATA
Jefferson, Thomas, 1743–1826.
Notes on the State of Virginia / Thomas Jefferson; edited with an
introduction and notes by Frank Shuffelton.
p. cm.—(Penguin classics)
Includes bibliographical references (p.).
ISBN 0 14 04.3667 7 (pbk.)
1. Virginia. 2. Jefferson, Thomas, 1743–1826—Political and
social views. I. Shuffelton, Frank, 1940– . II. Title.
III. Series.
F230.J5012 1998
975.5'03—dc21 98-28819

Printed in the United States of America
Set in Stempel Garamond
Designed by Sabrina Bowers

CONTENTS

INTRODUCTION

On November 30, 1780, Governor Thomas Jefferson of Virginia wrote to Charles-François D'Anmours, the French vice consul in Philadelphia, "I am at present busily employed for Monsr. Marbois without his knowing it, and have to acknolege to him the mysterious obligation for making me much better acquainted with my own country than I ever was before."[1] Jefferson's obligation was the consequence of his having received earlier that autumn a list of twenty-two questions drawn up by François Marbois, the secretary of the French legation to the United States. Marbois wished to collect information on each of the thirteen states for a report to his superiors, and he had distributed his questionnaire in Philadelphia to various possible informants, including Joseph Jones, a member of the Virginia congressional delegation, who in turn sent a copy of it, written in his own hand, to Jefferson. Jones would have recognized the particular suitability of Jefferson as the person best able to answer the range of Marbois's questions about Virginia, which were by turns historical, political, scientific, and ethnographic; at the same time, he would have known that Jefferson was the Virginian perhaps most capable of taking on the challenging task of speaking about the complicated circumstances and prospects of this largest of the thirteen original states. Jefferson's credentials as a man of learning had been marked by his election in January 1780 to the American Philosophical Society, the leading scientific organization in the young nation, and Jones also knew that Jefferson's interests in Virginia extended to its vast western land claims, which in 1780 included all of the present states of West Virginia and Kentucky as well as large parts of Ohio, Indiana, and Illinois. Thus Jefferson's fitness for answering Marbois's queries was measured both by the extent and variety of his knowledge and by the extent and variety of the land that he knew about. In the coming months and years this knowledge and experience would transform mere answers to a questionnaire into *Notes on the State of Virginia*, a classic statement about the promise and perils of the American experiment.

Jefferson was born on April 13, 1743, at Shadwell, Virginia, one of the plantations of his father, Peter Jefferson, who was an owner of extensive lands as well as a surveyor, mapmaker, and magistrate. Through his mother, Jane Randolph Jefferson, Thomas was connected to one of the most prominent land-owning and office-holding families in colonial Virginia. Jefferson remarked that his father's "education had been quite neglected; but being of strong mind, sound judgment and eager after information, he read much and improved himself."[2] During his lifetime Peter Jefferson saw that his son's education was more regular than his own had been, sending him to study with the Reverend William Douglas, whom Jefferson later remembered as "but a superficial Latinist, less instructed in Greek," although he was grateful that Douglas taught him French. After his father's death in 1757, Jefferson studied for two years with the Reverend James Maury, "a correct classical scholar," before going off to the College of William and Mary, where he met Dr. William Small, the professor of mathematics. The Scottish-born Small, a layman unlike the other professors at the college, introduced Jefferson to "my first views of the expansion of science and of the system of things in which we are placed." After the dismissal of the college's professor of moral philosophy, Small also taught him logic, ethics, rhetoric, and belles lettres. Small not only opened up the intellectual world of the European enlightenment to the young Jefferson, he also introduced him to an accomplished group of friends in Williamsburg who taught him perhaps more than any of his formal academic subjects. Along with Small, Jefferson found himself often at the "familiar table" of Governor Francis Fauquier, which also included George Wythe, the most learned lawyer of his time in Virginia. The conversations of this party of four were for Jefferson occasions of delight and instruction, a situation in which knowledge was not simply lore pulled out of dusty volumes in a library but a condition of sociability and friendship. Throughout his life Jefferson always saw learning as having a social end, whether as the means to bring about material improvements in the conditions of human life or as the stuff of conversations that for him made up a considerable part of the human pursuit of happiness.

After Small returned to England in 1762, Jefferson left college without taking a degree and began to study law under Wythe's direction, where, like his father, he read much. When he was only a few years past his own period of studying for the bar, he made light of the studying involved, telling the father of one would-be lawyer, "the only help a youth wants is to be directed which books to read, and in what order to read them."[3] Twenty years later he recommended a much more weighty period of study, putting lists of books into three columns and recommending that the student "should read those in the first column till 12. oclock every day: those in the 2d. from 12. to 2. those in the 3d. after candlelight, leaving the afternoon for exercise and recreation, which are as necessary as reading: I will rather say more necessary, because health is worth more than learning."[4] And twenty-four years later he recommended a truly daunting course and schedule of study for young men aspiring to become lawyers, in which time for recreation seems to have dropped out of the picture. He advised students to devote their morning hours before 8 A.M. to physical studies, ethics, religion, and natural law. After this initial session of mental stretching, they should read law from 8 until noon, then politics from noon until 1 P.M. In the afternoon they should read history, and "From Dark to Bed-time" belles lettres, criticism, rhetoric, and oratory. He prescribed a small library of titles, including Cicero, Lavoisier on chemistry, Locke on both human understanding and government, Vattel on natural law, Coke's *Institutes*, Blackstone's *Commentaries*, Gibbon, and Shakespeare. Before beginning any of this reading, the prospective student should already have mastered Latin and French as well as mathematics and natural philosophy, the latter two because they "are so useful in the most familiar occurrences of life, and are so peculiarly engaging and delightful as would induce every person to wish an acquaintance with them."[5] Jefferson's recommendations for students of the law become increasingly rigorous over the years because he became ever more aware of the need for citizens of a republic to be well versed in the legal history and codes that defined the very possibility of citizenship. We might suspect that Jefferson's own reading was most like the second course of study he recommended because while he knew too much law to be merely an off-handed reader, he also found time, unlike the student immersed in the legal grind of the third recommended course, to attend balls and frolics, visit friends, and flirt with the daughters of the Virginia gentry. Nevertheless, if he followed anything approaching his own recommendations, he led himself through a course of study more rigorous than anything most young men, then or now, would have encountered as university students. If Joseph Jones turned to Governor Jefferson with Marbois's questionnaire because of his public eminence, his reputation as a man of deep and varied scholarship equally supported his qualifications to speak for his state. Jones's choice was more significant than he thought, for, as Jefferson's development of an increasingly sophisticated and specific course of study for legal education demonstrates, he was not a person to make short work of an interesting problem, and in his hands Marbois's queries evolved into a text that became one of the most important and imaginative expressions of the cultural life of the early American republic.

After all, Jefferson never intended his learning to be merely a private hobby, but a preparation for taking part in the civic and political life of Virginia. Toward the end of 1765 he took his examination for the bar and sometime afterward began a successful law practice. He was elected to the Virginia House of Burgesses in 1769, where he served until it was closed by the Revolution in 1776, and he began to take a leading role in its deliberations as the political situation became more heated. In 1774 he proposed a set of instructions for the Virginia delegates to the first Continental Congress that was published later in the year as *A Summary View of the Rights of British America*.

The following year Jefferson went to Philadelphia himself as a delegate to Congress, and in June 1776, he was appointed to the committee to draft the Declaration of Independence, a document whose ultimate fame owes perhaps as much to Jefferson's wide reading in poetry and rhetoric as it does to his knowledge of law and political theory. He returned to Virginia after independence was declared, took up his seat in the state's revolutionary House of Delegates, and drafted a proposed new state constitution, although it was not adopted. He also became a member of a three-man "Committee of Revisors," charged with overhauling the laws of the Commonwealth of Virginia; the 126 laws proposed by the revisors were not enacted as a group, but among them was the "Statute for Establishing Religious Freedom" that Jefferson saw as one of the greatest accomplishments of his life. Finally, in 1779 he was elected to the first of two terms as governor of Virginia, a position less impressive for the political power it conveyed than for the respect it signified for its occupant.

Jefferson's 1780 letter to the Chevalier D'Anmours suggests that Marbois's inquiry had touched him deeply, stimulating him to organize and develop his impressive range of knowledge in order to become "much better acquainted with my own country." But it also touched him in some more secret part of himself that he typically concealed in letters and conversation. His obligation was "mysterious" certainly because Marbois, who had never met him, did not yet know that Jefferson had taken on the responsibility for answering his queries, but it is also tantalizing to discern, in his obvious pleasure of having taken on a "mysterious obligation," something like the gestures of secrecy that he took at other moments in his life when his most private feelings or sensibilities might be exposed. Jefferson, after all, destroyed his correspondence with his mother and with his wife after their deaths; he concealed emotionally or politically sensitive information behind codes and ciphers, and he typically refused to expose his sensitivities by responding to public attacks upon his character or actions. His enthusiastic letter to D'Anmours radiates his excitement over the project of enlightenment he has undertaken, a project that he sees as an energetic intellectual process, full of growth, hope, and boundless promise; for him, some of the mysteriousness of his "obligation" surely must have been in experiencing the aesthetic pleasure of imaginative discovery. This passion for learning that was at once factual and visionary, empirical yet always tried out under hypothetical schemes and explanations, at times threatened to consume him, for, as he told D'Anmours, "His queries as to this country . . . I take every occasion which presents itself of procuring answers to."

If Joseph Jones picked Jefferson to answer Marbois—to speak

for Virginia, "this country"—because of his knowledge and his experience, Jefferson paradoxically may have thrown himself into this public "obligation" of writing because of the troubled state of his private life between 1780 and 1784, during which he left for France on a diplomatic mission. His troubles began shortly after he wrote the exuberant letter to D'Anmours; at the end of December 1780, British military forces under the command of Benedict Arnold invaded Virginia, and, until his term as governor expired on June 2, 1781, Jefferson, without much in the way of resources, anxiously tried to organize the state's defenses. British forces moved seemingly at will up and down the James River, capturing and then abandoning Richmond, the state's capital. But the ultimate humiliation came on June 4, 1781, when Banastre Tarleton's troops overran Charlottesville, drove the House of Delegates over the Blue Ridge, and invaded Monticello itself, nearly capturing Governor Jefferson. A week later the Delegates voted to conduct an inquiry into Jefferson's behavior as governor, and although he was exonerated in December 1781 of negligence when they voted a resolution "to obviate and remove all unmerited Censure," he was deeply hurt by criticism of his administration, describing it to his friend James Monroe as "a wound on my spirit which will only be cured by the all-healing grave."[6] Adding injury to insult, he was recovering during these same months from the effects of a fall from his horse.

In the autumn of 1781, after his temporary departure from public life, Jefferson finished his answers to Marbois's queries and sent them off on December 20. He had seemingly fulfilled his "mysterious obligation" during the months in which he suffered a deep sense of pain and humiliation over the accusations of official negligence that had been laid against him, but he was at the end neither of his unhappiness nor of his work on Marbois's queries. While he continued to gather information from an informal circle of friends and acquaintances in order to improve and extend his text, serious work on the project was put aside in the fall of 1782. His wife, Martha Wayles Jefferson, had given birth to their sixth child in May 1782 but never regained her health. Jefferson watched by her bedside as she lingered throughout the summer, and her death on September 6 devastated him. His friends sought to distract him from his grief by persuading him to go to Europe as a commissioner to negotiate the treaty ending the war with Britain, but before he was able to leave, news arrived that a provisional treaty had already been reached.

Jefferson had recovered from his wife's death sufficiently by mid-November to write the Marquis de Chastellux about his plans to come to Philadelphia in the following month and discuss, among other subjects, the answers to Marbois. Thus, at more or less the same time that he may have been destroying the intimate correspondence he had exchanged with Martha, Jefferson was turning away from humiliation and sorrow to the public project of writing himself into a better acquaintance with his own country. The "Advertisement" to the 1787 London edition of *Notes on the State of Virginia* apologized for any deficiencies in them, but Jefferson went on to say, "To apologize for this by developing the circumstances of the time and place of their composition, would be to open wounds which have already bled enough." If Jefferson intended to close his wounds by writing and publishing *Notes*, he had set himself to a task whose end he would never see. Herman Melville's Ishmael might have been speaking Jefferson's case when he exclaimed, both ruefully and exuberantly, "This whole book is but a draught—nay, but the draught of a draught."[7]

On the same day in 1781 that he sent his manuscript to Marbois, Jefferson wrote his friend Charles Thomson, the secretary of Congress, "I received notice from the secretary of the American Philosophical society some time ago that they had done me the honour of appointing me a counsellor of that body. . . . In framing answers to some queries which Monsr. de Marbois sent me, it occurred to me that some of the subjects which I had then occasion to take up, might, if more fully handled, be a proper tribute to the Philosophical society, and . . . induced me to recur to you as my antient friend, to ask the favor of you to peruse those answers, and to take the trouble of communicating to me your opinion whether any and which of the subjects there treated would come within the scope of that learned institution, and to what degree of minuteness one should descend in treating it: perhaps also you would be so friendly as to give me some idea of the subjects which would at any time be admissible into their transactions."[8]

Rather than concluding his project, sending the manuscript answers to Marbois and Thomson only initiated a new stage of research and writing. Jefferson subsequently also circulated a copy of his manuscript among his friends and wrote to people as varied as his neighbor Thomas Walker, George Rogers Clark, who seized western British military outposts during the Revolution on joint behalf of the nation and of Virginia, and Thomas Hutchins, the Geographer of the United States. The information they supplied found its way into the text of *Notes*, sometimes silently absorbed in the at times almost overwhelming flood of Jefferson's information, and sometimes recognized in a footnote or a reference. Thomson's extensive responses became a part of the text on their own standing when Jefferson included them as the first "appendix" and inserted numbers in his text to show where Thomson's comments should be brought in. Early in 1784, Jefferson informed a friend, "I found some things should be omitted, many corrected, and more supplied and enlarged. They are swelled nearly to treble bulk. Being now too much for M.S. copies I think the ensuing spring to print a dozen or 20 copies."[9] Reconceived as a possible offering to the Philosophical Society, Jefferson's *Notes* was simultaneously becoming a text that could be viewed as a product of an invisible, informal learned society of his own devising, one that answered his needs for both information and friendship.

Since he had not gone to Europe as planned in late 1782, Jefferson was reelected as a delegate to Congress from Virginia in 1783 and 1784, and he worked on several legislative projects there that also enhanced his continuing revision of *Notes*. His proposal of a decimal system of money appeared in print as "Notes on the Establishment of a Money Unit, and of a Coinage for the United States," and he included it as an appendix in some copies of the first printing of *Notes on the State of Virginia*.[10] More important was his service on the committee appointed to plan a form of government for the western territories that Britain had surrendered in the Treaty of Paris that ended the War of the Revolution.[11] Virginia had earlier maintained extensive claims on these western lands, including all of the present state of Kentucky and large parts of Ohio, Indiana, and Illinois, but it ceded its claims on March 1, 1784. At the same time, Jefferson submitted a report he had drafted on "A Plan of Government for the Western Territories" that, after discussion in Congress and revision, was enacted as the Ordinance of 1784. The plan's central principle, that new states with republican governments should be formed out of the western territories and admitted to the Union on an equal standing to the original thirteen states, guided subsequent territorial expansion of the United States, but Jefferson's proposed states, with names like Assenisipia and Polypotamia, were rejected. His plan, however, relied on his extensive geographical knowledge of the territory concerned, and this information is reflected in Queries I and II of *Notes*, particularly the latter, with its sprawling account of the rivers of the western territories. In Query I Jefferson mentions Virginia's 1784 cession of claims to western territories as a condition of its own boundaries, but Query II, on rivers, is shaped by his state's earlier claims to a western empire. By preserving that vision here, even as he was working in Congress on a plan for independent governments for that territory that had already been given up, Jefferson implicitly enlarged the scope of his manuscript, transforming his vision from the merely local picture that Marbois wished to acquire to that of a landscape that was already national. His manuscript had subtly expanded its significance as it trebled in bulk.

In the busy months of spring 1784 Jefferson had also begun to inquire about the possibility of having his work printed but discovered that the cost of doing it in Philadelphia would be too high. However, following his appointment on May 7, 1784, as Minister Plenipotentiary to France, and before his departure, he wrote Thomson that he might "have a few copies struck off in Paris if there be an English Printer there."[12] By the end of the year, having at last made the voyage to France that he had planned eighteen months earlier, Jefferson had arranged with printer and bookseller Philippe Denis Pierres to have a small edition of 200 copies printed. After it was completed on May 10, 1785, he began to distribute them to a select list of European and American friends. The earliest copies he augmented with Charles Thomson's comments and with the "Draught of a Fundamental Constitution for the Commonwealth of Virginia," and these appendices appeared in subsequent editions as well. Some copies also had the "Notes on the Establishment of a Money Unit," but this appendix was not included in any later printings.

Jefferson continued to revise the main text even after Pierres had delivered the printed copies. In addition to adding the appendix on money and coinage to some copies, he also heavily revised four passages by replacing pages with new cancel sheets he had printed by Pierres in late 1786 and early 1787. At about this time he probably also had printed for inclusion "An Act for Establishing Religious Freedom," which had been passed by the Virginia Assembly in January 1786. Finally, he arranged to have engraved and printed a map, based on the famous work of his father, and he included this with a few copies.

Jefferson's invisible society of philosophical friends had contributed to *Notes*, either unobtrusively—such as the efforts, hidden from view in Appendix No. III, of James Madison and others who had some hand in the statute for religious freedom —or openly, such as Charles Thomson's comments, all of which supplied a harmonizing support for Jefferson's own words. He distributed this first edition to friends, acquaintances, and men of learning over a period of several years, and copies sent out later were layered over with increasing amounts of information and suggestion. The 1785 publication was less a completion of Jefferson's project than it was one more step in a continuously enlarging course of inquiry.

The trace of secrecy that had colored Jefferson's original sense of performing a "mysterious obligation" continued to reveal itself; in the dedication of each copy, he asked the recipient not to lend it to any person "on whose care and fidelity he cannot rely to guard them against publication." Jefferson wrote his friend the Marquis de Chastellux that he did not wish to make public "the strictures on slavery and on the constitution of Virginia . . . at least till I know whether their publication would do most harm or good. It is possible that in my own country these strictures might produce an irritation which would indispose the people towards the two great objects I have in view, that is the emancipation of their slaves, and the settlement of their constitution on a firmer and more permanent basis."[13] He might have added his comments on freedom of religion, which would be used against him by Federalist ministers during the election of 1800, because as of the publication of *Notes*, the Virginia Assembly had not yet passed his statute for religious freedom. Writing earlier to Madison, however, he had added more personal grounds for restricted circulation of his book: ". . . but there are sentiments on some subjects which I apprehend might be displeasing to the country, perhaps to the assembly or to some who lead it. I do not wish to be exposed to their censure."[14] Old wounds clearly were still fresh in memory.

His caution was effective for little more than nine months, when Louis François Barrois, a French bookseller, managed to obtain a copy of *Notes* from a recipient who had died, and he was preparing to publish a French translation "in the most injurious form possible," or so Jefferson informed Madison. Unable to stop Barrois, he tried to make the best he could of the situation by endorsing a translation by the Abbé André Morellet, a member of the Acadèmie Française, whom Jefferson knew and respected. Once a French edition appeared, however, there would be nothing to prevent a translation back into English, possibly doubling translation-related errors. Morellet's translation did not satisfy Jefferson's hopes in any case. His desire for a limited circulation of *Notes* had always been somewhat ambivalent; in the same letter to Madison enjoining him to restrict access to the book, Jefferson seemingly contradicted himself by envisioning a larger audience. "They were at first intended only for Marbois," he wrote Madison. "when I had enlarged them, I thought first of giving copies to three or four friends. I have since supposed they might set our young students into a useful train of thought."[15] After compiling seven pages of errors from Barrois's 1787 French edition, Jefferson offered *Notes* to John Stockdale, a London bookseller who had earlier proposed to publish an edition.

Stockdale gave Jefferson a chance to see that *Notes on the State of Virginia* would circulate in a reasonably correct form and with the author's latest improvements. Jefferson had revised four passages from the first edition by having new pages printed and substituted for the original text; there were also several smaller errors he wished to correct, and he wished to add more material to the book, notably a map and a third appendix containing the statute on religious freedom that had appeared in only some copies. The Stockdale edition, along with the major addition in 1800 of Appendix No. IV, provided the text followed by all subsequent printings before 1850 and most printings after that. Jefferson added the fourth appendix about the murder of the family of Logan, whose famous speech Jefferson had included in Query VI; as it had earlier, sensitivity to possible public censure became a factor in moving him to answer Luther Martin's attacks in the press upon his credibility. Martin, a former Maryland attorney general and Michael Cresap's son-in-law, attacked Jefferson's account of the Logan affair, particularly the blame placed on Cresap, and Jefferson once again began to collect new evidence with which to support or revise his text. In the letter to Governor John Henry of Maryland which opened the new appendix, he explained that had Martin "thought proper to suggest to me, that doubts might be entertained of the transaction respecting Logan," he would have felt "obliged by the enquiry" to answer personally, but since Martin "chose to step at once to the newspapers," Jefferson chose to answer through the supposedly more impersonal medium of print.

In the course of assembling the materials of Appendix No. IV, however, Jefferson only made more explicit the movement from secrecy to publicity that had marked the twenty-year-long *Notes* project. The private communications and contributions of his invisible philosophical society, a select group of gentlemen, were increasingly displaced by a public conversation about truth and justice carried on by ordinary citizens of the republic, represented here as the men of the West who testified about the 1774 murder of Logan's family. The evolving *Notes on the State of Virginia* was becoming an increasingly democratic text, and not only because after 1800 its author, now President Jefferson, was the nation's representative first democrat.

Although the printed text based on Stockdale and including the fourth appendix of 1800 was the version Jefferson's contemporaries were familiar with, he continued to revise and tinker with *Notes*. After his retirement from the presidency, he contemplated revising and enlarging *Notes* once again, but as he told a correspondent in 1809, "inquiries are still to be made, which will be more correct in proportion to the length of time they are continued. It is not unlikely that this may be through my life." He annotated his personal copy of the Stockdale edition by writing in the margins and by pasting in slips of paper, whole pages in one or two cases, with corrections, comments, further information, and citations. It is almost as if he had come to identify his life with the project; so long as he could pursue his enquiries, so long as could he maintain the "mysterious obligation" that had become his life. By 1815, however, he had given up the thought of publishing a new edition in his lifetime. Responding to a Philadelphia publisher of geographical books and maps, he stated, "I begin to see that it is impracticable for me. nearly forty years of additional experience in the affairs of mankind would lead me into dilations ending I know not where. . . . the work itself indeed is nothing more than the measure of a shadow, never stationary, but lengthening as the sun advances, and to be taken anew from hour to hour. it must remain therefore for some other hand to sketch it's appearance at another epoch."[16] Recognizing his own mortality, Jefferson came to see the invisible philosophical society that supported the beginnings of his project as extending in space and time beyond the mere limits of his personal identity. The life of *Notes on the State of Virginia* would not be his own life but the continuing discussion, the endless enquiries and critiques that originated with his attempt in 1780 to answer François Marbois's questions.

From the beginning, Jefferson ambitiously attempted to take on large issues of political, scientific, and moral significance that were merely implied by Marbois's queries, and his first "dilations" on the affairs of mankind transformed *Notes* from the local report that the Frenchman had hoped for into a scientific inquiry of a larger, American significance. Jefferson's impulse to expand the scope of his project first manifested itself in his revision and rearrangement of Marbois's original twenty-two queries into the twenty-three queries that now define the chapters of the book. Marbois's queries seem to be in somewhat random order, but Jefferson's rearrangement conducts his reader from a discussion of the landscape and natural features of Virginia through a discussion of the state's social characteristics—what we might describe as its civilization—ending in the final chapters with discussions of economic import and of the construction of a legal and historic tradition that established, in the spirit of the common law, the ultimate cultural boundaries of the state of Virginia. There are problems, however, with seeing Jefferson's reordering of the queries as simply ideological. Although this ordering seems to be in accord with a pattern of Enlightenment thinking that had been repeated from Montesquieu on—that geography and climate determined the forms of life, perhaps even imposing limits on human culture and civilization itself—it was precisely to refute this theory that Jefferson wrote his longest chapter in the book. On the other hand, we can see that the order of the chapters reflects some of the demands circumstances placed upon his attention as well as his greater readiness to write about some subjects over others. Thus he opens with the queries about the state's boundaries, rivers, and mountains because, when he began his answer to Marbois, he was also preoccupied with the issues surrounding Virginia's cession of its western claims. He places the queries about manufactures, commerce, money, and public revenue at the end of his book because he felt himself least prepared to write about these as he began his project; writing to Marbois on March 4, 1781, he was diffident about taking up these topics, particularly "the Commerce of the state, a subject with which I am wholly unacquainted."[17] By the time he comes to these queries, he seems to feel that he has gathered sufficient information to contribute a response, although even so his discussion of manufactures is less an account of the subject than an evasion, an eloquent statement about why Virginia should remain an agrarian society.

At the same time, Jefferson's concerns in any particular query are difficult to neatly categorize on a spectrum leading from nature to culture; discussions of land and landscape fall in turn under scientific, aesthetic, and economic perspectives. In discussing the western territories, Jefferson was sensitive to political issues that were unresolved at the time of his writing, and beneath his cataloguing of bodies of water lies a political agenda about the future of the West. Virginia was willing to cede her Ohio land claims to the nation, but she wanted to protect the titles of land she had sold or granted there, and she wanted to protect her commercial interests in the western settlements. Jefferson's discussion in Query II, "Rivers," laid an implicit claim to this vast territory, partly through the mere act of listing and describing, and partly through mentioning Kaskaskia and Vincennes, a subtle reminder that this territory had come into American hands during the Revolution because of the heroic efforts of an expedition from Virginia led by George Rogers Clark. The "Rivers" chapter closes with a discussion of the most likely routes for commerce between West and East and argues for the geographic and strategic advantages of the route from the Ohio River to the Potomac. In the early republic, commerce and development followed water routes, either rivers or canals, and a discussion of rivers was never mere travelogue but always the opening for an economic and political discussion.[18] Similarly, Jefferson's discussion of manufactures in Query XIX does not mention the iron-making business of his correspondent Isaac Zane, much less any other manufacturing enterprises, but instead becomes the moment when he indulges in a sentimental rhapsody on the value of a life spent cultivating one's own land. "Corruption of morals in the mass of cultivators is a phenomenon of which no age nor nation has furnished an example," he writes. "It is the mark set on those, who not looking up to heaven, to their own soil and industry, as does the husbandman, for their subsistence, depend for it on the casualties and caprice of customers." Thus, Jefferson's imaginative progress through *Notes on the State of Virginia* was dialectic rather than linear, playing over the complexity of his subjects in order to tease out a variety of meanings and possibilities of life in Virginia. As he brought his learning to bear on the long project of writing *Notes*, Jefferson found life in America more and more interesting and, in the process, the "hidden wounds" hinted at in the "Advertisement" remained closed.

But if the order of the queries, as Jefferson finally presented them in the published version of *Notes*, might have followed his life and the order of writing rather than an ideologically driven theoretical model, there is no doubt that at the center of his book he confronted what seemed to him to be the central challenge posed by Enlightenment science to the progress of human liberty. If Jefferson began his book with a consideration of the West because that was occupying his mind, he may have written the next set of chapters because the queries had been sent to him by a Frenchman seeking information for the French government, and, in 1780, it was French scientific thinking, particularly in the realm of biology or natural history, that seemed to cast shadows on the possible future of civilization in America. Indeed, Marbois's nationality may have been a sort of intellectual lightning rod for Jefferson, whose ultimate target was Georges Louis Leclerc, Comte de Buffon, director of the *Jardin du Roi* in Paris and author of the multivolume *Histoire Naturelle, Gènèrale et Particuliére*. Buffon was perhaps the most influential and widely known natural historian of the late eighteenth century.[19] His *Histoire* was encyclopedic in its scope and authoritative in reputation, but for Americans his conclusions were troubling. Buffon contended that New World animals were without exception smaller than their Old World counterparts (no elephants, rhinoceroses, hippopotamuses, camels, or giraffes in America), that species of quadrupeds were fewer in the New World (fewer than 70 to the Old World's 130, by his count), and that domestic animals introduced into America were diminished in size and quality from their European ancestors. Following up on Montesquieu's claims for the importance of climate to forms of life and culture, Buffon argued that nature in the New World was inherently hostile to life because it was colder and more humid, filled with moist, unhealthy vapors, where "everything languishes, decays, stifles."[20] Only insects and reptiles seemed to flourish in this climate, according to Buffon. More important, the environmental unsuitability for animal life also affected human beings, and as an example of what human life in America might become, Buffon described the typical Indian as so torpid as to be barely human. "Take from him hunger and thirst, and you will destroy at the same time the active cause of all his movements; he will remain either standing there stupidly or recumbent for days at a time,"[21] he wrote. Buffon's ideas were developed, often in more dogmatic terms than he had originally used, by the abbés Cornelius de Pauw and Guillaume Thomas François Raynal, the latter of whom Jefferson would meet in Paris. America thus described hardly seemed to be a promising landscape in which to attempt to establish a progressive society that claimed it would outgrow the old, backward political and social forms of the Old World. Jefferson sought to rebut this theory of natural decay both as a defense of his country's honor and, more important for a new nation with few allies, to create a confidence in the country's future that would encourage military and financial support from European countries—above all from France. The queries on rivers and seaports contained a commercial message, and the queries that followed would demonstrate that this was a country with a future worth investing in.

If at times the argument Jefferson waged with Buffon seems to be inordinately concerned with elephants and mammoths, this is because the French naturalist was much taken with sheer size as a measure of strength, beauty, and courage, theorizing that in unhealthy climates the abject "moist" species, such as insects and frogs, were more fecund than the larger, more "noble" species. Jefferson confronts Buffon most directly in Query VI on "Productions mineral, vegetable and animal," although the following chapters on "Climate" and "Aborigines" continue in a less explicit manner the preceding debate with French theory. Because Buffon's theories had several internal contradictions, which Jefferson readily points out in Query VI, the rebuttal pursues several threads of discourse rather than a single, focused assault. Jefferson counters the French theories of New World unhealthiness and degeneration by foregrounding aesthetic responses to American landscape; presenting the large variety of American species; establishing the presence of large animals in the New World; redeeming the cultural attainments of humans in America, among both the "savages" (as Buffon termed them) and the European settlers. Finally, by suggesting that climate is not immutable but can change over time, in part as a result of cultivation of the land. Jefferson operates here as a traveling theorist, taking up one issue and one kind of discourse after another, slowly, methodically drawing a noose around Buffon's assertions.

Jefferson sets up his critique by introducing the reader to several New World "wonders," because Buffon informs his distinctions between the climates and the life-forms of the Old and New Worlds with aesthetic and moral qualities. Thus, the accounts of the passage of the Potomac through the Blue Ridge, the natural bridge, and the burning spring and syphon fountains in the fourth, fifth, and sixth queries respectively affirm the American landscape as invested with wonders both sublime and curious. He begins Query VI with a discussion of mineral resources that leads him into a discussion of fossils as possible evidence for great deluges in the past, suggesting that the entire world was once much more moist and presumably more hostile to life. After thus subtly undermining Buffon's theory of the inevitable decline of life in a wet climate, Jefferson moves on to document the variety of New World species with a series of lists that constitute one of the major difficulties of this text for modern readers. The bare lists of animals and birds now might seem merely something to skip over, but these compiled details respond to one of Buffon's inconsistencies. As the author of a work intending to survey all of natural history, he could be quite dismissive of specific details ("The best crucible is the mind," he maintained, and people without "true talent" were competent to examine the "little objects" already explained by the natural historian of "genius"). Jefferson's lists are a methodological critique of Buffon that demolishes his assertions about the smaller number and size of New World species by amassing specific data collected by a community of industrious observers.

Jefferson annotated Query VI more heavily than any other in *Notes*, and if many of these refer to specific comments in the work of Buffon and his colleagues, they also bring into the discussion the work of other scientific observers, such as Peter Kalm, Francisco Clavigero, and Antonio de Ulloa. Where Jefferson solicited information from friends and acquaintances for the earlier chapters on the West, here his library fulfills the role played by his circle of informants. In all of these considerations he maintains an attitude of skepticism that is one of his chief weapons against Buffon's dogmatic assertions. If wonders excite admiration, they can also provoke questions about their status in the natural order of things; while both men rely on informants, the American is more aware finally of the complex problems of trust and caution necessarily involved when using second-hand information. Jefferson even went to considerable effort to mobilize his friends to provide him with various artifacts, including a moose skeleton and hide so that he could present Buffon with physical evidence of the size of American animals. He also counters Buffon's claims about the small size of New World animals by discussing the evidence for the mammoth as a distinctly American species, one fully the equal in size to the Old World elephant.

He argues most interestingly in Query VI, when he also defends the culture of the American Indian against the aspersions of Buffon and the Abbè Raynal. Here he takes on the French natural historian most directly by quoting a long passage in French that he first dismisses as derived from "fables," then refutes detail by detail. Since in the passage Buffon directs his scorn toward the moral development of American "savages," Jefferson brings his argument here to a climax by presenting the already well-known speech of the Mingo chief Logan, which is simultaneously an example of "eminence in oratory" equal to the best examples of the art from the Old World and of language charged with grief, moral seriousness, and dignity, all of which Buffon denied to the Indians.

Jefferson does not idealize the Indians into noble savages, however; he admits, for example, "The women are submitted to unjust drudgery." But where Buffon saw this as a sign of inherent moral inferiority, Jefferson describes it as an accident of history, as a consequence of the native American's position at this moment in a movement over time from barbarism to civilization, for "It is civilization alone which replaces women in the enjoyment of their natural equality." Buffon's belief that the "superior" animals were fixed and unchanging in form showed the resistance on his part to any tendency toward historicism, and Jefferson's insistence on placing the culture of red and white Americans in the context of historical change forms a critique of the Frenchman's method as important as the use of overwhelming lists of specific facts. Logan's speech is all the more remarkable coming from a representative of a not-yet-literate society, and, looking at the culture of transplanted Europeans, Jefferson argues that their own cultural achievements are equally remarkable in view of the brief history of their society, perhaps most remarkable in view of their much smaller population. Figures like General Washington, astronomer David Rittenhouse, and physicist Benjamin Franklin give "hopeful proofs of genius" at the same time as it seems that Great Britain's "glory is fast descending to the horizon." Jefferson implicitly charges Buffon and the Abbè Raynal with having written *Histoires* that lack a sense of history, a sense of the change of culture and land over time that must be taken into account when attempting a "scientific" description of culture.

Without referring to him specifically, Jefferson's response to Buffon continues in the next chapter, Query VII on "Climate." Again, Jefferson's seeming fondness for compiling statistics on rainfall and temperature might seem slightly cranky to readers without a compelling interest in the history of the science of meteorology, but it fulfills two important functions in *Notes*: First, it continues the refutation of Buffon's assertions about America's cold and humid climate, and, second, it collects information valuable to American farmers who want to know what crops to plant and when. With this chapter Jefferson in effect turns from questions about the impact of nature on culture to considerations of the impact of culture on nature, perhaps especially human nature, and sets the trajectory for the rest of his book. In contrast to his outburst of national chauvinism that seeped through in the exultation over Britain's fading glory, Jefferson does not portray a simple movement from barbarism to civilization in America in the second half of *Notes*. While he describes the progress of liberty and democratic government based upon the consent of the governed, he admits a troubling undertone that suggests a different story. For example, his discussion in Query XI on Virginia's Indians is on the one hand a triumph of eighteenth-century anthropological speculation and practice. He discusses the problematic status of questions about the origins of the human presence in the New World, examines the Indians' recent history in Virginia, offers one of the first descriptions of a stratigraphic excavation (one preserving the different layers of deposit laid down over time) of an archaeological site, and takes up the imperfect state of knowledge about Indian languages. However, while this description pays serious attention to the value of Indian history and culture as a worthy and important object of rational enquiry, it at the same time reduces the Indian subjects, the living men and women, to numbers on a list. And if Virginia is advancing in civilization and science, the chapter on "Aborigines" does not explicitly link that to the very obvious fact that the Indians were disappearing. The Chickahominies were gone; the Mattaponies had "three or four men only," and "Of the *Nottoways*, not a male is left." By having made, in the earlier queries, historical change out to be a part of the natural world, Jefferson can present the Indian disappearance as a natural and inevitable phenomenon and thus obscure the role of the European invasion in their demise. The transplantation of English law and culture to the New World, described at the beginning of Query XIII on the "Constitution," thus becomes a story of progress from the intrigues of the Elizabethan court that doomed Sir Walter Raleigh to the promise of the revolutionary revision of Virginia's laws described at the end of Query XIV. To Jefferson, the disappearance of the aborigines becomes a mere accident of history that displaced an interesting and admirable people who unfortunately still lived by the codes of a less sophisticated, less civilized culture. Interesting as their mounds are, they do not count as "monuments" in any sense which François Marbois would understand.[22]

If the narrative of the advance of civilization forced Jefferson to admit to losers in the shape of the vanished and vanishing Indians, the discussion of Virginia's laws in Query XIV involved Jefferson in difficulties that were to haunt the reputation of *Notes* long after his death. By his own reckoning, among the signs of civilized progress represented in Jefferson's own proposed revision of Virginia's laws were statutes in support of education, freedom of religion, a more equitable distribution of land bequeathed in wills, and the abolition of slavery. This latter was Jefferson's most radical proposition for legal reform in Virginia, but, unlike the others, it had not been brought forward to the legislature because of significant political opposition that had yet to be overcome. With his discussion in *Notes* of blacks and slavery that followed upon the mention of the proposed law, however, Jefferson did not greatly help his case for abolition. His forthright condemnation of the institution of slavery was wrapped around a description of blacks that concluded, however tentatively "as a suspicion only," that blacks "are inferior to the whites in the endowments both of body and mind."

He fell into this racist argument for several reasons. When he had earlier argued, against Buffon, that the New World climate and landscape was no bar to American political and cultural progress, he could point to the appearance of both red and white men of genius like Logan and Benjamin Franklin. Eloquence and science were thriving in the New World, and its cultivation by industrious farmers was changing its climate. But if Virginia's laws were so progressive, its legal culture so protective of liberty, Jefferson had to confront the difficult fact that descendants of the Africans did not seem to be partaking of his narrative of civilized progress. (It did not help that he rejected as inadequate what evidence he might have used, namely the writings of Phillis Wheatley and Ignatius Sancho.) Caught in this apparent contradiction, he took up Buffon's line of argument that he had earlier rejected, about necessary connections between body and mind, in order to explain Africans' apparent failure to excel in the arts and sciences. He first discounted the aesthetic qualities of the black race as compared to the "superior beauty" of the white, an intellectual move strikingly like Buffon's imputation of "nobility" to large animals and "cowardice" to small ones. He proceeded to other bodily differences, moved on to the crucial issue of emotional and intellectual differences, and concluded that after the abolition of slavery blacks "must be removed beyond the reach of mixture" with the whites.

The specific context in which he discussed blacks complicated his case. He had introduced his discussion of Indians in the context of an account of "Natural Productions," but he discussed blacks in the context of "Law," which immediately set limits on the kind of informed witness he had earlier received from correspondents and books. In all European colonies the discourse of the law had focused specifically on black bodies and addressed the possibility of blacks as producers of culture only insofar as to prevent them from creating it. Published accounts of travel in the colonies during the seventeenth and eighteenth centuries almost always focused on the laws regulating slavery and had very little to say about the lives of the slaves themselves beyond occasional brief mentions of their love for music and handiness with herbal medicines. The discourse of law in which Jefferson contextualized his discussion of blacks would not have encouraged him to inquire into the conditions of their private lives, or the content of their songs and stories, in the way in which the considerable literature about the American Indians had informed his earlier discussion. Because the slave codes considered blacks primarily as bodies under discipline and as property, they left open considerable space for the anxious play of white fantasies about miscegenation. Jefferson's comments about the necessity of removing freed black slaves beyond the reach of mixture with the white settlers consciously or unconsciously encouraged those fantasies for some readers and outraged others.

Finally, it has been difficult for many readers not to conclude that Jefferson was driven by underlying prejudices;[23] for them his "secret" has been not a patriotic obligation to his country, not an intellectual commitment to learning, but racism. Neither the term nor the concept "racism" was available to Jefferson's contemporaries, but a number of his acquaintances thought his description of black capacities was unjustified. David Ramsey, the historian of the Revolution, wrote to him, "You have depressed the negroes too low,"[24] and a fellow member of the American Philosophical Society commented, "These remarks upon the genius of the African negro appear to me to have so little foundation in true philosophy that few observations will be necessary to refute them."[25] Most of Jefferson's contemporary readers did not take vigorous exception to his description of blacks, however, but in later generations his words were more frequently deeply troubling. The problem was, of course, that the author of this account of supposed black inferiority was also the author of the Declaration of Independence, with its ringing words about human equality, and his scandalous language here also seemed to contradict his repeated attacks elsewhere in *Notes* on the institution of slavery. Indeed, one legacy of the book was its later selective use by the abolitionist movement.

Jefferson's criticism of slavery was as offensive to many Southern planters as his comments on black human nature were to readers like the black abolitionist David Walker. One anonymous Southern reader, for example, wrote in the margin next to one of Jefferson's antislavery passages, "This kind of morbid sensibility in our great men is the salient down from which abolitionism of the North took life and motion."[26] On the other hand, Walker found Jefferson's remarks on black inferiority profoundly dangerous because they came from a man "of such great learning combined with such excellent natural parts." Because "the assertions of such a man will [not] pass away into oblivion," he appealed to men of color to buy a copy of *Notes* and put it into the hands of their sons so that they might learn what calumnies they must confront in their struggle for respect.[27] However, Abraham Lincoln more than once cited antislavery passages from Query XVIII, on "Manners," claiming that "The principles of Jefferson are the definitions and axioms of a free society."[28]

The contradictions inherent in Jefferson's discourse about race and slavery have reappeared in the twentieth century as well. The sometimes exaggerated apotheosis of Jefferson as a high-minded champion of democracy that emerged in the years of the New Deal, World War II, and the Cold War inevitably produced harsh critiques in the 1960s, and through the present, that have focused on his comments on the nature of blacks.

While the controversies about his treatment of race have arisen mostly in the twentieth century, *Notes on the State of Virginia* provoked controversy enough in Jefferson's own lifetime, as he had feared, particularly for his comments in Query XVII, "Religion." His defense of freedom of religion, particularly the insouciant and memorable line about it doing "no injury for my neighbour to say there are twenty gods or no god," called down from political opponents in the elections of 1800 and 1804 furious charges of atheism in the White House. His praise of Logan's speech also generated public debate in which at least one issue was his generous treatment of Logan (whom his critics preferred to think of as "a blood-stained savage"). Controversy, particularly when it descended to the invective and scandal that characterized political contests in Jefferson's time, always pained him, sometimes to the extent of bringing on one of his debilitating migraine attacks. Yet controversy was precisely what he expected, perhaps even desired. When he began to expand his conception of the readership for *Notes*, he could hardly have expected that his scheme for distributing copies among the College of William and Mary students would not have begun debates. But these would have been debates conducted according to the conventions of a civilized exchange of opinion and argument, such as he had carried on in Query VI with Buffon and Raynal where the assumption of a shared commitment to truth prohibited personal censure. Like that exchange, a model of the conversation of enlightenment, the debates he hoped for would have been part of a process of drawing nearer to truth and to a democratic society. His account of Virginia's constitution and laws points to work that remained to be done and statutes yet to be enacted, but moving forward the process of improvement is unthinkable to him without the informed discussions of the people and their representatives. However, the actual political life of the early republic, with its emergent battles of party and section, was to be far less civil than he had hoped for, and was one very important reason why after 1800, he continued to develop *Notes* in the privacy of his library by making revisions and annotations that would not appear until after his death. What began as a secret obligation concluded in secrecy as well, at least for the author of *Notes on the State of Virginia*.

In the meantime, his book had become part of the new nation's stock of images of itself, going through at least eighteen editions before his death in 1826. It was and remains a challenging text in both form and content. Seeming at times to be a collection of discrete elements held together only by a nominal relationship to something called "Virginia," *Notes* seems at other times to be perhaps a form of writing that awaited a new technology, straining at print's linear organization of knowledge with its allusions, its illustrations and charts, and its enormous array of footnotes that use three different systems of placement in the text. One wonders what Jefferson would have done with a computer and the ability to make his own Web site. At the same time, many of the issues that Jefferson saw as unresolved in 1785 because people, including himself, lacked sufficient information or will to move them forward are still unresolved. Readers of *Notes on the State of Virginia* will find evidence of what has been the best and worst about America, the painful secrets that it has tried to keep from itself, and the aspirations to create a society in which freedom and human dignity find a place. What readers make of this will be their own responsibility, because Jefferson's ultimate hope was for a community of responsive and enlightened readers.

A NOTE ON THE TEXT

The first edition of *Notes on the State of Virginia* appeared in Paris in 1785 in a small edition of two hundred copies. Although Jefferson tried to restrict circulation of the book, a copy fell into the hands of a French bookseller, and a translation by the Abbé Morellet into French appeared in early 1787. Unhappy with this translation, Jefferson authorized the London printer John Stockdale to publish an English edition that appeared later in 1787. This edition included a number of revisions Jefferson had made to the 1785 printing, as well as the appendices containing Charles Thomson's comments, the "Draught of a Fundamental Constitution for . . . Virginia," and the "Act for Establishing Religious Freedom." The Stockdale edition also became the basis for all other printings of *Notes* in Jefferson's lifetime, but in 1800 he published separately a fourth appendix, *Relative to the Murder of Logan's Family*, after his account of these events had been sharply criticized. This appendix was included in printings after 1801. Jefferson extensively annotated his personal copy of the Stockdale edition, apparently with the intention of bringing out a new edition, but these annotations remained unpublished until 1853. In that year, Joseph W. Randolph included them in an edition of *Notes* he published in Richmond. Paul Leicester Ford later used this text to prepare the version of *Notes* he included in his 1894 edition of *The Notes of Thomas Jefferson.* Randolph and Ford kept Jefferson's annotations as footnotes, but in 1954 William Peden prepared an edition, working directly from Jefferson's personal copy, that included the annotations in the text, producing a work that supposedly conforms to the author's final intentions. This is a work of careful scholarship, but it presents a text read by no one in Jefferson's lifetime, nor in most of the nineteenth century for that matter.

The text that follows, based on the 1787 Stockdale edition and the 1800 appendix about the murder of Logan's family, aims to present a version of *Notes on the State of Virginia* that would have been familiar to most readers of the editions printed before

1954. It also seeks to indicate the nature of Jefferson's continuing attention to the text. His annotations in his personal copy of *Notes* are included here but are presented in the endnotes, where their source is identified. The attempt to present an edition of *Notes* that gives some sense of the 1787 printing's appearance entails some difficulties, however. This edition does not include the map based on the one by Joshua Fry and Jefferson's father, Peter Jefferson, and the fold-out chart listing the Indian tribes native to Virginia has been printed as part of the regular pagination. Second, Jefferson used a daunting array of quotations in languages other than English, both in the original text and in his annotations in his personal copy. Quotations of material in non-English languages that were a part of the 1787 Stockdale edition have been kept as they appeared there and in the early reprints, and translations are offered in the endnotes. Quotations in non-English languages in Jefferson's annotations in his personal copy, however, have been routinely translated with a notice of the languages in which he originally quoted.

Finally, reproducing Jefferson's own system of printed annotations to the Stockdale edition is challenging because he used at least three different systems. Numbers within parentheses, such as (1), refer to the comments of Charles Thomson contained in the first appendix; this system has been retained here. Jefferson also marked his own footnotes with various typographical symbols, such as *, †, and §; these marks are also retained, and the notes at the foot of the page are always Jefferson's own as they appeared in the Stockdale edition. In addition, Jefferson put abbreviated references to authoritative texts, such as those by Buffon, Linnaeus, and others, in the margins, particularly in Query VI; these have been moved to the endnotes in the interest of avoiding an excessively cluttered look. Since numbers within parentheses always refer to Thomson's comments that appear in the first appendix, the present editor's endnotes are linked to the text by page number and key words. Jefferson's original manuscript, now in the Massachusetts Historical Society, was also consulted in preparing this edition, and major differences between it and the printed text have been noted.

SUGGESTIONS FOR FURTHER READING

BIBLIOGRAPHY

Shuffelton, Frank. *Thomas Jefferson: A Comprehensive Annotated Bibliography of Writings About Him, 1826–1980.* New York: Garland, 1983.

———. *Thomas Jefferson: An Annotated Bibliography, 1981–1990.* New York: Garland, 1992.

Sowerby, E. Millicent. *A Catalogue of the Library of Thomas Jefferson.* 5 vols. Washington, D.C.: Library of Congress, 1952–59.

BIOGRAPHY

Ellis, Joseph E. *American Sphinx: The Character of Thomas Jefferson.* New York: Knopf, 1997.

Malone, Dumas. *Jefferson and His Times.* 6 vols. Boston: Little, Brown, 1948–81.

Peterson, Merrill D. *Thomas Jefferson and the New Nation.* New York: Oxford University Press, 1970.

SCHOLARSHIP AND CRITICISM

Breitwieser, Mitchell R. "Jefferson's Prospect." *Prospects* 10 (1985): 315–52.

Cohen, I. Bernard. *Science and the Founding Fathers: Science in the Political Thought of Jefferson, Franklin, Adams, and Madison.* New York: W. W. Norton, 1995.

Dumbauld, Edward. *Thomas Jefferson and the Law.* Norman, Okla.: University of Oklahoma Press, 1978.

Ferguson, Robert. "Mysterious Obligation: Jefferson's *Notes on the State of Virginia.*" In *Law and Letters in American Culture.* Cambridge: Harvard University Press, 1984.

Finkelman, Paul. "Thomas Jefferson and Slavery: The Myth Goes On," *Virginia Magazine of History and Biography* 102 (1994): 193–228.

Hellenbrand, Harold. "Roads to Happiness: Rhetorical and Philosophical Design in Jefferson's *Notes on the State of Virginia.*" *Early American Literature* 20 (1985): 3–23.

Manning, Susan. "Naming of Parts; or, The Comforts of Classification:

Thomas Jefferson's Construction of America as Fact and Myth." *Journal of American Studies* 30 (1996): 345–64.

Medlin, Dorothy. "Thomas Jefferson, Andre Morellet, and the French Version of *Notes on the State of Virginia.*" *William and Mary Quarterly* 35 (1978): 85–99.

Miller, Charles A. *Jefferson and Nature: An Interpretation.* Baltimore: Johns Hopkins University Press, 1988.

O'Callaghan, E. B. "The Revised Proofs of Jefferson's *Notes on Virginia.*" *Historical Magazine* 13 (1868): 96–98.

Onuf, Peter S., ed. *Jeffersonian Legacies.* Charlottesville: University Press of Virginia, 1993.

Quinby, Lee. "Thomas Jefferson: The Virtue of Aesthetics and the Aesthetics of Virtue." *American Historical Review* 87 (1982): 337–56.

Simpson, Lewis P. "Land, Slaves, and Mind: The High Culture of the Jeffersonian South." In *Mind and the American War*, 1–32. Baton Rouge: Louisiana State University Press, 1989.

Verner, Coolie. *A Further Checklist of the Separate Editions of Jefferson's Notes on the State of Virginia.* Charlottesville: Bibliographical Society of the University of Virginia, 1950.

———. "The Maps and Plates Appearing with the Several Editions of Mr. Jefferson's 'Notes on the State of Virginia.' " *Virginia Magazine of History and Biography* 59 (1951): 21–33.

———. "Mr. Jefferson Distributes His *Notes*: A Preliminary Checklist of the First Edition." *Bulletin of the New York Public Library* 56 (1952): 159–86.

Wilson, Douglas L. "Thomas Jefferson and the Character Issue." *Atlantic Monthly* 270 (November 1992): 57–74.

NOTES ON THE STATE OF VIRGINIA

ADVERTISEMENT

The following Notes were written in Virginia in the year 1781, and somewhat corrected and enlarged in the winter of 1782, in answer to Queries proposed to the Author, by a Foreigner of Distinction, then residing among us. The subjects are all treated imperfectly; some scarcely touched on. To apologize for this by developing the circumstances of the time and place of their composition, would be to open wounds which have already bled enough. To these circumstances some of their imperfections may with truth be ascribed; the great mass to the want of information and want of talents in the writer. He had a few copies printed, which he gave among his friends: and a translation of them has been lately published in France, but with such alterations as the laws of the press in that country rendered necessary. They are now offered to the public in their original form and language.

FEB. 27, 1787.

CONTENTS

QUERY I

AN EXACT DESCRIPTION OF THE LIMITS AND BOUNDARIES OF THE STATE OF VIRGINIA?

Limits

Virginia is bounded on the East by the Atlantic: on the North by a line of latitude, crossing the Eastern Shore through Watkins's Point, being about 37°. 57'. North latitude; from thence by a streight line to Cinquac, near the mouth of Patowmac; thence by the Patowmac, which is common to Virginia and Maryland, to the first fountain of its northern branch; thence by a meridian line, passing through that fountain till it intersects a line running East and West, in latitude 39°. 43'. 42.4" which divides Maryland from Pennsylvania, and which was marked by Messrs. Mason and Dixon;[1] thence by that line, and a continuation of it westwardly to the completion of five degrees of longitude from the eastern boundary of Pennsylvania, in the same latitude, and thence by a meridian line to the Ohio: On the West by the Ohio and Missisipi, to latitude 36°. 30'. North: and on the South by the line of latitude last-mentioned. By admeasurements through nearly the whole of this last line, and supplying the unmeasured parts from good data, the Atlantic and Missisipi, are found in this latitude to be 758 miles distant, equal to 13°. 38'. of longitude, reckoning 55 miles and 3144 feet to the degree. This being our comprehension of longitude, that of our latitude, taken between this and Mason and Dixon's line, is 3°. 13'. 42.4". equal to 223.3 miles, supposing a degree of a great circle to be 69 m. 864 f. as computed by Cassini.[2] These boundaries include an area somewhat triangular, of 121525 square miles, whereof 79650 lie westward of the Allegany mountains, and 57034 westward of the meridian of the mouth of the Great Kanhaway. This state is therefore one third larger than the islands of Great Britain and Ireland, which are reckoned at 88357 square miles.

These limits result from, 1. The antient charters from the crown of England. 2. The grant of Maryland to the Lord Baltimore, and the subsequent determinations of the British court as to the extent of that grant. 3. The grant of Pennsylvania to William Penn, and a compact between the general assemblies of the commonwealths of Virginia and Pennsylvania as to the extent of that grant. 4. The grant of Carolina, and actual location of its northern boundary, by consent of both parties. 5. The treaty of Paris of 1763. 6. The confirmation of the charters of the neighbouring states by the convention of Virginia at the time of constituting their commonwealth. 7. The cession made by Virginia to Congress of all the lands to which they had title on the North side of the Ohio.[3]

QUERY II

A NOTICE OF ITS RIVERS, RIVULETS, AND HOW FAR THEY ARE NAVIGABLE?

Rivers and Navigation

An inspection of a map of Virginia, will give a better idea of the geography of its rivers, than any description in writing. Their navigation may be imperfectly noted.

Roanoke, so far as it lies within this state, is no where navigable, but for canoes, or light batteaux; and, even for these, in such detached parcels as to have prevented the inhabitants from availing themselves of it at all.

James River, and its waters, afford navigation as follows.

The whole of *Elizabeth River,* the lowest of those which run into James River, is a harbour, and would contain upwards of 300 ships. The channel is from 150 to 200 fathom wide, and at common flood tide, affords 18 feet water to Norfolk. The Strafford, a 60 gun ship, went there, lightening herself to cross the bar at Sowell's point. The Fier Rodrigue, pierced for 64 guns, and carrying 50, went there without lightening. Craney island, at the mouth of this river, commands its channel tolerably well.

Nansemond River is navigable to Sleepy hole, for vessels of 250 tons; to Suffolk, for those of 100 tons; and to Milner's, for those of 25.

Pagan Creek affords 8 or 10 feet water to Smithfeild, which admits vessels of 20 ton.

Chickahominy has at its mouth a bar, on which is only 12 feet water at common flood tide. Vessels passing that, may go 8 miles up the river; those of 10 feet draught may go four miles further, and those of six tons burthen, 20 miles further.

Appamattox may be navigated as far as Broadways, by any vessel which has crossed Harrison's bar in James river; it keeps 8 or 9 feet water a mile or two higher up to Fisher's bar, and 4 feet on that and upwards to Petersburgh, where all navigation ceases.

James River itself affords harbour for vessels of any size in Hampton Road, but not in safety through the whole winter; and there is navigable water for them as far as Mulberry island. A 40 gun ship goes to James town, and, lightening herself, may pass to Harrison's bar, on which there is only 15 feet water. Vessels of 250 tons may go to Warwick; those of 125 go to Rocket's, a mile below Richmond; from thence is about 7 feet water to Richmond; and about the center of the town, four feet and a half, where the navigation is interrupted by falls, which in a course of six miles, descend about 80 feet perpendicular: above these it is resumed in canoes and batteaux, and is prosecuted safely and advantageously to within 10 miles of the Blue ridge; and even through the Blue ridge a ton weight has been brought; and the expence would not be great, when compared with its object, to open a tolerable navigation up Jackson's river and Carpenter's creek, to within 25 miles of Howard's creek of Green briar, both of which have then water enough to float vessels into the Great Kanhaway. In some future state of population, I think it possible, that its navigation may also be made to interlock with that of the Patowmac, and through that to communicate by a short portage with the Ohio. It is to be noted, that this river is called in the maps *James River,* only to its confluence with the Rivanna; thence to the Blue ridge it is called the Fluvanna; and thence to its source, Jackson's river. But in common speech, it is called James river to its source.

The *Rivanna,* a branch of James river, is navigable for canoes and batteaux to its intersection with the South West mountains, which is about 22 miles; and may easily be opened to navigation through those mountains to its fork above Charlottesville.

York River, at York town, affords the best harbour in the state for vessels of the largest size. The river there narrows to the width of a mile, and is contained within very high banks, close under which the vessels may ride. It holds 4 fathom water at high tide for 25 miles above York to the mouth of Poropotank, where the river is a mile and a half wide, and the channel only 75 fathom, and passing under a high bank. At the confluence of *Pamunkey* and *Mattapony,* it is reduced to 3 fathom depth, which continues up Pamunkey to Cumberland, where the width is 100 yards, and up Mattapony to within two miles of

Frazer's ferry, where it becomes 2½ fathom deep, and holds that about five miles. Pamunkey is then capable of navigation for loaded flats to Brockman's bridge, 50 miles above Hanover town, and Mattapony to Downer's bridge, 70 miles above its mouth.

Piankatank, the little rivers making out of *Mobjack bay* and those of the *Eastern shore,* receive only very small vessels, and these can but enter them.

Rappahanock affords 4 fathom water to Hobb's hole, and 2 fathom from thence to Fredericksburg.

Patowmac is 7½ miles wide at the mouth; 4½ at Nomony bay; 3 at Aquia; 1½ at Hallooing point; 1¼ at Alexandria. Its soundings are, 7 fathom at the mouth; 5 at St. George's island; 4½ at Lower Matchodic; 3 at Swan's point, and thence up to Alexandria; thence 10 feet water to the falls, which are 13 miles above Alexandria. These falls are 15 miles in length, and of very great descent, and the navigation above them for batteaux and canoes, is so much interrupted as to be little used. It is, however, used in a small degree up the Cohongoronta branch as far as Fort Cumberland, which was at the mouth of Wills's creek: and is capable, at no great expence, of being rendered very practicable. The Shenandoah branch interlocks with James river about the Blue ridge, and may perhaps in future be opened.

The *Missisipi* will be one of the principal channels of future commerce for the country westward of the Alleghaney. From the mouth of this river to where it receives the Ohio, is 1000 miles by water, but only 500 by land, passing through the Chickasaw country. From the mouth of the Ohio to that of the Missouri, is 230 miles by water, and 140 by land. From thence to the mouth of the Illinois river, is about 25 miles. The Missisipi, below the mouth of the Missouri, is always muddy, and abounding with sand bars, which frequently change their places. However, it carries 15 feet water to the mouth of the Ohio, to which place it is from one and a half to two miles wide, and thence to Kaskaskia from one mile to a mile and a quarter wide. Its current is so rapid, that it never can be stemmed by the force of the wind alone, acting on sails. Any vessel, however, navigated with oars, may come up at any time, and receive much aid from the wind. A batteau passes from the mouth of Ohio to the mouth of Missisipi in three weeks, and is from two to three months getting up again. During its floods, which are periodical as those of the Nile, the largest vessels may pass down it, if their steerage can be ensured. These floods begin in April, and the river returns into its banks early in August. The inundation extends further on the western than eastern side, covering the lands in some places for 50 miles from its banks. Above the mouth of the Missouri, it becomes much such a river as the Ohio, like it clear, and gentle in its current, not quite so wide, the period of its floods nearly the same, but not rising to so great a height. The streets of the village at Cohoes[4] are not more than 10 feet above the ordinary level of the water, and yet were never overflowed. Its bed deepens every year. Cohoes, in the memory of many people now living, was insulated by every flood of the river. What was the Eastern channel has now become a lake, 9 miles in length and one in width, into which the river at this day never flows. This river yields turtle of a peculiar kind, perch, trout, gar, pike, mullets, herrings, carp, spatula fish of 50 lb. weight, cat fish of an hundred pounds weight, buffalo fish, and sturgeon. Alligators or crocodiles have been seen as high up as the Acansas.[5] It also abounds in herons, cranes, ducks, brant, geese, and swans. Its passage is commanded by a fort established by this state, five miles below the mouth of Ohio, and ten miles above the Carolina boundary.

The Missouri, since the treaty of Paris,[6] the Illinois and Northern branches of the Ohio since the cession to Congress, are no longer within our limits. Yet having been so heretofore, and still opening to us channels of extensive communication with the western and north-western country, they shall be noted in their order.

The *Missouri* is, in fact, the principal river, contributing more to the common stream than does the Missisipi, even after its junction with the Illinois. It is remarkably cold, muddy and rapid. Its overflowings are considerable. They happen during the months of June and July. Their commencement being so much later than those of the Missisipi, would induce a belief that the sources of the Missouri are northward of those of the Missisipi, unless we suppose that the cold increases again with the ascent of the land from the Missisipi westwardly. That this ascent is great, is proved by the rapidity of the river. Six miles above the mouth it is brought within the compass of a quarter of a mile's width: yet the Spanish Merchants at Pancore, or St. Louis, say they go two thousand miles up it. It heads far westward of the Rio Norte, or North River.[7] There is, in the villages of Kaskaskia, Cohoes and St. Vincennes, no inconsiderable quantity of plate, said to have been plundered during the last war by the Indians from the churches and private houses of Santa Fé, on the North River, and brought to these villages for sale. From the mouth of Ohio to Santa Fé are forty days journey, or about 1000 miles. What is the shortest distance between the navigable waters of the Missouri, and those of the North River, or how far this is navigable[8] above Santa Fé, I could never learn. From Santa Fé to its mouth in the Gulph of Mexico is about 1200 miles. The road from New Orleans to Mexico crosses this river at the post of Rio Norte, 800 miles below Santa Fé: and from this post to New Orleans is about 1200 miles; thus making 2000 miles between Santa Fé and New Orleans, passing down the North river, Red river and Missisipi; whereas it is 2230 through the Missouri and Missisipi. From the same post of Rio Norte, passing near the mines of La Sierra and Laiguana, which are between the North river and the river Salina to Sartilla, is 375 miles; and from thence, passing the mines of Charcas, Zaccatecas and Potosi, to the city of Mexico is 375 miles; in all, 1550 miles from Santa Fé to the city of Mexico. From New Orleans to the city of Mexico is about 1950 miles: the roads, after setting out from the Red river, near Natchitoches, keeping generally parallel with the coast, and about two hundred miles from it, till it enters the city of Mexico.

The *Illinois* is a fine river, clear, gentle, and without rapids; insomuch that it is navigable for batteaux to its source. From thence is a portage of two miles only to the Chickago, which affords a batteau navigation of 16 miles to its entrance into lake Michigan. The Illinois, about 10 miles above its mouth, is 300 yards wide.

The *Kaskaskia* is 100 yards wide at its entrance into the Missisipi, and preserves that breadth to the Buffalo plains, 70 miles above. So far also it is navigable for loaded batteaux, and perhaps much further. It is not rapid.

The *Ohio* is the most beautiful river on earth. Its current gentle, waters clear, and bosom smooth and unbroken by rocks and rapids, a single instance only excepted.

It is ¼ of a mile wide at Fort Pitt:

500 yards at the mouth of the Great Kanhaway:

1 mile and 25 poles at Louisville:

¼ of a mile on the rapids, three or four miles below Louisville:

½ a mile where the low country begins, which is 20 miles above Green river:

1¼ at the receipt of the Tanissee:

And a mile wide at the mouth.

Its length, as measured according to its meanders by Capt. Hutchings,[9] is as follows:

From Fort Pitt

	MILES.		MILES.
To Log's town	18½	Little Miami	126¼
Big Beaver creek	10¾	Licking creek	8
Little Beaver cr.	13½	Great Miami	26¾
Yellow creek	11¾	Big Bones	32½
Two creeks	21¾	Kentuckey	44¼
Long reach	53¾	Rapids	77¼
End Long reach	16½	Low country	155¾
Muskingum	25½	Buffalo river	64½
Little Kanhaway	12¼	Wabash	97¼
Hockhocking	16	Big cave	42¾
Great Kanhaway	82½	Shawanee river	52½
Guiandot	43¾	Cherokee river	13
Sandy creek	14½	Massac	11
Sioto	48¾	Missisipi	46
			1188

In common winter and spring tides it affords 15 feet water to Louisville, 10 feet to La Tarte's rapids, 40 miles above the mouth of the great Kanhaway, and a sufficiency at all times for light batteaux and canoes to Fort Pitt. The rapids are in latitude 38°. 8'. The inundations of this river begin about the last of March, and subside in July. During these a first rate man of war may be carried from Louisville to New Orleans, if the sudden turns of the river and the strength of its current will admit a safe steerage. The rapids at Louisville descend about 30 feet in a length of a mile and a half. The bed of the river there is a solid rock, and is divided by an island into two branches, the southern of which is about 200 yards wide, and is dry four months in the year. The bed of the northern branch is worn into channels by the constant course of the water, and attrition of the pebble stones carried on with that, so as to be passable for batteaux through the greater part of the year. Yet it is thought that the southern arm may be the most easily opened for constant navigation. The rise of the waters in these rapids does not exceed 10 or 12 feet. A part of this island is so high as to have been never overflowed, and to command the settlement at Louisville, which is opposite to it. The fort, however, is situated at the head of the falls. The ground on the South side rises very gradually.

The *Tanissee,* Cherokee or Hogohege river is 600 yards wide at its mouth, ¼ of a mile at the mouth of Holston, and 200 yards at Chotee, which is 20 miles above Holston, and 300 miles above the mouth of the Tanissee. This river crosses the southern boundary of Virginia, 58 miles from the Missisipi. Its current is moderate. It is navigable for loaded boats of any burthen to the Muscleshoals, where the river passes through the Cumberland mountain. These shoals are 6 or 8 miles long, passable downwards for loaded canoes, but not upwards, unless there be a swell in the river. Above these the navigation for loaded canoes and batteaux continues to the Long island. This river has its inundations also. Above the Chickamogga towns is a whirlpool called the Sucking-pot, which takes in trunks of trees or boats, and throws them out again half a mile below. It is avoided by keeping very close to the bank, on the South side. There are but a few miles portage between a branch of this river and the navigable waters of the river Mobile, which runs into the gulph of Mexico.

Cumberland, or Shawanee river, intersects the boundary between Virginia and North Carolina 67 miles from the Missisipi, and again 198 miles from the same river, a little above the entrance of Obey's river into the Cumberland. Its clear fork crosses the same boundary about 300 miles from the Missisipi. Cumberland is a very gentle stream, navigable for loaded batteaux

800 miles, without interruption; then intervene some rapids of 15 miles in length, after which it is again navigable 70 miles upwards, which brings you within 10 miles of the Cumberland mountains. It is about 120 yards wide through its whole course, from the head of its navigation to its mouth.

The *Wabash* is a very beautiful river, 400 yards wide at the mouth, and 300 at St. Vincennes, which is a post 100 miles above the mouth, in a direct line. Within this space there are two small rapids, which give very little obstruction to the navigation. It is 400 yards wide at the mouth, and navigable 30 leagues upwards for canoes and small boats. From the mouth of Maple river to that of Eel river is about 80 miles in a direct line, the river continuing navigable, and from one to two hundred yards in width. The Eel river is 150 yards wide, and affords at all times navigation for periaguas, to within 18 miles of the Miami of the lake. The Wabash, from the mouth of Eel river to Little river, a distance of 50 miles direct, is interrupted with frequent rapids and shoals, which obstruct the navigation, except in a swell. Little river affords navigation during a swell to within 3 miles of the Miami, which thence affords a similar navigation into lake Erié, 100 miles distant in a direct line. The Wabash overflows periodically in correspondence with the Ohio, and in some places two leagues from its banks.

Green River is navigable for loaded batteaux at all times 50 miles upwards; but it is then interrupted by impassable rapids, above which the navigation again commences, and continues good 30 or 40 miles to the mouth of Barren river.

Kentucky river is 90 yards wide at the mouth, and also at Boonsborough, 80 miles above. It affords a navigation for loaded batteaux 180 miles in a direct line, in the winter tides.

The *Great Miami* of the Ohio, is 200 yards wide at the mouth. At the Piccawee towns, 75 miles above, it is reduced to 30 yards; it is, nevertheless, navigable for loaded canoes 50 miles above these towns. The portage from its western branch into the Miami of Lake Erié, is 5 miles; that from its eastern branch into Sandusky river, is of 9 miles.

Salt river is at all times navigable for loaded batteaux 70 or 80 miles. It is 80 yards wide at its mouth, and keeps that width to its fork, 25 miles above.

The *Little Miami* of the Ohio, is 60 or 70 yards wide at its mouth, 60 miles to its source, and affords no navigation.

The *Sioto* is 250 yards wide at its mouth, which is in latitude 38°. 22'. and at the Saltlick towns, 200 miles above the mouth, it is yet 100 yards wide. To these towns it is navigable for loaded batteaux, and its eastern branch affords navigation almost to its source.

Great Sandy river is about sixty yards wide, and navigable sixty miles for loaded batteaux.

Guiandot is about the width of the river last mentioned, but is more rapid. It may be navigated by canoes sixty miles.

The *Great Kanhaway* is a river of considerable note for the fertility of its lands, and still more, as leading towards the head-waters of James river.[10] Nevertheless, it is doubtful whether its great and numerous rapids will admit a navigation, but at an expence to which it will require ages to render its inhabitants equal. The great obstacles begin at what are called the great falls, 90 miles above the mouth, below which are only five or six rapids, and these passable, with some difficulty, even at low water. From the falls to the mouth of Greenbriar is 100 miles, and thence to the lead mines 120. It is 280 yards wide at its mouth.

Hock-hocking is 80 yards wide at its mouth, and yields navigation for loaded batteaux to the Press-place, 60 miles above its mouth.

The *Little Kanhaway* is 150 yards wide at the mouth. It yields a navigation of 10 miles only. Perhaps its northern branch, called Junius's creek, which interlocks with the western of Monongahela, may one day admit a shorter passage from the latter into the Ohio.

The *Muskingum* is 280 yards wide at its mouth, and 200 yards at the lower Indian towns, 150 miles upwards. It is navigable for small batteaux to within one mile of a navigable part of Cayahoga river, which runs into lake Erié.

At Fort Pitt the river Ohio loses its name, branching into the Monongahela and Alleghaney.

The *Monongahela* is 400 yards wide at its mouth. From thence is 12 or 15 miles to the mouth of Yohoganey, where it is 300 yards wide. Thence to Redstone by water is 50 miles, by land 30. Then to the mouth of Cheat river by water 40 miles, by land 28, the width continuing at 300 yards, and the navigation good for boats. Thence the width is about 200 yards to the western fork, 50 miles higher, and the navigation frequently interrupted by rapids; which however with a swell of two or three feet become very passable for boats. It then admits light boats, except in dry seasons, 65 miles further to the head of Tygarts valley, presenting only some small rapids and falls of one or two feet perpendicular, and lessening in its width to 20 yards. The *Western fork* is navigable in the winter 10 or 15 miles towards the northern of the Little Kanhaway, and will admit a good waggon road to it. The *Yohoganey* is the principal branch of this river. It passes through the Laurel mountain, about 30 miles from its mouth; is so far from 300 to 150 yards wide, and the navigation much obstructed in dry weather by rapids and shoals. In its passage through the mountain it makes very great falls, admitting no navigation for ten miles to the Turkey foot. Thence to the great crossing, about 20 miles, it is again navigable, except in dry seasons, and at this place is 200 yards wide. The sources of this river are divided from those of the Patowmac by the Alleghaney mountain. From the falls, where it intersects the Laurel mountain, to Fort Cumberland, the head of the navigation on the Patowmac, is 40 miles of very mountainous road. Wills's creek, at the mouth of which was Fort Cumberland, is 30 or 40 yards wide, but affords no navigation as yet. *Cheat* river, another considerable branch of the Monongahela, is 200 yards wide at its mouth, and 100 yards at the Dunkard's settlement, 50 miles higher. It is navigable for boats, except in dry seasons. The boundary between Virginia and Pennsylvania crosses it about three or four miles above its mouth.

The *Alleghaney* river, with a slight swell, affords navigation for light batteaux to Venango, at the mouth of French creek, where it is 200 yards wide; and it is practised even to Le Boeuf, from whence there is a portage of 15 miles to Presque Isle on Lake Erié.

The country watered by the Missisipi and its eastern branches, constitutes five-eighths of the United States, two of which five-eighths are occupied by the Ohio and its waters: the residuary streams which run into the Gulph of Mexico, the Atlantic, and the St. Laurence water, the remaining three-eighths.

Before we quit the subject of the western waters, we will take a view of their principal connections with the Atlantic. These are three; the Hudson's river, the Patowmac, and the Missisipi itself. Down the last will pass all heavy commodities. But the navigation through the Gulph of Mexico is so dangerous, and that up the Missisipi so difficult and tedious, that it is thought probable that European merchandize will not return through that channel. It is most likely that flour, timber, and other heavy articles will be floated on rafts, which will themselves be an article for sale as well as their loading, the navigators returning by land or in light batteaux. There will therefore be a competition between the Hudson and Patowmac rivers for the residue of the commerce of all the country westward of Lake Erié, on the waters of the lakes, of the Ohio, and upper parts of the Missisipi. To go to New-York, that part of the trade which comes from the lakes or their waters must first be brought into Lake Erié. Between Lake Superior and its waters and Huron are the rapids of St. Mary, which will permit boats to pass, but not larger vessels. Lakes Huron and Michigan afford communication with Lake Erié by vessels of 8 feet draught. That part of the trade which comes from the waters of the Missisipi must pass from them through some portage into the waters of the lakes. The portage from the Illinois river into a water of Michigan is of one mile only. From the Wabash, Miami, Muskingum, or Alleghaney, are portages into the waters of Lake Erié, of from one to fifteen miles. When the commodities are brought into, and have passed through Lake Erié, there is between that and Ontario an interruption by the falls of Niagara, where the portage is of 8 miles; and between Ontario and the Hudson's river are portages at the falls of Onondago, a little above Oswego, of a quarter of a mile; from Wood creek to the Mohawks river two miles; at the little falls of the Mohawks river half a mile, and from Schenectady to Albany 16 miles. Besides the increase of expence occasioned by frequent change of carriage, there is an increased risk of pillage produced by committing merchandize to a greater number of hands successively. The Patowmac offers itself under the following circumstances. For the trade of the lakes and their waters westward of Lake Erié, when it shall have entered that lake, it must coast along its southern shore, on account of the number and excellence of its harbours, the northern, though shortest, having few harbours, and these unsafe. Having reached Cayahoga, to proceed on to New-York it will have 825 miles and five portages: whereas it is but 425 miles to Alexandria, its emporium on the Patowmac, if it turns into the Cayahoga, and passes through that, Bigbeaver, Ohio, Yohoganey, (or Monongalia and Cheat) and Patowmac, and there are but two portages; the first of which between Cayahoga and Beaver may be removed by uniting the sources of these waters, which are lakes in the neighbourhood of each other, and in a champaign country; the other from the waters of Ohio to Patowmac will be from 15 to 40 miles, according to the trouble which shall be taken to approach the two navigations. For the trade of the Ohio, or that which shall come into it from its own waters or the Missisipi, it is nearer through the Patowmac to Alexandria than to New-York by 580 miles, and it is interrupted by one portage only. There is another circumstance of difference too. The lakes themselves never freeze, but the communications between them freeze, and the Hudson's river is itself shut up by the ice three months in the year; whereas the channel to the Chesapeak leads directly into a warmer climate. The southern parts of it very rarely freeze at all, and whenever the northern do, it is so near the sources of the rivers, that the frequent floods to which they are there liable break up the ice immediately, so that vessels may pass through the whole winter, subject only to accidental and short delays. Add to all this, that in case of a war with our neighbours the Anglo-Americans or the Indians, the route to New-York becomes a frontier through almost its whole length, and all commerce through it ceases from that moment.—But the channel to New-York is already known to practice; whereas the upper waters of the Ohio and the Patowmac, and the great falls of the latter, are yet to be cleared of their fixed obstructions (1).[11]

QUERY III

A NOTICE OF THE BEST SEA-PORTS OF THE STATE, AND HOW BIG ARE THE VESSELS THEY CAN RECEIVE?

Having no ports but our rivers and creeks, this Query has been answered under the preceding one.

QUERY IV

A NOTICE OF ITS MOUNTAINS?

Mountains

For the particular geography of our mountains I must refer to Fry and Jefferson's map of Virginia;[12] and to Evans's analysis of his map of America for a more philosophical view of them than is to be found in any other work.[13] It is worthy notice, that our mountains are not solitary and scattered confusedly over the face of the country; but that they commence at about 150 miles from the sea-coast, are disposed in ridges one behind another, running nearly parallel with the sea-coast, though rather approaching it as they advance north-eastwardly. To the south-west, as the tract of country between the sea-coast and the Missisipi becomes narrower, the mountains converge into a single ridge, which, as it approaches the Gulph of Mexico, subsides into plain country, and gives rise to some of the waters of that Gulph, and particularly to a river called the Apalachicola, probably from the Apalachies, an Indian nation formerly residing on it. Hence the mountains giving rise to that river, and seen from its various parts, were called the Apalachian mountains, being in fact the end or termination only of the great ridges passing through the continent. European geographers however extended the name northwardly as far as the mountains extended; some giving it, after their separation into different ridges, to the Blue ridge, others to the North mountain, others to the Alleghaney, others to the Laurel ridge, as may be seen in their different maps. But the fact I believe is, that none of these ridges were ever known by that name to the inhabitants, either native or emigrant, but as they saw them so called in European maps. In the same direction generally are the veins of lime-stone, coal and other minerals hitherto discovered: and so range the falls of our great rivers. But the courses of the great rivers are at right angles with these. James and Patowmac penetrate through all the ridges of mountains eastward of the Alleghaney; that is broken by no watercourse. It is in fact the spine of the country between the Atlantic on one side, and the Missisipi and St. Laurence on the other. The passage of the Patowmac through the Blue ridge[14] is perhaps one of the most stupendous scenes in nature. You stand on a very high point of land. On your right comes up the Shenandoah, having ranged along the foot of the mountain an hundred miles to seek a vent. On your left approaches the Patowmac, in quest of a passage also. In the moment of their junction they rush together against the mountain, rend it asunder, and pass off to the sea. The first glance of this scene hurries our senses into the opinion, that this earth has been created in time, that the mountains were formed first, that the rivers began to flow afterwards, that in this place particularly they have been dammed up by the Blue ridge of mountains, and have formed an ocean which filled the whole valley; that continuing to rise they have at length broken over at this spot, and have torn the mountain down from its summit to its base. The piles of rock on each hand, but particularly on the Shenandoah, the evident marks of their disrupture and avulsion from their beds by the most powerful agents of nature, corroborate the impression. But the distant finishing which nature has given to the picture is of a very different character. It is a true contrast to the fore-ground. It is as placid and delightful, as that is wild and tremendous. For the mountain being cloven asunder, she presents to your eye, through the cleft, a small catch of smooth blue horizon, at an infinite distance in the plain country, inviting you, as it were, from the riot and tumult roaring around, to pass through the breach and participate of the calm below. Here the eye ultimately composes itself; and that way too the road happens actually to lead. You cross the Patowmac above the junction, pass along its side through the base of the mountain for three miles, its terrible precipices hanging in fragments over you, and within about 20 miles reach Frederic town and the fine country round that. This scene is worth a voyage across the Atlantic. Yet here, as in the neighbourhood of the natural bridge, are people who have passed their lives within half a dozen miles, and have never been to survey these monuments of a war between rivers and mountains, which must have shaken the earth itself to its center (2).[15] —The height of our mountains has not yet been estimated with any degree of exactness. The Alleghaney being the great ridge which divides the waters of the Atlantic from those of the Missisipi, its summit is doubtless more elevated above the ocean than that of any other mountain. But its relative height, compared with the base on which it stands, is not so great as that of some others, the country rising behind the successive ridges like the steps of stairs. The mountains of the Blue ridge, and of these the Peaks of Otter,[16] are thought to be of a greater height, measured from their base, than any others in our country, and perhaps in North America. From data, which may found a tolerable conjecture, we suppose the highest peak to be about 4000 feet perpendicular, which is not a fifth part of the height of the mountains of South America,[17] nor one third of the height which would be necessary in our latitude to preserve ice in the open air unmelted through the year. The ridge of mountains next beyond the Blue ridge, called by us the North mountain, is of the greatest extent; for which reason they were named by the Indians the Endless mountains.[18]

A substance supposed to be Pumice, found floating on the Missisipi, has induced a conjecture, that there is a volcano on some of its waters: and as these are mostly known to their sources, except the Missouri, our expectations of verifying the conjecture would of course be led to the mountains which divide the waters of the Mexican Gulph from those of the South Sea; but no volcano having ever yet been known at such a distance from the sea, we must rather suppose that this floating substance has been erroneously deemed Pumice.[19]

QUERY V

ITS CASCADES AND CAVERNS?

Falling spring

The only remarkable Cascade in this country, is that of the Falling Spring in Augusta.[20] It is a water of James river, where it is called Jackson's river, rising in the warm spring mountains about twenty miles South West of the warm spring, and flowing into that valley.[21] About three quarters of a mile from its source, it falls over a rock 200 feet into the valley below. The sheet of water is broken in its breadth by the rock in two or three places, but not at all in its height. Between the sheet and rock, at the bottom, you may walk across dry. This Cataract will bear no comparison with that of Niagara, as to the quantity of water composing it; the sheet being only 12 or 15 feet wide above, and somewhat more spread below; but it is half as high again, the latter being only 156 feet, according to the mensuration made by order of M. Vaudreuil, Governor of Canada, and 130 according to a more recent account.[22]

Madison's cave

In the lime-stone country, there are many caverns of very considerable extent. The most noted is called Madison's Cave, and is on the North side of the Blue ridge, near the intersection of the Rockingham and Augusta line with the South fork of the southern river of Shenandoah. It is in a hill of about 200 feet perpendicular height, the ascent of which, on one side, is so steep, that you may pitch a biscuit from its summit into the river which washes its base. The entrance of the cave is, in this side, about two thirds of the way up. It extends into the earth about 300 feet, branching into subordinate caverns, sometimes ascending a little, but more generally descending, and at length terminates, in two different places, at basons of water of unknown extent, and which I should judge to be nearly on a level with the water of the river; however, I do not think they are formed

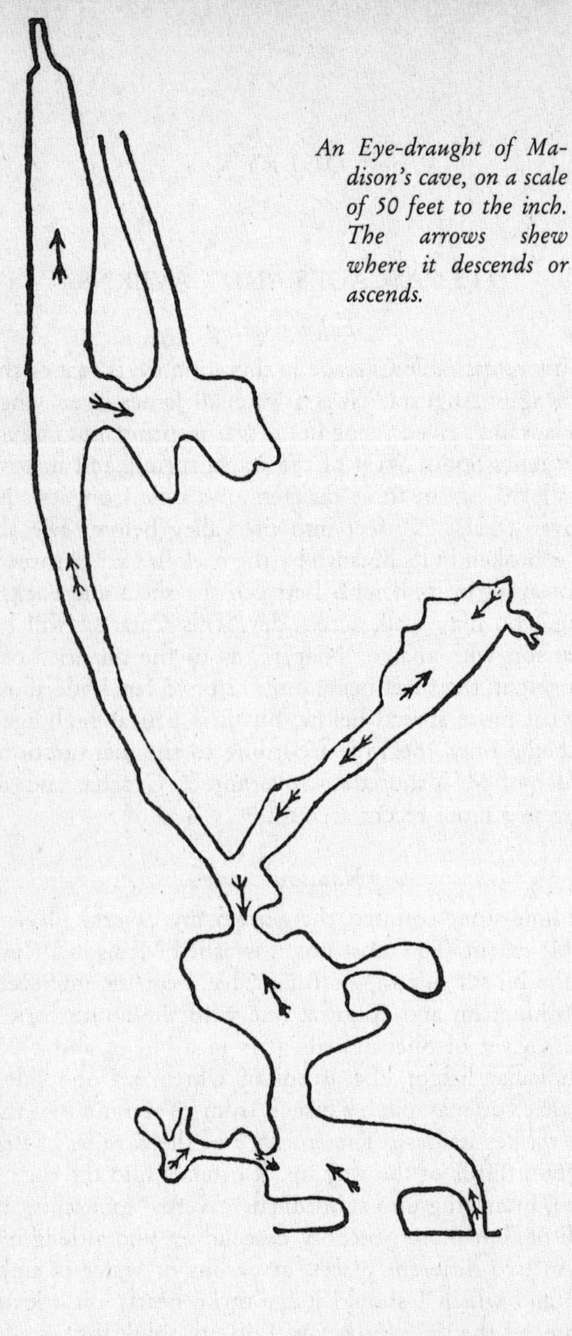

An Eye-draught of Madison's cave, on a scale of 50 feet to the inch. The arrows shew where it descends or ascends.

by refluent water from that, because they are never turbid; because they do not rise and fall in correspondence with that in times of flood, or of drought; and because the water is always cool. It is probably one of the many reservoirs with which the interior parts of the earth are supposed to abound, and which yield supplies to the fountains of water, distinguished from others only by its being accessible. The vault of this cave is of solid lime-stone, from 20 to 40 or 50 feet high, through which water is continually percolating. This, trickling down the sides of the cave, has incrusted them over in the form of elegant drapery; and dripping from the top of the vault generates on that, and on the base below, stalactites of a conical form, some of which have met and formed massive columns.

Another of these caves is near the North mountain, in the county of Frederick, on the lands of Mr. Zane.[23] The entrance into this is on the top of an extensive ridge. You descend 30 or 40 feet, as into a well, from whence the cave then extends, nearly horizontally, 400 feet into the earth, preserving a breadth of from 20 to 50 feet, and a height of from 5 to 12 feet. After entering this cave a few feet, the mercury, which in the open air was at 50°. rose to 57°. of Farenheit's thermometer, answering to 11°. of Reaumur's, and it continued at that to the remotest parts of the cave. The uniform temperature of the cellars of the observatory of Paris, which are 90 feet deep, and of all subterranean cavities of any depth, where no chymical agents may be supposed to produce a factitious heat, has been found to be 10°. of Reamur, equal to 54½°. of Farenheit. The temperature of the cave abovementioned so nearly corresponds with this, that the difference may be ascribed to a difference of instruments.

Blowing cave

At the Panther gap, in the ridge which divides the waters of the Cow and the Calf pasture, is what is called the *Blowing cave*. It is in the side of a hill, is of about 100 feet diameter, and emits constantly a current of air of such force, as to keep the weeds prostrate to the distance of twenty yards before it. This current is strongest in dry frosty weather, and in long spells of rain weakest. Regular inspirations and expirations of air, by caverns and fissures, have been probably enough accounted for, by supposing them combined with intermitting fountains; as they must of course inhale air while their reservoirs are emptying themselves, and again emit it while they are filling. But a constant issue of air, only varying in its force as the weather is drier or damper, will require a new hypothesis.[24] There is another blowing cave in the Cumberland mountain, about a mile from where it crosses the Carolina line. All we know of this is, that it is not constant, and that a fountain of water issues from it.

Natural bridge

The *Natural bridge,* the most sublime of Nature's works, though not comprehended under the present head, must not be pretermitted. It is on the ascent of a hill, which seems to have been cloven through its length by some great convulsion. The fissure, just at the bridge, is, by some admeasurements, 270 feet deep, by others only 205. It is about 45 feet wide at the bottom, and 90 feet at the top; this of course determines the length of the bridge, and its height from the water. Its breadth in the middle, is about 60 feet, but more at the ends, and the thickness of the mass at the summit of the arch, about 40 feet. A part of this thickness is constituted by a coat of earth, which gives growth to many large trees. The residue, with the hill on both sides, is one solid rock of lime-stone. The arch approaches the Semi-elliptical form; but the larger axis of the ellipsis, which would be the cord of the arch, is many times longer than the transverse.[25] Though the sides of this bridge are provided in some parts with a parapet of fixed rocks, yet few men have resolution to walk to them and look over into the abyss. You involuntarily fall on your hands and feet, creep to the parapet and peep over it. Looking down from this height about a minute, gave me a violent head ach. If the view from the top be painful and intolerable, that from below is delightful in an equal extreme. It is impossible for the emotions arising from the sublime, to be felt beyond what they are here: so beautiful an arch, so elevated, so light, and springing as it were up to heaven, the rapture of the spectator is really indescribable! The fissure continuing narrow, deep, and streight for a considerable distance above and below the bridge, opens a short but very pleasing view of the North mountain on one side, and Blue ridge on the other, at the distance each of them of about five miles.[26] This bridge is in the county of Rock bridge, to which it has given name, and affords a public and commodious passage over a valley, which cannot be crossed elsewhere for a considerable distance. The stream passing under it is called Cedar creek. It is a water of James river, and sufficient in the driest seasons to turn a grist-mill, though its fountain is not more than two miles above.*

---

*Don Ulloa mentions a break, similar to this, in the province of Angaraez, in South America. It is from 16 to 22 feet wide, 111 feet deep, and of 1.3 miles continuance, English measures. Its breadth at top is not sensibly greater than at bottom. But the following fact is remarkable, and will furnish some light for conjecturing the probable origin of our natural bridge. "Esta caxa, ó cauce[27] está cortada en péna viva con tanta precision, que las desigualdades del un lado entrantes, corresponden á las del otro lado salientes, como si aquella altura se hubiese abierto expresamente, con sus bueltas y tortuosidades, para darle transito á los aguas por entre los dos murallones que la forman; siendo tal su igualdad, que si llegasen á juntarse se endentarían uno con otro sin dexar hueco." Not. Amer. II. §. 10. Don Ulloa inclines to the opinion, that this channel has been affected by the wearing of the water which runs through it, rather than that the mountain should have been broken open by any convulsion of nature. But if it had been worn by the running of water, would not the rocks which form the sides, have been worn plane? or if, meeting in some parts with veins of harder stone, the water had left prominences on the one side, would not the same cause have sometimes, or perhaps generally, occasioned prominences on the other side also? Yet Don Ulloa tells us, that on the other side there are always corresponding cavities, and that these tally with the prominences so perfectly, that, were the two sides to come together, they would fit in all their indentures, without leaving any void. I think that this does not resemble the effect of running water, but looks rather as if the two sides had parted asunder. The sides of the break, over which is the Natural bridge of Virginia, consisting of a veiny rock which yields to time, the correspondence between the salient and re-entering inequalities, if it existed at all, has now disappeared. This break has the advantage of the one described by Don Ulloa in its finest circumstance; no portion in that instance having held together, during the separation of the other parts, so as to form a bridge over the Abyss.[28]

QUERY VI

A NOTICE OF THE MINES AND OTHER SUBTERRANEOUS RICHES; ITS TREES, PLANTS, FRUITS, &C.

1. *Minerals*

Gold

I knew a single instance of gold found in this state. It was interspersed in small specks through a lump of ore, of about four pounds weight, which yielded seventeen pennyweight of gold, of extraordinary ductility. This ore was found on the North side of Rappahanoc, about four miles below the falls. I never heard of any other indication of gold in its neighbourhood.

Lead

On the Great Kanhaway, opposite to the mouth of Cripple creek, and about twenty-five miles from our southern boundary, in the county of Montgomery, are mines of lead. The metal is mixed, some times with earth, and sometimes with rock, which requires the force of gunpowder to open it; and is accompanied with a portion of silver, too small to be worth separation under any process hitherto attempted there. The proportion yielded is from 50 to 80 lb. of pure metal from 100 lb. of washed ore. The most common is that of 60 to the 100 lb. The veins are at some times most flattering; at others they disappear suddenly and totally. They enter the side of the hill, and proceed horizontally. Two of them are wrought at present by the public, the best of which is 100 yards under the hill. These would employ about 50 labourers to advantage. We have not, however, more than 30 generally, and these cultivate their own corn. They have produced 60 tons of lead in the year; but the general quantity is from 20 to 25 tons. The present furnace is a mile from the orebank, and on the opposite side of the river. The ore is first waggoned to the river, a quarter of a mile, then laden on board of canoes and carried across the river, which is there about 200 yards wide, and then again taken into waggons and carried to the furnace. This mode was originally adopted, that they might avail themselves of a good situation on a creek, for a pounding mill: but it would be easy to have the furnace and pounding mill on the same side of the river, which would yield water, without any dam, by a canal of about half a mile in length. From the furnace the lead is transported 130 miles along a good road, leading through the peaks of Otter to Lynch's ferry, or Winston's, on James river, from whence it is carried by water about the same distance to Westham. This land carriage may be greatly shortened, by delivering the lead on James river, above the Blue ridge, from whence a ton weight has been brought on two canoes. The Great Kanhaway has considerable falls in the neighbourhood of the mines. About seven miles below are three falls, of three or four feet perpendicular each; and three miles above is a rapid of three miles continuance, which has been compared in its descent to the great fall of James river. Yet it is the opinion, that they may be laid open for useful navigation, so as to reduce very much the portage between the Kanhaway and James river.

A valuable lead mine is said to have been lately discovered on Cumberland,[29] below the mouth of Red river. The greatest, however, known in the western country, are on the Missisipi, extending from the mouth of Rock river 150 miles upwards. These are not wrought, the lead used in that country being from the banks on the Spanish side of the Missisipi, opposite to Kaskaskia.

Copper

A mine of copper was once opened in the county of Amherst, on the North side of James river, and another in the opposite country, on the South side. However, either from bad management or the poverty of the veins, they were discontinued. We are told of a rich mine of native copper on the Ouabache, below the upper Wiaw.

Iron

The mines of iron worked at present are Callaway's, Ross's, and Ballendine's, on the South side of James river; Old's on the

North side, in Albemarle; Millar's in Augusta, and Zane's in Frederic. These two last are in the valley between the Blue ridge and North mountain. Callaway's, Ross's, Millar's, and Zane's, make about 150 tons of bar iron each, in the year. Ross's makes also about 1600 tons of pig iron annually; Ballendine's 1000; Callaway's, Millar's, and Zane's, about 600 each. Besides these, a forge of Mr. Hunter's, at Fredericksburgh, makes about 300 tons a year of bar iron, from pigs imported from Maryland; and Taylor's forge on Neapsco of Patowmac, works in the same way, but to what extent I am not informed. The indications of iron in other places are numerous, and dispersed through all the middle country. The toughness of the cast iron of Ross's and Zane's furnaces is very remarkable. Pots and other utensils, cast thinner than usual, of this iron, may be safely thrown into, or out of the waggons in which they are transported. Salt-pans made of the same, and no longer wanted for that purpose, cannot be broken up, in order to be melted again, unless previously drilled in many parts.

In the western country, we are told of iron mines between the Muskingum and Ohio; of others on Kentucky, between the Cumberland and Barren rivers, between Cumberland and Tannissee, on Reedy creek, near the Long island, and on Chesnut creek, a branch of the Great Kanhaway, near where it crosses the Carolina line. What are called the iron banks, on the Missisipi, are believed, by a good judge, to have no iron in them. In general, from what is hitherto known of that country, it seems to want iron.

Black lead

Considerable quantities of black lead are taken occasionally for use from Winterham, in the county of Amelia. I am not able, however, to give a particular state of the mine. There is no work established at it, those who want, going and procuring it for themselves.

Pit coal

The country on James river, from 15 to 20 miles above Richmond, and for several miles northward and southward, is replete with mineral coal of a very excellent quality. Being in the hands of many proprietors, pits have been opened, and before the interruption of our commerce were worked to an extent equal to the demand.

In the western country coal is known to be in so many places, as to have induced an opinion, that the whole tract between the Laurel mountain, Missisipi, and Ohio, yields coal. It is also known in many places on the North side of the Ohio. The coal at Pittsburg is of very superior quality. A bed of it at that place has been a-fire since the year 1765. Another coal-hill on the Pike-run of Monongahela has been a-fire ten years; yet it has burnt away about twenty yards only.

Precious stones

I have known one instance of an Emerald found in this country. Amethysts have been frequent, and chrystals common; yet not in such numbers any of them as to be worth seeking.

Marble

There is very good marble, and in very great abundance, on James river, at the mouth of Rockfish. The samples I have seen, were some of them of a white as pure as one might expect to find on the surface of the earth: but most of them were variegated with red, blue, and purple. None of it has been ever worked. It forms a very large precipice, which hangs over a navigable part of the river. It is said there is marble at Kentucky.[30]

Limestone

But one vein of lime-stone is known below the Blue ridge. Its first appearance, in our country, is in Prince William, two miles below the Pignut ridge of mountains; thence it passes on nearly parallel with that, and crosses the Rivanna about five miles below it, where it is called the South-west ridge. It then crosses Hardware, above the mouth of Hudson's creek, James river at the mouth of Rockfish, at the marble quarry before spoken of, probably runs up that river to where it appears again at Ross's ironworks, and so passes off south-westwardly by Flat creek of Otter river. It is never more than one hundred yards wide. From the Blue ridge westwardly the whole country seems to be founded on a rock of lime-stone, besides infinite quantities on the surface, both loose and fixed. This is cut into beds, which range, as the mountains and sea-coast do, from south-west to north-east, the lamina of each bed declining from the horizon towards a parallelism with the axis of the earth. Being struck with this observation, I made, with a quadrant, a great number of trials on the angles of their declination, and found them to vary from 22°. to 60°. but averaging all my trials, the result was within one-third of a degree of the elevation of the pole or latitude of the place, and much the greatest part of them taken separately were little different from that: by which it appears, that these lamina are, in the main, parallel with the axis of the earth. In some instances, indeed, I found them perpendicular, and even reclining the other way: but these were extremely rare, and always attended with signs of convulsion, or other circumstances of singularity, which admitted a possibility of removal from their original position. These trials were made between Madison's cave and the Patowmac. We hear of lime-stone on the Missisipi and Ohio, and in all the mountainous country between the eastern and western waters, not on the mountains themselves, but occupying the vallies between them.[31]

Near the eastern foot of the North mountain are immense bodies of *Schist*, containing impressions of shells in a variety of forms. I have received petrified shells of very different kinds from the first sources of the Kentucky, which bear no resemblance to any I have ever seen on the tide-waters. It is said that shells are found in the Andes, in South-America, fifteen thousand feet above the level of the ocean.[32] This is considered by many, both of the learned and unlearned, as a proof of an universal deluge. To the many considerations opposing this opinion, the following may be added. The atmosphere, and all its contents, whether of water, air, or other matters, gravitate to the earth; that is to say, they have weight. Experience tells us, that the weight of all these together never exceeds that of a column of mercury of 31 inches height, which is equal to one of rainwater of 35 feet high. If the whole contents of the atmosphere then were water, instead of what they are, it would cover the globe but 35 feet deep; but as these waters, as they fell, would run into the seas, the superficial measure of which is to that of the dry parts of the globe as two to one, the seas would be raised only 52½ feet above their present level, and of course would overflow the lands to that height only.[33] In Virginia this would be a very small proportion even of the champaign country, the banks of our tide-waters being frequently, if not generally, of a greater height. Deluges beyond this extent then, as for instance, to the North mountain or to Kentucky, seem out of the laws of nature. But within it they may have taken place to a greater or less degree, in proportion to the combination of natural causes which may be supposed to have produced them. History renders probable some instances of a partial deluge in the country lying round the Mediterranean sea. It has been often *supposed, and is not unlikely, that that sea was once a lake. While such, let us admit an extraordinary collection of the waters of the atmosphere from the other parts of the globe to have been discharged over that and the countries whose waters run into it. Or without supposing it a lake, admit such an extraordinary collection of the waters of the atmosphere, and an influx of waters from the Atlantic ocean, forced by long continued Western winds.[34] That lake, or that sea, may thus have been so raised as to overflow the low lands adjacent to it, as those of Egypt and Armenia, which, according to a tradition of the Egyptians and Hebrews, were overflowed about 2300 years before the Christian aera; those of Attica, said to have been overflowed in the time of Ogyges, about 500 years later; and those of Thessaly, in the time of Deucalion, still 300 years posterior.[35] But such deluges as these will not account for the shells found in the higher lands. A second opinion has been entertained,[36] which is, that, in times anterior to the records either of history or tradition, the bed of the ocean, the principal residence of the shelled tribe, has, by some great convulsion of nature, been heaved to the heights at which we now find shells and other remains of marine animals. The favourers of this opinion do well to suppose the great events on which it rests to have taken place beyond all the aeras of history;

---

*2. Buffon Epoques, 96.

for within these, certainly none such are to be found: and we may venture to say further, that no fact has taken place, either in our own days, or in the thousands of years recorded in history, which proves the existence of any natural agents, within or without the bowels of the earth, of force sufficient to heave, to the height of 15,000 feet, such masses as the Andes. The difference between the power necessary to produce such an effect, and that which shuffled together the different parts of Calabria in our days, is so immense, that, from the existence of the latter we are not authorised to infer that of the former.

M. de Voltaire has suggested a third solution of this difficulty (Quest. encycl. Coquilles).[37] He cites an instance in Touraine, where, in the space of 80 years, a particular spot of earth had been twice metamorphosed into soft stone, which had become hard when employed in building. In this stone shells of various kinds were produced, discoverable at first only with the microscope, but afterwards growing with the stone. From this fact, I suppose, he would have us infer, that, besides the usual process for generating shells by the elaboration of earth and water in animal vessels, nature may have provided an equivalent operation, by passing the same materials through the pores of calcareous earths and stones: as we see calcareous dropstones generating every day by the percolation of water through limestone, and new marble forming in the quarries from which the old has been taken out; and it might be asked, whether it is more difficult for nature to shoot the calcareous juice into the form of a shell, than other juices into the forms of chrystals, plants, animals, according to the construction of the vessels through which they pass? There is a wonder somewhere. Is it greatest on this branch of the dilemma; on that which supposes the existence of a power, of which we have no evidence in any other case; or on the first, which requires us to believe the creation of a body of water, and its subsequent annihilation? The establishment of the instance, cited by M. de Voltaire, of the growth of shells unattached to animal bodies, would have been that of his theory. But he has not established it. He has not even left it on ground so respectable as to have rendered it an object of enquiry to the literati of his own country. Abandoning this fact, therefore, the three hypotheses are equally unsatisfactory; and we must be contented to acknowledge, that this great phaenomenon is as yet unsolved. Ignorance is preferable to error; and he is less remote from the truth who believes nothing, then he who believes what is wrong.

Stone

There is great abundance (more especially when you approach the mountains) of stone, white, blue, brown, &c. fit for the chissel, good mill-stone, such also as stands the fire, and slate-stone. We are told of flint, fit for gun-flints, on the Meherrin in Brunswic, on the Missisipi between the mouth of Ohio and Kaskaskia, and on others of the western waters. Isinglass or mica is in several places; load-stone also, and an Asbestos of a ligneous texture, is sometimes to be met with.

Earths

Marle abounds generally. A clay, of which, like the Sturbridge in England, bricks are made, which will resist long the violent action of fire, has been found on Tuckahoe creek of James river, and no doubt will be found in other places. Chalk is said to be in Botetourt and Bedford. In the latter county is some earth, believed to be Gypseous. Ochres are found in various parts.

Nitre

In the lime-stone country are many caves, the earthy floors of which are impregnated with nitre. On Rich creek, a branch of the Great Kanhaway, about 60 miles below the lead mines, is a very large one, about 20 yards wide, and entering a hill a quarter or half a mile. The vault is of rock, from 9 to 15 or 20 feet above the floor. A Mr. Lynch, who gives me this account, undertook to extract the nitre. Besides a coat of the salt which had formed on the vault and floor, he found the earth highly impregnated to the depth of seven feet in some places, and generally of three, every bushel yielding on an average three pounds of nitre. Mr. Lynch having made about 1000 lb. of the salt from it, consigned it to some others, who have since made 10,000 lb. They have done this by pursuing the cave into the hill, never trying a second time the earth they have once exhausted, to see how far or soon it receives another impregnation. At least fifty of these caves are worked on the Greenbriar. There are many of them known on Cumberland river.

Salt

The country westward of the Alleghaney abounds with springs of common salt. The most remarkable we have heard of are at Bullet's lick, the Big bones, the Blue licks, and on the North fork of Holston. The area of Bullet's lick is of many acres. Digging the earth to the depth of three feet, the water begins to boil up, and the deeper you go, and the drier the weather, the stronger is the brine. A thousand gallons of water yield from a bushel to a bushel and a half of salt, which is about 80 lb. of water to one lb. of salt; but of sea-water 25 lb. yield one lb. of salt. So that sea-water is more than three times as strong as that of these springs. A salt spring has been lately discovered at the Turkey foot on Yohogany, by which river it is overflowed, except at very low water. Its merit is not yet known. Duning's lick is also as yet untried, but it is supposed to be the best on this side the Ohio. The salt springs on the margin of the Onondago lake are said to give a saline taste to the waters of the lake.

Medicinal springs

There are several Medicinal springs, some of which are indubitably efficacious, while others seem to owe their reputation as much to fancy, and change of air and regimen, as to their real virtues. None of them having undergone a chemical analysis in skilful hands, nor been so far the subject of observations as to have produced a reduction into classes of the disorders which they relieve, it is in my power to give little more than an enumeration of them.

The most efficacious of these are two springs in Augusta, near the first sources of James river, where it is called Jackson's river. They rise near the foot of the ridge of mountains, generally called the Warm spring mountain, but in the maps Jackson's mountains. The one is distinguished by the name of the Warm spring, and the other of the Hot spring. The Warm spring issues with a very bold stream, sufficient to work a grist-mill, and to keep the waters of its bason, which is 30 feet in diameter, at the vital warmth, viz. 96°. of Farenheit's thermometer. The matter with which these waters is allied is very volatile; its smell indicates it to be sulphureous, as also does the circumstance of its turning silver black. They relieve rheumatisms. Other complaints also of very different natures have been removed or lessened by them. It rains here four or five days in every week.

The *Hot spring* is about six miles from the Warm, is much smaller, and has been so hot as to have boiled an egg. Some believe its degree of heat to be lessened. It raises the mercury in Farenheit's thermometer to 112 degrees, which is fever heat. It sometimes relieves where the Warm spring fails. A fountain of common water, issuing within a few inches of its margin, gives it a singular appearance. Comparing the temperature of these with that of the Hot springs of Kamschatka, of which Krachininnikow[38] gives an account, the difference is very great, the latter raising the mercury to 200°. which is within 12°. of boiling water. These springs are very much resorted to in spite of a total want of accommodation for the sick. Their waters are strongest in the hottest months, which occasions their being visited in July and August principally.

The Sweet springs are in the county of Botetourt, at the eastern foot of the Alleghaney, about 42 miles from the Warm springs. They are still less known. Having been found to relieve cases in which the others had been ineffectually tried, it is probable their composition is different. They are different also in their temperature, being as cold as common water: which is not mentioned, however, as a proof of a distinct impregnation. This is among the first sources of James river.

On Patowmac river, in Berkeley county, above the North mountain, are Medicinal springs, much more frequented than those of Augusta. Their powers, however, are less, the waters weakly mineralized, and scarcely warm. They are more visited, because situated in a fertile, plentiful, and populous country, better provided with accommodations, always safe from the Indians, and nearest to the more populous states.

In Louisa county, on the head waters of the South Anna branch of York river, are springs of some medicinal virtue. They are not much used however. There is a weak chalybeate at Richmond; and many others in various parts of the country, which are of too little worth, or too little note, to be enumerated after those before-mentioned.

We are told of a Sulphur spring on Howard's creek of Greenbriar, and another at Boonsborough on Kentuckey.

Burning spring

In the low grounds of the Great Kanhaway, 7 miles above the mouth of Elk river, and 67 above that of the Kanhaway itself, is a hole in the earth of the capacity of 30 or 40 gallons, from which issues constantly a bituminous vapour in so strong a current,[39] as to give to the sand about its orifice the motion which it has in a boiling spring. On presenting a lighted candle or torch within 18 inches of the hole, it flames up in a column of 18 inches diameter, and four or five feet height, which sometimes burns out within 20 minutes, and at other times has been known to continue three days, and then has been left still burning. The flame is unsteady, of the density of that of burning spirits, and smells like burning pit coal. Water sometimes collects in the bason, which is remarkably cold, and is kept in ebullition by the vapour issuing[40] through it. If the vapour[41] be fired in that state, the water soon becomes so warm that the hand cannot bear it, and evaporates wholly in a short time. This, with the circumjacent lands, is the property of his Excellency General Washington and of General Lewis.[42]

There is a similar one on Sandy river, the flame of which is a column of about 12 inches diameter, and 3 feet high. General Clarke,[43] who informs me of it, kindled the vapour, staid about an hour, and left it burning.

Syphon fountains

The mention of uncommon springs leads me to that of Syphon fountains. There is one of these near the intersection of the Lord Fairfax's boundary with the North mountain, not far from Brock's gap, on the stream of which is a grist-mill, which grinds two bushel of grain at every flood of the spring. Another, near the Cow-pasture river, a mile and a half below its confluence with the Bull-pasture river, and 16 or 17 miles from the Hot springs, which intermits once in every twelve hours. One also near the mouth of the North Holston.[44]

After these may be mentioned the *Natural Well*, on the lands of a Mr. Lewis in Frederick county. It is somewhat larger than a common well: the water rises in it as near the surface of the earth as in the neighbouring artificial wells, and is of a depth as yet unknown. It is said there is a current in it tending sensibly downwards. If this be true, it probably feeds some fountain, of which it is the natural reservoir, distinguished from others, like that of Madison's cave, by being accessible. It is used with a bucket and windlass as an ordinary well.

Vegetables

A complete catalogue of the trees, plants, fruits, &c. is probably not desired. I will sketch out those which would principally attract notice, as being 1. Medicinal, 2. Esculent, 3. Ornamental, or 4. Useful for fabrication; adding the Linnaean[45] to the popular names, as the latter might not convey precise information to a foreigner. I shall confine myself too to native plants.

1. Senna. *Cassia ligustrina.*
Arsmart. *Polygonum Sagittatum.*
Clivers, or goose-grass. *Galium spurium.*
Lobelia of several species.
Palma Christi. *Ricinus.*
James-town weed. *Datura Stramonium* (3).
Mallow. *Malva rotundifolia.*
Syrian mallow. *Hibiscus moschentos.*
Hibiscus virginicus.
Indian mallow. *Sida rhombifolia.*
Sida abutilon.
Virginia Marshmallow. *Napaea hermaphrodita.*
Napaea dioica.
Indian physic. *Spiraea trifoliata.*
Euphorbia Ipecacuanhae.
Pleurisy root. *Asclepias decumbens.*
Virginia snake-root. *Aristolochia serpentaria.*

Black snake-root. *Actaea racemosa.*
Seneca rattlesnake-root. *Polygala Senega.*
Valerian. *Valeriana locusta radiata.*
Gentiana, Saponaria, Villosa & Centaurium.
Ginseng. *Panax quinquefolium.*
Angelica. *Angelica sylvestris.*
Cassava. *Jatropha urens.*

2. Tuckahoe. *Lycoperdon tuber.*
Jerusalem artichoke. *Helianthus tuberosus.*
Long potatoes. *Convolvulas batatas.*
Granadillas. Maycocks. Maracocks. *Passiflora incarnata.*
Panic. *Panicum* of many species.
Indian millet. *Holcus laxus.*
Holcus striosus.
Wild oat. *Zizania aquatica.*
Wild pea. Dolichos of Clayton.
Lupine. *Lupinus perennis.*
Wild hop. *Humulus lupulus.*
Wild cherry. *Prunus Virginiana.*
Cherokee plumb. *Prunus sylvestris fructu majori.* } Clayton.[46]
Wild plumb. *Prunus sylvestris fructu minori.* }
Wild crab-apple. *Pyrus coronaria.*
Red mulberry. *Morus rubra.*
Persimmon. *Diospyros Virginiana.*
Sugar maple. *Acer saccharinum.*
Scaly bark hiccory. *Juglans alba cortice squamoso.* Clayton.
Common hiccory. *Juglans alba, fructu minore rancido.* Clayton.
Paccan, or Illinois nut. Not described by Linnaeus, Millar, or Clayton.[47] Were I to venture to describe this, speaking of the fruit from memory, and of the leaf from plants of two years growth, I should specify it as the *Juglans alba,*[48] *foliolis lanceolatis, acuminatis, serratis, tomentosis, fructu minore, ovato, compresso, vix insculpto, dulci, putamine, tenerrimo.* It grows on the Illinois, Wabash, Ohio, and Missisipi. It is spoken of by Don Ulloa under the name of Pacanos, in his Noticis Americanas. Entret. 6.
Black walnut. *Juglans nigra.*
White walnut. *Juglans alba.*
Chesnut. *Fagus castanea.*
Chinquapin. *Fagus pumila.*
Hazlenut. *Corylus avellana.*

Grapes. *Vitis.* Various kinds, though only three described by Clayton.
Scarlet Strawberries. *Fragaria Virginiana* of Millar.
Whortleberries. *Vaccinium uliginosum?*
Wild gooseberries. *Ribes grossularia.*
Cranberries. *Vaccinium oxycoccos.*
Black raspberries. *Rubus occidentalis.*
Blackberries. *Rubus fruticosus.*
Dewberries. *Rubus caesius.*
Cloud-berries. *Rubus chamaemorus.*

3. Plane-tree. *Platanus occidentalis.*
Popular. *Liriodendron tulipifera.*
Populus heterophylla.
Black poplar. *Populus nigra.*
Aspen. *Populus tremula.*
Linden, or lime. *Tilia Americana.*
Red flowering maple. *Acer rubrum.*
Horse-chesnut, or Buck's-eye. *Aesculus pavia.*
Catalpa. *Bignonia catalpa.*
Umbrella. *Magnolia tripetala.*
Swamp laurel. *Magnolia glauca.*
Cucumber-tree. *Magnolia acuminata.*
Portugal bay. *Laurus indica.*
Red bay. *Laurus borbonia.*
Dwarf-rose bay. *Rhododendron maximum.*
Laurel of the western country. Qu. species?
Wild pimento. *Laurus benzoin.*
Sassafras. *Laurus sassafras.*
Locust. *Robinia pseudo-acacia.*
Honey-locust. *Gleditsia.* 1. ß.
Dogwood. *Cornus florida.*
Fringe or snow-drop tree. *Chionanthus Virginica.*
Barberry. *Berberis vulgaris.*
Redbud, or Judas-tree. *Cercis Canadensis.*
Holly. *Ilex aquifolium.*
Cockspur hawthorn. *Crataegus coccinea.*
Spindle-tree. *Euonymus Europaeus.*
Evergreen spindle-tree. *Euonymus Americanus.*
Itea Virginica.
Elder. *Sambacus nigra.*

Papaw. *Annona triloba.*
Candleberry myrtle. *Myrica cerifera.*
Dwarf-laurel. *Kalmia angustifolia.* } called ivy
Kalmia latifolia } with us.
Ivy. *Hedera quinquefolia.*
Trumpet honeysuckle. *Lonicera sempervirens.*
Upright honeysuckle. *Azalea nudiflora.*
Yellow jasmine. *Bignonia sempervirens.*
Calycanthus floridus.
American aloe. *Agave Virginica.*
Sumach. *Rhus.* Qu. species?
Poke. *Phytolacca decandra.*
Long moss. *Tillandsia Usneoides.*

4. Reed. *Arundo phragmitis.*
Virginia hemp. *Acnida cannabina.*
Flax. *Linum Virginianum.*
Black, or pitch-pine. *Pinus taeda.*
White pine. *Pinus strobus.*
Yellow pine. *Pinus Virginica.*
Spruce pine. *Pinus foliis singularibus.* Clayton.
Hemlock spruce fir. *Pinus Canadensis.*
Arbor vitae. *Thuya occidentalis.*
Juniper. *Juniperus virginica* (call cedar with us).
Cypress. *Cupressus disticha.*
White cedar. *Cupressus Thyoides.*
Black oak. *Quercus nigra.*
White oak. *Quercus alba.*
Red oak. *Quercus rubra.*
Willow oak. *Quercus phellos.*
Chesnut oak. *Quercus prinus.*
Black jack oak. *Quercus aquatica.* Clayton. Query?
Ground oak. *Quercus pumila.* Clayton.
Live oak. *Quercus Virginiana.* Millar.
Black Birch. *Betula nigra.*
White birch. *Betula alba.*
Beach. *Fagus sylvatica.*
Ash. *Fraxinus Americana.*
Fraxinus Novae Angliae Millar.
Elm. *Ulmus Americana.*
Willow. *Salix.* Query species?[49]
Sweet Gum. *Liquidambar styraciflua.*

The following were found in Virginia when first visited by the English; but it is not said whether of spontaneous growth, or by cultivation only. Most probably they were natives of more southern climates, and handed along the continent from one nation to another of the savages.

Tobacco. *Nicotiana.*
Maize.[50] *Zea mays.*
Round potatoes.[51] *Solanum tuberosum.*
Pumpkins. *Cucurbita pepo.*
Cymlings. *Cucurbita verrucosa.*
Squashes. *Cucurbita melopepo.*

There is an infinitude of other plants and flowers, for an enumeration and scientific description of which I must refer to the Flora Virginica of our great botanist Dr. Clayton, published by Gronovius[52] at Leyden, in 1762. This accurate observer was a native and resident of this state, passed a long life in exploring and describing its plants, and is supposed to have enlarged the botanical catalogue as much as almost any man who has lived.

Besides these plants, which are native, our *Farms* produce wheat, rye, barley, oats, buck wheat, broom corn, and Indian corn.[53] The climate suits rice well enough wherever the lands do. Tobacco, hemp, flax, and cotton, are staple commodities. Indico yields two cuttings. The silk-worm is a native, and the mulberry, proper for its food, grows kindly.

We cultivate also potatoes, both the long and the round, turnips, carrots, parsneps, pumpkins, and ground nuts (*Arachis*). Our grasses are Lucerne, St. Foin, Burnet, Timothy, ray and orchard grass; red, white, and yellow clover; greensward, blue grass, and crab grass.

The *gardens* yield musk melons, water melons, tomatas, okra, pomegranates, figs, and the esculent plants of Europe.

The *orchards* produce apples, pears, cherries, quinces, peaches, nectarines, apricots, almonds, and plumbs.

Animals

Our quadrupeds have been mostly described by Linnaeus and Mons. de Buffon.[54] Of these the Mammoth, or big buffalo, as called by the Indians, must certainly have been the largest. Their tradition is, that he was carnivorous, and still exists in the northern parts of America. A delegation of warriors from the Delaware tribe[55] having visited the governor of Virginia, during the present revolution, on matters of business, after these had been discussed and settled in council, the governor asked them some questions relative to their country, and, among others, what they knew or had heard of the animal whose bones were found at the Saltlicks, on the Ohio. Their chief speaker immediately put himself into an attitude of oratory, and with a pomp suited to what he conceived the elevation of his subject, informed him that it was a tradition handed down from their fathers, "That in antient times a herd of these tremendous animals came to the Big-bone licks, and began an universal destruction of the bear, deer, elks, buffaloes, and other animals, which had been created for the use of the Indians: that the Great Man above, looking down and seeing this, was so enraged that he seized his lightning, descended on the earth, seated himself on a neighbouring mountain, on a rock, of which his seat and the print of his feet are still to be seen, and hurled his bolts among them till the whole were slaughtered, except the big bull, who presenting his forehead to the shafts, shook them off as they fell; but missing one at length, it wounded him in the side; whereon, springing round, he bounded over the Ohio, over the Wabash, the Illinois, and finally over the great lakes, where he is living at this day." It is well known that on the Ohio, and in many parts of America further north, tusks, grinders, and skeletons of unparalleled magnitude, are found in great numbers, some lying on the surface of the earth, and some a little below it. A Mr. Stanley,[56] taken prisoner by the Indians near the mouth of the Tanissee, relates, that, after being transferred through several tribes, from one to another, he was at length carried over the mountains west of the Missouri to a river which runs westwardly; that these bones abounded there; and that the natives described to him the animal to which they belonged as still existing in the northern parts of their country; from which description he judged it to be an elephant. Bones of the same kind have been lately found, some feet below the surface of the earth, in salines opened on the

North Holston, a branch of the Tanissee, about the latitude of 36½°. North. From the accounts published in Europe, I suppose it to be decided, that these are of the same kind with those found in Siberia.[57] Instances are mentioned of like animal remains found in the more southern climates of both hemispheres;[58] but they are either so loosely mentioned as to leave a doubt of the fact, so inaccurately described as not to authorize the classing them with the great northern bones, or so rare as to found a suspicion that they have been carried thither as curiosities from more northern regions. So that on the whole there seem to be no certain vestiges of the existence of this animal further south than the salines last mentioned.[59] It is remarkable that the tusks and skeletons have been ascribed by the naturalists of Europe to the elephant, while the grinders have been given to the hippopotamus, or river-horse.[60] Yet it is acknowledged, that the tusks and skeletons are much larger than those of the elephant, and the grinders many times greater than those of the hippopotamus, and essentially different in form. Wherever these grinders are found, there also we find the tusks and skeleton; but no skeleton of the hippopotamus nor grinders of the elephant. It will not be said that the hippopotamus and elephant came always to the same spot, the former to deposit his grinders, and the latter his tusks and skeleton. For what became of the parts not deposited there? We must agree then that these remains belong to each other, that they are of one and the same animal, that this was not a hippopotamus, because the hippopotamus had no tusks nor such a frame, and because the grinders differ in their size as well as in the number and form of their points. That it was not an elephant, I think ascertained by proofs equally decisive. I will not avail myself of the authority of the celebrated* anatomist,[61] who, from an examination of the form and structure of the tusks, has declared they were essentially different from those of the elephant; because another† anatomist,[62] equally celebrated, has declared, on a like examination, that they are precisely the same. Between two such authorities I will suppose this circumstance

*Hunter.
†D'Aubenton.

equivocal. But, 1. The skeleton of the mammoth (for so the incognitum has been called) bespeaks an animal of five or six times the cubic volume of the elephant, as Mons. de Buffon has admitted.[63] 2. The grinders are five times as large, are square, and the grinding surface studded with four or five rows of blunt points: whereas those of the elephant are broad and thin, and their grinding surface flat.[64] 3. I have never heard an instance, and suppose there has been none, of the grinder of an elephant being found in America. 4. From the known temperature and constitution of the elephant he could never have existed in those regions where the remains of the mammoth have been found. The elephant is a native only of the torrid zone and its vicinities: if, with the assistance of warm apartments and warm clothing, he has been preserved in life in the temperate climates of Europe, it has only been for a small portion of what would have been his natural period, and no instance of his multiplication in them has ever been known. But no bones of the mammoth, as I have before observed, have been ever found further south than the salines of the Holston, and they have been found as far north as the Arctic circle. Those, therefore, who are of opinion that the elephant and mammoth are the same, must believe, 1. That the elephant known to us can exist and multiply in the frozen zone; or, 2. That an internal fire may once have warmed those regions, and since abandoned them, of which, however, the globe exhibits no unequivocal indications; or, 3. That the obliquity of the ecliptic, when these elephants lived, was so great as to include within the tropics all those regions in which the bones are found; the tropics being, as is before observed, the natural limits of habitation for the elephant.[65] But if it be admitted that this obliquity has really decreased, and we adopt the highest rate of decrease yet pretended, that is, of one minute in a century, to transfer the northern tropic to the Arctic circle, would carry the existence of these supposed elephants 250,000 years back; a period far beyond our conception of the duration of animal bones left exposed to the open air, as these are in many instances. Besides, though these regions would then be supposed within the tropics, yet their winters would have been too severe for the sensibility of the elephant. They would have had too but one day and one night in the year, a circumstance to which we have no reason to suppose the nature of the elephant fitted. However, it has been demonstrated, that, if a variation of obliquity in the ecliptic takes place at all, it is vibratory, and never exceeds the limits of 9 degrees, which is not sufficient to bring these bones within the tropics. One of these hypotheses, or some other equally voluntary and inadmissible to cautious philosophy, must be adopted to support the opinion that these are the bones of the elephant. For my own part, I find it easier to believe that an animal may have existed, resembling the elephant in his tusks, and general anatomy, while his nature was in other respects extremely different. From the 30th degree of South latitude to the 30th of North, are nearly the limits which nature has fixed for the existence and multiplication of the elephant known to us. Proceeding thence northwardly to 36½ degrees, we enter those assigned to the mammoth. The further we advance North, the more their vestiges multiply as far as the earth has been explored in that direction; and it is as probable as otherwise, that this progression continues to the pole itself, if land extends so far. The center of the Frozen zone then may be the Achmé of their vigour, as that of the Torrid is of the elephant. Thus nature seems to have drawn a belt of separation between these two tremendous animals, whose breadth indeed is not precisely known, though at present we may suppose it about 6½ degrees of latitude; to have assigned to the elephant the regions South of these confines, and those North to the mammoth, founding the constitution of the one in her extreme of heat, and that of the other in the extreme of cold. When the Creator has therefore separated their nature as far as the extent of the scale of animal life allowed to this planet would permit, it seems perverse to declare it the same, from a partial resemblance of their tusks and bones. But to whatever animal we ascribe these remains, it is certain such a one has existed in America, and that it has been the largest of all terrestrial beings. It should have sufficed to have rescued the earth it inhabited, and the atmosphere it breathed, from the imputation of impotence in the conception and nourishment of animal life on a large scale: to have stifled, in its birth, the opinion of a writer, the most learned too of all others in the science of animal history, that in the new world, "La nature vivante est beaucoup moins agissante, beaucoup moins forte":[66] that nature is less active, less energetic on one side of the globe than she is on the other. As if both sides were not warmed by the same genial sun; as if a soil of the same chemical composition, was less capable of elaboration into animal nutriment; as if the fruits and grains from that soil and sun, yielded a less rich chyle, gave less extension to the solids and fluids of the body, or produced sooner in the cartilages, membranes, and fibres, that rigidity which restrains all further extension, and terminates animal growth. The truth is, that a Pigmy and a Patagonian, a Mouse and a Mammoth, derive their dimensions from the same nutritive juices. The difference of increment depends on circumstances unsearchable to beings with our capacities. Every race of animals seems to have received from their Maker certain laws of extension at the time of their formation. Their elaborative organs were formed to produce this, while proper obstacles were opposed to its further progress. Below these limits they cannot fall, nor rise above them. What intermediate station they shall take may depend on soil, on climate, on food, on a careful choice of breeders. But all the manna of heaven would never raise the Mouse to the bulk of the Mammoth.

The opinion advanced by the Count de Buffon,[67] is 1. That the animals common both to the old and new world, are smaller in the latter. 2. That those peculiar to the new, are on a smaller scale. 3. That those which have been domesticated in both, have degenerated in America: and 4. That on the whole it exhibits fewer species. And the reason he thinks is, that the heats of America are less; that more waters are spread over its surface by nature, and fewer of these drained off by the hand of man. In other words, that *heat* is friendly, and *moisture* adverse to the production and developement of large quadrupeds. I will not meet this hypothesis on its first doubtful ground, whether the climate of America be comparatively more humid? Because we are not furnished with observations sufficient to decide this question. And though, till it be decided, we are as free to deny, as others are to affirm the fact, yet for a moment let it be supposed. The hypothesis, after this supposition, proceeds to another; that *moisture* is unfriendly to animal growth. The truth of this is inscrutable to us by reasonings a priori. Nature has hidden from us her modus agendi. Our only appeal on such questions is to experience; and I think that experience is against the supposition. It is by the assistance of *heat* and *moisture* that vegetables are elaborated from the elements of earth, air, water, and fire. We accordingly see the more humid climates produce the greater quantity of vegetables. Vegetables are mediately or immediately the food of every animal: and in proportion to the quantity of food, we see animals not only multiplied in their numbers, but improved in their bulk, as far as the laws of their nature will admit. Of this opinion is the Count de Buffon himself in another part of his work: "en general il paroit que les pays un peu *froids* conviennent mieux à nos boeufs que les pays chauds, et qu'ils sont d'autant plus gros et plus grands que le climat est plus *humide* et plus abondans en paturages. Les boeufs de Danemarck, de la Podolie, de l'Ukraine et de la Tartarie qu'habitent les Calmouques sont les plus grands de tous."[68] Here then a race of animals, and one of the largest too, has been increased in its dimensions by *cold* and *moisture*, in direct opposition to the hypothesis, which supposes that these two circumstances diminish animal bulk, and that it is their contraries *heat* and *dryness* which enlarge it. But when we appeal to experience, we are not to rest satisfied with a single fact. Let us therefore try our question on more general ground. Let us take two portions of the earth, Europe and America for instance, sufficiently extensive to give operation to general causes; let us consider the circumstances peculiar to each, and observe their effect on animal nature. America, running through the torrid as well as temperate zone, has more *heat*, collectively taken, than Europe. But Europe, according to our hypothesis, is the *dryest*. They are equally adapted then to animal productions; each being endowed with one of those causes which befriend animal growth, and with one which opposes it. If it be thought unequal to compare Europe with America, which is so much larger, I answer, not more so than to compare America with the whole world. Besides, the purpose of the comparison is to try an hypothesis, which makes the size of animals depend on the *heat* and *moisture* of climate. If therefore we take a region, so extensive as to comprehend a sensible distinction of climate, and so extensive too as that local accidents, or the intercourse of animals on its borders, may not materially affect the size of those in its interior parts, we shall comply with those conditions which the hypothesis may reasonably demand. The objection would be the weaker in the present case, because any intercourse of animals which may take place on the confines of Europe and Asia, is to the advantage of the former, Asia producing certainly larger animals than Europe. Let us then take a comparative view of the Quadrupeds of Europe and America, presenting them to the eye in three different tables, in one of which shall be enumerated those found in both countries; in a second those found in one only; in a third those which have been domesticated in both. To facilitate the comparison, let those of each table be arranged in gradation according to their sizes, from the greatest to the smallest, so far as their sizes can be conjectured. The weights of the large animals shall be expressed in the English avoirdupoise pound and its decimals: those of the smaller in the ounce and its decimals. Those which are marked thus *, are actual weights of particular subjects, deemed among the largest of their species. Those marked thus †, are furnished by judicious persons, well acquainted with the species, and saying, from conjecture only, what the largest individual they had seen would probably have weighed. The other weights are taken from Messrs. Buffon and D'Aubenton, and are of such subjects as came casually to their hands for dissection. This circumstance must be remembered where their weights and mine stand opposed: the latter being stated, not to produce a conclusion in favour of the American species, but to justify a suspension of opinion until we are better informed, and a suspicion in the mean time that there is no uniform difference in favour of either; which is all I pretend.

A Comparative View of the Quadrupeds of Europe and of America.

I. Aboriginals of both.

	Europe	America
	lb.	lb.
Mammoth		
Buffalo. Bison		*1800
White bear. Ours blanc		
Caribou. Renne		
Bear. Ours	153.7	*410
Elk. Elan. Orignal, palmated		
Red deer. Cerf	288.8	*273
Fallow deer. Daim	167.8	
Wolf. Loup	69.8	
Roe, Chevreuil	56.7	
Glutton. Glouton. Carcajour		
Wild cat. Chat sauvage		†30
Lynx. Loup cervier	25.	
Beaver. Castor	18.5	*45
Badger. Blaireau	13.6	
Red Fox. Renard	13.5	
Grey Fox. Isatis		
Otter. Loutre	8.9	†12
Monax. Marmotte	6.5	
Vison. Fouine	2.8	
Hedgehog. Herisson	2.2	
Martin. Marte	1.9	†6
	oz.	
Water rat. Rat d'eau	7.5	
Wesel. Belette	2.2	oz.
Flying squirrel. Polatouche	2.2	†4
Shrew mouse. Musaraigne	1.	

II. Aboriginals of one only.			
Europe		**America**	
	lb.		**lb.**
Sanglier. Wild boar	280.	Tapir	534.
Mouflon. Wild sheep	56.	Elk, round horned	†450.
Bouquetin. Wild goat		Puma	
Lievre. Hare[69]	7.6	Jaguar	218.
Lapin. Rabbet	3.4	Cabiai	109.
Putois. Polecat	3.3	Tamanoir	109.
Genette	3.1	Tamandua	65.4
Desman. Muskrat	oz.	Cougar of N. Amer.	75.
Ecureuil. Squirrel	12.	Cougar of S. Amer.	59.4
Hermine. Ermin	8.2	Ocelot	
Rat. Rat	7.5	Pecari	46.3
Loirs	3.1	Jaguaret	43.6
Lerot. Dormouse	1.8	Alco	
Taupe. Mole	1.2	Lama	
Hamster	.9	Paco	
Zisel		Paca	32.7
Leming		Serval	
Souris. Mouse	.6	Sloth. Unau	27¼
		Saricovienne	
		Kincajou	
		Tatou Kabassou	21.8
		Urson. Urchin	
		Raccoon. Raton	16.5
		Coati	
		Coendou	16.3
		Sloth. Aï	13.
		Sapajou Ouarini	
		Sapajou Coaita	9.8
		Tatou Encubert	
		Tatou Apar	
		Tatou Cachica	7.
		Little Coendou	6.5
		Opossum. Sarigue	
		Tapeti	
		Margay	
		Crabier	
		Agouti	4.2

[continued]

II. *Aboriginals of one only.*			
Europe		**America**	
		Sapajou Saï	3.5
		Tatou Cirquinçon	
		Tatou Tatouate	3.3
		Mouffette Squash	
		Mouffette Chinche	
		Mouffette Conepate. Scunk	
		Mouffette. Zorilla	
		Whabus. Hare. Rabbet	
		Aperea	
		Akouchi	
		Ondatra. Muskrat	
		Pilori	
		Great grey squirrel	†2.7
		Fox squirrel of Virginia	†2.625
		Surikate	2.
		Mink	†2.
		Sapajou. Sajou	1.8
		Indian pig. Cochon d'Inde	1.6
		Sapajou. Saïmiri	1.5
		Phalanger	
		Coquallin	
		Lesser grey squirrel	†1.5
		Black squirrel	†1.5
		Red squirrel	10. oz.
		Sagoin Saki	
		Sagoin Pinche	
		Sagoin Tamarin	oz.
		Sagoin Ouistiti	4.4
		Sagoin Marikine	
		Sagoin Mico	
		Cayopollin	
		Fourmillier	
		Marmose	
		Sarigue of Cayenne	
		Tucan	
		Red mole	oz.
		Ground squirrel	4.

III. Domesticated in both.		
	Europe	**America**
	lb.	lb.
Cow	763.	*2500
Horse		*1366
Ass		
Hog		*1200
Sheep		*125
Goat		*80
Dog	67.6	
Cat	7.	

I have not inserted in the first table the *Phoca nor leather-winged bat, because the one living half the year in the water, and the other being a winged animal, the individuals of each species may visit both continents.

Of the animals in the 1st table Mons. de Buffon himself informs us, [XXVII. 130. XXX. 213.] that the beaver, the otter,[70] and shrew mouse, though of the same species, are larger in America than Europe. This should therefore have corrected the generality of his expressions XVIII. 145. and elsewhere, that the animals common to the two countries, are considerably less in America than in Europe, "& cela sans aucune exception."[71] He tells us too, [Quadrup. VIII. 334. edit. Paris, 1777] that on examining a bear from America, he remarked no difference, "dans *la forme* de cet ours d'Amerique comparé a celui d'Europe."[72] But adds from Bartram's journal, that an American bear weighed 400 lb. English, equal to 367 lb. French: whereas we find the European bear examined by Mons. D'Aubenton, [XVII. 82.]

---

*It is said, that this animal is seldom seen above 30 miles from shore, or beyond the 56th degree of latitude. The interjacent islands between Asia and America admit his passing from one continent to the other without exceeding these bounds. And, in fact, travellers tell us that these islands are places of principal resort for them, and especially in the season of bringing forth their young.

weighed but 141 lb. French. That the palmated Elk is larger in America than Europe we are informed by Kalm, a Naturalist who visited the former by public appointment for the express purpose of examining the subjects of Natural history. In this fact Pennant concurs with him. [Barrington's Miscellanies.] The same Kalm tells us that the Black Moose, or Renne of America, is as high as a tall horse; and Catesby, that it is about the bigness of a middle sized ox. The same account of their size has been given me by many who have seen them.[73] But Mons. D'Aubenton says[74] that the Renne of Europe is but about the size of a Red-deer. The wesel is larger in America than in Europe, as may be seen by comparing its dimensions as reported by Mons. D'Aubenton and Kalm. The latter tells us, that the lynx, badger, red fox, and flying squirrel, are the *same* in America as in Europe: by which expression I understand, they are the same in all material circumstances, in size as well as others: for if they were smaller, they would differ from the European. Our grey fox is, by Catesby's account, little different in size and shape from the European fox. I presume he means the red fox of Europe, as does Kalm, where he says, that in size "they do not quite come up to our foxes." For proceeding next to the red fox of America, he says "they are entirely the same with the European sort." Which shews he had in view one European sort only, which was the red. So that the result of their testimony is, that the American grey fox is somewhat less than the European red; which is equally true of the grey fox of Europe, as may be seen by comparing the measures of the Count de Buffon and Mons. D'Aubenton.[75] The white bear of America is as large as that of Europe. The bones of the Mammoth which have been found in America, are as large as those found in the old world. It may be asked, why I insert the Mammoth, as if it still existed? I ask in return, why I should omit it, as if it did not exist? Such is the oeconomy of nature, that no instance can be produced of her having permitted any one race of her animals to become extinct; of her having formed any link in her great work so weak as to be broken. To add to this, the traditionary testimony of the Indians, that this animal still exists in the northern and western parts of America, would be adding the light of a taper to that of the meridian sun. Those parts still remain in their aboriginal state, unexplored and undisturbed by us, or by others for us. He may as well exist there now, as he did formerly where we find his bones. If he be a carnivorous animal, as some Anatomists have conjectured, and the Indians affirm, his early retirement may be accounted for from the general destruction of the wild game by the Indians, which commences in the first instant of their connection with us, for the purpose of purchasing matchcoats, hatchets, and fire locks, with their skins. There remain then the buffalo, red deer, fallow deer, wolf, roe, glutton,[76] wild cat, monax, vison, hedge-hog, martin, and water rat, of the comparative sizes of which we have not sufficient testimony. It does not appear that Messrs. de Buffon and D'Aubenton have measured, weighed, or seen those of America. It is said of some of them, by some travellers, that they are smaller than the European. But who were these travellers? Have they not been men of a very different description from those who have laid open to us the other three quarters of the world? Was natural history the object of their travels? Did they measure or weigh the animals they speak of? or did they not judge of them by sight, or perhaps even from report only? Were they acquainted with the animals of their own country, with which they undertake to compare them? Have they not been so ignorant as often to mistake the species?[77] A true answer to these questions would probably lighten their authority, so as to render it insufficient for the foundation of an hypothesis. How unripe we yet are, for an accurate comparison of the animals of the two countries, will appear from the work of Mons. de Buffon. The ideas we should have formed of the sizes of some animals, from the information he had received at his first publications concerning them, are very different from what his subsequent communications give us. And indeed his candour in this can never be too much praised. One sentence of his book must do him immortal honour. "J'aime autant une personne qui me releve d'une erreur, qu'une autre qui m'apprend une verité, parce qu'en effet une erreur corrigée est une verité."[78] He seems to have thought the Cabiai he first examined wanted little of its full growth. "Il n'etoit pas encore tout-a-fait adulte."[79] Yet he weighed but 46½ lb. and he found afterwards, that these animals, when full grown, weigh 100 lb. He had supposed, from the examination of a jaguar, said to be two years old, which weighed but 16 lb. 12 oz. that, when he should have acquired his full growth, he would not be larger than a middle sized dog. But a subsequent account[80] raises his weight to 200 lb. Further information will, doubtless, produce further corrections. The wonder is, not that there is yet something in this great work to correct, but that there is so little. The result of this view then is, that of 26 quadrupeds common to both countries, 7 are said to be larger in America, 7 of equal size, and 12 not sufficiently examined. So that the first table impeaches the first member of the assertion, that of the animals common to both countries, the American are smallest, "et cela sans aucune exception." It shews it not just, in all the latitude in which its author has advanced it, and probably not to such a degree as to found a distinction between the two countries.

Proceeding to the second table, which arranges the animals found in one of the two countries only, Mons. de Buffon observes, that the tapir, the elephant of America, is but of the size of a small cow. To preserve our comparison, I will add that the wild boar, the elephant of Europe, is little more than half that size. I have made an elk with round or cylindrical horns, an animal of America, and peculiar to it; because I have seen many of them myself, and more of their horns; and because I can say, from the best information, that, in Virginia, this kind of elk has abounded much, and still exists in smaller numbers; and I could never learn that the palmated kind had been seen here at all. I suppose this confined to the more Northern latitudes*.[81] I have

---

*The descriptions of Theodat, Denys and La Hontan,[82] cited by Mons. de Buffon under the article Elan, authorize the supposition, that the flat-horned elk is found in the northern parts of America. It has not however extended to our latitudes. On the other hand, I could never learn that the round-horned elk has been seen further North than the Hudson's river. This agrees with the former elk in its general character, being, like that, when compared with a deer, very much larger, its ears longer, broader, and thicker in proportion, its hair much longer, neck and tail shorter, having a dewlap before the breast (caruncula gutturalis Linnaei) a white spot often, if not always; of a foot diameter, on the hinder part of the buttocks round the tail; its gait a trot, and attended with a rattling of the hoofs: but distinguished from that decisively by its horns, which are not palmated, but round and pointed. This is the animal described by Catesby as the Cervus major Americanus, the Stag of America, le Cerf de l'Amerique. But it differs from the Cervus

made our hare or rabbet peculiar, believing it to be different from both the European animals of those denominations, and calling it therefore by its Algonquin name Whabus, to keep it distinct from these. Kalm is of the same opinion.[83] I have enumerated the squirrels according to our own knowledge, derived from daily sight of them, because I am not able to reconcile with that the European appellations and descriptions. I have heard of other species, but they have never come within my own notice. These, I think, are the only instances in which I have departed from the authority of Mons. de Buffon in the construction of this table. I take him for my ground work, because I think him the best informed of any Naturalist who has ever written. The result is, that there are 18 quadrupeds peculiar to Europe; more than four times as many, to wit 74, peculiar to America; that the

---

as totally, as does the palmated elk from the dama. And in fact it seems to stand in the same relation to the palmated elk, as the red deer does to the fallow. It has abounded in Virginia, has been seen, within my knowledge, on the Eastern side of the Blue ridge since the year 1765, is now common beyond those mountains, has been often brought to us and tamed, and their horns are in the hands of many. I should designate it as the "Alces Americanus cornibus teretibus." It were to be wished, that Naturalists, who are acquainted with the renne and elk of Europe, and who may hereafter visit the northern parts of America, would examine well the animals called there by the names of grey and black moose, caribou, orignal, and elk. Mons. de Buffon has done what could be done from the materials in his hands, towards clearing up the confusion introduced by the loose application of these names among the animals they are meant to designate. He reduces the whole to the renne and flat-horned elk. From all the information I have been able to collect, I strongly suspect they will be found to cover three, if not four distinct species of animals. I have seen skins of a moose, and of the caribou: they differ more from each other, and from that of the round-horned elk, than I ever saw two skins differ which belonged to different individuals of any wild species. These differences are in the colour, length, and coarseness of the hair, and in the size, texture, and marks of the skin. Perhaps it will be found that there is, 1. the moose, black and grey, the former being said to be the male, and the latter the female. 2. The caribou or renne. 3. The flat-horned elk, or orignal. 4. The round-horned elk. Should this last, though possessing so nearly the characters of the elk, be found to be the same with the Cerf d'Ardennes or Brandhirtz of Germany, still there will remain the three species first enumerated.

*first of these 74 weighs more than the whole column of Europeans; and consequently this second table disproves the second member of the assertion, that the animals peculiar to the new world are on a smaller scale, so far as that assertion relied on European animals for support: and it is in full opposition to the theory which makes the animal volume to depend on the circumstances of *heat* and *moisture*.

The IIId. table comprehends those quadrupeds only which are domestic in both countries. That some of these, in some parts of America, have become less than their original stock, is doubtless true; and the reason is very obvious. In a thinly peopled country, the spontaneous productions of the forests and waste fields are sufficient to support indifferently the domestic animals of the farmer, with a very little aid from him in the severest and scarcest season. He therefore finds it more convenient to receive them from the hand of nature in that indifferent state, than to keep up their size by a care and nourishment which would cost him much labour. If, on this low fare, these animals dwindle, it is no more than they do in those parts of Europe where the poverty of the soil, or poverty of the owner, reduces them to the same scanty subsistance. It is the uniform effect of one and the same cause, whether acting on this or that side of the globe. It would be erring therefore against that rule of philosophy, which teaches us to ascribe like effects to like causes, should we impute this diminution of size in America to any imbecility or want of uniformity in the operations of nature. It may be affirmed with truth that, in those countries, and with those individuals of America, where necessity or curiosity has produced equal attention as in Europe to the nourishment of animals, the

---

*The Tapir is the largest of the animals peculiar to America. I collect his weight thus. Mons. de Buffon says, XXIII. 274. that he is of the size of a Zebu, or a small cow. He gives us the measures of a Zebu, ib. 94. as taken by himself, viz. 5 feet 7 inches from the muzzle to the root of the tail, and 5 feet 1 inch circumference behind the fore legs. A bull, measuring in the same way 6 feet 9 inches and 5 feet 2 inches, weighed 600 lb. VIII. 153. The Zebu then, and of course the Tapir, would weigh about 500 lb. But one individual of every species of European peculiars would probably weigh less than 400 lb. These are French measures and weights.

horses, cattle, sheep, and hogs of the one continent are as large as those of the other. There are particular instances, well attested, where individuals of this country have imported good breeders from England, and have improved their size by care in the course of some years. To make a fair comparison between the two countries, it will not answer to bring together animals of what might be deemed the middle or ordinary size of their species; because an error in judging of that middle or ordinary size would vary the result of the comparison. Thus Monsieur D'Aubenton[84] considers a horse of 4 feet 5 inches high and 400 lb. weight French, equal to 4 feet 8.6 inches and 436 lb. English, as a middle sized horse. Such a one is deemed a small horse in America. The extremes must therefore be resorted to. The same anatomist dissected a horse of 5 feet 9 inches height, French measure, equal to 6 feet 1.7 English. This is near 6 inches higher than any horse I have seen: and could it be supposed that I had seen the largest horses in America, the conclusion would be, that ours have diminished, or that we have bred from a smaller stock. In Connecticut and Rhode-Island, where the climate is favorable to the production of grass, bullocks have been slaughtered which weighed 2500, 2200, and 2100 lb. nett; and those of 1800 lb. have been frequent. I have seen a *hog weigh 1050 lb. after the blood, bowels, and hair had been taken from him. Before he was killed an attempt was made to weigh him with a pair of steel-yards, graduated to 1200 lb. but he weighed more. Yet this hog was probably not within fifty generations of the European stock. I am well informed of another which weighed 1100 lb. gross. Asses have been still more neglected than any other domestic animal in America. They are neither fed nor housed in the most rigorous season of the year. Yet they are larger than those measured by Mons. D'Aubenton, of 3 feet 7¼ inches, 3 feet 4 inches, and 3 feet 2½ inches, the latter weighing only 215.8 lb.[85] These sizes, I suppose, have been produced by the same negligence in Europe, which has produced a like diminution here. Where care has been taken of them on that side of the water, they have been raised to a size bordering on that of the horse; not by the *heat* and *dryness* of the climate, but by good food and shelter. Goats

---

*In Williamsburg, April, 1769.

have been also much neglected in America. Yet they are very prolific here, bearing twice or three times a year, and from one to five kids at a birth. Mons. de Buffon has been sensible of a difference in this circumstance in favour of America.[86] But what are their greatest weights I cannot say. A large sheep here weighs 100 lb. I observe Mons. D'Aubenton calls a ram of 62 lb. one of the middle size.[87] But to say what are the extremes of growth in these and the other domestic animals of America, would require information of which no one individual is possessed.[88] The weights actually known and stated in the third table preceding will suffice to shew, that we may conclude, on probable grounds, that, with equal food and care, the climate of America will preserve the races of domestic animals as large as the European stock from which they are derived; and consequently that the third member of Mons. de Buffon's assertion, that the domestic animals are subject to degeneration from the climate of America, is as probably wrong as the first and second were certainly so.

That the last part of it is erroneous, which affirms that the species of American quadrupeds are comparatively few, is evident from the tables taken all together. By these it appears that there are an hundred species aboriginal of America. Mons. de Buffon supposes about double that number existing on the whole earth.[89] Of these Europe, Asia, and Africa, furnish suppose 126; that is, the 26 common to Europe and America, and about 100 which are not in America at all. The American species then are to those of the rest of the earth, as 100 to 126, or 4 to 5. But the residue of the earth being double the extent of America, the exact proportion would have been but as 4 to 8.

Hitherto I have considered this hypothesis as applied to brute animals only, and not in its extension to the man of America, whether aboriginal or transplanted. It is the opinion of Mons. de Buffon that the former furnishes no exception to it.[90] "Quoique le sauvage du nouveau monde soit à-peu-près de même stature que l'homme de notre monde, cela ne suffit pas pour qu'il puisse faire une exception au fait général du rapetissement de la nature vivante dans tout ce continent: le sauvage est foible & petit par les organes de la génération; il n'a ni poil, ni barbe, & nulle ardeur pour sa femelle; quoique plus léger que l'Européen parce qu'il a plus d'habitude à courir, il est cependant beaucoup moins fort de corps; il est aussi bien moins sensible, & cependant plus craintif & plus lâche; il n'a nulle vivacité, nulle activité dans l'ame; celle du corps est moins un exercice, un mouvement volontaire qu'une nécessité d'action causée par le besoin; otez lui la faim & la soif, vous détruirez en meme temps le principe actif de tous ses mouvemens; il demeurera stupidement en repos sur ses jambes ou couché pendant des jours entiers. Il ne faut pas aller chercher plus loin la cause de la vie dispersée des sauvages & de leur éloignement pour la société: la plus precieuse étincelle du feu de la nature leur a été refusée; ils manquent d'ardeur pour leur femelle, & par consequent d'amour pour leur semblables: ne connoissant pas l'attachement le plus vif, le plus tendre de tous, leurs autres sentimens de ce genre sont froids & languissans; ils aiment foiblement leurs pères & leurs enfans; la société la plus intime de toutes, celle de la même famille, n'a donc chez eux que de foibles liens; la société d'une famille à l'autre n'en a point du tout: dès lors nulle réunion, nulle république, nulle état social. La physique de l'amour fait chez eux le moral des moeurs; leur coeur est glacé, leur société froide, & leur empire dur. Ils ne regardent leurs femmes que comme des servantes de peine ou des bêtes de somme qu'ils chargent, sans ménagement, du fardeau de leur chasse, & qu'ils forcent sans pitié, sans reconnoissance, à des ouvrages qui souvent sont audessus de leurs forces: ils n'ont que peu d'enfans; ils en ont peu de soin; tout se ressent de leur premier défaut; ils en ont peu de soin; tout se ressent de leur premier défaut; ils sont indifférents parce qu'ils sont peu puissans, & cette indifférence pour le sexe est la tâche originelle qui flétrit la nature, qui l'empêche de s'épanouir, & qui détruisant les germes de la vie, coupe en même temps la racine de la société. L'homme ne fait donc point d'exception ici. La nature en lui refusant les puissances de l'amour l'a plus maltraité & plus rapetissé qu'aucun des animaux."[91] An afflicting picture indeed, which, for the honor of human nature, I am glad to believe has no original. Of the Indian of South America I know nothing; for I would not honor with the appellation of knowledge, what I derive from the fables published of them. These I believe to be just as true as the fables of Aesop. This belief is founded on what I have seen of man, white, red, and black, and what has been written of him by authors, enlightened themselves, and writing amidst an enlightened people. The Indian of North America being more within our reach, I can speak of him somewhat from my own knowledge, but more from the information of others better acquainted with him, and on whose truth and judgment I can rely. From these sources I am able to say, in contradiction to this representation, that he is neither more defective in ardor, nor more impotent with his female, than the white reduced to the same diet and exercise:[92] that he is brave, when an enterprize depends on bravery; education with him making the point of honor consist in the destruction of an enemy by stratagem, and in the preservation of his own person free from injury; or perhaps this is nature; while it is education which teaches us to *honor force more than finesse: that he will defend himself against an host of enemies, always chusing to be killed, rather than to †surrender, though it be to the whites, who he

---

*Sol Rodomonte[93] sprezza di venire
Se non, dove la via meno è sicura. Ariosto. 14. 117.

†In so judicious an author as Don Ulloa, and one to whom we are indebted for the most precise information we have of South America, I did not expect to find such assertions as the following. "Los Indios vencidos son los mas cobardes y pusilanimes que se peuden vér:—se hacen inocentes, se humillan hasta el desprecio, disculpan su inconsiderado arrojo, y con las súplicas y los ruegos dán seguras pruebas de su pusilanimidad.—ó lo que resieren las historias de la Conquista, sobre sus grandes acciones, es en un sentido figurado, ó el caracter de estas gentes no es ahora segun era entonces; pero lo que no tiene duda es, que las Naciones de la parte Septentrional subsisten en la misma libertad que siempre han tenido, sin haber sido sojuzgados por algun Principe extrano, y que viven segun su régimen y costumbres de toda la vida, sin que haya habido motivo para que muden de caracter; y en estos se vé lo mismo, que sucede en los del Peru, y de toda la América Meridional, reducidos, y que nunca lo han estado."[94] Noticias Americanas. Entretenimiento XVIII. §. 1. Don Ulloa here admits, that the authors who have described the Indians of South America, before they were enslaved, had represented them as a brave people, and therefore seems to have suspected that the cowardice which he had observed in those of the present race might be the effect of subjugation. But, supposing the Indians of North America to be cowards also, he concludes the ancestors of those of South America to have been so too, and therefore that those authors have given fictions for truths. He was probably not acquainted himself with the Indians of North America, and had formed his opinion of them from hear-say. Great numbers of French, of English, and of Americans, are perfectly acquainted with these people. Had he had an opportunity of enquiring of any of these, they would

knows will treat him well: that in other situations also he meets death with more deliberation, and endures tortures with a firmness unknown almost to religious enthusiasm with us: that he is affectionate to his children, careful of them, and indulgent in the extreme: that his affections comprehend his other connections, weakening, as with us, from circle to circle, as they recede from the center: that his friendships are strong and faithful to the uttermost *extremity: that his sensibility is keen,[96] even the warriors weeping most bitterly on the loss of their children, though in general they endeavour to appear superior to human events: that his vivacity and activity of mind is equal to ours in the same situation; hence his eagerness for hunting, and for games of chance.[97] The women are submitted to unjust drudgery. This I believe is the case with every barbarous people. With such, force is law. The stronger sex therefore imposes on the weaker. It is civilization alone which replaces women in the enjoyment of their natural equality. That first teaches us to subdue the selfish

---

have told him, that there never was an instance known of an Indian begging his life when in the power of his enemies: on the contrary, that he courts death by every possible insult and provocation. His reasoning then would have been reversed thus. "Since the present Indian of North America is brave, and authors tell us, that the ancestors of those of South America were brave also; it must follow, that the cowardice of their descendants is the effect of subjugation and ill treatment." For he observes, ib. §. 27. that "los obrages los aniquilan por la inhumanidad con que se les trata."[95]

*A remarkable instance of this appeared in the case of the late Col. Byrd,[98] who was sent to the Cherokee nation to transact some business with them. It happened that some of our disorderly people had just killed one or two of that nation. It was therefore proposed in the council of the Cherokees that Col. Byrd should be put to death, in revenge for the loss of their countrymen. Among them was a chief called Silòuee, who, on some former occasion, had contracted an acquaintance and friendship with Col. Byrd. He came to him every night in his tent, and told him not to be afraid, they should not kill him. After many days deliberation, however, the determination was, contrary to Silòuee's expectation, that Byrd should be put to death, and some warriors were dispatched as executioners. Silòuee attended them, and when they entered the tent, he threw himself between them and Byrd, and said to the warriors, "this man is my friend: before you get at him, you must kill me." On which they returned, and the council respected the principle so much as to recede from their determination.

passions, and to respect those rights in others which we value in ourselves. Were we in equal barbarism, our females would be equal drudges. The man with them is less strong than with us, but their woman stronger than ours; and both for the same obvious reason; because our man and their woman is habituated to labour, and formed by it. With both races the sex which is indulged with ease is least athletic. An Indian man is small in the hand and wrist for the same reason for which a sailor is large and strong in the arms and shoulders, and a porter in the legs and thighs.—They raise fewer children than we do. The causes of this are to be found, not in a difference of nature, but of circumstance. The women very frequently attending the men in their parties of war and of hunting, child-bearing becomes extremely inconvenient to them. It is said, therefore, that they have learnt the practice of procuring abortion by the use of some vegetable; and that it even extends to prevent conception for a considerable time after.[99] During these parties they are exposed to numerous hazards, to excessive exertions, to the greatest extremities of hunger. Even at their homes the nation depends for food, through a certain part of every year, on the gleanings of the forest: that is, they experience a famine once in every year. With all animals, if the female be badly fed, or not fed at all, her young perish: and if both male and female be reduced to like want, generation becomes less active, less productive. To the obstacles then of want and hazard, which nature has opposed to the multiplication of wild animals, for the purpose of restraining their numbers within certain bounds, those of labour and of voluntary abortion are added with the Indian. No wonder then if they multiply less than we do. Where food is regularly supplied, a single farm will shew more of cattle, than a whole country of forests can of buffaloes. The same Indian women, when married to white traders, who feed them and their children plentifully and regularly, who exempt them from excessive drudgery, who keep them stationary and unexposed to accident, produce and raise as many children as the white women.[100] Instances are known, under these circumstances, of their rearing a dozen children. An inhuman practice once prevailed in this country of making slaves of the Indians.[101] It is a fact well known with us, that the Indian women so enslaved produced and raised as numerous families as either the whites or blacks among whom they lived.—It has been said, that Indians have less hair than the whites, except on the head.[102] But this is a fact of which fair proof can scarcely be had. With them it is disgraceful to be hairy on the body. They say it likens them to hogs. They therefore pluck the hair as fast as it appears. But the traders who marry their women, and prevail on them to discontinue this practice, say, that nature is the same with them as with the whites. Nor, if the fact be true, is the consequence necessary which has been drawn from it. Negroes have notoriously less hair than the whites; yet they are more ardent. But if cold and moisture be the agents of nature for diminishing the races of animals, how comes she all at once to suspend their operation as to the physical man of the new world, whom the Count acknowledges to be "à peu près de même stature que l'homme de notre monde,"[103] and to let loose their influence on his moral faculties? How has this "combination of the elements and other physical causes, so contrary to the enlargement of animal nature in this new world, these obstacles to the development and formation of great germs,"[104] been arrested and suspended, so as to permit the human body to acquire its just dimensions, and by what inconceivable process has their action been directed on his mind alone? To judge of the truth of this, to form a just estimate of their genius and mental powers, more facts are wanting, and great allowance to be made for those circumstances of their situation which call for a display of particular talents only. This done, we shall probably find that they are formed in mind as well as in body, on the same module with the *"Homo sapiens Europaeus." The principles of their society forbidding all compulsion, they are to be led to duty and to enterprize by personal influence and persuasion. Hence eloquence in council, bravery and address in war, become the foundations of all consequence with them. To these acquirements all their faculties are directed. Of their bravery and address in war we have multiplied proofs, because we have been the subjects on which they were exercised. Of their eminence in

*Linn. Syst.[105] Definition of a Man.

oratory we have fewer examples, because it is displayed chiefly in their own councils. Some, however, we have of very superior lustre. I may challenge the whole orations of Demosthenes and Cicero, and of any more eminent orator, if Europe has furnished more eminent, to produce a single passage, superior to the speech of Logan,[106] a Mingo chief, to Lord Dunmore, when governor of this state. And, as a testimony of their talents in this line, I beg leave to introduce it, first stating the incidents necessary for understanding it. In the spring of the year 1774,[107] a robbery and murder were committed on an inhabitant of the frontiers of Virginia, by two Indians of the Shawanee tribe. The neighbouring whites, according to their custom, undertook to punish this outrage in a summary way. Col. Cresap,[108] a man infamous for the many murders he had committed on those much-injured people, collected a party, and proceeded down the Kanhaway in quest of vengeance. Unfortunately a canoe of women and children, with one man only, was seen coming from the opposite shore, unarmed, and unsuspecting an hostile attack from the whites. Cresap and his party concealed themselves on the bank of the river, and the moment the canoe reached the shore, singled out their objects, and, at one fire, killed every person in it. This happened to be the family of Logan, who had long been distinguished as a friend of the whites. This unworthy return provoked his vengeance. He accordingly signalized himself in the war which ensued. In the autumn of the same year, a decisive battle was fought at the mouth of the Great Kanhaway, between the collected forces of the Shawanees, Mingoes, and Delawares, and a detachment of the Virginia militia. The Indians were defeated, and sued for peace. Logan however disdained to be seen among the suppliants. But, lest the sincerity of a treaty should be distrusted, from which so distinguished a chief absented himself, he sent by a messenger the following speech to be delivered to Lord Dunmore.[109]

"I appeal to any white man to say, if ever he entered Logan's cabin hungry, and he gave him not meat; if ever he came cold and naked, and he clothed him not. During the course of the last long and bloody war, Logan remained idle in his cabin, an advocate for peace. Such was my love for the whites, that my countrymen pointed as they passed, and said, "Logan is the friend of white men." I had even thought to have lived with you, but for the injuries of one man. Col. Cresap, the last spring, in cold blood, and unprovoked, murdered all the relations of Logan, not sparing even my women and children. There runs not a drop of my blood in the veins of any living creature. This called on me for revenge. I have sought it: I have killed many: I have fully glutted my vengeance. For my country, I rejoice at the beams of peace. But do not harbour a thought that mine is the joy of fear. Logan never felt fear. He will not turn on his heel to save his life. Who is there to mourn for Logan?—Not one."

Before we condemn the Indians of this continent as wanting genius, we must consider that letters have not yet been introduced among them.[110] Were we to compare them in their present state with the Europeans North of the Alps, when the Roman arms and arts first crossed those mountains, the comparison would be unequal, because, at that time, those parts of Europe were swarming with numbers; because numbers produce emulation, and multiply the chances of improvement, and one improvement begets another. Yet I may safely ask, How many good poets, how many able mathematicians, how many great inventors in arts or sciences, had Europe North of the Alps then produced? And it was sixteen centuries after this before a Newton could be formed. I do not mean to deny, that there are varieties in the race of man, distinguished by their powers both of body and mind. I believe there are, as I see to be the case in the races of other animals. I only mean to suggest a doubt, whether the bulk and faculties of animals depend on the side of the Atlantic on which their food happens to grow, or which furnishes the elements of which they are compounded? Whether nature has enlisted herself as a Cis or Trans-Atlantic partisan? I am induced to suspect, there has been more eloquence than sound reasoning displayed in support of this theory; that it is one of those cases where the judgment has been seduced by a glowing pen: and whilst I render every tribute of honor and esteem to the celebrated Zoologist, who has added, and is still adding, so many precious things to the treasures of science, I must doubt whether in this instance he has not cherished error also, by lending her for a moment his vivid imagination and bewitching language.[111] (4)

So far the Count de Buffon has carried this new theory of the tendency of nature to belittle her productions on this side the Atlantic. Its application to the race of whites, transplanted from Europe, remained for the Abbé Raynal. "On doit etre etonné (he says) que l'Amerique n'ait pas encore produit un bon poëte, un habile mathematicien, un homme de genie dans un seul art, ou une seule science."[112] 7. Hist. Philos. p. 92. ed. Maestricht. 1774. "America has not yet produced one good poet." When we shall have existed as a people as long as the Greeks did before they produced a Homer, the Romans a Virgil, the French a Racine and Voltaire, the English a Shakespeare and Milton, should this reproach be still true, we will enquire from what unfriendly causes it has proceeded, that the other countries of Europe and quarters of the earth shall not have inscribed any name in the roll of poets*. But neither has America produced "one able mathematician, one man of genius in a single art or a single science." In war we have produced a Washington, whose memory will be adored while liberty shall have votaries, whose name will triumph over time, and will in future ages assume its just station among the most celebrated worthies of the world, when that wretched philosophy shall be forgotten which would have arranged him among the degeneracies of nature. In physics we have produced a Franklin, than whom no one of the present age has made more important discoveries, nor has enriched philosophy with more, or more ingenious solutions of the phaenomena of nature. We have supposed Mr. Rittenhouse[113] second to no astronomer living: that in genius he must be the first, because he is self-taught. As an artist he has exhibited as great a proof of

---

*Has the world as yet produced more than two poets, acknowledged to be such by all nations? An Englishman, only, reads Milton with delight,[114] an Italian Tasso, a Frenchman the Henriade, a Portuguese Camouens: but Homer and Virgil have been the rapture of every age and nation: they are read with enthusiasm in their originals by those who can read the originals, and in translations by those who cannot.

mechanical genius as the world has ever produced. He has not indeed made a world; but he has by imitation approached nearer its Maker than any man who has lived from the creation to this day*. As in philosophy and war, so in government, in oratory, in painting, in the plastic art, we might shew that America, though but a child of yesterday, has already given hopeful proofs of genius, as well of the nobler kinds, which arouse the best feelings of man, which call him into action, which substantiate his freedom, and conduct him to happiness, as of the subordinate, which serve to amuse him only. We therefore suppose, that this reproach is as unjust as it is unkind; and that, of the geniuses which adorn the present age, America contributes its full share. For comparing it with those countries, where genius is most cultivated, where are the most excellent models for art, and scaffoldings for the attainment of science, as France and England for instance, we calculate thus. The United States contain three millions of inhabitants; France twenty millions; and the British islands ten. We produce a Washington, a Franklin, a Rittenhouse. France then should have half a dozen in each of these lines, and Great-Britain half that number, equally eminent. It may be true, that France has: we are but just becoming acquainted with her, and our acquaintance so far gives us high ideas of the genius of her inhabitants. It would be injuring too many of them to name particularly a Voltaire, a Buffon, the constellation of Encyclopedists,[116] the Abbé Raynal himself, &c. &c. We therefore have reason to believe she can produce her full quota of genius. The present war having so long cut off all communication with Great-Britain, we are not able to make a fair estimate of the state of science in that country. The spirit in which she wages war is the only sample before our eyes, and that does not seem the legitimate offspring either of science or of civilization. The sun of her glory is fast descending to the horizon. Her philosophy has crossed the Channel, her freedom the Atlantic, and herself

*There are various ways[115] of keeping truth out of sight. Mr. Rittenhouse's model of the planetary system has the plagiary appellation of an Orrery; and the quadrant invented by Godfrey, an American also, and with the aid of which the European nations traverse the globe, is called Hadley's quadrant.

seems passing to that awful dissolution, whose issue is not given human foresight to scan*.

Having given a sketch of our minerals, vegetables, and quadrupeds, and being led by a proud theory to make a comparison of the latter with those of Europe, and to extend it to the Man of America, both aboriginal and emigrant, I will proceed to the remaining articles comprehended under the present query.

Between ninety and an hundred of our birds have been described by Catesby. His drawings are better as to form and attitude, than colouring, which is generally too high. They are the following.

---

*In a later edition of the Abbé Raynal's work, he has withdrawn his censure from that part of the new world inhabited by the Federo-Americans; but has left it still on the other parts. North America has always been more accessible to strangers than South. If he was mistaken then as to the former, he may be so as to the latter. The glimmerings which reach us from South America enable us only to see that its inhabitants are held under the accumulated pressure of slavery, superstition, and ignorance. Whenever they shall be able to rise under this weight, and to shew themselves to the rest of the world, they will probably shew they are like the rest of the world. We have not yet sufficient evidence that there are more *lakes* and *fogs* in South America than in other parts of the earth. As little do we know what would be their operation on the mind of man. That country has been visited by Spaniards and Portugueze chiefly, and almost exclusively. These, going from a country of the old world remarkably dry in its soil and climate, fancied there were more lakes and fogs in South America than in Europe. An inhabitant of Ireland, Sweden, or Finland,[117] would have formed the contrary opinion. Had South America then been discovered and seated by a people from a fenny country, it would probably have been represented as much drier than the old world. A patient pursuit of facts, and cautious combination and comparison of them, is the drudgery to which man is subjected by his Maker, if he wishes to attain sure knowledge.

BIRDS OF VIRGINIA.

LINNEAN DESIGNATION	CATESBY'S DESIGNATION		POPULAR NAMES	BUFFON OISEAUX.[118]
Lanius tyrannus	*Muscicapa coronâ rubrâ*	1.55	Tyrant. Field martin	8.398
Vultur aura	*Buteo specie Gallo-pavonis*	1.6	Turkey buzzard	1.246
Falco leucocephalus	*Aquila capite albo*	1.1	Bald eagle	1.138
Falco sparverius	*Accipiter minor*	1.5	Little hawk. Sparrow hawk	
Falco columbarius	*Accipiter palumbarius*	1.3	Pigeon hawk	1.338
Falco furcatus	*Accipiter caudâ furcatâ*	1.4	Forked tail hawk	1.286.312
	Accipiter piscatorius	1.2	Fishing hawk	1.199
Strix asio	*Noctua aurita minor*	1.7	Little owl	1.141
Psittacus Caroliniensis	*Psitticus Caroliniensis*	1.11	Parrot of Carolina. Perroquet	11.383
Corvus cristatus	*Pica glandaria, caerulea. cristata*	1.15	Blue jay	5.164
Oriolus Baltimore	*Icterus ex aureo nigroque varius*	1.48	Baltimore bird	5.318
Oriolus spurius	*Icterus minor*	1.49	Bastard Baltimore	5.321
Gracula quiscula	*Monedula purpurea*	1.12	Purple jackdaw. Crow blackbird	5.134
Cuculus Americanus	*Cuculus Caroliniensis*	1.9	Carolina cuckow	12.62
Picus principalis	*Picus maximus rostro albo*	1.16	White bill woodpecker	13.69
Picus pileatus	*Picus niger maximus, capite rubro*	1.17	Larger red-crested woodpecker	13.72
Picus erythrocephalus	*Picus capite toto rubro*	1.20	Red-headed woodpecker	13.83
Picus auratus	*Picus major alis aureis*	1.18	Gold winged woodpecker. Yucker	13.59
Picus Carolinus	*Picus ventre rubro*	1.19	Red bellied woodpecker	13.105
Picus pubescens	*Picus varius minimus*	1.21	Smallest spotted woodpecker	13.113
Picus villosus	*Picus medius quasi-villosus*	1.19	Hairy woodpecker. Speck. woodpec.	13.111
Picus varius	*Picus varius minor ventre luteo*	1.21	Yellow bellied woodpecker	13.115

Linnean Designation	*Catesby's Designation*		*Popular Names*	*Buffon oiseaux*
Sitta Europaea	*Sitta capite nigro*	1.22	Nuthatch	10.213
	Sitta capite fusco	1.22	Small Nuthatch	10.214
Alcedo alcyon	*Ispida*	1.69	Kingfisher	13.310
Certhia pinus	*Parus Americanus lutescens*	1.61	Pinecreeper	9.433
Trochilus colubris	*Mellivora avis Caroliniensis*	1.65	Humming bird	11.16
Anas Canadensis	*Anser Canadensis*	1.92	Wild goose	17.122
Anas bucephala	*Anas minor purpureo capite*	1.95	Buffel's head duck	17.356
Anas rustica	*Anas minor ex albo & fusco vario*	1.98	Little brown duck	17.413
Anas discors	*Querquedula Americana variegata*	1.100	White face teal	17.403
Anas discors. β	*Querquedula Americana fusca*	1.99	Blue wing teal	17.405
Anas sponsa	*Anas Americanus cristatus elegans*	1.97	Summer duck	17.351
	Anas Americanus lato rostro	1.96	Blue wing shoveler	17.275
Mergus cucullatus	*Anas cristatus*	1.94	Round crested duck	15.437
Colymbus podiceps	*Prodicipes minor rostro vario*	1.91	Pied bill dopchick	15.383
Ardea Herodias	*Ardea cristata maxima Americana*	3.10	Largest crested heron	14.113
Ardea violacea	*Ardea stellaris cristata Americana*	1.79	Crested bittern	14.134
Ardea caerulea	*Ardea caerulea*	1.76	Blue heron. Crane	14.131
Ardea virescens	*Ardea stellaris minima*	1.80	Small bittern	14.142
Ardea aequinoctialis	*Ardea alba minor Caroliniensis*	1.77	Little white heron	14.136
	Ardea stellaris Americana	1.78	Brown bittern. Indian hen	14.175

Linnean Designation	Catesby's Designation		Popular Names	Buffon oiseaux
Tantalus loculator	*Pelicanus Americanus*	1.81	Wood pelican	13.403
Tantalus alber	*Numenius albus*	1.82	White curlew	15.62
Tantalus fuscus	*Numenius fuscus*	1.83	Brown curlew	15.64
Charadrius vociferus	*Pluvialis vociferus*	1.71	Chattering plover. Kildee	15.151
Haematopus ostralegus	*Haematopus*	1.85	Oyster Catcher	15.185
Rallus Virginianus	*Gallinula Americana*	1.70	Soree. Ral-bird	15.256
Meleagris Gallopavo[119]	*Gallopavo Sylvestris*	xliv.	Wild turkey	3.187.229
Tetrao Virginianus	*Perdix Sylvestris Virginiana*	3.12	American partridge. American quail	4.237
	Urogallus minor, or a kind of *Lagopus*	3.1	Pheasant.[120] Mountain partridge	3.409
Columba passerina	*Turtur minimus guttatus*	1.26	Ground dove	4.404
Columba migratoria	*Palumbus migratorius*	1.23	Pigeon of passage. Wild pigeon	4.351
Columba Caroliniensis	*Turtur Caroliniensis*	1.24	Turtle. Turtle dove	4.401
Alauda alpestris	*Alauda gutture flavo*	1.32	Lark. Sky lark	9.79
Alauda magna	*Alauda magna*	1.33	Field lark. Large lark	6.59
	Sturnus niger alis suprené rubentibus	1.13	Red winged starling. Marsh blackbird	5.293
Turdus migratorius	*Tardus pilaris migratorius*	1.29	Fieldfare of Carolina. Robin redbreast	5.426 / 9.257
Turdus rufus	*Turdus ruffus*	1.28	Fox coloured thrush. Thrush	5.449
Turdus polyglottos[121]	*Turdus minor albus non maculatus*	1.27	Mocking bird	5.451
	Tardus minimus	1.31	Little thrush	5.400
Ampelis garrulus. β.	*Garrulus Caroliniensis*	1.46	Chatterer	6.162
Loxia Cardinalis	*Coccothrausters rubra*	1.38	Red bird. Virginia nightingale	6.185

LINNEAN DESIGNATION	CATESBY'S DESIGNATION		POPULAR NAMES	BUFFON OISEAUX
Loxia Caerulea	*Coccothraustes caerulea*	1.39	Blue gross beak	8.125
Emberiza hyemalis	*Passer nivalis*	1.36	Snow bird	8.47
Emberiza Oryzivora	*Hortulanus Caroliniensis*	1.14	Rice bird	8.49
Emberiza Ciris	*Pringilla tricolor*	1.44	Painted finch	7.247
Tanagra cyanea	*Linaria caerulea*	1.45	Blue linnet	7.122
	Passerculus	1.35	Little sparrow	7.120
	Passer fuscus	1.34	Cowpen bird	7.196
Fringilla crythrophthalma	*Passer niger oculis rubris*	1.34	Towhe bird	7.201
Fringilla tristis	*Carduelis Americanus*	1.43	American goldfinch. Lettuce bird	7.297
	Fringilla purpurea	1.41	Purple finch	8.129
Muscicapa crinita	*Muscicapa cristata ventre luteo*	1.52	Crested flycatcher	8.379
Muscicapa rubra	*Muscicapa rubra*	1.56	Summer red bird	8.410
Muscicapa ruticilla	*Ruticilla Americana*	1.67	Red start	8.349 9.259
Muscicapa Caroliniensis	*Muscicapa vertice nigro*	1.66	Cat bird	8.372
	Muscicapa nigrescens	1.53	Black-cap flycatcher	8.341
	Muscicapa fusca	1.54	Little brown flycatcher	8.344
	Muscicapa oculis rubris	1.54	Red-eye flycatcher	8.337
Motacilla Sialis	*Rubicula Americana caerulea*	1.47	Blue bird	9.308
Motacilla regulus	*Regulus cristatus*	3.13	Wren	10.58
Motacilla trochilus. β.	*Oenanthe Americana pectore luteo*	1.50	Yellow-breasted chat	6.96
Parus bicolor	*Parus cristatus*	1.57	Crested titmouse	10.181
Parus Americanus	*Parus fringillaris*	1.64	Finch creeper	9.442

LINNEAN DESIGNATION	CATESBY'S DESIGNATION		POPULAR NAMES	BUFFON OISEAUX
Parus Virginianus	*Parus uropygeo luteo*	1.58	Yellow rump	10.184
	Parus cucullo nigro	1.60	Hooded titmouse	10.183
	Parus Americanus gutture luteo	1.62	Yellow-throated creeper	
	Parus Caroliniensis	1.63	Yellow titmouse	9.431
Hirundo Pelasgia	*Hirundo cauda aculeata Americana*	3.8	American swallow	12.478
Hirundo purpurea	*Hirundo purpurea*	1.51	Purple martin. House martin	12.445
Caprimulgus Europaeus α	*Caprimulgus*	1.8	Goatsucker. Great bat	12.243
Caprimulgus Europaeus β	*Caprimulgus minor Americanus*	3.16	Whip-poor Will	12.246

Besides these, we have

The Royston crow. *Corvus cornix.*
Crane. *Ardea Canadensis.*
House swallow. *Hirundo rustica.*
Ground swallow. *Hirundo riparia.*
Greatest grey eagle.
Smaller turkey buzzard, with a feathered head.
Greatest owl, or night-hawk.
Wethawk, which feeds flying.
Raven.
Water pelican of the Missisipi, whose pouch holds a peck.
Swan.
Loon.

The Cormorant.
Duck and Mallard.
Widgeon.
Sheldrach, or Canvas back.
Black head.
Ballcoot.[122]
Sprigtail.
Didapper, or Dopchick.
Spoon billed duck.
Water-witch.
Water-pheasant.
Mow-bird.
Blue peter.
Water wagtail.
Yellow-legged snipe.
Squatting snipe.
Small plover.
Whistling plover.
Woodcock.
Red bird, with black head, wings and tail.

And doubtless many others which have not yet been described and classed.

To this catalogue of our indigenous animals, I will add a short account of an anomaly of nature, taking place sometimes in the race of negroes brought from Africa, who, though black themselves, have in rare instances, white children, called Albinos. I have known four of these myself, and have faithful accounts of three others. The circumstances in which all the individuals agree are these. They are of a pallid cadaverous white, untinged with red, without any coloured spots or seams; their hair of the same kind of white, short, coarse, and curled as is that of the negro; all of them well formed, strong, healthy, perfect in their senses, except that of sight, and born of parents who had no mixture of white blood. Three of these Albinos were sisters, having two other full sisters, who were black. The youngest of the three was killed by lightning, at twelve years of age. The eldest died at about 27 years of age, in child-bed, with her second child. The middle one is now alive in health, and has issue, as the eldest had, by a black man, which issue was black. They are uncommonly shrewd, quick in their apprehensions and in reply. Their eyes are in a perpetual tremulous vibration, very weak, and much affected by the sun: but they see better in the night than we do. They are of the property of Col. Skipwith, of Cumberland. The fourth is a negro woman, whose parents came from Guinea, and had three other children, who were of their own colour. She is freckled, her eye-sight so weak that she is obliged to wear a bonnet in the summer; but it is better in the night than day. She had an Albino child by a black man. It died at the age of a few weeks. These were the property of Col. Carter, of Albemarle. A sixth instance is a woman of the property of a Mr. Butler, near Petersburgh. She is stout and robust, has issue a daughter, jet black, by a black man. I am not informed as to her eye sight. The seventh instance is of a male belonging to a Mr. Lee, of Cumberland. His eyes are tremulous and weak. He is tall of stature, and now advanced in years. He is the only male of the Albinos which have come within my information. Whatever be the cause of the disease in the skin, or in its colouring matter, which produces this change, it seems more incident to the female than male sex. To these I may add the mention of a negro man within my own knowledge, born black, and of black parents; on whose chin, when a boy, a white spot appeared. This continued to increase till he became a man, by which time it had extended over his chin, lips, one cheek, the under jaw and neck on that side. It is of the Albino white, without any mixture of red, and has for several years been stationary. He is robust and healthy, and the change of colour was not accompanied with any sensible disease, either general or topical.

Of our fish and insects there has been nothing like a full description or collection. More of them are described in Catesby than in any other work. Many also are to be found in Sir Hans Sloane's Jamaica,[123] as being common to that and this country. The honey-bee is not a native of our continent. Marcgrave indeed mentions a species of honey-bee in Brasil.[124] But this has no sting, and is therefore different from the one we have, which resembles perfectly that of Europe. The Indians concur with us in the tradition that it was brought from Europe; but when, and by whom, we know not. The bees have generally extended themselves into the country, a little in advance of the white settlers.[125] The Indians therefore call them the white man's fly, and consider their approach as indicating the approach of the settlements of the whites. A question here occurs, How far northwardly have these insects been found? That they are unknown in Lapland, I infer from Scheffer's information, that the Laplanders eat the pine bark, prepared in a certain way, instead of those things sweetened with sugar. "Hoc comedunt pro rebus saccharo conditis."[126] Scheff.. Lapp. c. 18. Certainly, if they had honey, it would be a better substitute for sugar than any preparation of the pine bark. Kalm tells us the honey bee cannot live through the winter in Canada.[127] They furnish then an additional proof of the remarkable fact first observed by the Count de Buffon, and which has thrown such a blaze of light on the field of natural history, that no animals are found in both continents, but those which are able to bear the cold of those regions where they probably join.[128]

QUERY VII

A NOTICE OF ALL WHAT CAN INCREASE THE PROGRESS OF HUMAN KNOWLEDGE?

Climate

Under the latitude of this query, I will presume it not improper nor unacceptable to furnish some data for estimating the climate of Virginia. Journals of observations on the quantity of rain, and degree of heat, being lengthy, confused, and too minute to produce general and distinct ideas, I have taken five years observations, to wit, from 1772 to 1777, made in Williamsburgh and its neighbourhood, have reduced them to an average for every month in the year, and stated those averages in the following table, adding an analytical view of the winds during the same period.

The rains of every month, (as of January for instance) through the whole period of years, were added separately, and an average drawn from them. The coolest and warmest point of the same day in each year of the period were added separately, and an average of the greatest cold and greatest heat of that day, was formed. From the averages of every day in the month, a general average for the whole month was formed. The point from which the wind blew was observed two or three times in every day. These observations, in the month of January for instance, through the whole period amounted to 337. At 73 of these, the wind was from the North; at 47, from the North-east, &c. So that it will be easy to see in what proportion each wind usually prevails in each month: or, taking the whole year, the total of observations through the whole period having been 3698, it will be observed that 611 of them were from the North, 558 from the North-east, &c.

Though by this table it appears we have on an average 47 inches of rain annually, which is considerably more than usually falls in Europe, yet from the information I have collected, I suppose we have a much greater proportion of sunshine here than there. Perhaps it will be found there are twice as many cloudy days in the middle parts of Europe, as in the United States of America. I mention the middle parts of Europe, because my information does not extend to its northern or southern parts.

In an extensive country, it will of course be expected that the climate is not the same in all its parts. It is remarkable that, proceeding on the same parallel of latitude westwardly, the climate becomes colder in like manner as when you proceed northwardly. This continues to be the case till you attain the summit of the Alleghaney, which is the highest land between the ocean and the Missisipi. From thence, descending in the same latitude to the Missisipi, the change reverses; and, if we may believe travellers, it becomes warmer there than it is in the same latitude on the sea side. Their testimony is strengthened by the vegetables and animals which subsist and multiply there naturally, and do not on our sea coast. Thus Catalpas grow spontaneously on the Missisipi, as far as the latitude of 37°. and reeds as far as 38°. Perroquets even winter on the Sioto, in the 39th degree of latitude. In the summer of 1779, when the thermometer was at 90°. at Monticello, and 96 at Williamsburgh, it was 110°. at Kaskaskia. Perhaps the mountain, which overhangs this village on the North side, may, by its reflexion, have contributed somewhat to produce this heat. The difference of temperature of the air at the sea coast, or on Chesapeak bay, and at the Alleghaney, has not been ascertained; but cotemporary observations, made at Williamsburgh, or in its neighbourhood, and at Monticello, which is on the most eastern ridge of mountains, called the South West, where they are intersected by the Rivanna, have furnished a ratio by which that difference may in some degree be conjectured. These observations make the difference between Williamsburgh and the nearest mountains, at the position before mentioned, to be on an average 6⅛ degrees of Farenheit's thermometer. Some allowance however is to be made for the difference of latitude between these two places, the latter being 38°. 8'. 17". which is 52'. 22". North of the former. By cotemporary observations of between five and six weeks, the averaged and almost unvaried difference of the height of mercury in the barometer, at those two places, was .784 of an inch, the atmosphere at Monticello being so much the lightest, that is to say, about 1/37 of its whole

	Fall of rain, &c. in inches.	Least & greatest daily heat by Farenheit's thermometer.		WINDS[129]								
				N.	N. E.	E.	S. E.	S.	S. W.	W.	N. W.	TOTAL.
Jan.	3.192	38½ to	44	73	47	32	10	11	78	40	46	337
Feb.	2.049	41	47½	61	52	24	11	4	63	30	31	276
Mar.	3.95	48	54½	49	44	38	28	14	83	29	33	318
April	3.68	56	62½	35	44	54	19	9	58	18	20	257
May	2.871	63	70½	27	36	62	23	7	74	32	20	281
June	3.751	71½	78¼	22	34	43	24	13	81	25	25	267
July	4.497	77	82½	41	44	75	15	7	95	32	19	328
Aug.	9.153	76¼	81	43	52	40	30	9	103	27	30	334
Sept.	4.761	69½	74¼	70	60	51	18	10	81	18	37	345
Oct.	3.633	61¼	66½	52	77	64	15	6	56	23	34	327
Nov.	2.617	47¾	53½	74	21	20	14	9	63	35	58	294
Dec.	2.877	43	48¾	64	37	18	16	10	91	42	56	334
Total.	47.038	8 A.M.	4 P.M.	611	548	521	223	109	926	351	409	3698

weight. It should be observed, however, that the hill of Monticello is of 500 feet perpendicular height above the river which washes its base. This position being nearly central between our northern and southern boundaries, and between the bay and Alleghaney, may be considered as furnishing the best average of the temperature of our climate. Williamsburgh is much too near the South-eastern corner to give a fair idea of our general temperature.

But a more remarkable difference is in the winds which prevail in the different parts of the country. The following table exhibits a comparative view of the winds prevailing at Williamsburgh, and at Monticello. It is formed by reducing nine months observations at Monticello to four principal points, to wit, the North-east, South-east, South-west, and North-west; these points being perpendicular to, or parallel with our coast, mountains and rivers: and by reducing, in like manner, an equal number of observations, to wit, 421. from the preceding table of winds at Williamsburgh, taking them proportionably from every point.

	N. E.	S. E.	S. W.	N. W.	Total.
Williamsburgh	127	61	132	101	421
Monticello	32	91	126	172	421

By this it may be seen that the South-west wind prevails equally at both places; that the North-east is, next to this, the principal wind towards the sea coast, and the North-west is the predominant wind at the mountains. The difference between these two winds to sensation, and in fact, is very great. The North-east is loaded with vapour, insomuch, that the salt makers have found that their crystals would not shoot while that blows; it brings a distressing chill, is heavy and oppressive to the spirits: the North-west is dry, cooling, elastic and animating. The Eastern and South-eastern breezes come on generally in the afternoon. They have advanced into the country very sensibly within the memory of people now living. They formerly did not penetrate far above Williamsburgh. They are now frequent at Richmond, and every now and then reach the mountains. They deposit most of their moisture however before they get that far. As the lands become more cleared, it is probable they will extend still further westward.

Going out into the open air, in the temperate, and in the warm months of the year, we often meet with bodies of warm air, which, passing by us in two or three seconds, do not afford time to the most sensible thermometer to seize their temperature. Judging from my feelings only, I think they approach the ordinary heat of the human body. Some of them perhaps go a little beyond it. They are of about 20 or 30 feet diameter horizontally. Of their height we have no experience; but probably they are globular volumes wafted or rolled along with the wind. But whence taken, where found, or how generated? They are not to be ascribed to Volcanos, because we have none. They do not happen in the winter when the farmers kindle large fires in clearing up their grounds. They are not confined to the spring season, when we have fires which traverse whole counties, consuming the leaves which have fallen from the trees. And they are too frequent and general to be ascribed to accidental fires. I am persuaded their cause must be sought for in the atmosphere itself, to aid us in which I know but of these constant circumstances; a dry air; a temperature as warm at least as that of the spring or autumn; and a moderate current of wind. They are most frequent about sun-set; rare in the middle parts of the day; and I do not recollect having ever met with them in the morning.

The variation in the weight of our atmosphere, as indicated by the barometer, is not equal to two inches of mercury. During twelve months observation at Williamsburgh, the extremes were 29, and 30.86 inches, the difference being 1.86 of an inch: and in nine months, during which the height of the mercury was noted at Monticello, the extremes were 28.48 and 29.69 inches, the variation being 1.21 of an inch. A gentleman, who has observed his barometer many years, assures me it has never varied two inches. Cotemporary observations, made at Monticello and Williamsburgh, proved the variations in the weight of air to be simultaneous and corresponding in these two places.

Our changes from heat to cold, and cold to heat, are very sudden and great. The mercury in Farenheit's thermometer has been known to descend from 92°. to 47°. in thirteen hours.[130]

It is taken for granted, that the preceding table of averaged heat will not give a false idea on this subject, as it proposes to state only the ordinary heat and cold of each month, and not those which are extraordinary. At Williamsburgh in August 1766, the mercury in Farenheit's thermometer was at 98°. corresponding with 29⅓ of Reaumur.[131] At the same place in January 1780, it was at 6°. corresponding with 11½ below 0. of Reaumur. I believe *these may be considered to be nearly the extremes of heat and cold in that part of the country. The latter may most certainly, as, at that time, York river, at York town, was frozen over, so that people walked across it; a circumstance which proves it to have been colder than the winter of 1740, 1741, usually called the cold winter, when York river did not freeze over at that place. In the same season of 1780, Chesapeak bay was solid, from its head to the mouth of Patowmac. At Annapolis, where it is 5¼ miles over between the nearest points of land, the ice was from 5 to 7 inches thick quite across, so that loaded carriages went over on it. Those, our extremes of heat and cold, of 6°. and 98°. were indeed very distressing to us, and were thought to put the extent of the human constitution to considerable trial. Yet a Siberian would have considered them as scarcely a sensible variation. At Jenniseitz in that country, in latitude 58°. 27'. we are told, that the cold in 1735 sunk the mercury by Farenheit's scale to 126°. below nothing; and the inhabitants of the same country use stove rooms two or three times a week, in which they stay two hours at a time, the atmosphere of which raises the mercury to 135°. above nothing. Late experiments shew that the human body will exist in rooms heated to 140°. of Reaumur, equal to 347°. of Farenheit, and 135°. above boiling water.[132] The hottest point of the 24 hours is about four o'clock, P.M. and the dawn of day the coldest.

The access of frost in autumn, and its recess in the spring, do not seem to depend merely on the degree of cold; much less on the air's being at the freezing point. White frosts are frequent

---

*At Paris, in 1753, the mercury in Reaumur's thermometer was at 30½ above 0, and in 1776, it was at 16 below 0. The extremities of heat and cold therefore at Paris, are greater than at Williamsburgh, which is in the hottest part of Virginia.

when the thermometer is at 47°. have killed young plants of Indian corn at 48°. and have been known at 54°. Black frost, and even ice, have been produced at 38½°. which is 6½ degrees above the freezing point.[133] That other circumstances must be combined with the cold to produce frost, is evident from this also, that on the higher parts of mountains, where it is absolutely colder than in the plains on which they stand, frosts do not appear so early by a considerable space of time in autumn, and go off sooner in the spring, than in the plains. I have known frosts so severe as to kill the hiccory trees round about Monticello, and yet not injure the tender fruit blossoms then in bloom on the top and higher parts of the mountain; and in the course of 40 years, during which it has been settled, there have been but two instances of a general loss of fruit on it: while, in the circumjacent country, the fruit has escaped but twice in the last seven years. The plants of tobacco, which grow from the roots of those which have been cut off in the summer, are frequently green here at Christmas. This privilege against the frost is undoubtedly combined with the want of dew on the mountains. That the dew is very rare on their higher parts, I may say with certainty, from 12 years observations, having scarcely ever, during that time, seen an unequivocal proof of its existence on them at all during summer.[134] Severe frosts in the depth of winter prove that the region of dews extends higher in that season than the tops of the mountains: but certainly, in the summer season, the vapours, by the time they attain that height, are become so attenuated as not to subside and form a dew when the sun retires.

The weavil has not yet ascended the high mountains.

A more satisfactory estimate of our climate to some, may perhaps be formed, by noting the plants which grow here, subject however to be killed by our severest colds. These are the fig, pomegranate, artichoke, and European walnut. In mild winters, lettuce and endive require no shelter; but generally they need a slight covering. I do not know that the want of long moss, reed, myrtle, swamp laurel, holly and cypress, in the upper country, proceeds from a greater degree of cold, nor that they were ever killed with any degree of cold in the lower country. The aloe lived in Williamsburgh in the open air through the severe winter of 1779, 1780.

A change in our climate however is taking place very sensibly. Both heats and colds are become much more moderate within the memory even of the middle-aged. Snows are less frequent and less deep. They do not often lie, below the mountains, more than one, two, or three days, and very rarely a week. They are remembered to have been formerly frequent, deep, and of long continuance. The elderly inform me the earth used to be covered with snow about three months in every year. The rivers, which then seldom failed to freeze over in the course of the winter, scarcely ever do so now. This change has produced an unfortunate fluctuation between heat and cold, in the spring of the year, which is very fatal to fruits. From the year 1741 to 1769, an interval of twenty-eight years, there was no instance of fruit killed by the frost in the neighbourhood of Monticello. An intense cold, produced by constant snows, kept the buds locked up till the sun could obtain, in the spring of the year, so fixed an ascendency as to dissolve those snows, and protect the buds, during their developement, from every danger of returning cold. The accumulated snows of the winter remaining to be dissolved all together in the spring, produced those overflowings of our rivers, so frequent then, and so rare now.

Having had occasion to mention the particular situation of Monticello for other purposes, I will just take notice that its elevation affords an opportunity of seeing a phaenomenon which is rare at land, though frequent at sea. The seamen call it *looming*. Philosophy is as yet in the rear of the seamen, for so far from having accounted for it, she has not given it a name. Its principal effect is to make distant objects appear larger, in opposition to the general law of vision, by which they are diminished.[135] I knew an instance, at York town, from whence the water prospect eastwardly is without termination, wherein a canoe with three men, at a great distance, was taken for a ship with its three masts. I am little acquainted with the phaenomenon as it shews itself at sea; but at Monticello it is familiar. There is a solitary mountain about 40 miles off,[136] in the South, whose natural shape, as presented to view there, is a regular cone; but, by the effect of looming, it sometimes subsides almost totally into the horizon; sometimes it rises more acute and more elevated; sometimes it is hemispherical; and sometimes its sides are perpendicular, its top flat, and as broad as its base. In short it assumes at times the most whimsical shapes, and all these perhaps successively in the same morning. The Blue ridge of mountains comes into view, in the North East, at about 100 miles distance, and, approaching in a direct line, passes by within 20 miles, and goes off to the Southwest. This phaenomenon begins to shew itself on these mountains, at about 50 miles distance, and continues beyond that as far as they are seen. I remark no particular state, either in the weight, moisture, or heat of the atmosphere, necessary to produce this. The only constant circumstances are, its appearance in the morning only, and on objects at least 40 or 50 miles distant. In this latter circumstance, if not in both, it differs from the looming on the water. Refraction will not account for this metamorphosis. That only changes the proportions of length and breadth, base and altitude, preserving the general outlines. Thus it may make a circle appear elliptical, raise or depress a cone, but by none of its laws, as yet developed, will it make a circle appear a square, or a cone a sphere.

QUERY VIII

THE NUMBER OF ITS INHABITANTS?

Population

The following table shews the number of persons imported for the establishment of our colony in its infant state, and the census of inhabitants at different periods, extracted from our historians and public records, as particularly as I have had opportunities and leisure to examine them. Successive lines in the same year shew successive periods of time in that year. I have stated the census in two different columns, the whole inhabitants having been sometimes numbered, and sometimes the *tythes* only. This term, with us, includes the free males above 16 years of age, and slaves above that age of both sexes. A further examination of our records would render this history of our population much more satisfactory and perfect, by furnishing a greater number of intermediate terms. Those however which are here stated will enable us to calculate, with a considerable degree of precision, the rate at which we have increased. During the infancy of the colony, while numbers were small, wars, importations, and other accidental circumstances render the progression fluctuating and irregular. By the year 1654, however, it becomes tolerably uniform, importations having in a great measure ceased from the dissolution of the company, and the inhabitants become too numerous to be sensibly affected by Indian wars. Beginning at that period, therefore, we find that from thence to the year 1772, our tythes had increased from 7209 to 153,000. The whole term being of 118 years, yields a duplication once in every 27¼ years. The intermediate enumerations taken in 1700, 1748, and 1759, furnish proofs of the uniformity of this progression. Should this rate of increase continue, we shall have between six and seven millions of inhabitants within 95 years. If we suppose our country to be bounded, at some future day, by the meridian of the mouth of the Great Kanhaway, (within which it has been before conjectured, are 64,491 square miles) there will then be 100

Years	Settlers imported.	Census of Inhabitants.[137]	Census of Tythes.
1607	100		
		40	
	120		
1608		130	
	70		
1609		490	
	16		
		60	
1610	150		
		200	
1611	3 ship loads		
	300		
1612	80		
1617		400	
1618	200		
	40		
		600	
1619	1216		
1621	1300		
1622		3800	
		2500	
1628		3000	
1632			2000
1644			4822
1645			5000
1652			7000
1654			7209
1700			22,000
1748			82,100
1759			105,000
1772			153,000
1782		567,614	

inhabitants for every square mile, which is nearly the state of population in the British islands.

Here I will beg leave to propose a doubt. The present desire of America is to produce rapid population by as great importations of foreigners as possible. But is this founded in good policy? The advantage proposed is the multiplication of numbers. Now let us suppose (for example only) that, in this state, we could double our numbers in one year by the importation of foreigners; and this is a greater accession than the most sanguine advocate for emigration has a right to expect. Then I say, beginning with a double stock, we shall attain any given degree of population only 27 years and 3 months sooner than if we proceed on our single stock. If we propose four millions and a half as a competent population for this state, we should be 54½ years attaining it, could we at once double our numbers; and 81¾ years, if we rely on natural propagation, as may be seen by the following table [page 92].

In the first column are

stated periods of 27¼ years; in the second are our numbers, at each period, as they will be if we proceed on our actual stock; and in the third are what they would be, at the same periods, were we to set out from the double of our present stock. I have taken the term of four millions and a half of inhabitants for example's sake only. Yet I am persuaded it is a greater number than the country spoken of, considering how much inarrable land it contains, can clothe and feed, without a material change in the quality of their diet. But are there no inconveniences to be thrown into the scale against the advantage expected from a multiplication of numbers by the importation of foreigners? It is for the happiness of those united in society to harmonize as much as possible in matters which they must of necessity transact together. Civil government being the sole object of forming societies, its administration must be conducted by common consent. Every species of government has its specific principles. Ours perhaps are more peculiar than those of any other in the universe. It is a composition of the freest principles of the English constitution, with others derived from natural right and natural reason. To these nothing can be more opposed than the maxims of absolute monarchies. Yet, from such, we are to expect the greatest number of emigrants. They will bring with them the principles of the governments they leave, imbibed in their early youth; or, if able to throw them off, it will be in exchange for an unbounded licentiousness, passing, as is usual, from one extreme to another. It would be a miracle were they to stop precisely at the point of temperate liberty. These principles, with their language, they will transmit to their children. In proportion to their numbers, they will share with us the legislation. They will infuse into it their spirit, warp and bias its direction, and render it a heterogeneous, incoherent, distracted mass. I may appeal to experience, during the present contest, for a verification of these conjectures. But, if they be not certain in event, are they not possible, are they not probable? Is it not safer to wait with patience 27 years and three months longer, for the attainment of any degree of population desired, or expected? May not our government be more homogeneous, more peaceable, more durable? Suppose 20 millions of republican Americans thrown all of a sudden into France, what would be the condition of that king-

	Proceeding on our present stock.	Proceeding on a double stock.
1781	567,614	1,135,228
1808¼	1,135,228	2,270,456
1835½	2,270,456	4,540,912
1862¾	4,540,912	

dom? If it would be more turbulent, less happy, less strong, we may believe that the addition of half a million of foreigners to our present numbers would produce a similar effect here. If they come of themselves, they are entitled to all the rights of citizenship: but I doubt the expediency of inviting them by extraordinary encouragements. I mean not that these doubts should be extended to the importation of useful artificers. The policy of that measure depends on very different considerations. Spare no expence in obtaining them. They will after a while go to the plough and the hoe; but, in the mean time, they will teach us something we do not know. It is not so in agriculture. The indifferent state of that among us does not proceed from a want of knowledge merely; it is from our having such quantities of land to waste as we please. In Europe the object is to make the most of their land, labour being abundant: here it is to make the most of our labour, land being abundant.[138]

It will be proper to explain how the numbers for the year 1782 have been obtained; as it was not from a perfect census of the inhabitants. It will at the same time develope the proportion between the free inhabitants and slaves. The following return of taxable articles for that year was given in.

53,289	free males above 21 years of age.
211,698	slaves of all ages and sexes.
23,766	not distinguished in the returns, but said to be titheable slaves.
195,439	horses.
609,734	cattle.
5,126	wheels of riding-carriages.
191	taverns.

There were no returns from the 8 counties of Lincoln, Jefferson, Fayette, Monongalia, Yohogania, Ohio, Northampton, and York. To find the number of slaves which should have been returned instead of the 23,766 titheables, we must mention that some observations on a former census had given reason to believe that the numbers above and below 16 years of age were equal. The double of this number, therefore, to wit, 47,532 must be added to 211,698, which will give us 259,230 slaves of all ages and sexes. To find the number of free inhabitants, we must repeat the observation, that those above and below 16 are nearly equal. But as the number 53,289 omits the males between 16 and 21, we must supply them from conjecture. On a former experiment it had appeared that about one-third of our militia, that is, of the males between 16 and 50, were unmarried. Knowing how early marriage takes place here, we shall not be far wrong in supposing that the unmarried part of our militia are those between 16 and 21. If there be young men who do not marry till after 21, there are as many who marry before that age. But as the men above 50 were not included in the militia, we will suppose the unmarried, or those between 16 and 21, to be one-fourth of the whole number above 16, then we have the following calculation:

53,289	free males above 21 years of age.
17,763	free males between 16 and 21.
71,052	free males under 16.
142,104	free females of all ages.
284,208	free inhabitants of all ages.
259,230	slaves of all ages.

543,438 inhabitants, exclusive of the 8 counties from which were no returns. In these 8 counties in the years 1779 and 1780 were 3,161 militia. Say then,

3,161	free males above the age of 16.
3,161	ditto under 16.
6,322	free females.

12,644 free inhabitants in these 8 counties. To find the number of slaves, say, as 284,208 to 259,230, so is 12,644 to 11,532. Adding the third of these numbers to the first, and the fourth to the second, we have,

296,852 free inhabitants.
270,762 slaves.

567,614 inhabitants of every age, sex, and condition. But 296,852, the number of free inhabitants, are to 270,762, the number of slaves, nearly as 11 to 10. Under the mild treatment our slaves experience, and their wholesome, though coarse, food, this blot in our country increases as fast, or faster, than the whites. During the regal government, we had at one time obtained a law, which imposed such a duty on the importation of slaves, as amounted nearly to a prohibition, when one inconsiderate assembly, placed under a peculiarity of circumstance, repealed the law. This repeal met a joyful sanction from the then sovereign, and no devices, no expedients, which could ever after be attempted by subsequent assemblies, and they seldom met without attempting them, could succeed in getting the royal assent to a renewal of the duty. In the very first session held under the republican government, the assembly passed a law for the perpetual prohibition of the importation of slaves. This will in some measure stop the increase of this great political and moral evil, while the minds of our citizens may be ripening for a complete emancipation of human nature.[139]

QUERY IX

THE NUMBER AND CONDITION OF THE MILITIA AND REGULAR TROOPS, AND THEIR PAY?

Military

The following is a state of the militia, taken from returns of 1780 and 1781, except in those counties marked with an asterisk, the returns from which are somewhat older.

Every able-bodied freeman, between the ages of 16 and 50, is enrolled in the militia. Those of every county are formed into companies, and these again into one or more battalions, according to the numbers in the county. They are commanded by colonels, and other subordinate officers, as in the regular service. In every county is a county-lieutenant, who commands the whole militia of his county, but ranks only as a colonel in the field. We have no general officers always existing. These are appointed occasionally, when an invasion or insurrection happens, and their commission determines with the occasion. The governor is head of the military, as well as civil power. The law requires every militia-man to provide himself with the arms usual in the regular service. But this injunction was always indifferently complied with, and the arms they had have been so frequently called for to arm the regulars, that in the lower parts of the country they are entirely disarmed. In the middle country a fourth or fifth part of them may have such firelocks as they had provided to destroy the noxious animals which infest their farms; and on the western side of the Blue ridge they are generally armed with rifles. The pay of our militia, as well as of our regulars, is that of the Continental regulars. The condition of our regulars, of whom we have none but Continentals, and part of a battalion of state troops, is so constantly on the change, that a state of it at this day would not be its state a month hence. It is much the same with the condition of the other Continental troops, which is well enough known.

Situation.	Counties.	Militia.
Westward of the Allegany. 4458.	Lincoln	600
	Jefferson	300
	Fayette	156
	Ohio	
	Monongalia	*1000
	Washington	*829
	Montgomery	1071
	Green-briar	502
Between the Allegany and Blue ridge. 7673.	Hampshire	930
	Berkeley	*1110
	Frederick	1143
	Shenando	*925
	Rockingham	875
	Augusta	1375
	Rockbridge	*625
	Botetourt	*700
Between the Blue ridge and Tide waters. 18,828	Loudoun	1746
	Fauquier	1078
	Culpeper	1513
	Spotsylvania	480
	Orange	*600
	Louisa	603
	Goochland	*550
	Fluvanna	*296
	Albemarle	873
	Amherst	896
	Buckingham	*625
	Bedford	1300
	Henry	1004
	Pittsylvania	*725
	Halifax	*1139
	Charlotte	612
	Prince Edward	589
	Cumberland	408
	Powhatan	330
	Amelia	*1125
	Lunenberg	677
	Mecklenburg	1100
	Brunswic	559
On the Tide Waters and in that Parallel. 19,012. — Between James river and Carolina. 6959.	Greenesville	500
	Dinwiddie	*750
	Chesterfield	655
	Prince George	382
	Surry	380
	Sussex	*700
	Southampton	874
	Isle of Wight	*600
	Nansemond	*644
	Norfolk	*880
	Princess Anne	*594
On the Tide Waters and in that Parallel. 19,012. — Between James and York rivers. 3009.	Henrico	619
	Hanover	796
	New Kent	*418
	Charles City	286
	James City	235
	Williamsburg	129
	York	*244
	Warwick	*100
	Elizabeth City	182
On the Tide Waters and in that Parallel. 19,012. — Between York and Rappahanock. 3269.	Caroline	805
	King William	436
	King & Queen	500
	Essex	468
	Middlesex	*210
	Gloucester	850
On the Tide Waters and in that Parallel. 19,012. — Between Rappahnoc & Patowamac. 4137.	Fairfax	652
	Prince William	614
	Stafford	*500
	King George	483
	Richmond	412
	Westmoreland	544
	Northumberl.	630
	Lancaster	302
On the Tide Waters and in that Parallel. 19,012. — East Shore. 1638.	Accomac	*1208
	Northampton	*430
Whole Militia of the State		49,971

QUERY X

THE MARINE?

Marine

Before the present invasion of this state by the British under the command of General Phillips,[140] we had three vessels of 16 guns, one of 14, five small gallies, and two or three armed boats. They were generally so badly manned as seldom to be in condition for service. Since the perfect possession of our rivers assumed by the enemy, I believe we are left with a single armed boat only.

QUERY XI

A DESCRIPTION OF THE INDIANS ESTABLISHED IN THAT STATE?

Aborigines

When the first effectual settlement of our colony was made, which was in 1607, the country from the sea-coast to the mountains, and from Patowmac to the most southern waters of James river, was occupied by upwards of forty different tribes of Indians. Of these the *Powhatans*, the *Mannahoacs*, and *Monacans*, were the most powerful. Those between the sea-coast and falls of the rivers, were in amity with one another, and attached to the *Powhatans* as their link of union. Those between the falls of the rivers and the mountains, were divided into two confederacies; the tribes inhabiting the head waters of Patowmac and Rappahanoc being attached to the *Mannahoacs*; and those on the upper parts of James river to the *Monacans*. But the *Monacans* and their friends were in amity with the *Mannahoacs* and their friends, and waged joint and perpetual war against the *Powhatans*. We are told that the *Powhatans, Mannahoacs*, and *Monacans*, spoke languages so radically different, that interpreters were necessary when they transacted business. Hence we may conjecture, that this was not the case between all the tribes, and probably that each spoke the language of the nation to which it was attached; which we know to have been the case in many particular instances. Very possibly there may have been antiently three different stocks, each of which multiplying in a long course of time, had separated into so many little societies.[141] This practice results from the circumstance of their having never submitted themselves to any laws, any coercive power, any shadow of government. Their only controuls are their manners, and that moral sense of right and wrong, which, like the sense of tasting and feeling, in every man makes a part of his nature. An offence against these is punished by contempt, by exclusion from society, or, where the case is serious, as that of murder, by the individuals whom it concerns. Imperfect as this species of coercion may seem, crimes are very rare among them: insomuch that were it made a question, whether no law, as among the savage Americans, or too much law, as among the civilized Europeans, submits man to the greatest evil, one who has seen both conditions of existence would pronounce it to be the last: and that the sheep are happier of themselves, than under care of the wolves. It will be said, that great societies cannot exist without government. The Savages therefore break them into small ones.

The territories of the *Powhatan* confederacy, south of the Patowmac, comprehended about 8000 square miles, 30 tribes, and 2400 warriors. Capt. Smith[142] tells us, that within 60 miles of James town were 5000 people, of whom 1500 were warriors. From this we find the proportion of their warriors to their whole inhabitants, was as 3 to 10. The *Powhatan* confederacy then would consist of about 8000 inhabitants, which was one for every square mile; being about the twentieth part of our present population in the same territory, and the hundredth of that of the British islands.

Besides these, were the *Nottoways*, living on Nottoway river, the *Meherrins* and *Tuteloes* on Meherrin river, who were connected with the Indians of Carolina, probably with the Chowanocs.

WEST.	MANNAHOACS.					
	TRIBES.	COUNTRY.	CHIEF TOWN.	WARRIORS. 1607	WARRIORS. 1669	TRIBES.
Between PATOWMAC and RAPPAHANOC.	Whonkenties Tegninaties Ontponies Tauxitanians Hassinungaes	Fauquier Culpeper Orange Fauquier Culpeper				Tauxenents Patówomekes Cuttatawomans Pissasecs Onaumanients Rappahànocs Moràughtacunds Secacaonies Wighcocòmicoes Cuttatawomans
Between RAPPAHANOC and YORK.	Stegarakies Shackakonies Mannahoacs	Orange Spotsylvania Stafford Spotsylvania				Nantaughtacunds Màttapomènts Pamùnkies Wèrowocòmicos Payànkatanks
	MONACANS.					Youghtanunds
Between YORK and JAMES.	Monacans Monasiccapanoes	James R. above the falls Louisa. Fluvanna	Fork of James R.		30	Chickahòminies Powhatàns Arrowhàtocs Wèanoes Paspahèghes Chiskiacs Kecoughtáns
Between JAMES and CAROLINA.	Monahassanoes Massinacacs Mohemenchoes	Bedford. Buckingham Cumberland Powhatan				Appamáttocs Quiocohànocs Wàrrasqeaks Nansamònds Chèsapeaks
EASTERN SHORE.						Accohanocs Accomàcks

NORTH.

POWHATANS.				
COUNTRY.	CHIEF TOWN.	WARRIORS.		
		1607	1669	
Fairfax	About General Washington's	40		
Stafford. King George	Patowmac creek	200		By the name of
King George	About Lamb creek	20		Matchotics, U.
King Geo. Richmond	Above Leeds town	—	60	Matchodic, Nan-
Westmoreland	Nomony river	100		zatico. Appamatox
Richmond county	Rappahanoc creek	100	30	Matox.
Lancaster. Richmond	Moratico river	80	40	
Northumberland	Coan river	30		by the name of
Northumberland	Wicocomico river	130	70	Totuskeys.
Lancaster	Corotoman	30		
Essex. Caroline	Port tobacco creek	150	60	
Mattapony river	— — — —	30	20	
King William	Romuncock	300	30	
Gloucester	About Rosewell	40		
Piankatank river	Turk's Ferry, Grimesby	55		
Pamunkey river	— — — —	60		
Chickahominy river	Orapaks	250	60	
Henrico	Powhatan. Mayo's	40	10	
Henrico	Arrohatocs	30		
Charles city	Weynoke	100	15	
Charles city. James city	Sandy point	40		
York	Chiskiac	45	15	
Elizabeth city	Roscows	20		
Chesterfield	Bermuda hundred	60	30	
Surry	About Upper Chipoak	25	3 Pohics	Nottoways 1669 / 90
Isle of Wight	Warrasqueac			
Nansamond	About the mouth of West. branch	200		Meherrics
Princess Anne	About Lynhaven river	100	45	Tutcloes 30
Accom. Northampton	Accohanoc river	40		
Northampton	About Cheriton's	80		

EAST.

SOUTH.

The preceding table contains a state of these several tribes, according to their confederacies and geographical situation, with their numbers when we first became acquainted with them, where these numbers are known. The numbers of some of them are again stated as they were in the year 1669, when an attempt was made by the assembly to enumerate them. Probably the enumeration is imperfect, and in some measure conjectural, and that a further search into the records would furnish many more particulars. What would be the melancholy sequel of their history, may however be augured from the census of 1669; by which we discover that the tribes therein enumerated were, in the space of 62 years, reduced to about one-third of their former numbers. Spirituous liquors, the small-pox, war, and an abridgment of territory, to a people who lived principally on the spontaneous productions of nature, had committed terrible havock among them, which generation,[143] under the obstacles opposed to it among them, was not likely to make good. That the lands of this country were taken from them by conquest, is not so general a truth as is supposed. I find in our historians and records, repeated proofs of purchase, which cover a considerable part of the lower country; and many more would doubtless be found on further search.[144] The upper country we know has been acquired altogether by purchases made in the most unexceptionable form.

Westward of all these tribes, beyond the mountains, and extending to the great lakes, were the *Massawomecs*, a most powerful confederacy, who harrassed unremittingly the *Powhatans* and *Manahoacs*. These were probably the ancestors of the tribes known at present by the name of the *Six Nations*.

Very little can now be discovered of the subsequent history of these tribes severally. The *Chickahominies* removed, about the year 1661, to Mattapony river. Their chief, with one from each of the tribes of the Pamunkies and Mattaponies, attended the treaty of Albany in 1685. This seems to have been the last chapter in their history. They retained however their separate name so late as 1705, and were at length blended with the Pamunkies and Mattaponies, and exist at present only under their names. There remain of the *Mattaponies* three or four men only, and they have more negro than Indian blood in them. They have lost their language, have reduced themselves, by voluntary sales, to about fifty acres of land, which lie on the river of their own name, and have, from time to time, been joining the Pamunkies, from whom they are distant but 10 miles. The *Pamunkies* are reduced to about 10 or 12 men, tolerably pure from mixture with other colours. The older ones among them preserve their language in a small degree, which are the last vestiges on earth, as far as we know, of the Powhatan language. They have about 300 acres of very fertile land, on Pamunkey river, so encompassed by water that a gate shuts in the whole. Of the *Nottoways*, not a male is left. A few women constitute the remains of that tribe. They are seated on Nottoway river, in Southampton county, on very fertile lands. At a very early period, certain lands were marked out and appropriated to these tribes, and were kept from encroachment by the authority of the laws. They have usually had trustees appointed, whose duty was to watch over their interests, and guard them from insult and injury.

The *Monacans* and their friends, better known latterly by the name of *Tuscaroras*, were probably connected with the Massawomecs, or Five Nations. For though we are *told their languages were so different that the intervention of interpreters was necessary between them, yet do we also †learn that the Erigas, a nation formerly inhabiting on the Ohio, were of the same original stock with the Five Nations, and that they partook also of the Tuscarora language. Their dialects might, by long separation, have become so unlike as to be unintelligible to one another. We know that in 1712, the Five Nations received the Tuscaroras into their confederacy, and made them the Sixth Nation. They received the Meherrins and Tuteloes also into their protection: and it is most probable, that the remains of many other of the tribes, of whom we find no particular account, retired westwardly in like manner, and were incorporated with one or other of the western tribes (5).

I know of no such thing existing as an Indian monument: for I would not honour with that name arrow points, stone hatchets, stone pipes, and half-shapen images. Of labour on the large scale, I think there is no remain as respectable as would be a common

*Smith.
†Evans.[145]

ditch for the draining of lands: unless indeed it be the Barrows, of which many are to be found all over this country. These are of different sizes, some of them constructed of earth, and some of loose stones. That they were repositories of the dead, has been obvious to all: but on what particular occasion constructed, was matter of doubt. Some have thought they covered the bones of those who have fallen in battles fought on the spot of interment. Some ascribed them to the custom, said to prevail among the Indians, of collecting, at certain periods, the bones of all their dead, wheresoever deposited at the time of death. Others again supposed them the general sepulchres for towns, conjectured to have been on or near these grounds; and this opinion was supported by the quality of the lands in which they are found, (those constructed of earth being generally in the softest and most fertile meadow-grounds on river sides) and by a tradition, said to be handed down from the Aboriginal Indians, that, when they settled in a town, the first person who died was placed erect, and earth put about him, so as to cover and support him; that, when another died, a narrow passage was dug to the first, the second reclined against him, and the cover of earth replaced, and so on. There being one of these in my neighbourhood, I wished to satisfy myself whether any, and which of these opinions were just. For this purpose I determined to open and examine it thoroughly. It was situated on the low grounds of the Rivanna, about two miles above its principal fork, and opposite to some hills, on which had been an Indian town. It was of a spheroidical form, of about 40 feet diameter at the base, and had been of about twelve feet altitude, though now reduced by the plough to seven and a half, having been under cultivation about a dozen years. Before this it was covered with trees of twelve inches diameter, and round the base was an excavation of five feet depth and width, from whence the earth had been taken of which the hillock was formed. I first dug superficially in several parts of it, and came to collections of human bones, at different depths, from six inches to three feet below the surface. These were lying in the utmost confusion, some vertical, some oblique, some horizontal, and directed to every point of the compass, entangled, and held together in clusters by the earth. Bones of the most distant parts were found together, as, for instance, the small bones of the foot in the hollow of a scull, many sculls would sometimes be in contact, lying on the face, on the side, on the back, top or bottom, so as, on the whole, to give the idea of bones emptied promiscuously from a bag or basket, and covered over with earth, without any attention to their order. The bones of which the greatest numbers remained, were sculls, jaw-bones, teeth, the bones of the arms, thighs, legs, feet, and hands. A few ribs remained, some vertebrae of the neck and spine, without their processes, and one instance only of the *bone which serves as a base to the vertebral column. The sculls were so tender, that they generally fell to pieces on being touched. The other bones were stronger. There were some teeth which were judged to be smaller than those of an adult; a scull, which, on a slight view, appeared to be that of an infant, but it fell to pieces on being taken out, so as to prevent satisfactory examination; a rib, and a fragment of the under-jaw of a person about half grown; another rib of an infant; and part of the jaw of a child, which had not yet cut its teeth. This last furnishing the most decisive proof of the burial of children here, I was particular in my attention to it. It was part of the right-half of the under-jaw. The processes, by which it was articulated to the temporal bones, were entire; and the bone itself firm to where it had been broken off, which, as nearly as I could judge, was about the place of the eye-tooth. Its upper edge, wherein would have been the sockets of the teeth, was perfectly smooth. Measuring it with that of an adult, by placing their hinder processes together, its broken end extended to the penultimate grinder of the adult. This bone was white, all the others of a sand colour. The bones of infants being soft, they probably decay sooner, which might be the cause so few were found here. I proceeded then to make a perpendicular cut through the body of the barrow, that I might examine its internal structure. This passed about three feet from its center, was opened to the former surface of the earth, and was wide enough for a man to walk through and examine its sides. At the bottom, that is, on the level of the circumjacent plain, I found bones; above these a few stones, brought from a cliff a quarter of a mile off, and from the river one-eighth of a mile off; then a large

*The os sacrum.

interval of earth, then a stratum of bones, and so on. At one end of the section were four strata of bones plainly distinguishable; at the other, three; the strata in one part not ranging with those in another. The bones nearest the surface were least decayed. No holes were discovered in any of them, as if made with bullets, arrows, or other weapons. I conjectured that in this barrow might have been a thousand skeletons. Every one will readily seize the circumstances above related, which militate against the opinion, that it covered the bones only of persons fallen in battle; and against the tradition also, which would make it the common sepulchre of a town, in which the bodies were placed upright, and touching each other. Appearances certainly indicate that it has derived both origin and growth from the accustomary collection of bones, and deposition of them together; that the first collection had been deposited on the common surface of the earth, a few stones put over it, and then a covering of earth, that the second had been laid on this, had covered more or less of it in proportion to the number of bones, and was then also covered with earth; and so on. The following are the particular circumstances which give it this aspect. 1. The number of bones. 2. Their confused position. 3. Their being in different strata. 4. The strata in one part having no correspondence with those in another. 5. The different states of decay in these strata, which seem to indicate a difference in the time of inhumation. 6. The existence of infant bones among them.[146]

But on whatever occasion they may have been made, they are of considerable notoriety among the Indians: for a party passing, about thirty years ago, through the part of the country where this barrow is, went through the woods directly to it, without any instructions or enquiry, and having staid about it some time, with expressions which were construed to be those of sorrow, they returned to the high road, which they had left about half a dozen miles to pay this visit, and pursued their journey. There is another barrow, much resembling this in the low grounds of the South branch of Shenandoah, where it is crossed by the road leading from the Rock-fish gap to Staunton. Both of these have, within these dozen years, been cleared of their trees and put under cultivation, are much reduced in their height, and spread in width, by the plough, and will probably disappear in time.

There is another on a hill in the Blue ridge of mountains, a few miles North of Wood's gap, which is made up of small stones thrown together. This has been opened and found to contain human bones, as the others do. There are also many others in other parts of the country (6).

Great question has arisen from whence came those aboriginal inhabitants of America?[147] Discoveries, long ago made, were sufficient to shew that a passage from Europe to America was always practicable, even to the imperfect navigation of ancient times. In going from Norway to Iceland, from Iceland to Groenland, from Groenland to Labrador, the first traject is the widest: and this having been practised from the earliest times of which we have any account of that part of the earth, it is not difficult to suppose that the subsequent trajects may have been sometimes passed. Again, the late discoveries of Captain Cook,[148] coasting from Kamschatka to California, have proved that, if the two continents of Asia and America be separated at all, it is only by a narrow streight. So that from this side also, inhabitants may have passed into America: and the resemblance between the Indians of America and the Eastern inhabitants of Asia, would induce us to conjecture, that the former are the descendants of the latter, or the latter of the former: excepting indeed the Eskimaux, who, from the same circumstance of resemblance, and from identity of language, must be derived from the Groenlanders, and these probably from some of the northern parts of the old continent. A knowledge of their several languages would be the most certain evidence of their derivation which could be produced. In fact, it is the best proof of the affinity of nations[149] which ever can be referred to. How many ages have elapsed since the English, the Dutch, the Germans, the Swiss, the Norwegians, Danes and Swedes have separated from their common stock? Yet how many more must elapse before the proofs of their common origin, which exist in their several languages, will disappear? It is to be lamented then, very much to be lamented, that we have suffered so many of the Indian tribes already to extinguish, without our having previously collected and deposited in the records of literature, the general rudiments at least of the languages they spoke. Were vocabularies formed of all the languages spoken in North and South America, preserving their appellations of the most common objects in nature, of those which must be present to every nation barbarous or civilised, with the inflections of their nouns and verbs, their principles of regimen and concord, and these deposited in all the public libraries, it would furnish opportunities to those skilled in the languages of the old world to compare them with these, now, or at any future time, and hence to construct the best evidence of the derivation of this part of the human race.[150]

But imperfect as is our knowledge of the tongues spoken in America, it suffices to discover the following remarkable fact.[151] Arranging them under the radical ones to which they may be palpably traced, and doing the same by those of the red men of Asia, there will be found probably twenty in America, for one in Asia, of those radical languages, so called because, if they were ever the same, they have lost all resemblance to one another. A separation into dialects may be the work of a few ages only, but for two dialects to recede from one another till they have lost all vestiges of their common origin, must require an immense course of time; perhaps not less than many people give to the age of the earth. A greater number of those radical changes of language having taken place among the red men of America, proves them of greater antiquity than those of Asia.[152]

I will now proceed to state the nations and numbers of the Aborigines which still exist in a respectable and independant form. And as their undefined boundaries would render it difficult to specify those only which may be within any certain limits, and it may not be unacceptable to present a more general view of them, I will reduce within the form of a Catalogue all those within, and circumjacent to, the United States, whose names and numbers have come to my notice. These are taken from four different lists, the first of which was given in the year 1759 to General Stanwix by George Croghan, Deputy agent for Indian affairs under Sir William Johnson; the second was drawn up by a French trader of considerable note, resident among the Indians many years, and annexed to Colonel Bouquet's printed account of his expedition in 1764. The third was made out by Captain Hutchins, who visited most of the tribes, by order, for the purpose of learning their numbers in 1768. And the fourth by John Dodge, an Indian trader, in 1779, except the numbers marked *, which are from other information.[153]

Northward and Westward of the United States.

TRIBES	Croghan. 1759.	Bouquet. 1764.	Hutchins. 1768.	Where they reside.
Oswegatchies	--	--	100	At Swagatchy, on the river St. Laurence
Connasedagoes	--	--	300	Near Montreal
Cohunnewagoes	--	200		
Orondocs	--	--	100	Near Trois Rivieres
Abenakies	--	350	150	Near Trois Rivieres
Little Algonkins	--	--	100	Near Trois Rivieres
Michmacs	--	700	--	River St. Laurence
Amelistes	--	550	--	River St. Laurence
Chalas	--	130	--	River St. Laurence
Nipissins	--	400	--	Towards the head of the Ottawas river
Algonquins	--	300	--	Towards the heads of the Ottawas river
Round heads	--	2500	--	Riviere aux Tetes boules on the East side of Lake Superior
Messasagues	--	2000	--	Lakes Huron and Superior
Christinaux. Kris	--	3000	--	Lake Christinaux
Assinaboes	--	1500	--	Lake Assinaboes
Blancs, or Barbus	--	1500	--	
Sious of the Meadows		2500		
Sioux of the Woods	10,000	1800	10,000	On the heads of the Missisipi and Westward of that river
Sioux		--		
Ajoues	--	1100	--	North of the Padoucas
Panis. White	--	2000	--	South of the Missouri
Panis. Freckled	--	1700	--	South of the Missouri
Padoucas	--	500	--	South of the Missouri
Grandes eaux	--	1000	--	
Canses	--	1600	--	South of the Missouri
Osages	--	600	--	South of the Missouri
Missouris	400	3000	--	On the river Missouri
Arkanzas	--	2000	--	On the river Arkanzas
Caouitas	--	700	--	East of the Alibamous

	TRIBES	Croghan. 1759.	Bouquet. 1764.	Hutchins. 1768.	Dodge. 1779.	Where they reside.
Within the Limits of the United States.	Mohocks	–	--	160	100	Mohocks river [of Susquehanna.
	Onèidas	–	--	300	400	E. side of Oneida L. and head branches
	Tuscaròras	–	--	200		Between the Oneidas and Onondagoes.
	Onondàgoes	–	1550	260	230	Near Onondago L. [of Susquehanna.
	Cayùgas	–	--	200	220	On the Cayuga L. near the N. branch
	Sènecas	–	--	1000	650	On the waters of Susquehanna, of Ontario, and the heads of the Ohio.
	Aughquàgahs	–	--	150	–	East branch of Susquehanna, and on Aughquagah.
	Nánticocs	–	--	100	–	Utsanango, Chaghtnet, and Owegy, on the East branch of Susquehanna.
	Mohìccons	–	--	100	–	In the same parts.
	Conòies	–	--	30	–	In the same parts.
	Sapòonies	–	--	30	–	At Diahago and other villages up the N. branch of Susquehanna.
	Mùnsies	–	--	150	*150	At Diahago and other villages up the N. branch of Susquehanna.
	Delawares, or Linnelinopies	–	–	150	*500	At Diahago and other villages up the N. branch of Susquehanna.
	Delawares, or Linnelinopies	600	600	600		Between Ohio and L. Erie and the branches of Beaver creek, Cayahoga and Muskingham.
	Shàwanees	400	500	300	300	Sioto and the branches of Muskingham.
	Mìngoes	–	–	--	60	On a branch of Sioto.
	Mohìccons	–	–		*60	
	Cohunnewagos	–	–	300	–	Near Sandusky.
	Wyandots	300	300		180	Near Fort St. Joseph's and Detroit.
	Wyandots			250		

Within the limits of the United States.

TRIBES	Croghan. 1759.	Bouquet. 1764.	Hutchins. 1768.	Dodge. 1779.	Where they reside.
Twightwees	300	–	250	–	Miami river near Fort Miami.
Miamis	–	350	––	300	Miami river, about Fort St. Joseph.
Ouiàtonons	200	400	300	*300	On the banks of the Wabash, near Fort Ouiatonon.
Piànkishas	300	250	300	*400	On the banks of the Wabash, near Fort Ouiatonon.
Shàkies	–	–	200	–	On the banks of the Wabash, near Fort Ouiatonon.
Kaskaskias	–	600	300	–	Near Kaskaskia.
Illinois	400		300	–	Near Cahokia. Qu. If not the same with the Mitchigamis?
Piorias	–	800	––	–	On the Illinois R. called Pianrias, but supposed to mean Piorias.
Pouteòtamies	–	350	300	450	Near St. Joseph's and Fort Detroit.
Ottàwas	–	–	550	*300	Near St. Joseph's and Fort Detroit.
Chippawas	–	–		–	On Saguinam bay of Lake Huron.
Ottawas	–	–	200	–	On Saguinam bay of Lake Huron.
Chippawas	–	–	400	–	Near Michillimakinac.
Ottawas	–	–	250	5450	Near Michillimakinac.
Chippawas	2000	5900	400		Near Fort St. Mary's on Lake Superior.
Chippawas	–	–	––	–	Several other villages along the banks of Lake Superior. Numbers unknown.
Chippawas	–	–	––	–	Near Puans bay, on Lake Michigan.
Shakies	200	400	550	–	Near Puans bay, on Lake Michigan.
Mynonàmies	–	–	––	–	Near Puans bay, on Lake Michigan.

	TRIBES	Croghan. 1759.	Bouquet. 1764.	Hutchins. 1768.	Dodge. 1779.	Where they reside.
Within the Limits of the United States.	Ouisconsings	–	550	--	–	Ouisconsing River.
	Kìckapous	600	300	--	250	
	Otogamies.	–	–	--	–	
	Foxes					
	Màscoutens	–	500		–	On Lake Michigan, and between that and the Missisipi.
	Miscòthins	–	–	4000	–	
	Outimacs	–	–	--	–	
	Musquakies	200	250	--	250	
	Sioux. Eastern	–	–	--	500	On the Eastern heads of Missisipi, and the islands of Lake Superior.
				Galphin. 1768.		
	Cherokees	1500	2500	3000	–	Western parts of North Carolina.
	Chickasaws	–	750	500	–	Western parts of Georgia.
	Catawbas	–	150	--	–	On the Catawba R. in S. Carolina.
	Chacktaws	2000	4500	6000	–	Western parts of Georgia.
	Upper Creeks	–	–	3000	–	Western parts of Georgia.
	Lower Creeks	–	1180			
	Natchez	–	150	--	–	
	Alibamous	–	600	--	–	Alibama R. in the Western parts of Georgia.

The following tribes are also mentioned:

Croghan's catal.	Lezar	400	From the mouth of Ohio to the mouth of Wabash.
	Webings	200	On the Missisipi below the Shakies.
	Ousasoys. Grand Tuc.	4000	On White creek, a branch of the Missisipi.
	Linways	1000	On the Missisipi.

Bouquet's.	Les Puans	700	Near Puans bay.
	Folle avoine	350	Near Puans bay.
	Quanakina	300	Conjectured to be tribes of the creeks.
	Chiakanessou	350	
	Machecous	800	
	Souikilas	200	
Dodge's.	Mineamis	2000	North-west of L. Michigan, to the heads of Missisipi, and up to L. Superior.
	Piankishas Mascoutins Vermillions	800	On and near the Wabash, towards the Illinois.

But, apprehending these might be different appellations for some of the tribes already enumerated, I have not inserted them in the table, but state them separately as worthy of further inquiry. The variations observable in numbering the same tribe may sometimes be ascribed to imperfect information, and sometimes to a greater or less comprehension of settlements under the same name (7).

QUERY XII

A NOTICE OF THE COUNTIES, CITIES, TOWNSHIPS, AND VILLAGES?

Counties, Towns

The counties have been enumerated under Query IX. They are 74 in number, of very unequal size and population. Of these 35 are on the tide waters, or in that parallel; 23 are in the Midlands, between the tide waters and Blue ridge of mountains; 8 between the Blue ridge and Alleghaney; and 8 westward of the Alleghaney.

The state, by another division, is formed into parishes, many of which are commensurate with the counties: but sometimes a county comprehends more than one parish, and sometimes a parish more than one county. This division had relation to the religion of the state, a Parson of the Anglican church, with a fixed salary, having been heretofore established in each parish. The care of the poor was another object of the parochial division.

We have no townships. Our country being much intersected with navigable waters, and trade brought generally to our doors, instead of our being obliged to go in quest of it, has probably been one of the causes why we have no towns of any consequence. Williamsburgh, which, till the year 1780, was the seat of our government, never contained above 1800 inhabitants; and Norfolk, the most populous town we ever had, contained but 6000. Our towns, but more properly our villages or hamlets, are as follows.

On *James river* and its waters, Norfolk, Portsmouth, Hampton, Suffolk, Smithfield, Williamsburgh, Petersburg, Richmond the seat of our government, Manchester, Charlottesville, New London.

On *York river* and its waters, York, Newcastle, Hanover.

On *Rappahannoc*, Urbanna, Portroyal, Fredericksburg, Falmouth.

On *Patowmac* and its waters, Dumfries, Colchester, Alexandria, Winchester, Staunton.

On *Ohio*, Louisville.

There are other places at which, like some of the foregoing, the *laws* have said there shall be towns; but *Nature* has said there shall not, and they remain unworthy of enumeration. *Norfolk* will probably be the emporium for all the trade of the Chesapeak bay and its waters; and a canal of 8 or 10 miles will bring to it all that of Albemarle sound and its waters. Secondary to this place, are the towns at the head of the tidewaters, to wit, Petersburgh on Appamattox, Richmond on James river, Newcastle on York river, Alexandria on Patowmac, and Baltimore on the Patapsco. From these the distribution will be to subordinate situations in the country. Accidental circumstances however may controul the indications of nature, and in no instances do they do it more frequently than in the rise and fall of towns.

QUERY XIII

THE CONSTITUTION OF THE STATE, AND ITS SEVERAL CHARTERS?

Constitution

Queen Elizabeth by her letters-patent, bearing date March 25, 1584, licensed Sir Walter Raleigh to search for remote heathen lands, not inhabited by Christian people, and granted to him, in fee simple, all the soil within 200 leagues of the places where his people should, within 6 years, make their dwellings or abidings; reserving only, to herself and her successors, their allegiance and one fifth part of all the gold and silver ore they should obtain. Sir Walter immediately sent out two ships which visited Wococon island in North Carolina, and the next year dispatched seven with 107 men, who settled in Roanoke island, about latitude 35°. 50'. Here Okisko, king of the Weopomeiocs, in a full council of his people, is said to have acknowledged himself the homager of the Queen of England, and, after her, of Sir Walter Raleigh. A supply of 50 men were sent in 1586, and 150 in 1587. With these last, Sir Walter sent a Governor, appointed him twelve assistants, gave them a charter of incorporation, and instructed them to settle on Chesapeak bay. They landed however at Hatorask. In 1588, when a fleet was ready to sail with a new supply of colonists and necessaries, they were detained by the Queen to assist against the Spanish Armada. Sir Walter having now expended 40,000 l. in these enterprizes, obstructed occasionally by the crown, without a shilling of aid from it, was under a necessity of engaging others to adventure their money. He therefore, by deed bearing date the 7th of March 1589, by the name of Sir Walter Raleigh, Chief Governor of Assamàcomòc, (probably Acomàc), alias Wingadacoia, alias Virginia, granted to Thomas Smith and others, in consideration of their adventuring certain sums of money, liberty of trade to his new country, free from all customs and taxes for seven years, excepting the fifth part of the gold and silver ore to be obtained;

and stipulated with them, and the other assistants, then in Virginia, that he would confirm the deed of incorporation which he had given in 1587, with all the prerogatives, jurisdictions, royalties and privileges granted to him by the Queen. Sir Walter, at different times, sent five other adventures hither, the last of which was in 1602: for in 1603 he was attainted, and put into close imprisonment, which put an end to his cares over his infant colony. What was the particular fate of the colonists he had before sent and seated, has never been known: whether they were murdered, or incorporated with the savages.

Some gentlemen and merchants, supposing that by the attainder of Sir Walter Raleigh the grant to him was forfeited, not enquiring over carefully whether the sentence of an English court could affect lands not within the jurisdiction of that court, petitioned king James for a new grant of Virginia to them. He accordingly executed a grant to Sir Thomas Gates and others, bearing date the 9th of March 1607, under which, in the same year a settlement was effected at Jamestown and ever after maintained. Of this grant however no particular notice need be taken, as it was superseded by letters-patent of the same king, of May 23, 1609, to the Earl of Salisbury and others, incorporating them by the name of "the Treasurer and Company of adventurers and planters of the City of London for the first colony in Virginia," granting to them and their successors all the lands in Virginia from Point Comfort along the sea coast to the northward 200 miles, and from the same point along the sea coast to the southward 200 miles, and all the space from this precinct on the sea coast up into the land, West and North-west, from sea to sea, and the islands within one hundred miles of it, with all the commodities, jurisdictions, royalties, privileges, franchises and preeminences within the same, and thereto and thereabouts, by sea and land, appertaining, in as ample manner as had before been granted to any adventurer: to be held of the king and his successors, in common soccage, yielding one fifth part of the gold and silver ore to be therein found, for all manner of services; establishing a council in England for the direction of the enterprise, the members of which were to be chosen and displaced by the voice of the majority of the company and adventurers, and were to have the nomination and revocation of governors, officers, and ministers, which by them should be thought needful for the colony, the power of establishing laws and forms of government and magistracy, obligatory not only within the colony, but also on the seas in going and coming to and from it; authorising them to carry thither any persons who should consent to go, freeing them for ever from all taxes and impositions on any goods or merchandize on importation into the colony, or exportation out of it, except the five per cent. due for custom on all goods imported into the British dominions, according to the ancient trade of merchants; which five per cent. only being paid, they might, within 13 months, re-export the same goods into foreign parts, without any custom, tax, or other duty, to the king or any his officers or deputies: with powers of waging war against those who should annoy them: giving to the inhabitants of the colony all the rights of natural subjects, as if born and abiding in England; and declaring that these letters should be construed, in all doubtful parts, in such manner as should be most for the benefit of the grantees.

Afterwards, on the 12th of March 1612, by other letters-patent, the king added to his former grants, all islands in any part of the ocean between the 30th and 41st degrees of latitude, and within 300 leagues of any of the parts before granted to the Treasurer and company, not being possessed or inhabited by any other christian prince or state, nor within the limits of the northern colony.

In pursuance of the authorities given to the company by these charters, and more especially of that part in the charter of 1609, which authorised them to establish a form of government, they on the 24th of July 1621, by charter under their common seal, declared that from thenceforward there should be two supreme councils in Virginia, the one to be called the council of state, to be placed and displaced by the treasurer, council in England, and company, from time to time, whose office was to be that of assisting and advising the governor; the other to be called the general assembly, to be convened by the governor once yearly or oftener, which was to consist of the council of state, and two burgesses out of every town, hundred, or plantation, to be respectively chosen by the inhabitants. In this all matters were to be decided by the greater part of the votes present; reserving to the governor a negative voice; and they were to have power to treat, consult, and conclude all emergent occasions concerning the public weal, and to make laws for the behoof and government of the colony, imitating and following the laws and policy of England as nearly as might be: providing that these laws should have no force till ratified in a general quarter court of the company in England, and returned under their common seal, and declaring that, after the government of the colony should be well framed and settled, no orders of the council in England should bind the colony unless ratified in the said general assembly. The king and company quarrelled, and, by a mixture of law and force, the latter were ousted of all their rights, without retribution, after having expended 100,000 l. in establishing the colony, without the smallest aid from government. King James suspended their powers by proclamation of July 15, 1624, and Charles I. took the government into his own hands. Both sides had their partisans in the colony: but in truth the people of the colony in general thought themselves little concerned in the dispute. There being three parties interested in these several charters, what passed between the first and second it was thought could not affect the third. If the king seized on the powers of the company, they only passed into other hands, without increase or diminution, while the rights of the people remained as they were. But they did not remain so long. The northern parts of their country were granted away to the Lords Baltimore and Fairfax, the first of these obtaining also the rights of separate jurisdiction and government. And in 1650 the parliament, considering itself as standing in the place of their deposed king, and as having succeeded to all his powers, without as well as within the realm, began to assume a right over the colonies, passing an act for inhibiting their trade with foreign nations. This succession to the exercise of the kingly authority gave the first colour for parliamentary interference with the colonies, and produced that fatal precedent which they continued to follow after they had retired, in other respects, within their proper functions. When this colony, therefore, which still maintained its opposition to Cromwell and the parliament, was induced in 1651 to lay down their arms, they previously secured their most essential rights, by a solemn convention, which having never seen in print, I will here insert literally from the records.

"ARTICLES agreed on & concluded at James Cittie in Virginia for the surrendering and settling of that plantation under the obedience & government of the common wealth of England by the Commissioners of the Council of state by authoritie of the parliamt. of England & by the Grand assembly of the Governour, Councill & Burgesses of that countrey.

"First it is agreed and consted that the plantation of Virginia, and all the inhabitants thereof shall be and remaine in due obedience and subjection to the Comon wealth of England, according to the lawes there established, and that this submission and subscription bee acknowledged a voluntary act not forced nor constrained by a conquest upon the countrey, and that they shall have & enjoy such freedomes and priviledges as belong to the free borne people of England, and that the former government by the Comissions and Instructions be void and null.

"2ly, Secondly that the Grand assembly as formerly shall convene & transact the affairs of Virginia wherein nothing is to be acted or done contrarie to the government of the Comon wealth of England & the lawes there established.

"3ly, That there shall be a full & totall remission and indempnitie of all acts, words, or writeings done or spoken against the parliament of England in relation to the same.

"4ly, That Virginia shall have & enjoy the antient bounds and Lymitts granted by the charters of the former kings, and that we shall seek a new charter from the parliament to that purpose against any that have intrencht upon the rights thereof.

"5ly, That all the pattents of land granted under the collony seale by any of the precedent governours shall be & remaine in their full force & strength.

"6ly, That the priviledge of haveing ffiftie acres of land for every person transported in that collonie shall continue as formerly granted.

"7ly, That the people of Virginia have free trade as the people of England do enjoy to all places and with all nations according to the lawes of that common wealth, and that Virginia shall enjoy all priviledges equall with any English plantations in America.

"8ly, That Virginia shall be free from all taxes, customs & impositions whatsoever, & none to be imposed on them without consent of the Grand assembly, And soe that neither ffortes nor castles bee erected or garrisons maintained without their consent.

"9ly, That noe charge shall be required from this country in respect of this present ffleet.

"10ly, That for the future settlement of the countrey in their due obedience, the Engagement shall be tendred to all the inhabitants according to act of parliament made to that purpose, that all persons who shall refuse to subscribe the said engagement, shall have a yeare's time if they please to remove themselves & their estates out of Virginia, and in the mean time during the said yeare to have equall justice as formerly.

"11ly, That the use of the booke of common prayer shall be permitted for one yeare ensueinge with referrence to the consent of the major part of the parishes, provided that those things which relate to kingshipp or that government be not used publiquely, and the continuance of ministers in their places, they not misdemeaning themselves, and the payment of their accustomed dues and agreements made with them respectively shall be left as they now stand dureing this ensueing yeare.

"12ly, That no man's cattell shall be questioned as the companies unles such as have been entrusted with them or have disposed of them without order.

"13ly, That all ammunition, powder & armes, other then for private use, shall be delivered up, securitie being given to make satisfaction for it.

"14ly, That all goods allreadie brought hither by the Dutch or others which are now on shoar shall be free from surprizall.

"15ly, That the quittrents granted unto us by the late kinge for seaven yeares bee confirmed.

"16ly, That the commissioners for the parliament subscribeing these articles engage themselves & the honour of the parliament for the full performance thereof: and that the present governour & the councill & the burgesses do likewise subscribe & engage the whole collony on their parts.

RICH. BENNETT.———Seale.
W^{m}. CLAIBORNE.———Seale.
EDMOND CURTIS.[154]———Seale.

"Theise articles were signed & sealed by the Commissioners of the Councill of state for the Commonwealth of England the twelveth day of March 1651."

Then follow the articles stipulated by the governor and council, which relate merely to their own persons and property, and then the ensuing instrument:

> "An act of indempnitie made att the surrender of the countrey.
>
> "Whereas by the authoritie of the parliament of England wee the commissioners appointed by the councill of state authorized thereto having brought a fleete & force before James cittie in Virginia to reduce that collonie under the obedience of the commonwealth of England, & findeing force raised by the Governour & countrey to make opposition against the said ffleet whereby assured danger appearinge of the ruine & destruction of the plantation, for prevention whereof the Burgesses of all the severall plantations being called to advise & assist therein, uppon long & serious debate, and in sad contemplation of the greate miseries & certaine destruction which were soe neerely hovering over the whole countrey; Wee the said Comissioners have thought fitt & condescended and granted to signe & confirme under our hands, seales, & by our oath, Articles bearinge date with theise presents, and do further declare that by the authoritie of the parliament & commonwealth of England derived unto us theire Comissioners, that according to the articles in generall wee have granted an act of indempnitie and oblivion to all the inhabitants of this colloney from all words, actions, or writings that have been spoken acted or writt against the parliament or commonwealth of England or any other person from the beginning of the world to this daye. And this wee have done that all the inhabitants of the collonie may live quietly & securely under the comonwealth of England. And wee do promise that the parliament and commonwealth of England shall confirme & make good all those transactions of ours. Wittnes our hands & seales this 12th of March 1651. Richard Bennett—Seale. W^{m}. Claiborne—Seale. Edm. Curtis—Seale."

The colony supposed, that, by this solemn convention, entered into with arms in their hands, they had secured the *antient

*Art. 4.

limits of their country, *its free trade, its exemption from †taxation but by their own assembly, and exclusion of ‡military force from among them. Yet in every of these points was this convention violated by subsequent kings and parliaments, and other infractions of their constitution, equally dangerous, committed. Their General Assembly, which was composed of the council of state and burgesses, sitting together and deciding by plurality of voices, was split into two houses, by which the council obtained a separate negative on their laws. Appeals from their supreme court, which had been fixed by law in their General Assembly, were arbitrarily revoked to England, to be there heard before the king and council. Instead of four hundred miles on the sea coast, they were reduced, in the space of thirty years, to about one hundred miles. Their trade with foreigners was totally suppressed, and, when carried to Great-Britain, was there loaded with imposts.[155] It is unnecessary, however, to glean up the several instances of injury, as scattered through American and British history, and the more especially as, by passing on to the accession of the present king, we shall find specimens of them all, aggravated, multiplied and crouded within a small compass of time, so as to evince a fixed design of considering our rights natural, conventional and chartered as mere nullities.[156] The following is an epitome of the first fifteen years of his reign. The colonies were taxed internally and externally; their essential interests sacrificed to individuals in Great-Britain; their legislatures suspended; charters annulled; trials by juries taken away; their persons subjected to transportation across the Atlantic, and to trial before foreign judicatories; their supplications for redress thought beneath answer; themselves published as cowards in the councils of their mother country and courts of Europe; armed troops sent among them to enforce submission to these violences; and actual hostilities commenced against them. No alternative was presented but resistance, or unconditional submission. Between these could be no hesitation. They closed in the appeal to arms. They declared themselves independent

---

*Art. 7.
†Art. 8.
‡Art. 8.

States. They confederated together into one great republic; thus securing to every state the benefit of an union of their whole force. In each state separately a new form of government was established. Of ours particularly the following are the outlines. The executive powers are lodged in the hands of a governor, chosen annually, and incapable of acting more than three years in seven. He is assisted by a council of eight members. The judiciary powers are divided among several courts, as will be hereafter explained. Legislation is exercised by two houses of assembly, the one called the house of Delegates, composed of two members from each county, chosen annually by the citizens possessing an estate for life in 100 acres of uninhabited land, or 25 acres with a house on it, or in a house or lot in some town: the other called the Senate, consisting of 24 members, chosen quadrennially by the same electors, who for this purpose are distributed into 24 districts. The concurrence of both houses is necessary to the passage of a law. They have the appointment of the governor and council, the judges of the superior courts, auditors, attorney-general, treasurer, register of the land office, and delegates to congress. As the dismemberment of the state had never had its confirmation, but, on the contrary, had always been the subject of protestation and complaint, that it might never be in our own power to raise scruples on that subject, or to disturb the harmony of our new confederacy, the grants to Maryland, Pennsylvania, and the two Carolinas, were ratified.

This constitution was formed when we were new and unexperienced in the science of government. It was the first too which was formed in the whole United States. No wonder then that time and trial have discovered very capital defects in it.

1. The majority of the men in the state, who pay and fight for its support, are unrepresented in the legislature, the roll of freeholders intitled to vote, not including generally the half of those on the roll of the militia, or of the tax-gatherers.

2. Among those who share the representation, the shares are very unequal. Thus the county of Warwick, with only one hundred fighting men, has an equal representation with the county of Loudon, which has 1746. So that every man in Warwick has as much influence in the government as 17 men in Loudon. But lest it should be thought that an equal interspersion of small

among large counties, through the whole state, may prevent any danger of injury to particular parts of it,*† we will divide it into districts, and shew the proportions of land, of fighting men, and of representation in each.

	Square miles.	Fighting men.	Delegates.	Senators.
Between the sea-coast and falls of the rivers	*11,205	19,012	71	12
Between the falls of the rivers and the Blue ridge of mountains	18,759	18,828	46	8
Between the Blue ridge and the Alleghaney	11,911	7,673	16	2
Between the Alleghaney and the Ohio	†79,650	4,458	16	2
Total	121,525	49,971	149	24

An inspection of this table will supply the place of commentaries on it. It will appear at once that nineteen thousand men, living below the falls of the rivers, possess half the senate, and want four members only of possessing a majority of the house of delegates; a want more than supplied by the vicinity of their situation to the seat of government, and of course the greater degree of convenience and punctuality with which their members may and will attend in the legislature. These nineteen thousand, therefore, living in one part of the country, give law to upwards of thirty thousand, living in another, and appoint all their chief officers executive and judiciary. From the difference of their situation and circumstances, their interests will often be very different.

3. The senate is, by its constitution, too homogeneous with the house of delegates. Being chosen by the same electors, at the same time, and out of the same subjects, the choice falls of course on men of the same description. The purpose of establishing different houses of legislation is to introduce the influence of different interests or different principles. Thus in Great-Britain it is said their constitution relies on the house of commons for honesty, and the lords for wisdom; which would be a rational reliance if honesty were to be bought with money, and if wisdom

---

*Of these, 542 are on the Eastern shore.

†Of these, 22,616 are Eastward of the meridian of the mouth of the Great Kanhaway.

were hereditary. In some of the American states the delegates and senators are so chosen, as that the first represent the persons, and the second the property of the state. But with us, wealth and wisdom have equal chance for admission into both houses. We do not therefore derive from the separation of our legislature into two houses, those benefits which a proper complication of principles is capable of producing, and those which alone can compensate the evils which may be produced by their dissensions.

4. All the powers of government, legislative, executive, and judiciary, result to the legislative body. The concentrating these in the same hands is precisely the definition of despotic government. It will be no alleviation that these powers will be exercised by a plurality of hands, and not by a single one. 173 despots would surely be as oppressive as one. Let those who doubt it turn their eyes on the republic of Venice. As little will it avail us that they are chosen by ourselves. An *elective despotism* was not the government we fought for; but one which should not only be founded on free principles, but in which the powers of government should be so divided and balanced among several bodies of magistracy, as that no one could transcend their legal limits, without being effectually checked and restrained by the others. For this reason that convention, which passed the ordinance of government, laid its foundation on this basis, that the legislative, executive and judiciary departments should be separate and distinct, so that no person should exercise the powers of more than one of them at the same time. But no barrier was provided between these several powers. The judiciary and executive members were left dependant on the legislative, for their subsistence in office, and some of them for their continuance in it. If therefore the legislature assumes executive and judiciary powers, no opposition is likely to be made; nor, if made, can it be effectual; because in that case they may put their proceedings into the form of an act of assembly, which will render them obligatory on the other branches. They have accordingly, in many instances, decided rights which should have been left to judiciary controversy: and the direction of the executive, during the whole time of their session, is becoming habitual and familiar. And this is done with no ill intention. The views of the

present members are perfectly upright. When they are led out of their regular province, it is by art in others, and inadvertence in themselves. And this will probably be the case for some time to come. But it will not be a very long time. Mankind soon learn to make interested uses of every right and power which they possess, or may assume. The public money and public liberty, intended to have been deposited with three branches of magistracy, but found inadvertently to be in the hands of one only, will soon be discovered to be sources of wealth and dominion to those who hold them; distinguished too by this tempting circumstance, that they are the instrument, as well as the object of acquisition. With money we will get men, said Caesar, and with men we will get money. Nor should our assembly be deluded by the integrity of their own purposes, and conclude that these unlimited powers will never be abused, because themselves are not disposed to abuse them. They should look forward to a time, and that not a distant one, when corruption in this, as in the country from which we derive our origin, will have seized the heads of government, and be spread by them through the body of the people; when they will purchase the voices of the people, and make them pay the price. Human nature is the same on every side of the Atlantic, and will be alike influenced by the same causes. The time to guard against corruption and tyranny, is before they shall have gotten hold on us. It is better to keep the wolf out of the fold, than to trust to drawing his teeth and talons after he shall have entered. To render these considerations the more cogent, we must observe in addition,

5. That the ordinary legislature may alter the constitution itself. On the discontinuance of assemblies, it became necessary to substitute in their place some other body, competent to the ordinary business of government, and to the calling forth the powers of the state for the maintenance of our opposition to Great-Britain. Conventions were therefore introduced, consisting of two delegates from each county, meeting together and forming one house, on the plan of the former house of Burgesses, to whose places they succeeded. These were at first chosen anew for every particular session. But in March 1775, they recommended to the people to chuse a convention, which should continue in office a year. This was done accordingly in April

1775, and in the July following that convention passed an ordinance for the election of delegates in the month of April annually. It is well known, that in July 1775, a separation from Great-Britain and establishment of Republican government had never yet entered into any person's mind. A convention therefore, chosen under that ordinance, cannot be said to have been chosen for purposes which certainly did not exist in the minds of those who passed it. Under this ordinance, at the annual election in April 1776, a convention for the year was chosen. Independance, and the establishment of a new form of government, were not even yet the objects of the people at large. One extract from the pamphlet called Common Sense had appeared in the Virginia papers in February, and copies of the pamphlet itself had got into a few hands. But the idea had not been opened to the mass of the people in April, much less can it be said that they had made up their minds in its favor. So that the electors of April 1776, no more than the legislators of July 1775, not thinking of independance and a permanent republic, could not mean to vest in these delegates powers of establishing them, or any authorities other than those of the ordinary legislature. So far as a temporary organization of government was necessary to render our opposition energetic, so far their organization was valid. But they received in their creation no powers but what were given to every legislature before and since. They could not therefore pass an act transcendant to the powers of other legislatures. If the present assembly pass any act, and declare it shall be irrevocable by subsequent assemblies, the declaration is merely void, and the act repealable, as other acts are. So far, and no farther authorized, they organized the government by the ordinance entitled a Constitution or Form of government. It pretends to no higher authority than the other ordinances of the same session; it does not say, that it shall be perpetual; that it shall be unalterable by other legislatures; that it shall be transcendant above the powers of those, who they knew would have equal power with themselves. Not only the silence of the instrument is a proof they thought it would be alterable, but their own practice also: for this very convention, meeting as a House of Delegates in General Assembly with the new Senate in the autumn of that year, passed acts of assembly in contradiction to their ordinance of government; and every assembly from that time to this has done the same. I am safe therefore in the position, that the constitution itself is alterable by the ordinary legislature. Though this opinion seems founded on the first elements of common sense, yet is the contrary maintained by some persons. 1. Because, say they, the conventions were vested with every power necessary to make effectual opposition to Great-Britain. But to complete this argument, they must go on, and say further, that effectual opposition could not be made to Great-Britain, without establishing a form of government perpetual and unalterable by the legislature; which is not true. An opposition which at some time or other was to come to an end, could not need a perpetual institution to carry it on: and a government, amendable as its defects should be discovered, was as likely to make effectual resistance, as one which should be unalterably wrong. Besides, the assemblies were as much vested with all powers requisite for resistance as the conventions were. If therefore these powers included that of modelling the form of government in the one case, they did so in the other. The assemblies then as well as the conventions may model the government; that is, they may alter the ordinance of government. 2. They urge, that if the convention had meant that this instrument should be alterable, as their other ordinances were, they would have called it an ordinance: but they have called it a *constitution*, which ex vi termini[157] means "an act above the power of the ordinary legislature." I answer that *constitutio, constitutum, statutum, lex*, are convertible terms. "*Constitutio* dicitur jus quod a principe conditur." "*Constitutum*, quod ab imperatoribus rescriptum statutumve est." "*Statutum*, idem quod lex."[158] Calvini Lexicon juridicum. *Constitution* and *statute* were originally terms of the *civil law, and from thence introduced by Ecclesiastics into the English law. Thus in the statute 25 Hen. 8. c. 19. §. 1.[160] "*Constitutions* and *ordinances*" are used as synonimous. The term *constitution* has many other significations in physics and in politics; but in Jurisprudence, whenever it is applied to any act of the legislature, it invariably means a statute, law, or

*To *bid*, to *set*, was the antient legislative word of the English. Ll. Hlotharii & Eadrici. Ll. Inae. Ll. Eadwerdi. Ll. Aathelstani.[159]

ordinance, which is the present case. No inference then of a different meaning can be drawn from the adoption of this title: on the contrary, we might conclude, that, by their affixing to it a term synonimous with ordinance, or statute, they meant it to be an ordinance or statute. But of what consequence is their meaning, where their power is denied? If they meant to do more than they had power to do, did this give them power? It is not the name, but the authority which renders an act obligatory. Lord Coke[161] says, "an article of the statute 11 R. 2. c. 5. that no person should attempt to revoke any ordinance then made, is repealed, for that such restraint is against the jurisdiction and power of the parliament." 4. inst. 42. and again, "though divers parliaments have attempted to restrain subsequent parliaments, yet could they never effect it; for the latter parliament hath ever power to abrogate, suspend, qualify, explain, or make void the former in the whole or in any part thereof, notwithstanding any words of restraint, prohibition, or penalty, in the former: for it is a maxim in the laws of the parliament, quod leges posteriores priores contrarias abrogant."[162] 4. inst. 43.—To get rid of the magic supposed to be in the word *constitution*, let us translate it into its definition as given by those who think it above the power of the law; and let us suppose the convention instead of saying, "We, the ordinary legislature, establish a *constitution*," had said, "We, the ordinary legislature, establish an act *above the power of the ordinary legislature*." Does not this expose the absurdity of the attempt? 3. But, say they, the people have acquiesced, and this has given it an authority superior to the laws. It is true, that the people did not rebel against it: and was that a time for the people to rise in rebellion? Should a prudent acquiescence, at a critical time, be construed into a confirmation of every illegal thing done during that period? Besides, why should they rebel? At an annual election, they had chosen delegates for the year, to exercise the ordinary powers of legislation, and to manage the great contest in which they were engaged. These delegates thought the contest would be best managed by an organized government. They therefore, among others, passed an ordinance of government. They did not presume to call it perpetual and unalterable. They well knew they had no power to make it so; that our choice of them had been for no such purpose, and at a time when we could have no such purpose in contemplation. Had an unalterable form of government been meditated, perhaps we should have chosen a different set of people. There was no cause then for the people to rise in rebellion. But to what dangerous lengths will this argument lead? Did the acquiescence of the colonies under the various acts of power exercised by Great-Britain in our infant state, confirm these acts, and so far invest them with the authority of the people as to render them unalterable, and our present resistance wrong? On every unauthoritative exercise of power by the legislature, must the people rise in rebellion, or their silence be construed into a surrender of that power to them? If so, how many rebellions should we have had already? One certainly for every session of assembly. The other states in the Union have been of opinion, that to render a form of government unalterable by ordinary acts of assembly, the people must delegate persons with special powers. They have accordingly chosen special conventions to form and fix their governments. The individuals then who maintain the contrary opinion in this country, should have the modesty to suppose it possible that they may be wrong and the rest of America right. But if there be only a possibility of their being wrong, if only a plausible doubt remains of the validity of the ordinance of government, is it not better to remove that doubt, by placing it on a bottom which none will dispute? If they be right, we shall only have the unnecessary trouble of meeting once in convention. If they be wrong, they expose us to the hazard of having no fundamental rights at all. True it is, this is no time for deliberating on forms of government. While an enemy is within our bowels, the first object is to expel him. But when this shall be done, when peace shall be established, and leisure given us for intrenching within good forms, the rights for which we have bled, let no man be found indolent enough to decline a little more trouble for placing them beyond the reach of question. If any thing more be requisite to produce a conviction of the expediency of calling a convention, at a proper season, to fix our form of government, let it be the reflection,

6. That the assembly exercises a power of determining the Quorum of their own body which may legislate for us. After the establishment of the new form they adhered to the *Lex ma-*

joris partis,[163] founded in *common law as well as common right. It is the †natural law[164] of every assembly of men, whose numbers are not fixed by any other law. They continued for some time to require the presence of a majority of their whole number, to pass an act. But the British parliament fixes its own quorum: our former assemblies fixed their own quorum: and one precedent in favour of power is stronger than an hundred against it. The house of delegates therefore have ‡lately voted that, during the present dangerous invasion, forty members shall be a house to proceed to business. They have been moved to this by the fear of not being able to collect a house.[165] But this danger could not authorize them to call that a house which was none: and if they may fix it at one number, they may at another, till it loses its fundamental character of being a representative body. As this vote expires with the present invasion, it is probable the former rule will be permitted to revive: because at present no ill is meant. The power however of fixing their own quorum has been avowed, and a precedent set. From forty it may be reduced to four, and from four to one: from a house to a committee, from a committee to a chairman or speaker, and thus an oligarchy or monarchy be substituted under forms supposed to be regular. "Omnia mala exempla ex bonis orta sunt: sed ubi imperium ad ignaros aut minus bonos pervenit, novum illud exemplum ab dignis et idoneis ad indignos et non idoneos fertur."[166] When therefore it is considered, that there is no legal obstacle to the assumption by the assembly of all the powers legislative, executive, and judiciary, and that these may come to the hands of the smallest rag of delegation, surely the people will say, and their representatives, while yet they have honest representatives, will advise them to say, that they will not acknowledge as laws any acts not considered and assented to by the major part of their delegates.

In enumerating the defects of the constitution, it would be wrong to count among them what is only the error of particular persons. In December 1776, our circumstances being much dis-

---

*Bro. abr. Corporations. 31. 34. Hakewell, 93.
†Puff. Off. hom. l. 2. c. 6. §. 12.
‡June 4, 1781.

tressed, it was proposed in the house of delegates to create a *dictator*, invested with every power legislative, executive and judiciary, civil and military, of life and of death, over our persons and over our properties: and in June 1781,[167] again under calamity, the same proposition was repeated, and wanted a few votes only of being passed.—One who entered into this contest from a pure love of liberty, and a sense of injured rights, who determined to make every sacrifice, and to meet every danger, for the re-establishment of those rights on a firm basis, who did not mean to expend his blood and substance for the wretched purpose of changing this master for that, but to place the powers of governing him in a plurality of hands of his own choice, so that the corrupt will of no one man might in future oppress him, must stand confounded and dismayed when he is told, that a considerable portion of that plurality had meditated the surrender of them into a single hand, and, in lieu of a limited monarch, to deliver him over to a despotic one! How must we find his efforts and sacrifices abused and baffled, if he may still by a single vote be laid prostrate at the feet of one man! In God's name, from whence have they derived this power? Is it from our ancient laws? None such can be produced. Is it from any principle in our new constitution, expressed or implied? Every lineament of that expressed or implied, is in full opposition to it. Its fundamental principle is, that the state shall be governed as a commonwealth. It provides a republican organization, proscribes under the name of *prerogative* the exercise of all powers undefined by the laws; places on this basis the whole system of our laws; and, by consolidating them together, chuses that they shall be left to stand or fall together, never providing for any circumstances, nor admitting that such could arise, wherein either should be suspended, no, not for a moment. Our antient laws expressly declare, that those who are but delegates themselves shall not delegate to others powers which require judgment and integrity in their exercise.—Or was this proposition moved on a supposed right in the movers of abandoning their posts in a moment of distress? The same laws forbid the abandonment of that post, even on ordinary occasions; and much more a transfer of their powers into other hands and other forms, without consulting the people. They never admit the idea that these, like sheep or cattle, may be given from hand to hand without an appeal to their own will.—Was it from the necessity of the case? Necessities which dissolve a government, do not convey its authority to an oligarchy or a monarchy. They throw back, into the hands of the people, the powers they had delegated, and leave them as individuals to shift for themselves. A leader may offer, but not impose himself, nor be imposed on them. Much less can their necks be submitted to his sword, their breath be held at his will or caprice. The necessity which should operate these tremendous effects should at least be palpable and irresistible. Yet in both instances, where it was feared, or pretended with us, it was belied by the event. It was belied too by the preceding experience of our sister states, several of whom had grappled through greater difficulties without abandoning their forms of government. When the proposition was first made, Massachusets had found even the government of committees sufficient to carry them through an invasion. But we at the time of that proposition were under no invasion. When the second was made, there had been added to this example those of Rhode-Island, New-York, New-Jersey, and Pennsylvania, in all of which the republican form had been found equal to the task of carrying them through the severest trials. In this state alone did there exist so little virtue, that fear was to be fixed in the hearts of the people, and to become the motive of their exertions and the principle of their government? The very thought alone was treason against the people; was treason against mankind in general; as rivetting for ever the chains which bow down their necks, by giving to their oppressors a proof, which they would have trumpeted through the universe, of the imbecility of republican government, in times of pressing danger, to shield them from harm. Those who assume the right of giving away the reins of government in any case, must be sure that the herd, whom they hand on to the rods and hatchet of the dictator, will lay their necks on the block when he shall nod to them. But if our assemblies supposed such a resignation in the people, I hope they mistook their character. I am of opinion, that the government, instead of being braced and invigorated for greater exertions under their difficulties, would have been thrown back upon the bungling machinery of county committees for administration, till a convention could have been called, and its wheels again set into regular motion. What a cruel moment was this for creating such an embarrassment, for putting to the proof the attachment of our countrymen to republican government! Those who meant well, of the advocates for this measure, (and most of them meant well, for I know them personally, had been their fellow-labourers in the common cause, and had often proved the purity of their principles), had been seduced in their judgment by the example of an ancient republic, whose constitution and circumstances were fundamentally different. They had sought this precedent in the history of Rome, where alone it was to be found, and where at length too it had proved fatal. They had taken it from a republic, rent by the most bitter factions and tumults, where the government was of a heavy-handed unfeeling aristocracy, over a people ferocious, and rendered desperate by poverty and wretchedness; tumults which could not be allayed under the most trying circumstances, but by the omnipotent hand of a single despot. Their constitution therefore allowed a temporary tyrant to be erected, under the name of a Dictator; and that temporary tyrant, after a few examples, became perpetual. They misapplied this precedent to a people, mild in their dispositions, patient under their trial, united for the public liberty, and affectionate to their leaders. But if from the constitution of the Roman government there resulted to their Senate a power of submitting all their rights to the will of one man, does it follow, that the assembly of Virginia have the same authority? What clause in our constitution has substituted that of Rome, by way of residuary provision, for all cases not otherwise provided for? Or if they may step ad libitum into any other form of government for precedents to rule us by, for what oppression may not a precedent be found in this world of the bellum omnium in omnia[168]?—Searching for the foundations of this proposition, I can find none which may pretend a colour of right or reason, but the defect before developed, that there being no barrier between the legislative, executive, and judiciary departments, the legislature may seize the whole: that having seized it, and possessing a right to fix their own quorum, they may reduce that quorum to one, whom they may call a chairman, speaker, dictator, or by any other name they please.—Our situation is indeed perilous,[169] and I hope my countrymen will be sensible of it, and will apply, at a proper season, the proper remedy; which is a convention to fix the constitution, to amend its defects, to bind up the several branches of government by certain laws, which when they transgress their acts shall become nullities; to render unnecessary an appeal to the people, or in other words a rebellion, on every infraction of their rights, on the peril that their acquiescence shall be construed into an intention to surrender those rights.

QUERY XIV

THE ADMINISTRATION OF JUSTICE AND DESCRIPTION OF THE LAWS?

Laws

The state is divided into counties. In every county are appointed magistrates, called justices of the peace, usually from eight to thirty or forty in number, in proportion to the size of the county, of the most discreet and honest inhabitants. They are nominated by their fellows, but commissioned by the governor, and act without reward. These magistrates have jurisdiction both criminal and civil. If the question before them be a question of law only, they decide on it themselves: but if it be of fact, or of fact and law combined, it must be referred to a jury. In the latter case, of a combination of law and fact, it is usual for the jurors to decide the fact, and to refer the law arising on it to the decision of the judges. But this division of the subject lies with their discretion only. And if the question relate to any point of public liberty, or if it be one of those in which the judges may be suspected of bias, the jury undertake to decide both law and fact. If they be mistaken, a decision against right, which is casual only, is less dangerous to the state, and less afflicting to the loser, than one which makes part of a regular and uniform system. In truth, it is better to toss up cross and pile[170] in a cause, than to refer it to a judge whose mind is warped by any motive whatever, in that particular case. But the common sense of twelve honest men gives still a better chance of just decision, than the hazard of cross and pile. These judges execute their process by the sheriff or coroner of the county, or by constables of their own appointment. If any free person commit an offence against the commonwealth, if it be below the degree of felony, he is bound by a justice to appear before their court, to answer it on indictment or information. If it amount to felony, he is committed to jail, a court of these justices is called; if they on examination think him guilty, they send him to the jail of the general court, before which court he is to be tried first by a grand jury of 24, of whom 13 must concur in opinion: if they find him guilty, he is then tried by a jury of 12 men of the county where the offence was committed, and by their verdict, which must be unanimous, he is acquitted or condemned without appeal. If the criminal be a slave the trial by the county court is final. In every case however, except that of high treason, there resides in the governor a power of pardon. In high treason, the pardon can only flow from the general assembly. In civil matters these justices have jurisdiction in all cases of whatever value, not appertaining to the department of the admiralty. This jurisdiction is twofold. If the matter in dispute be of less value than 4⅙ dollars, a single member may try it at any time and place within his county, and may award execution on the goods of the party cast. If it be of that or greater value, it is determinable before the county court, which consists of four at the least of those justices, and assembles at the court-house of the county on a certain day in every month. From their determination, if the matter be of the value of ten pounds sterling, or concern the title or bounds of lands, an appeal lies to one of the superior courts.

There are three superior courts, to wit, the high-court of chancery, the general court, and court of admiralty. The first and second of these receive appeals from the county courts, and also have original jurisdiction where the subject of controversy is of the value of ten pounds sterling, or where it concerns the title or bounds of land. The jurisdiction of the admiralty is original altogether. The high-court of chancery is composed of three judges, the general court of five, and the court of admiralty of three. The two first hold their sessions at Richmond at stated times, the chancery twice in the year, and the general court twice for business civil and criminal, and twice more for criminal only. The court of admiralty sits at Williamsburgh whenever a controversy arises.

There is one supreme court, called the court of appeals, composed of the judges of the three superior courts, assembling twice a year at stated times at Richmond. This court receives appeals in all civil cases from each of the superior courts, and determines them finally. But it has no original jurisdiction.

If a controversy arise between two foreigners of a nation in alliance with the United States, it is decided by the Consul for their State, or, if both parties chuse it, by the ordinary courts of justice. If one of the parties only be such a foreigner, it is triable before the courts of justice of the country. But if it shall have been instituted in a county court, the foreigner may remove it into the general court, or court of chancery, who are to determine it at their first sessions, as they must also do if it be originally commenced before them. In cases of life and death, such foreigners have a right to be tried by a jury, the one half foreigners, the other natives.

All public accounts are settled with a board of auditors, consisting of three members, appointed by the general assembly, any two of whom may act. But an individual, dissatisfied with the determination of that board, may carry his case into the proper superior court.

A description of the laws.

The general assembly was constituted, as has been already shewn, by letters-patent of March the 9th, 1607, in the 4th year of the reign of James the First. The laws of England seem to have been adopted by consent of the settlers, which might easily enough be done whilst they were few and living all together. Of such adoption however we have no other proof than their practice, till the year 1661, when they were expressly adopted by an act of the assembly, except so far as "a difference of condition" rendered them inapplicable. Under this adoption, the rule, in our courts of judicature was, that the common law of England, and the general statutes previous to the 4th of James, were in force here; but that no subsequent statutes were, *unless we were named in them*, said the judges and other partisans of the crown, but *named or not named*, said those who reflected freely. It will be unnecessary to attempt a description of the laws of England, as that may be found in English publications. To those which were established here, by the adoption of the legislature, have been since added a number of acts of assembly passed during the monarchy, and ordinances of convention and acts of assembly enacted since the establishment of the republic. The following variations from the British model are perhaps worthy of being specified.

Debtors unable to pay their debts, and making faithful delivery of their whole effects, are released from confinement, and their persons for ever discharged from restraint for such previous debts: but any property they may afterwards acquire will be subject to their creditors.

The poor, unable to support themselves, are maintained by an assessment on the titheable persons in their parish. This assessment is levied and administered by twelve persons in each parish, called vestrymen, originally chosen by the housekeepers of the parish, but afterwards filling vacancies in their own body by their own choice. These are usually the most discreet farmers, so distributed through their parish, that every part of it may be under the immediate eye of some one of them. They are well acquainted with the details and oeconomy of private life, and they find sufficient inducements to execute their charge well, in their philanthropy, in the approbation of their neighbours, and the distinction which that gives them. The poor who have neither property, friends, nor strength to labour, are boarded in the houses of good farmers, to whom a stipulated sum is annually paid. To those who are able to help themselves a little, or have friends from whom they derive some succours, inadequate however to their full maintenance, supplementory aids are given, which enable them to live comfortably in their own houses, or in the houses of their friends. Vagabonds, without visible property or vocation, are placed in workhouses, where they are well cloathed, fed, lodged, and made to labour. Nearly the same method of providing for the poor prevails through all our states; and from Savannah to Portsmouth you will seldom meet a beggar. In the larger towns indeed they sometimes present themselves. These are usually foreigners, who have never obtained a settlement in any parish. I never yet saw a native American begging in the streets or highways. A subsistence is easily gained here: and if, by misfortunes, they are thrown on the charities of the world, those provided by their own country are so comfortable and so certain, that they never think of relinquishing them to become strolling beggars. Their situation too, when sick, in the family of a good farmer, where every member is emulous to do them kind offices, where they are visited by all the neighbours, who bring them the little rarities which their sickly appetites may crave, and who take by rotation the nightly watch over them, when their condition requires it, is without comparison better than in a general hospital, where the sick, the dying, and the dead are crammed together, in the same rooms, and often in the same beds. The disadvantages, inseparable from general hospitals, are such as can never be counterpoised by all the regularities of medicine and regimen. Nature and kind nursing save a much greater proportion in our plain way, at a smaller expence, and with less abuse. One branch only of hospital institution is wanting with us; that is, a general establishment for those labouring under difficult cases of chirurgery. The aids of this art are not equivocal. But an able chirurgeon cannot be had in every parish. Such a receptacle should therefore be provided for those patients: but no others should be admitted.

Marriages must be solemnized either on special licence, granted by the first magistrate of the county, on proof of the consent of the parent or guardian of either party under age, or after solemn publication, on three several Sundays, at some place of religious worship, in the parishes where the parties reside. The act of solemnization may be by the minister of any society of Christians, who shall have been previously licensed for this purpose by the court of the county. Quakers and Menonists however are exempted from all these conditions, and marriage among them is to be solemnized by the society itself.

A foreigner of any nation, not in open war with us, becomes naturalized by removing to the state to reside, and taking an oath of fidelity: and thereupon acquires every right of a native citizen: and citizens may divest themselves of that character, by declaring, by solemn deed, or in open court, that they mean to expatriate themselves, and no longer to be citizens of this state.

Conveyances of land must be registered in the court of the county wherein they lie, or in the general court, or they are void, as to creditors, and subsequent purchasers.

Slaves pass by descent and dower as lands do. Where the descent is from a parent, the heir is bound to pay an equal share of their value in money to each of his brothers and sisters.

Slaves, as well as lands, were entailable during the monarchy: but, by an act of the first republican assembly, all donees in tail, present and future, were vested with the absolute dominion of the entailed subject.

Bills of exchange, being protested, carry 10 per cent. interest from their date.

No person is allowed, in any other case, to take more than five per cent. per annum simple interest, for the loan of monies.

Gaming debts are made void, and monies actually paid to discharge such debts (if they exceeded 40 shillings) may be recovered by the payer within three months, or by any other person afterwards.

Tobacco, flour, beef, pork, tar, pitch, and turpentine, must be inspected by persons publicly appointed, before they can be exported.

The erecting iron-works and mills is encouraged by many privileges; with necessary cautions however to prevent their dams from obstructing the navigation of the water-courses. The general assembly have on several occasions shewn a great desire to encourage the opening the great falls of James and Patowmac rivers. As yet, however, neither of these have been effected.

The laws have also descended to the preservation and improvement of the races of useful animals, such as horses, cattle, deer; to the extirpation of those which are noxious, as wolves, squirrels, crows, blackbirds; and to the guarding our citizens against infectious disorders, by obliging suspected vessels coming into the state, to perform quarantine, and by regulating the conduct of persons having such disorders within the state.

The mode of acquiring lands, in the earliest times of our settlement, was by petition to the general assembly. If the lands prayed for were already cleared of the Indian title, and the assembly thought the prayer reasonable, they passed the property by their vote to the petitioner. But if they had not yet been ceded by the Indians, it was necessary that the petitioner should previously purchase their right. This purchase the assembly verified, by enquiries of the Indian proprietors; and being satisfied of its reality and fairness, proceeded further to examine the reasonableness of the petition, and its consistence with policy; and, according to the result, either granted or rejected the petition. The company also sometimes, though very rarely, granted lands, independantly of the general assembly. As the colony increased, and individual applications for land multiplied, it was found to give too much occupation to the general assembly to enquire into and execute the grant in every special case. They therefore thought it better to establish general rules, according to which all grants should be made, and to leave to the governor the execution of them, under these rules. This they did by what have been usually called the land laws, amending them from time to time, as their defects were developed. According to these laws, when an individual wished a portion of unappropriated land, he was to locate and survey it by a public officer, appointed for that purpose: its breadth was to bear a certain proportion to its length: the grant was to be executed by the governor: and the lands were to be improved in a certain manner, within a given time. From these regulations there resulted to the state a sole and exclusive power of taking conveyances of the Indian right of soil: since, according to them, an Indian conveyance alone could give no right to an individual, which the laws would acknowledge. The state, or the crown, thereafter, made general purchases of the Indians from time to time, and the governor parcelled them out by special grants, conformed to the rules before described, which it was not in his power, or in that of the crown, to dispense with. Grants, unaccompanied by their proper legal circumstances, were set aside regularly by *scire facias*,[171] or by bill in Chancery. Since the establishment of our new government, this order of things is but little changed. An individual, wishing to appropriate to himself lands still unappropriated by any other, pays to the public treasurer a sum of money proportioned to the quantity he wants. He carries the treasurer's receipt to the auditors of public accompts, who thereupon debit the treasurer with the sum, and order the register of the land-office to give the party a warrant for his land. With this warrant from the register, he goes to the surveyor of the county where the land lies on which he has cast his eye. The surveyor lays it off for him, gives him its exact description, in the form of a certificate, which certificate he returns to the land-office, where a grant is made out, and is signed by the governor. This vests in him a perfect dominion in his lands, transmissible to whom he pleases by deed or will, or by descent to his heirs if he die intestate.

Many of the laws which were in force during the monarchy being relative merely to that form of government, or inculcating principles inconsistent with republicanism, the first assembly which met after the establishment of the commonwealth appointed a committee to revise the whole code, to reduce it into proper form and volume, and report it to the assembly. This work has been executed by three gentlemen, and reported; but probably will not be taken up till a restoration of peace shall leave to the legislature leisure to go through such a work.

The plan of the revisal[172] was this. The common law of England, by which is meant, that part of the English law which was anterior to the date of the oldest statutes extant, is made the basis of the work. It was thought dangerous to attempt to reduce it to a text: it was therefore left to be collected from the usual monuments of it. Necessary alterations in that, and so much of the whole body of the British statutes, and of acts of assembly, as were thought proper to be retained, were digested into 126 new acts, in which simplicity of stile was aimed at, as far as was safe. The following are the most remarkable alterations proposed:

To change the rules of descent, so as that the lands of any person dying intestate shall be divisible equally among all his children, or other representatives, in equal degree.

To make slaves distributable among the next of kin, as other moveables.

To have all public expences, whether of the general treasury, or of a parish or county, (as for the maintenance of the poor, building bridges, court-houses, &c.) supplied by assessments on the citizens, in proportion to their property.

To hire undertakers for keeping the public roads in repair, and indemnify individuals through whose lands new roads shall be opened.

To define with precision the rules whereby aliens should become citizens, and citizens make themselves aliens.

To establish religious freedom on the broadest bottom.

To emancipate all slaves born after passing the act. The bill reported by the revisors does not itself contain this proposition; but an amendment containing it was prepared, to be offered to the legislature whenever the bill should be taken up, and further directing, that they should continue with their parents to a certain age, then be brought up, at the public expence, to tillage, arts or sciences, according to their geniusses, till the females should be eighteen, and the males twenty-one years of age, when they should be colonized to such place as the circumstances of the time should render most proper, sending them out with arms, implements of houshold and of the handicraft arts, feeds, pairs of the useful domestic animals, &c. to declare them a free and independant people, and extend to them our alliance and protection, till they shall have acquired strength; and to send vessels at the same time to other parts of the world for an equal number of white inhabitants; to induce whom to migrate hither, proper encouragements were to be proposed. It will probably be asked, Why not retain and incorporate the blacks into the state, and thus save the expence of supplying, by importation of white settlers, the vacancies they will leave? Deep rooted prejudices entertained by the whites; ten thousand recollections, by the blacks, of the injuries they have sustained; new provocations; the real distinctions which nature has made; and many other circumstances, will divide us into parties, and produce convulsions which will probably never end but in the extermination of the one or the other race.—To these objections, which are political, may be added others, which are physical and moral. The first difference which strikes us is that of colour. Whether the black of the negro resides in the reticular membrane between the skin and scarf-skin, or in the scarf-skin itself; whether it proceeds from the colour of the blood, the colour of the bile, or from that of some other secretion, the difference is fixed in nature, and is as real as if its seat and cause were better known to us. And is this difference of no importance? Is it not the foundation of a greater or less share of beauty in the two races? Are not the fine mixtures of red and white, the expressions of every passion by greater or less suffusions of colour in the one, preferable to that eternal monotony, which reigns in the countenances, that immoveable veil of black which covers all the emotions of the other race? Add to these, flowing hair, a more elegant symmetry of form, their own judgment in favour of the whites, declared by their preference of them, as uniformly as is the preference of the Oranootan for the black women over those of his own species. The circumstance of superior beauty, is thought worthy attention in the propagation of our horses, dogs, and other domestic animals; why not in that of man? Besides those of colour, figure, and hair, there are other physical distinctions proving a difference of race. They have less hair on the face and body. They secrete less by the kidnies, and more by the glands of the skin, which gives them a very strong and disagreeable odour. This greater degree of transpiration renders them more tolerant of heat, and less so of cold, than the whites. Perhaps too a difference of structure in the pulmonary apparatus, which a late ingenious *experimentalist has discovered to be the principal regulator of animal heat, may have disabled them from extricating, in the act of inspiration, so much of that fluid from the outer air, or obliged them in expiration, to part with more of it. They seem to require less sleep. A black, after hard labour through the day, will be induced by the slightest amusements to sit up till midnight,[174] or later, though knowing he must be out with the first dawn of the morning. They are at least as brave, and more adventuresome. But this may perhaps proceed from a want of forethought, which prevents their seeing a danger till it be present. When present, they do not go through it with more coolness or steadiness than the whites. They are more ardent after their female: but love seems with them to be more an eager desire, than a tender delicate mixture of sentiment and sensation.[175] Their griefs are transient. Those numberless afflictions, which render it doubtful whether heaven has given life to us in mercy or in wrath, are less felt, and sooner forgotten with them. In general, their existence appears to participate more of sensation than reflection. To this must be ascribed their disposition to sleep when abstracted from their diversions, and unemployed in labour. An animal whose body is at rest, and who does not reflect, must be disposed to sleep of course. Comparing them by their faculties of memory, reason, and imagination, it appears to me, that in memory they are equal to the whites; in reason much inferior, as I think one could scarcely be found capable of tracing and comprehending the investigations of Euclid; and that in imagination they are dull, tasteless, and anomalous. It would be unfair to follow them to Africa for this investigation. We will consider them here, on the same stage with the whites, and

---

*Crawford.[173]

where the facts are not apocryphal on which a judgment is to be formed. It will be right to make great allowances for the difference of condition, of education, of conversation, of the sphere in which they move. Many millions of them have been brought to, and born in America. Most of them indeed have been confined to tillage, to their own homes, and their own society: yet many have been so situated, that they might have availed themselves of the conversation of their masters; many have been brought up to the handicraft arts, and from that circumstance have always been associated with the whites. Some have been liberally educated, and all have lived in countries where the arts and sciences are cultivated to a considerable degree, and have had before their eyes samples of the best works from abroad. The Indians, with no advantages of this kind, will often carve figures on their pipes not destitute of design and merit. They will crayon out an animal, a plant, or a country, so as to prove the existence of a germ in their minds which only wants cultivation. They astonish you with strokes of the most sublime oratory; such as prove their reason and sentiment strong, their imagination glowing and elevated. But never yet could I find that a black had uttered a thought above the level of plain narration; never see even an elementary trait of painting or sculpture. In music they are more generally gifted than the whites with accurate ears for tune and time, and they have been found capable of imagining a small catch*. Whether they will be equal to the composition of a more extensive run of melody, or of complicated harmony, is yet to be proved. Misery is often the parent of the most affecting touches in poetry.—Among the blacks is misery enough, God knows, but no poetry. Love is the peculiar oestrum of the poet. Their love is ardent, but it kindles the senses only, not the imagination. Religion indeed has produced a Phyllis Whately;[176] but it could not produce a poet. The compositions published under her name are below the dignity of criticism. The heroes of the Dunciad[177] are to her, as Hercules to the author of that poem. Ignatius Sancho[178] has approached nearer to merit in

---

*The instrument proper to them is the Banjar, which they brought hither from Africa, and which is the original of the guitar, its chords being precisely the four lower chords of the guitar.

composition; yet his letters do more honour to the heart than the head. They breathe the purest effusions of friendship and general philanthropy, and shew how great a degree of the latter may be compounded with strong religious zeal. He is often happy in the turn of his compliments, and his stile is easy and familiar, except when he affects a Shandean fabrication of words. But his imagination is wild and extravagant, escapes incessantly from every restraint of reason and taste, and, in the course of its vagaries, leaves a tract of thought as incoherent and eccentric, as is the course of a meteor through the sky. His subjects should often have led him to a process of sober reasoning: yet we find him always substituting sentiment for demonstration. Upon the whole, though we admit him to the first place among those of his own colour who have presented themselves to the public judgment, yet when we compare him with the writers of the race among whom he lived, and particularly with the epistolary class, in which he has taken his own stand, we are compelled to enroll him at the bottom of the column. This criticism supposes the letters published under his name to be genuine, and to have received amendment from no other hand; points which would not be of easy investigation.[179] The improvement of the blacks in body and mind, in the first instance of their mixture with the whites, has been observed by every one, and proves that their inferiority is not the effect merely of their condition of life. We know that among the Romans, about the Augustan age especially, the condition of their slaves was much more deplorable than that of the blacks on the continent of America. The two sexes were confined in separate apartments, because to raise a child cost the master more than to buy one. Cato, for a very restricted indulgence to his slaves in this particular, *took from them a certain price. But in this country the slaves multiply as fast as the free inhabitants. Their situation and manners place the commerce between the two sexes almost without restraint.—The same Cato, on a principle of oeconomy, always sold his sick and superannuated slaves. He gives it as a standing precept to a master visiting his farm, to sell his old oxen, old waggons, old tools,

---

* Τȣς δȣλȣς εταξεν ὡρισμενȣ νομισματος ὁμιλειν ταις θεραπαινισιν. —Plutarch.[180] Cato.

old and diseased servants, and every thing else become useless. "Vendat boves vetulos, plaustrum vetus, ferramenta vetera, servum senem, servum morbosum, & si quid aliud supersit vendat."[181] Cato de re rusticâ. c. 2. The American slaves cannot enumerate this among the injuries and insults they receive. It was the common practice to expose in the island of Aesculapius, in the Tyber, diseased slaves, whose cure was like to become tedious.[182] The Emperor Claudius, by an edict, gave freedom to such of them as should recover, and first declared, that if any person chose to kill rather than to expose them, it should be deemed homicide. The exposing them is a crime of which no instance has existed with us; and were it to be followed by death, it would be punished capitally. We are told of a certain Vedius Pollio, who, in the presence of Augustus, would have given a slave as food to his fish, for having broken a glass.[183] With the Romans, the regular method of taking the evidence of their slaves was under torture. Here it has been thought better never to resort to their evidence. When a master was murdered, all his slaves, in the same house, or within hearing, were condemned to death. Here punishment falls on the guilty only, and as precise proof is required against him as against a freeman. Yet notwithstanding these and other discouraging circumstances among the Romans, their slaves were often their rarest artists. They excelled too in science, insomuch as to be usually employed as tutors to their master's children. Epictetus, Terence, and Phaedrus,[184] were slaves. But they were of the race of whites. It is not their condition then, but nature, which has produced the distinction.—Whether further observation will or will not verify the conjecture, that nature has been less bountiful to them in the endowments of the head, I believe that in those of the heart she will be found to have done them justice. That disposition to theft with which they have been branded, must be ascribed to their situation, and not to any depravity of the moral sense. The man, in whose favour no laws of property exist, probably feels himself less bound to respect those made in favour of others. When arguing for ourselves, we lay it down as a fundamental, that laws, to be just, must give a reciprocation of right: that, without this, they are mere arbitrary rules of conduct, founded in force, and not in conscience: and it is a problem which I give to the master to solve,[185] whether the religious precepts against the violation of property were not framed for him as well as his slave? And whether the slave may not as justifiably take a little from one, who has taken all from him, as he may slay one who would slay him? That a change in the relations in which a man is placed should change his ideas of moral right and wrong, is neither new, nor peculiar to the colour of the blacks. Homer tells us it was so 2600 years ago.

'Ημιου, γαζ τ' ἀρετῆς ἀποαίνυ͡ιαι εὐρύθπα Ζεὺς
'Ανερος, ευτ' ἄν μιν κατὰ δὅλιον ἤμαζ ἔλησιν.
Od. 17, 323.

Jove fix'd it certain, that whatever day
Makes man a slave, takes half his worth away.[186]

But the slaves of which Homer speaks were whites. Notwithstanding these considerations which must weaken their respect for the laws of property, we find among them numerous instances of the most rigid integrity, and as many as among their better instructed masters, of benevolence, gratitude, and unshaken fidelity.—The opinion, that they are inferior in the faculties of reason and imagination, must be hazarded with great diffidence. To justify a general conclusion, requires many observations, even where the subject may be submitted to the Anatomical knife, to Optical glasses, to analysis by fire, or by solvents. How much more then where it is a faculty, not a substance, we are examining; where it eludes the research of all the senses; where the conditions of its existence are various and variously combined; where the effects of those which are present or absent bid defiance to calculation; let me add too, as a circumstance of great tenderness, where our conclusion would degrade a whole race of men from the rank in the scale of beings which their Creator may perhaps have given them. To our reproach it must be said, that though for a century and a half we have had under our eyes the races of black and of red men, they have never yet been viewed by us as subjects of natural history. I advance it therefore as a suspicion only, that the blacks, whether originally a distinct race, or made distinct by time and circumstances, are inferior to the whites in the endowments both of body and mind. It is not against experience to suppose, that different species of the same genus, or varieties of the same species, may possess different qualifications. Will not a lover of natural history then, one who views the gradations in all the races of animals with the eye of philosophy, excuse an effort to keep those in the department of man as distinct as nature has formed them? This unfortunate difference of colour, and perhaps of faculty, is a powerful obstacle to the emancipation of these people. Many of their advocates, while they wish to vindicate the liberty of human nature, are anxious also to preserve its dignity and beauty. Some of these, embarrassed by the question "What further is to be done with them?" join themselves in opposition with those who are actuated by sordid avarice only. Among the Romans emancipation required but one effort. The slave, when made free, might mix with, without staining the blood of his master. But with us a second is necessary, unknown to history. When freed, he is to be removed beyond the reach of mixture.

The revised code further proposes to proportion crimes and punishments. This is attempted on the following scale.

I. Crimes whose punishment extends to *Life*.

1. High treason. — Death by hanging.
Forfeiture of lands and goods to the commonwealth.
2. Petty treason. — Death by hanging. Dissection.
Forfeiture of half the lands and goods to the representatives of the party slain.
3. Murder.
    1. by poison. — Death by poison.
Forfeiture of one-half as before.
    2. in Duel. — Death by hanging. Gibbeting, if the challenger.
Forfeiture of one-half as before, unless it be the party challenged, then the forfeiture is to the commonwealth.
    3. in any other way. — Death by hanging.
Forfeiture of one-half as before.
4. Manslaughter. — The second offence is murder.

II. Crimes whose punishment goes to *Limb*.

1. Rape,
2. Sodomy, } Dismemberment.
3. Maiming,
4. Disfiguring, } Retaliation, and the forfeiture of half the lands and goods to the sufferer.

III. Crimes punishable by *Labour*.

1. Manslaughter, 1st offence.	Labour VII. years for the public.	Forfeiture of half as in murder.
2. Counterfeiting money.	Labour VI. years.	Forfeiture of lands and goods to the commonwealth.
3. Arson. 4. Asportation of vessels.	Labour V. years.	Reparation threefold.
5. Robbery. 6. Burglary.	Labour IV. years.	Reparation double.
7. Housebreaking. 8. Horse-stealing.	Labour III. years.	Reparation.
9. Grand Larcency.	Labour II. years.	Reparation. Pillory.
10. Petty Larcency.	Labour I. year.	Reparation. Pillory.
11. Pretensions to witch-craft, &c.	Ducking.	Stripes.
12. Excusable homicide. 13. Suicide. 14. Apostacy, Heresy.	to be pitied, not punished.	

Pardon and privilege of clergy are proposed to be abolished; but if the verdict be against the defendant, the court in their discretion, may allow a new trial. No attainder to cause a corruption of blood, or forfeiture of dower. Slaves guilty of offences punishable in others by labour, to be transported to Africa, or elsewhere, as the circumstances of the time admit, there to be continued in slavery. A rigorous regimen proposed for those condemned to labour.

Another object of the revisal is, to diffuse knowledge more generally through the mass of the people. This bill proposes to lay off every county into small districts of five or six miles square, called hundreds, and in each of them to establish a school for teaching reading, writing, and arithmetic. The tutor to be supported by the hundred, and every person in it entitled to send their children three years gratis, and as much longer as they please, paying for it. These schools to be under a visitor, who is annually to chuse the boy, of best genius in the school, of those whose parents are too poor to give them further education, and to send him forward to one of the grammar schools, of which twenty are proposed to be erected in different parts of the country, for teaching Greek, Latin, geography, and the higher branches of numerical arithmetic. Of the boys thus sent in any one year, trial is to be made at the grammar schools one or two years, and the best genius of the whole selected, and continued six years, and the residue dismissed. By this means twenty of the best geniusses will be raked from the rubbish annually, and be instructed, at the public expence, so far as the grammar schools go. At the end of six years instruction, one half are to be discontinued (from among whom the grammar schools will probably be supplied with future masters); and the other half, who are to be chosen for the superiority of their parts and disposition, are to be sent and continued three years in the study of such sciences as they shall chuse, at William and Mary college, the plan of which is proposed to be enlarged, as will be hereafter explained, and extended to all the useful sciences. The ultimate result of the whole scheme of education would be the teaching all the children of the state reading, writing, and common arithmetic: turning out ten annually of superior genius, well taught in Greek, Latin, geography, and the higher branches of arithmetic: turning out ten others annually, of still superior parts, who, to those branches of learning, shall have added such of the sciences as their genius shall have led them to: the furnishing to the wealthier part of the people convenient schools, at which their children may be educated, at their own expence.—The general objects of this law are to provide an education adapted to the years, to the capacity, and the condition of every one, and directed to their freedom and happiness. Specific details were not proper for the law. These must be the business of the visitors entrusted with its execution. The first stage of this education being the schools of the hundreds, wherein the great mass of the people will receive their instruction, the principal foundations of future order will be laid here. Instead therefore of putting the Bible and Testament into the hands of the children, at an age when their judgments are not sufficiently matured for religious enquiries, their memories may here be stored with the most useful facts from Grecian, Roman, European and American history.[187] The first elements of morality too may be instilled into their minds; such as, when further developed as their judgments advance in strength, may teach them how to work out their own greatest happiness, by shewing them that it does not depend on the condition of life in which chance has placed them, but is always the result of a good conscience, good health, occupation, and freedom in all just pursuits.—Those whom either the wealth of their parents or the adoption of the state shall destine to higher degrees of learning, will go on to the grammar schools, which constitute the next stage, there to be instructed in the languages. The learning Greek and Latin, I am told, is going into disuse in Europe. I know not what their manners and occupations may call for: but it would be very ill-judged in us to follow their example in this instance. There is a certain period of life, say from eight to fifteen or sixteen years of age, when the mind, like the body, is not yet firm enough for laborious and close operations. If applied to such, it falls an early victim to premature exertion; exhibiting indeed at first, in these young and tender subjects, the flattering appearance of their being men while they are yet children, but ending in reducing them to be children when they should be men. The memory is then most susceptible and tenacious of impressions; and the learning of languages being chiefly a work of memory, it seems precisely fitted to the powers of this period, which is long enough too for acquiring the most useful languages antient and modern. I do not pretend that language is science. It is only an instrument for the attainment of science. But that time is not lost which is employed in providing tools for future operation: more especially as in this case the books put into the hands of the youth for this purpose may be such as will at the same time impress their minds with useful facts and good principles. If this period be suffered to pass in idleness, the mind becomes lethargic and impotent, as would the body it inhabits if unexercised during the same time. The sympathy between body and mind during their rise, progress and decline, is too strict and obvious to endanger our being misled while we reason from the one to the other.—As soon as they are of sufficient age, it is supposed they will be sent on from the grammar schools to the university, which constitutes our third and last stage, there to study those sciences which may be adapted to their views.—By that part of our plan which prescribes the selection of the youths of genius from among the classes of the poor, we hope to avail the state of those talents which nature has sown as liberally among the poor as the rich, but which perish without use, if not sought for and cultivated.-

—But of all the views of this law none is more important, none more legitimate, than that of rendering the people the safe, as they are the ultimate, guardians of their own liberty. For this purpose the reading in the first stage, where *they* will receive their whole education, is proposed, as has been said, to be chiefly historical. History by apprising them of the past will enable them to judge of the future; it will avail them of the experience of other times and other nations; it will qualify them as judges of the actions and designs of men; it will enable them to know ambition under every disguise it may assume; and knowing it, to defeat its views. In every government on earth is some trace of human weakness, some germ of corruption and degeneracy, which cunning will discover, and wickedness insensibly open, cultivate, and improve. Every government degenerates when trusted to the rulers of the people alone. The people themselves therefore are its only safe depositories. And to render even them safe their minds must be improved to a certain degree. This indeed is not all that is necessary, though it be essentially necessary. An amendment of our constitution must here come in aid of the public education. The influence over government must be shared among all the people. If every individual which composes their mass participates of the ultimate authority, the government will be safe; because the corrupting the whole mass will exceed any private resources of wealth: and public ones cannot be provided but by levies on the people. In this case every man would have to pay his own price. The government of Great-Britain has been corrupted, because but one man in ten has a right to vote for members of parliament. The sellers of the government therefore get nine-tenths of their price clear. It has been thought that corruption is restrained by confining the right of suffrage to a few of the wealthier of the people: but it would be more effectually restrained by an extension of that right to such numbers as would bid defiance to the means of corruption.

Lastly, it is proposed, by a bill in this revisal, to begin a public library and gallery, by laying out a certain sum annually in books, paintings, and statues.

QUERY XV

THE COLLEGES AND PUBLIC ESTABLISHMENTS, THE ROADS, BUILDINGS, &C?

Colleges, buildings, roads, &c.

The college of William and Mary is the only public seminary of learning in this state. It was founded in the time of king William and queen Mary, who granted to it 20,000 acres of land, and a penny a pound duty on certain tobaccoes exported from Virginia and Maryland, which had been levied by the statute of 25 Car. 2. The assembly also gave it, by temporary laws, a duty on liquors imported, and skins and firs exported. From these resources it received upwards of 3000 l. communibus annis. The buildings are of brick, sufficient for an indifferent accommodation of perhaps an hundred students. By its charter it was to be under the government of twenty visitors, who were to be its legislators, and to have a president and six professors, who were incorporated. It was allowed a representative in the general assembly. Under this charter, a professorship of the Greek and Latin languages, a professorship of mathematics, one of moral philosophy, and two of divinity, were established. To these were annexed, for a sixth professorship, a considerable donation by Mr. Boyle of England,[188] for the instruction of the Indians, and their conversion to Christianity. This was called the professorship of Brafferton, from an estate of that name in England, purchased with the monies given. The admission of the learners of Latin and Greek filled the college with children. This rendering it disagreeable and degrading to young gentlemen already prepared for entering on the sciences, they were discouraged from resorting to it, and thus the schools for mathematics and moral philosophy, which might have been of some service, became of very little. The revenues too were exhausted in accommodating those who came only to acquire the rudiments of science. After the present revolution, the visitors, having no power to change those circumstances in the constitution of the college which were fixed by the charter, and being therefore confined in the number of professorships, undertook to change the objects of the professorships. They excluded the two schools for divinity, and that for the Greek and Latin languages, and substituted others; so that at present they stand thus:

A Professorship for Law and Police:
Anatomy and Medicine:
Natural Philosophy and Mathematics:
Moral Philosophy, the Law of Nature
and Nations, the Fine Arts:
Modern Languages:
For the Brafferton.

And it is proposed, so soon as the legislature shall have leisure to take up this subject, to desire authority from them to increase the number of professorships, as well for the purpose of subdividing those already instituted, as of adding others for other branches of science. To the professorships usually established in the universities of Europe, it would seem proper to add one for the antient languages and literature of the North, on account of their connection with our own language, laws, customs, and history. The purposes of the Brafferton institution would be better answered by maintaining a perpetual mission among the Indian tribes, the object of which, besides instructing them in the principles of Christianity, as the founder requires, should be to collect their traditions, laws, customs, languages, and other circumstances which might lead to a discovery of their relation with one another, or descent from other nations. When these objects are accomplished with one tribe, the missionary might pass on to another.

The roads are under the government of the county courts, subject to be controuled by the general court. They order new roads to be opened wherever they think them necessary. The inhabitants of the county are by them laid off into precincts, to each of which they allot a convenient portion of the public roads to be kept in repair. Such bridges as may be built without the assistance of artificers, they are to build. If the stream be such as to require a bridge of regular workmanship, the court employs workmen to build it, at the expence of the whole county. If it be too great for the county, application is made to the general assembly, who authorize individuals to build it, and to take a fixed toll from all passengers, or give sanction to such other proposition as to them appears reasonable.

Ferries are admitted only at such places as are particularly pointed out by law, and the rates of ferriage are fixed.

Taverns are licensed by the courts, who fix their rates from time to time.

The private buildings are very rarely constructed of stone or brick; much the greatest proportion being of scantling and boards, plaistered with lime. It is impossible to devise things more ugly, uncomfortable, and happily more perishable. There are two or three plans, on one of which, according to its size, most of the houses in the state are built. The poorest people build huts of logs, laid horizontally in pens, stopping the interstices with mud. These are warmer in winter, and cooler in summer, than the more expensive constructions of scantling and plank. The wealthy are attentive to the raising of vegetables, but very little so to fruits. The poorer people attend to neither, living principally on milk and animal diet. This is the more inexcusable, as the climate requires indispensably a free use of vegetable food, for health as well as comfort, and is very friendly to the raising of fruits.—The only public buildings worthy mention are the Capitol, the Palace, the College, and the Hospital for Lunatics, all of them in Williamsburg, heretofore the seat of our government. The Capitol is a light and airy structure, with a portico in front of two orders, the lower of which, being Doric, is tolerably just in its proportions and ornaments, save only that the intercolonnations are too large. The upper is Ionic, much too small for that on which it is mounted, its ornaments not proper to the order, nor proportioned within themselves. It is crowned with a pediment, which is too high for its span. Yet, on the whole, it is the most pleasing piece of architecture we have. The Palace is not handsome without: but it is spacious and commodious within, is prettily situated, and, with the grounds annexed to it, is capable of being made an elegant seat. The College and Hospital are rude, mis-shapen piles, which, but that they have roofs, would be taken for brick-kilns. There are no other public buildings but churches and court-houses, in which no attempts are made at elegance. Indeed it would not be easy to execute such an attempt, as a workman could scarcely be found here capable of drawing an order. The genius of architecture seems to have shed its maledictions over this land. Buildings are often erected, by individuals, of considerable expence. To give these symmetry and taste would not increase their cost. It would only change the arrangement of the materials, the form and combination of the members. This would often cost less than the burthen of barbarous ornaments with which these buildings are sometimes charged. But the first principles of the art are unknown, and there exists scarcely a model among us sufficiently chaste to give an idea of them. Architecture being one of the fine arts, and as such within the department of a professor of the college, according to the new arrangement, perhaps a spark may fall on some young subjects of natural taste, kindle up their genius, and produce a reformation in this elegant and useful art. But all we shall do in this way will produce no permanent improvement to our country, while the unhappy prejudice prevails that houses of brick or stone are less wholesome than those of wood. A dew is often observed on the walls of the former in rainy weather, and the most obvious solution is, that the rain has penetrated through these walls. The following facts however are sufficient to prove the error of this solution. 1. This dew on the walls appears when there is no rain, if the state of the atmosphere be moist. 2. It appears on the partition as well as the exterior walls. 3. So also on pavements of brick or stone. 4. It is more copious in proportion as the walls are thicker; the reverse of which ought to be the case, if this hypothesis were just. If cold water be poured into a vessel of stone, or glass, a dew forms instantly on the outside: but if it be poured into a vessel of wood, there is no such appearance. It is not supposed, in the first case, that the water has exuded through the glass, but that it is precipitated from the circumambient air; as the humid particles of vapour, passing from the boiler of an alembic through its refrigerant, are precipitated from the air, in which they were suspended, on the internal surface of the refrigerant. Walls of brick or stone act as the refrigerant in this instance. They are sufficiently cold to condense and precipitate the moisture suspended in the air of the room, when it is heavily charged therewith. But walls of wood are not so. The question then is, whether air in which this moisture is left floating, or that which is deprived of it, be most wholesome? In both cases the remedy is easy. A little fire kindled in the room, whenever the air is damp, prevents the precipitation on the walls: and this practice, found healthy in the warmest as well as coldest seasons, is as necessary in a wooden as in a stone or a brick house. I do not mean to say, that the rain never penetrates through walls of brick. On the contrary I have seen instances of it. But with us it is only through the northern and eastern walls of the house, after a north-easterly storm, these being the only ones which continue long enough to force through the walls. This however happens too rarely to give a just character of unwholesomeness to such houses. In a house, the walls of which are of well-burnt brick and good mortar, I have seen the rain penetrate through but twice in a dozen or fifteen years. The inhabitants of Europe, who dwell chiefly in houses of stone or brick, are surely as healthy as those of Virginia. These houses have the advantage too of being warmer in winter and cooler in summer than those of wood, of being cheaper in their first construction, where lime is convenient, and infinitely more durable. The latter consideration renders it of great importance to eradicate this prejudice from the minds of our countrymen. A country whose buildings are of wood, can never increase in its improvements to any considerable degree. Their duration is highly estimated at 50 years. Every half century then our country becomes a tabula rasa, whereon we have to set out anew, as in the first moment of seating it. Whereas when buildings are of durable materials, every new edifice is an actual and permanent acquisition to the state, adding to its value as well as to its ornament.

QUERY XVI

THE MEASURES TAKEN WITH REGARD OF THE ESTATES AND POSSESSIONS OF THE REBELS, COMMONLY CALLED TORIES?

Tories

A Tory has been properly defined to be a traitor in thought, but not in deed. The only description, by which the laws have endeavoured to come at them, was that of non-jurors, or persons refusing to take the oath of fidelity to the state. Persons of this description were at one time subjected to double taxation, at another to treble, and lastly were allowed retribution, and placed on a level with good citizens. It may be mentioned as a proof both of the lenity of our government, and unanimity of its inhabitants, that though this war has now raged near seven years, not a single execution for treason has taken place.

Under this query I will state the measures which have been adopted as to British property, the owners of which stand on a much fairer footing than the Tories. By our laws, the same as the English in this respect, no alien can hold lands, nor alien enemy maintain an action for money, or other moveable thing. Lands acquired or held by aliens become forfeited to the state; and, on an action by an alien enemy to recover money, or other moveable property, the defendant may plead that he is an alien enemy. This extinguishes his right in the hands of the debtor or holder of his moveable property. By our separation from Great-Britain, British subjects became aliens, and being at war, they were alien enemies. Their lands were of course forfeited, and their debts irrecoverable. The assembly however passed laws, at various times, for saving their property. They first sequestered their lands, slaves, and other property on their farms, in the hands of commissioners, who were mostly the confidential friends or agents of the owners, and directed their clear profits to be paid into the treasury: and they gave leave to all persons owing debts to British subjects to pay them also into the treasury. The monies so to be brought in were declared to remain the property of the British subject, and, if used by the state, were to be repaid, unless an improper conduct in Great-Britain should render a detention of it reasonable. Depreciation had at that time, though unacknowledged and unperceived by the Whigs, begun in some small degree. Great sums of money were paid in by debtors. At a later period, the assembly, adhering to the political principles which forbid an alien to hold lands in the state, ordered all British property to be sold: and, become sensible of the real progress of depreciation, and of the losses which would thence occur, if not guarded against, they ordered that the proceeds of the sales should be converted into their then worth in tobacco, subject to the future direction of the legislature. This act has left the question of retribution more problematical. In May 1780 another act took away the permission to pay into the public treasury debts due to British subjects.

QUERY XVII

THE DIFFERENT RELIGIONS RECEIVED INTO THAT STATE?

Religion

The first settlers in this country were emigrants from England, of the English church, just at a point of time when it was flushed with complete victory over the religious of all other persuasions. Possessed, as they became, of the powers of making, administering, and executing the laws, they shewed equal intolerance in this country with their Presbyterian brethren, who had emigrated to the northern government. The poor Quakers were flying from persecution in England. They cast their eyes on these new countries as asylums of civil and religious freedom; but they found them free only for the reigning sect. Several acts of the Virginia assembly of 1659, 1662, and 1693, had made it penal in parents to refuse to have their children baptized; had prohibited the unlawful assembling of Quakers; had made it penal for any master of a vessel to bring a Quaker into the state; had ordered those already here, and such as should come thereafter, to be imprisoned till they should abjure the country; provided a milder punishment for their first and second return, but death for their third; had inhibited all persons from suffering their meetings in or near their houses, entertaining them individually, or disposing of books which supported their tenets. If no capital execution took place here, as did in New-England, it was not owing to the moderation of the church, or spirit of the legislature, as may be inferred from the law itself; but to historical circumstances which have not been handed down to us. The Anglicans retained full possession of the country about a century. Other opinions began then to creep in, and the great care of the government to support their own church, having begotten an equal degree of indolence in its clergy, two-thirds of the people had become dissenters at the commencement of the present revolution. The laws indeed were still oppressive on them, but the spirit of the one party had subsided into moderation, and of the other had risen to a degree of determination which commanded respect.

The present state of our laws[189] on the subject of religion is this. The convention of May 1776, in their declaration of rights, declared it to be a truth, and a natural right, that the exercise of religion should be free; but when they proceeded to form on that declaration the ordinance of government, instead of taking up every principle declared in the bill of rights, and guarding it by legislative sanction, they passed over that which asserted our religious rights, leaving them as they found them. The same convention, however, when they met as a member of the general assembly in October 1776, repealed all *acts of parliament* which had rendered criminal the maintaining any opinions in matters of religion, the forbearing to repair to church, and the exercising any mode of worship; and suspended the laws giving salaries to the clergy, which suspension was made perpetual in October 1779. Statutory oppressions in religion being thus wiped away, we remain at present under those only imposed by the common law, or by our own acts of assembly. At the common law, *heresy* was a capital offence, punishable by burning. Its definition was left to the ecclesiastical judges, before whom the conviction was, till the statute of the 1 El. c. 1.[190] circumscribed it, by declaring, that nothing should be deemed heresy, but what had been so determined by authority of the canonical scriptures, or by one of the four first general councils, or by some other council having for the grounds of their declaration the express and plain words of the scriptures. Heresy, thus circumscribed, being an offence at the common law, our act of assembly of October 1777, c. 17. gives cognizance of it to the general court, by declaring, that the jurisdiction of that court shall be general in all matters at the common law. The execution is by the writ *De haeretico comburendo*.[191] By our own act of assembly of 1705, c. 30, if a person brought up in the Christian religion denies the being of a God, or the Trinity, or asserts there are more Gods than one, or denies the Christian religion to be true, or the scriptures to be of divine authority, he is punishable on the first offence by incapacity to hold any office or employment ecclesiastical, civil, or military; on the second by disability to sue, to take any gift or legacy, to be guardian, executor, or administrator, and by three years imprisonment, without bail. A father's right to the custody of his own children being founded in law on his right of guardianship, this being taken away, they may of course be severed from him, and put, by the authority of a court, into more orthodox hands. This is a summary view of that religious slavery, under which a people have been willing to remain, who have lavished their lives and fortunes for the establishment of their civil freedom.* The error seems not sufficiently eradicated, that the operations of the mind, as well as the acts of the body, are subject to the coercion of the laws. But our rulers can have authority over such natural rights only as we have submitted to them. The rights of conscience we never submitted, we could not submit. We are answerable for them to our God. The legitimate powers of government extend to such acts only as are injurious to others.[193] But it does me no injury for my neighbour to say there are twenty gods, or no god. It neither picks my pocket nor breaks my leg. If it be said, his testimony in a court of justice cannot be relied on, reject it then, and be the stigma on him. Constraint may make him worse by making him a hypocrite, but it will never make him a truer man. It may fix him obstinately in his errors, but will not cure them. Reason and free enquiry are the only effectual agents against error. Give a loose to them, they will support the true religion, by bringing every false one to their tribunal, to the test of their investigation. They are the natural enemies of error, and of error only. Had not the Roman government permitted free enquiry, Christianity could never have been introduced. Had not free enquiry been indulged, at the aera of the reformation, the corruptions of Christianity could not have been purged away. If it be restrained now, the present corruptions will be protected, and new ones encouraged. Was the government to prescribe to us our medicine and diet, our bodies would be in such keeping as our souls are now. Thus in France the emetic was once forbidden as a medicine, and the potatoe as an article of food.[194] Government is just as infallible too when it fixes systems in physics. Galileo was sent to the inquisition for affirming that the earth was a sphere: the government had declared it to be as flat as a

*Furneaux passim.[192]

trencher, and Galileo was obliged to abjure his error. This error however at length prevailed, the earth became a globe, and Descartes declared it was whirled round its axis by a vortex. The government in which he lived was wise enough to see that this was no question of civil jurisdiction, or we should all have been involved by authority in vortices. In fact, the vortices have been exploded, and the Newtonian principle of gravitation is now more firmly established, on the basis of reason, than it would be were the government to step in, and to make it an article of necessary faith. Reason and experiment have been indulged, and error has fled before them. It is error alone which needs the support of government.[195] Truth can stand by itself. Subject opinion to coercion: whom will you make your inquisitors? Fallible men; men governed by bad passions, by private as well as public reasons. And why subject it to coercion? To produce uniformity. But is uniformity of opinion desireable? No more than of face and stature. Introduce the bed of Procrustes then, and as there is danger that the large men may beat the small, make us all of a size, by lopping the former and stretching the latter. Difference of opinion is advantageous in religion. The several sects perform the office of a Censor morum over each other. Is uniformity attainable? Millions of innocent men, women, and children, since the introduction of Christianity, have been burnt, tortured, fined, imprisoned; yet we have not advanced one inch towards uniformity. What has been the effect of coercion? To make one half the world fools, and the other half hypocrites. To support roguery and error all over the earth. Let us reflect that it is inhabited by a thousand millions of people. That these profess probably a thousand different systems of religion. That ours is but one of that thousand. That if there be but one right, and ours that one, we should wish to see the 999 wandering sects gathered into the fold of truth. But against such a majority we cannot effect this by force. Reason and persuasion are the only practicable instruments. To make way for these, free enquiry must be indulged; and how can we wish others to indulge it while we refuse it ourselves. But every state, says an inquisitor, has established some religion. No two, say I, have established the same. Is this a proof of the infallibility of establishments? Our sister states of Pennsylvania and New York, however, have long subsisted without any establishment at all. The experiment was new and doubtful when they made it. It has answered beyond conception. They flourish infinitely. Religion is well supported; of various kinds, indeed, but all good enough; all sufficient to preserve peace and order: or if a sect arises, whose tenets would subvert morals, good sense has fair play, and reasons and laughs it out of doors, without suffering the state to be troubled with it. They do not hang more malefactors than we do. They are not more disturbed with religious dissensions. On the contrary, their harmony is unparalleled, and can be ascribed to nothing but their unbounded tolerance, because there is no other circumstance in which they differ from every nation on earth. They have made the happy discovery, that the way to silence religious disputes, is to take no notice of them. Let us too give this experiment fair play, and get rid, while we may, of those tyrannical laws. It is true, we are as yet secured against them by the spirit of the times. I doubt whether the people of this country would suffer an execution for heresy, or a three years imprisonment for not comprehending the mysteries of the Trinity. But is the spirit of the people an infallible, a permanent reliance? Is it government? Is this the kind of protection we receive in return for the rights we give up? Besides, the spirit of the times may alter, will alter. Our rulers will become corrupt, our people careless. A single zealot may commence persecutor, and better men be his victims. It can never be too often repeated, that the time for fixing every essential right on a legal basis is while our rulers are honest, and ourselves united. From the conclusion of this war we shall be going down hill. It will not then be necessary to resort every moment to the people for support. They will be forgotten, therefore, and their rights disregarded. They will forget themselves, but in the sole faculty of making money, and will never think of uniting to effect a due respect for their rights. The shackles, therefore, which shall not be knocked off at the conclusion of this war, will remain on us long, will be made heavier and heavier, till our rights shall revive or expire in a convulsion.

QUERY XVIII

THE *PARTICULAR* CUSTOMS AND MANNERS THAT MAY HAPPEN TO BE RECEIVED IN THAT STATE?

Manners

It is difficult to determine on the standard by which the manners of a nation may be tried, whether *catholic*, or *particular*. It is more difficult for a native to bring to that standard the manners of his own nation, familiarized to him by habit. There must doubtless be an unhappy influence on the manners of our people produced by the existence of slavery among us. The whole commerce between master and slave is a perpetual exercise of the most boisterous passions, the most unremitting despotism on the one part, and degrading submissions on the other. Our children see this, and learn to imitate it; for man is an imitative animal. This quality is the germ of all education in him. From his cradle to his grave he is learning to do what he sees others do. If a parent could find no motive either in his philanthropy or his self-love, for restraining the intemperance of passion towards his slave, it should always be a sufficient one that his child is present. But generally it is not sufficient. The parent storms, the child looks on, catches the lineaments of wrath, puts on the same airs in the circle of smaller slaves, gives a loose to his worst of passions, and thus nursed, educated, and daily exercised in tyranny, cannot but be stamped by it with odious peculiarities. The man must be a prodigy who can retain his manners and morals undepraved by such circumstances. And with what execration should the statesman be loaded, who permitting one half the citizens thus to trample on the rights of the other, transforms those into despots, and these into enemies, destroys the morals of the one part, and the amor patriae of the other. For if a slave can have a country in this world, it must be any other in preference to that in which he is born to live and labour for another: in which he must lock up the faculties of his nature, contribute as far as depends on his individual endeavours to the evanishment of the human race, or entail his own miserable condition on the endless generations proceeding from him. With the morals of the people, their industry also is destroyed. For in a warm climate, no man will labour for himself who can make another labour for him. This is so true, that of the proprietors of slaves a very small proportion indeed are ever seen to labour. And can the liberties of a nation be thought secure when we have removed their only firm basis, a conviction in the minds of the people that these liberties are of the gift of God? That they are not to be violated but with his wrath? Indeed I tremble for my country when I reflect that God is just: that his justice cannot sleep for ever: that considering numbers, nature and natural means only, a revolution of the wheel of fortune, an exchange of situation, is among possible events: that it may become probable by supernatural interference! The Almighty has no attribute which can take side with us in such a contest.—But it is impossible to be temperate and to pursue this subject through the various considerations of policy, of morals, of history natural and civil. We must be contented to hope they will force their way into every one's mind. I think a change already perceptible, since the origin of the present revolution. The spirit of the master is abating, that of the slave rising from the dust, his condition mollifying, the way I hope preparing, under the auspices of heaven, for a total emancipation, and that this is disposed, in the order of events, to be with the consent of the masters, rather than by their extirpation.

QUERY XIX

THE PRESENT STATE OF MANUFACTURES, COMMERCE, INTERIOR AND EXTERIOR TRADE?

Manufactures

We never had an interior trade of any importance. Our exterior commerce has suffered very much from the beginning of the present contest. During this time we have manufactured within our families the most necessary articles of cloathing. Those of cotton will bear some comparison with the same kinds of manufacture in Europe; but those of wool, flax and hemp are very coarse, unsightly, and unpleasant: and such is our attachment to agriculture, and such our preference for foreign manufactures, that be it wise or unwise, our people will certainly return as soon as they can, to the raising raw materials, and exchanging them for finer manufactures than they are able to execute themselves.

The political oeconomists of Europe have established it as a principle that every state should endeavour to manufacture for itself: and this principle, like many others, we transfer to America, without calculating the difference of circumstance which should often produce a difference of result. In Europe the lands are either cultivated, or locked up against the cultivator. Manufacture must therefore be resorted to of necessity not of choice, to support the surplus of their people. But we have an immensity of land courting the industry of the husbandman. Is it best then that all our citizens should be employed in its improvement, or that one half should be called off from that to exercise manufactures and handicraft arts for the other? Those who labour in the earth are the chosen people of God, if ever he had a chosen people, whose breasts he has made his peculiar deposit for substantial and genuine virtue. It is the focus in which he keeps alive that sacred fire, which otherwise might escape from the face of the earth. Corruption of morals in the mass of cultivators is a phaenomenon of which no age nor nation has furnished an example. It is the mark set on those, who not looking up to heaven, to their own soil and industry, as does the husbandman, for their subsistance, depend for it on the casualties and caprice of customers. Dependance begets subservience and venality, suffocates the germ of virtue, and prepares fit tools for the designs of ambition. This, the natural progress and consequence of the arts, has sometimes perhaps been retarded by accidental circumstances: but, generally speaking, the proportion which the aggregate of the other classes of citizens bears in any state to that of its husbandmen, is the proportion of its unsound to its healthy parts, and is a good-enough barometer whereby to measure its degree of corruption. While we have land to labour then, let us never wish to see our citizens occupied at a work-bench, or twirling a distaff. Carpenters, masons, smiths, are wanting in husbandry: but, for the general operations of manufacture, let our work-shops remain in Europe. It is better to carry provisions and materials to workmen there, than bring them to the provisions and materials, and with them their manners and principles. The loss by the transportation of commodities across the Atlantic will be made up in happiness and permanence of government. The mobs of great cities add just so much to the support of pure government, as sores do to the strength of the human body. It is the manners and spirit of a people which preserve a republic in vigour. A degeneracy in these is a canker which soon eats to the heart of its laws and constitution.

QUERY XX

A NOTICE OF THE COMMERCIAL PRODUCTIONS PARTICULAR TO THE STATE, AND OF THOSE OBJECTS WHICH THE INHABITANTS ARE OBLIGED TO GET FROM EUROPE AND FROM OTHER PARTS OF THE WORLD?

Commercial productions

Before the present war we exported, communibus annis,[196] according to the best information I can get, nearly as follows:

ARTICLES.	Quantity.	Price in dollars.	Am. in dollars.
Tobacco	55,000 hhds. of 1000 lb.	at 30 d. per hhd.	1,650,000
Wheat	800,000 bushels	at 5/6 d. per bush.	666,666⅔
Indian corn	600,000 bushels	at ⅓ d. per bush.	200,000
Shipping	---	--	100,000
Masts, planks, skantling, shingles, staves	---	--	66,666⅔
Tar, pitch, turpentine	30,000 barrels	at 1⅓ d. per bar.	40,000
Peltry, viz. skins of deer, beavers, otters, muskrats, racoons, foxes	180 hhds. of 600 lb.	at 5/12 d. per lb.	42,000
Pork	4,000 barrels	at 10 d. per bar.	40,000
Flax-seed, hemp, cotton	---	--	8,000
Pit-coal, pig-iron	---	--	6,666⅔
Peas	5,000 bushels	at ⅔ d. per bush.	3,333⅓
Beef	1,000 barrels	at 3⅓ d. per bar.	3,333⅓
Sturgeon, white shad, herring	---	--	3,333⅓
Brandy from peaches and apples, and whiskey	---	--	1,666⅔
Horses	---	--	1,666⅔
This sum is equal to 850,000 l. Virginia money, 607,142 guineas.			2,833,333⅓ D.

In the year 1758 we exported seventy thousand hogsheads of tobacco, which was the greatest quantity ever produced in this country in one year. But its culture was fast declining at the commencement of this war and that of wheat taking its place: and it must continue to decline on the return of peace. I suspect that the change in the temperature of our climate has become sensible to that plant, which, to be good, requires an extraordinary degree of heat. But it requires still more indispensably an uncommon fertility of soil: and the price which it commands at market will not enable the planter to produce this by manure. Was the supply still to depend on Virginia and Maryland alone, as its culture becomes more difficult, the price would rise, so as to enable the planter to surmount those difficulties and to live. But the western country on the Missisipi, and the midlands of Georgia, having fresh and fertile lands in abundance, and a hotter sun, will be able to undersell these two states, and will oblige them to abandon the raising tobacco altogether. And a happy obligation for them it will be. It is a culture productive of infinite wretchedness. Those employed in it are in a continued state of exertion beyond the powers of nature to support. Little food of any kind is raised by them; so that the men and animals on these farms are badly fed, and the earth is rapidly impoverished. The cultivation of wheat is the reverse in every circumstance. Besides cloathing the earth with herbage, and preserving its fertility, it feeds the labourers plentifully, requires from them only a moderate toil, except in the season of harvest, raises great numbers of animals for food and service, and diffuses plenty and happiness among the whole. We find it easier to make an hundred bushels of wheat than a thousand weight of tobacco, and they are worth more when made. The weavil indeed is a formidable obstacle to the cultivation of this grain with us. But principles are already known which must lead to a remedy. Thus a certain degree of heat, to wit, that of the common air in summer, is necessary to hatch the egg. If subterranean granaries, or others, therefore, can be contrived below that temperature, the evil will be cured by cold. A degree of heat beyond that which hatches the egg, we know will kill it. But in aiming at this we easily run into that which produces putrefaction. To produce putrefaction, however, three agents are requisite, heat, moisture, and the external air. If the absence of any one of these be secured, the other two may safely be admitted. Heat is the one we want. Moisture then, or external air, must be excluded. The former has been done by exposing the grain in kilns to the action of fire, which produces heat, and extracts moisture at the same time: the latter, by putting the grain into hogsheads, covering it with a coat of lime, and heading it up. In this situation its bulk produces a heat sufficient to kill the egg; the moisture is suffered to remain indeed, but the external air is excluded. A nicer operation yet has been attempted; that is, to produce an intermediate temperature of heat between that which kills the egg, and that which produces putrefaction. The threshing the grain as soon as it is cut, and laying it in its chaff in large heaps, has been found very nearly to hit this temperature, though not perfectly, nor always. The heap generates heat sufficient to kill most of the eggs, whilst the chaff commonly restrains it from rising into putrefaction. But all these methods abridge too much the quantity which the farmer can manage, and enable other countries to undersell him which are not infested with this insect. There is still a desideratum then to give with us decisive triumph to this branch of agriculture over that of tobacco.—The culture of wheat, by enlarging our pasture, will render the Arabian horse an article of very considerable profit. Experience has shewn that ours is the particular climate of America where he may be raised without degeneracy. Southwardly the heat of the sun occasions a deficiency of pasture, and northwardly the winters are too cold for the short and fine hair, the particular sensibility and constitution of that race. Animals transplanted into unfriendly climates, either change their nature and acquire new fences against the new difficulties in which they are placed, or they multiply poorly and become extinct. A good foundation is laid for their propagation here by our possessing already great numbers of horses of that blood, and by a decided taste and preference for them established among the people. Their patience of heat without injury, their superior wind, fit them better in this and the more southern climates even for the drudgeries of the plough and waggon. Northwardly they will become an object only to persons of taste and fortune, for the saddle and light carriages. To these, and for these uses, their fleetness and beauty will recommend them.—

Besides these there will be other valuable substitutes when the cultivation of tobacco shall be discontinued, such as cotton in the eastern parts of the state, and hemp and flax in the western.

It is not easy to say what are the articles either of necessity, comfort, or luxury, which we cannot raise, and which we therefore shall be under a necessity of importing from abroad, as every thing hardier than the olive, and as hardy as the fig, may be raised here in the open air. Sugar, coffee and tea, indeed, are not between these limits; and habit having placed them among the necessaries of life with the wealthy part of our citizens, as long as these habits remain, we must go for them to those countries which are able to furnish them.

QUERY XXI

THE WEIGHTS, MEASURES, AND THE CURRENCY OF THE HARD MONEY? SOME DETAILS RELATING TO THE EXCHANGE WITH EUROPE?

Weights, Measures, Money

Our weights and measures are the same which are fixed by acts of parliament in England.—How it has happened that in this as well as the other American states the nominal value of coin was made to differ from what it was in the country we had left, and to differ among ourselves too, I am not able to say with certainty. I find that in 1631 our house of burgesses desired of the privy council in England, a coin debased to twenty-five per cent: that in 1645 they forbid dealing by barter for tobacco, and established the Spanish piece of eight at six shillings, as the standard of their currency: that in 1655 they changed it to five shillings sterling. In 1680 they sent an address to the king, in consequence of which, by proclamation in 1683, he fixed the value of French crowns, rixdollars[197] and pieces of eight at six shillings, and the coin of New-England at one shilling. That in 1710, 1714, 1727, and 1762, other regulations were made, which will be better presented to the eye stated in the form of a table as follows:[198]

	1710.	1714.	1727.	1762.
Guineas	--	26s		
British gold coin not milled, coined gold of Spain and France, chequins, Arabian gold, moidores of Portugal	--	5s the dwt.		
Coined gold of the empire	--	5s the dwt.	--	4s3 the dwt.
English milled silver money, in proportion to the crown, at	--	5s10	6s3	
Pieces of eight of Mexico, Seville, and Pillar, ducatoons of Flanders, French ecus, or silver Louis, crusados of Portugal	3¾ d. the dwt.	--	4 d. the dwt.	
Peru pieces, cross dollars, and old rixdollars of the empire	3½ d. the dwt.	--	3¾ d. the dwt.	
Old British silver coin not milled	--	3¾ d. the dwt.		

The first symptom of the depreciation of our present paper-money, was that of silver dollars selling at six shillings, which had before been worth but five shillings and ninepence. The assembly thereupon raised them by law to six shillings. As the dollar is now likely to become the money-unit of America, as it passes at this rate in some of our sister-states, and as it facilitates their computation in pounds and shillings, & e converso,[199] this seems to be more convenient than it's former denomination. But as this particular coin now stands higher than any other in the proportion of 133⅓ to 125, or 16 to 15, it will be necessary to raise the others in the same proportion.

QUERY XXII

THE PUBLIC INCOME AND EXPENCES?

Revenue

The nominal amount of these varying constantly and rapidly, with the constant and rapid depreciation of our paper-money, it becomes impracticable to say what they are. We find ourselves cheated in every essay by the depreciation intervening between the declaration of the tax and its actual receipt. It will therefore be more satisfactory to consider what our income may be when we shall find means of collecting what the people may spare. I should estimate the whole taxable property of this state at an hundred millions of dollars, or thirty millions of pounds our money. One per cent on this, compared with any thing we ever yet paid, would be deemed a very heavy tax. Yet I think that those who manage well, and use reasonable oeconomy, could pay one and a half per cent, and maintain their houshould comfortably in the mean time, without aliening any part of their principal, and that the people would submit to this willingly for the purpose of supporting their present contest. We may say then, that we could raise, and ought to raise, from one million to one million and a half of dollars annually, that is from three hundred to four hundred and fifty thousand pounds, Virginia money.

Of our expences it is equally difficult to give an exact state, and for the same reason. They are mostly stated in paper money, which varying continually, the legislature endeavours at every session, by new corrections, to adapt the nominal sums to the value it is wished they should bear. I will state them therefore in real coin, at the point at which they endeavour to keep them.

	Dollars.
The annual expenses of the general assembly are about	20,000
The governor	3,333⅓
The council of state	10,666⅔
Their clerks	1,166⅔

Eleven judges	11,000
The clerk of the chancery	666⅔
The attorney general	1,000
Three auditors and a solicitor	5,333⅓
Their clerks	2,000
The treasurer	2,000
His clerks	2,000
The keeper of the public jail	1,000
The public printer	1,666⅔
Clerks of the inferior courts	43,333⅓
Public levy: this is chiefly for the expences of criminal justice	40,000
County levy, for bridges, court houses, prisons, &c.	40,000
Members of congress	7,000
Quota of the Federal civil list, supposed ⅙ of about 78,000 dollars	13,000
Expences of collection, 6 per cent. on the above	12,310
The clergy receive only voluntary contributions: suppose them on an average ⅛ of a dollar a tythe on 200,000 tythes	25,000
Contingencies, to make round numbers not far from truth	7,523⅓
	250,000

Dollars, or 53,571 guineas. This estimate is exclusive of the military expence. That varies with the force actually employed, and in time of peace will probably be little or nothing. It is exclusive also of the public debts, which are growing while I am writing, and cannot therefore be now fixed. So it is of the maintenance of the poor, which being merely a matter of charity, cannot be deemed expended in the administration of government. And if we strike out the 25,000 dollars for the services of the clergy,[200] which neither makes part of that administration, more than what is paid to physicians or lawyers, and being voluntary, is either much or nothing as every one pleases, it leaves 225,000 dollars, equal to 48,208 guineas, the real cost of the apparatus of government with us. This, divided among the actual inhabitants of our country, comes to about two-fifths of a dollar, 21d sterling, or 42 sols, the price which each pays annually for the protection of the residue of his property, that of his person, and the other advantages of a free government. The public revenues of Great Britain divided in like manner on its inhabitants would be sixteen times greater. Deducting even the double of the expences of government, as before estimated, from the million and a half of dollars which we before supposed might be annually paid without distress, we may conclude that this state can contribute one million of dollars annually towards supporting the federal army, paying the federal debt, building a federal navy, or opening roads, clearing rivers, forming safe ports, and other useful works.

To this estimate of our abilities, let me add a word as to the application of them, if, when cleared of the present contest, and of the debts with which that will charge us, we come to measure force hereafter with any European power. Such events are devoutly to be deprecated. Young as we are, and with such a country before us to fill with people and with happiness, we should point in that direction the whole generative force of nature, wasting none of it in efforts of mutual destruction. It should be our endeavour to cultivate the peace and friendship of every nation, even of that which has injured us most, when we shall have carried our point against her. Our interest will be to throw open the doors of commerce, and to knock off all its shackles, giving perfect freedom to all persons for the vent of whatever they may chuse to bring into our ports, and asking the same in theirs. Never was so much false arithmetic employed on any subject, as that which has been employed to persuade nations that it is their interest to go to war. Were the money which it has cost to gain, at the close of a long war, a little town, or a little territory, the right to cut wood here, or to catch fish there, expended in improving what they already possess, in making roads, opening rivers, building ports, improving the arts, and finding employment for their idle poor, it would render them much stronger, much wealthier and happier. This I hope will be our wisdom. And, perhaps, to remove as much as possible the occasions of making war, it might be better for us to abandon the ocean altogether, that being the element whereon we shall be principally exposed to jostle with other nations: to leave to others to bring what we shall want, and to carry what we can spare. This would make us invulnerable to Europe, by offering none of our property to their prize, and would turn all our citizens to the cultivation of the earth; and, I repeat it again, cultivators of the earth are the most virtuous and independant citizens. It might be time enough to seek employment for them at sea, when the land no longer offers it. But the actual habits of our countrymen attach them to commerce. They will exercise it for themselves. Wars then must sometimes be our lot; and all the wise can do, will be to avoid that half of them which would be produced by our own follies, and our own acts of injustice; and to make for the other half the best preparations we can. Of what nature should these be? A land army would be useless for offence, and not the best nor safest instrument of defence. For either of these purposes, the sea is the field on which we should meet an European enemy. On that element it is necessary we should possess some power. To aim at such a navy as the greater nations of Europe possess, would be a foolish and wicked waste of the energies of our countrymen. It would be to pull on our own heads that load of military expence, which makes the European labourer go supperless to bed, and moistens his bread with the sweat of his brows. It will be enough if we enable ourselves to prevent insults from those nations of Europe which are weak on the sea, because circumstances exist, which render even the stronger ones weak as to us. Providence has placed their richest and most defenceless possessions at our door; has obliged their most precious commerce to pass as it were in review before us. To protect this, or to assail us, a small part only of their naval force will ever be risqued across the Atlantic. The dangers to which the elements expose them here are too well known, and the greater dangers to which they would be exposed at home, were any general calamity to involve their whole fleet. They can attack us by detachment only; and it will suffice to make ourselves equal to what they may detach. Even a smaller force than they may detach will be rendered equal or superior by the quickness with which any check may be repaired with us, while losses with them will be irreparable till too late. A small naval force then is sufficient for us, and a small one is necessary. What this should be, I will not undertake to say. I will only say, it should by no means be so great as we are able to make it. Suppose the million of dollars, or 300,000 pounds, which Virginia could annually spare without distress, to be applied to the creating of a navy. A single year's contribution would build, equip, man, and send to sea a force which should carry 300 guns. The rest of the confederacy, exerting themselves in the same proportion, would equip in the same time 1500 guns more. So that one year's contributions would set up a navy of 1800 guns. The British ships of the line average 76 guns; their frigates 38. 1800 guns then would form a fleet of 30 ships, 18 of which might be of the line, and 12 frigates. Allowing 8 men, the British average, for every gun, their annual expence, including subsistence, cloathing, pay, and ordinary repairs, would be about 1280 dollars for every gun, or 2,304,000 dollars for the whole. I state this only as one year's possible exertion, without deciding whether more or less than a year's exertion should be thus applied.

The value of our lands and slaves, taken conjunctly, doubles in about twenty years. This arises from the multiplication of our slaves, from the extension of culture, and increased demand for lands. The amount of what may be raised will of course rise in the same proportion.

QUERY XXIII[201]

THE HISTORIES OF THE STATE, THE MEMORIALS PUBLISHED IN ITS NAME IN THE TIME OF ITS BEING A COLONY, AND THE PAMPHLETS RELATING TO ITS INTERIOR OR EXTERIOR AFFAIRS PRESENT OR ANTIENT?

Histories, &c.

Captain Smith, who next to Sir Walter Raleigh may be considered as the founder of our colony, has written its history, from the first adventures to it till the year 1624. He was a member of the council, and afterwards president of the colony; and to his efforts principally may be ascribed its support against the opposition of the natives. He was honest, sensible, and well informed; but his style is barbarous and uncouth. His history, however, is almost the only source from which we derive any knowledge of the infancy of our state.

The reverend William Stith,[202] a native of Virginia, and president of its college, has also written the history of the same period, in a large octavo volume of small print. He was a man of classical learning, and very exact, but of no taste in style. He is inelegant, therefore, and his details often too minute to be tolerable, even to a native of the country, whose history he writes.

Beverley,[203] a native also, has run into the other extreme; he has comprised our history, from the first propositions of Sir Walter Raleigh to the year 1700, in the hundredth part of the space which Stith employs for the fourth part of the period.

Sir William Keith[204] has taken it up at its earliest period, and continued it to the year 1725. He is agreeable enough in style, and passes over events of little importance. Of course he is short, and would be preferred by a foreigner.

During the regal government, some contest arose on the exaction of an illegal fee by governor Dinwiddie,[205] and doubtless there were others on other occasions not at present recollected.

It is supposed, that these are not sufficiently interesting to a foreigner to merit a detail.

The petition of the council and burgesses of Virginia to the king, their memorial to the lords, and remonstrance to the commons in the year 1764, began the present contest: and these having proved ineffectual to prevent the passage of the stamp-act, the resolutions of the house of burgesses of 1765 were passed, declaring the independance of the people of Virginia on the parliament of Great-Britain, in matters of taxation. From that time till the declaration of independance by congress in 1776, their journals are filled with assertions of the public rights.

The pamphlets published in this state on the controverted question were,

1766, An Enquiry into the Rights of the British Colonies, by Richard Bland.
1769, The Monitor's Letters, by Dr. Arthur Lee.
1774, *A summary View of the Rights of British America.
——Considerations, &c. by Robert Carter Nicholas.

Since the declaration of independance this state has had no controversy with any other, except with that of Pennsylvania, on their common boundary. Some papers on this subject passed between the executive and legislative bodies of the two states, the result of which was a happy accommodation of their rights.

To this account of our historians, memorials, and pamphlets, it may not be unuseful to add a chronological catalogue of American state-papers, as far as I have been able to collect their titles. It is far from being either complete or correct. Where the title alone, and not the paper itself, has come under my observation, I cannot answer for the exactness of the date. Sometimes I have not been able to find any date at all, and sometimes have not been satisfied that such a paper exists. An extensive collection of papers of this description has been for some time in a course of preparation by a †gentleman fully equal to the task, and from whom, therefore, we may hope ere long to receive it. In the mean time accept this as the result of my labours, and as

*By the author of these Notes.
†Mr. Hazard.[206]

closing the tedious detail which you have so undesignedly drawn upon yourself.

Pro Johanne Caboto et filiis suis super terra incognita investiganda. 12. Ry. 595. 3. Hakl. 4. 2. Mem. Am. 409.	*1496, Mar. 5.*	*11. H. 7.*[207]
Billa signata anno 13. Henrici septimi. 3. Hakluyt's voiages 5.	*1498, Feb. 3.*	*13. H. 7.*
De potestatibus ad terras incognitas investigandum. 13. Rymer. 37.	*1502, Dec. 19.*	*18. H. 7.*
Commission de François I. à Jacques Cartier pour l'establissement du Canada. L'Escarbot. 397. 2. Mem. Am. 416.	*1540, Oct. 17.*	
An act against the exaction of money, or any other thing, by any officer for license to traffique into Iseland and Newfoundland, made in An. 2. Edwardi sexti. 3. Hakl. 131.	*1548,*	*2. E. 6.*
The letters-patent granted by her Majestie to Sir Humphrey Gilbert, knight, for the inhabiting and planting of our people in America. 3. Hakl. 135.	*1578, June 11,*	*20. El.*
Letters-patents of Queen Elizabeth to Adrian Gilbert and others, to discover the Northwest passage to China. 3. Hakl. 96.	*1583, Feb. 6.*	
The letters-patents granted by the Queen's majestie to M. Walter Raleigh, now knight, for the discovering and planting of new lands and countries, to continue the space of 6 years and no more. 3. Hakl. 243.	*1584, Mar. 25,*	*26 El.*
An assignment by Sir Walter Raleigh for continuing the action of inhabiting and planting his people in Virginia. Hakl. 1st. ed. publ. in 1589, p. 815.	*Mar. 7.*	*31. El.*
Lettres de Lieutenant General de l'Acadie & pays circonvoisins pour le Sieur de Monts. L'Escarbot. 417.	*1603, Nov. 8.*	
Letters-patent to Sir Thomas Gates, Sir George Somers and others, for two several colonies to be made in Virginia and other parts of America. Stith. Append. No. 1.	*1606, Apr. 10,*	*4. Jac. 1.*
An ordinance and constitution enlarging the council of the two colonies in Virginia and	*1607, Mar. 9,*	*4. Jac. 1.*

		America, and augmenting their authority, M. S.
1609, May 23.	*7. Jac. 1.*	The second charter to the treasurer and company for Virginia, erecting them into a body politick. Stith. Ap. 2.
1610, Apr. 10.	*Jac. 1.*	Letters-patents to the E. of Northampton, granting part of the island of Newfoundland. 1. Harris. 861.
1611, Mar. 12.	*9. Jac. 1.*	A third charter to the treasurer and company for Virginia.—Stith. App. 3.
1617,	*Jac. 1.*	A commission to Sir Walter Raleigh. Qu.?
1620, Apr. 7.	*18. Jac. 1.*	Commissio specialis concernens le garbling herbae Nicotianae. 17. Rym. 190.
1620, June 29.	*18. Jac. 1.*	A proclamation for restraint of the disordered trading of tobacco. 17. Rym. 233.
1620, Nov. 3.	*Jac. 1.*	A grant of New England to the council of Plymouth.
1621, July 24.	*Jac. 1.*	An ordinance and constitution of the treasurer, council and company in England, for a council of state and general assembly in Virginia. Stith. App. 4.
1621, Sep. 10–20.	*Jac. 1.*	A grant of Nova Scotia to Sir William Alexander. 2. Mem. de l'Amerique. 193.
1622, Nov. 6.	*20. Jac. 1.*	A proclamation prohibiting interloping and disorderly trading to New England in America. 17. Rym. 416.
1623, May 9.	*21. Jac. 1.*	De Commissione speciali Willielmo Jones militi directa. 17. Rym. 490.
1623.		A grant to Sir Edmund Ployden, of New Albion. Mentioned in Smith's examination. 82.
1624, July 15.	*22. Jac. 1.*	De Commissione Henrico vice-comiti Mandevill & aliis. 17. Rym. 609.
1624, Aug. 26.	*22. Jac. 1.*	De Commissione speciali concernenti gubernationem in Virginia. 17. Rym. 618.
1624, Sep. 29.	*22. Jac. 1.*	A proclamation concerning tobacco. 17. Rym. 621.
1624, Nov. 9.	*22. Jac. 1.*	De concessione demiss. Edwardo Dichfield et aliis. 17. Rym. 633.
1625, Mar. 2.	*22. Jac. 1.*	A proclamation for the utter prohibiting the importation and use of all tobacco which is not of the proper growth of the colony of Virginia and the Somer islands, or one of them. 17. Rym. 668.

De commissione directa Georgio Yardeley militi et aliis. 18. Rym. 311.	*1625, Mar. 4.*	*1. Car. 1.*
Proclamation de herba Nicotianâ. 18. Rym. 19.	*1625, Apr. 9.*	*1. Car. 1.*
A proclamation for settlinge the plantation of Virginia. 18. Rym. 72.	*1625, May 13.*	*1. Car. 1.*
A grant of the soil, barony, and domains of Nova Scotia to Sir Wm. Alexander of Minstrie. 2. Mem. Am. 226.	*1625, July 12.*	
Commissio directa Johanni Wostenholme militi et aliis. 18. Ry. 831.	*1625, Jan. 31.*	*2. Car. 1.*
A proclamation touching tobacco. Ry. 848.	*1625, Feb. 17.*	*2. Car. 1.*
A grant of Massachuset's bay by the council of Plymouth to Sir Henry Roswell and others.	*1627, Mar. 19. qu.?*	*2. Car. 1.*
De concessione commissionis specialis pro concilio in Virginia. 18. Ry. 980.	*1627, Mar. 26.*	*3. Car. 1.*
De proclamatione de signatione de tobacco. 18. Ry. 886.	*1627, Mar. 30.*	*3. Car. 1.*
De proclamatione pro ordinatione de tobacco. 18. Ry. 920.	*1627, Aug. 9.*	*3. Car. 1.*
A confirmation of the grant of Massachuset's bay by the crown.	*1628, Mar. 4.*	*3. Car. 1.*
The capitulation of Quebec. Champlain part. 2. 216. 2. Mem. Am. 489.	*1629, Aug. 19.*	
A proclamation concerning tobacco. 19. Ry. 235.	*1630, Jan. 6.*	*5. Car. 1.*
Conveyance of Nova Scotia (Port-royal excepted) by Sir William Alexander to Sir Claude St. Etienne Lord of la Tour and of Uarre and to his son Sir Charles de St. Etienne Lord of St. Denniscourt, on condition that they continue subjects to the king of Scotland under the great seal of Scotland.	*1630, April 30.*	
A proclamation forbidding the disorderly trading with the savages in New England in America, especially the furnishing the natives in those and other parts of America by the English with weapons and habiliments of warre. 19. Ry. 210. 3. Rushw. 82.	*1630–31, Nov. 24.*	*6. Car. 1.*
A proclamation prohibiting the selling arms, &c. to the savages in America. Mentioned 3. Rushw. 75.	*1630, Dec. 5.*	*6. Car. 1.*

1630,	*Car. 1.*	A grant of Connecticut by the council of Plymouth to the E. of Warwick.
1630,	*Car. 1.*	A confirmation by the crown of the grant of Connecticut [said to be in the petty bag office in England].
1631, Mar. 19.	*6. Car. 1.*	A conveiance of Connecticut by the E. of Warwick to Lord Say and Seal and others. Smith's examination, App. No. 1.
1631, June 27.	*7. Car. 1.*	A special commission to Edward Earle of Dorsett and others for the better plantation of the colony of Virginia. 19. Ry. 301.
1631, June 29.	*7. Car. 1.*	Litere continentes promissionem regis ad tradendum castrum et habitationem de Kebec in Canada ad regem Francorum. 19. Ry. 303.
1632, Mar. 29.	*8. Car. 1.*	Traité entre le roy Louis XIII. et Charles roi d'Angleterre pour la restitution de la nouvelle France, la Cadie et Canada et des navires et merchandises pris de part et d'autre. Fait a St. Germain. 19. Ry. 361. 2. Mem. Am. 5.
1632, June 20.	*8. Car. 1.*	A grant of Maryland to Caecilius Calvert, Baron of Baltimore in Ireland.
1633, July 3.	*9. Car. 1.*	A petition of the planters of Virginia against the grant to Lord Baltimore.
1633, July 3.		Order of council upon the dispute between the Virginia planters and lord Baltimore. Votes of repres. of Pennsylvania. V.
1633, Aug. 13.	*9. Car. 1.*	A proclamation to prevent abuses growing by the unordered retailing of tobacco. Mentioned 3. Rushw. 191.
1633, Sept. 23.	*9. Car. 1.*	A special commission to Thomas Young to search, discover and find out what parts are not yet inhabited in Virginia and America and other parts thereunto adjoining. 19. Ry. 472.
1633, Oct. 13.	*9. Car. 1.*	A proclamation for preventing of the abuses growing by the unordered retailing of tobacco. 19. Ry. 474.
1634, Mar. 13.	*Car. 1.*	A proclamation restraining the abusive venting of tobacco. 19. Rym. 522.

A proclamation concerning the landing of tobacco, and also forbidding the planting thereof in the king's dominions. 19. Ry. 553.	*1634, May 19. 10. Car. 1.*
A commission to the Archbishop of Canterbury and 11 others, for governing the American colonies.	*1634, Car. 1.*
A commission concerning tobacco. Ḿ. S.	*1634, June 19. 10. Car. 1.*
A commission from Lord Say and Seal, and others, to John Winthrop to be governor of Connecticut. Smith's App.	*1635, July 18. 11. Car. 1.*
A grant to Duke Hamilton.	*1635, Car. 1.*
De commissione speciali Johanni Harvey militi pro meliori regimine coloniae in Virginia. 20. Ry. 3.	*1636, Apr. 2. 12. Car. 1.*
A proclamation concerning tobacco. Title in 3. Rush. 617.	*1637, Mar. 14. Car. 1.*
De commissione speciali Georgio domino Goring et aliis concessâ concernente venditionem de tobacco absque licentiâ regiâ. 20. Ry. 116.	*1636–7, Mar. 16. 12. Car. 1.*
A proclamation against the disorderly transporting his Majesty's subjects to the plantations within the parts of America. 20. Ry. 143. 3. Rush. 409.	*1637, Apr. 30. Car. 1.*
An order of the privy council to stay 8 ships now in the Thames from going to New-England. 3. Rush. 409.	*1637, May 1. 13. Car. 1.*
A warrant of the Lord Admiral to stop uncomformable ministers from going beyond sea. 3. Rush. 410.	*1637, Car. 1.*
Order of council upon Claiborne's petition against Lord Baltimore. Votes of representatives of Pennsylvania. vi.	*1638, Apr. 4. Car. 1.*
An order of the king and council that the attorney-general draw up a proclamation to prohibit transportation of passengers to New-England without license. 3. Rush. 718.	*1638, Apr. 6. 14. Car. 1.*
A proclamation to restrain the transporting of passengers and provisions to New-England without licence. 20. Ry. 223.	*1638, May 1. 14. Car. 1.*

1639, Mar. 25.	*Car. 1.*	A proclamation concerning tobacco. Title 4. Rush. 1060.
1639, Aug. 19.	*15. Car. 1.*	A proclamation declaring his majesty's pleasure to continue his commission and letters patents for licensing retailers of tobacco. 20. Ry. 348.
1639, Dec. 16.	*15. Car. 1.*	De commissione speciali Henrico Ashton armigero et aliis ad amovendum Henricum Hawley gubernatorem de Barbadoes. 20. Ry. 357.
1639,	*Car. 1.*	A proclamation concerning retailers of tobacco. 4. Rush. 966.
1641, Aug. 9.	*17. Car. 1.*	De constitutione gubernatoris et concilii pro Virginia. 20. Ry. 484.
1643,	*Car. 1.*	Articles of union and confederacy entered into by Massachusets, Plymouth, Connecticut and New-haven. 1. Neale. 223.
1644,	*Car. 1.*	Deed from George Fenwick to the old Connecticut jurisdiction.
		An ordinance of the lords and commons assembled in parliament, for exempting from custom and imposition all commodities exported for, or imported from New-England, which has been very prosperous and without any public charge to this state, and is likely to prove very happy for the propagation of the gospel in those parts. Tit. in Amer. library 90. 5. No date. But seems by the neighbouring articles to have been in 1644.
1644, June 20.	*Car. 2.*	An act for charging of tobacco brought from New-England with custom and excise. Title in American library. 99. 8.
1644, Aug. 1.	*Car. 2.*	An act for the advancing and regulating the trade of this commonwealth. Tit. Amer. libr. 99. 9.
Sept. 18.	*1. Car. 2.*	Grant of the Northern neck of Virginia to Lord Hopton, Lord Jermyn, Lord Culpeper, Sir John Berkely, Sir William Moreton, Sir Dudly Wyatt, and Thomas Culpeper.
1650, Oct. 3.	*2. Car. 2.*	An act prohibiting trade with the Barbadoes, Virginia, Bermudas and Antego. Scoble's Acts. 1027.

A declaration of Lord Willoughby, governor of Barbadoes, and of his council, against an act of parliament of 3d of October 1650. 4. Polit. register. 2. cited from 4. Neale. hist. of the Puritans. App. No. 12. but not there.	*1650,*	*Car. 2.*
A final settlement of boundaries between the Dutch New Netherlands and Connecticut.	*1650,*	*Car. 2.*
Instructions for Captain Robert Dennis, Mr. Richard Bennet, Mr. Thomas Stagge, and Capt. William Clabourne, appointed commissioners for the reducing of Virginia and the inhabitants thereof to their due obedience to the commonwealth of England. 1. Thurloe's state papers. 197.	*1651, Sept. 26.*	*3. Car. 2.*
An act for increase of shipping and encouragement of the navigation of this nation. Scobell's acts. 1449.	*1651, Oct. 9.*	*3. Car. 2.*
Articles agreed on and concluded at James cittie in Virginia for the surrendering and settling of that plantation under the obedience and government of the commonwealth of England, by the commissioners of the council of state, by authoritie of the parliament of England, and by the grand assembly of the governor, council, and burgesse of that state. M. S. [Ante. pa. 201.]	*1651–2, Mar. 12.*	*4. Car. 2.*
An act of indempnitie made at the surrender of the countrey [of Virginia.] [Ante. p. 206.]	*1651–2, Mar. 12.*	*4. Car. 2.*
Capitulation de Port-Royal. mem. Am. 507.	*1654, Aug. 16.*	
A proclamation of the protector relating to Jamaica. 3. Thurl. 75.	*1655,*	*Car. 2.*
The protector to the commissioners of Maryland. A letter. 4. Thurl. 55.	*1655, Sept. 26.*	*7. Car. 2.*
An instrument made at the council of Jamaica, Oct. 8, 1655, for the better carrying on of affairs there. 4. Thurl. 71.	*1655, Oct. 8.*	*7. Car. 2.*
Treaty of Westminster between France and England. 6. corps diplom. part 2. p. 121. 2. Mem. Am. 10.	*1655, Nov. 3.*	

1656, Mar. 27.	*8. Car. 2.*	The assembly at Barbadoes to the Protector. 4. Thurl. 651.
1656, Aug. 9.		A grant by Cromwell to Sir Charles de Saint Etienne, a baron of Scotland, Crowne and Temple. A French translation of it. 2. Mem. Am. 511.
1656,	*Car. 2.*	A paper concerning the advancement of trade. 5. Thurl. 80.
1656,	*Car. 2.*	A brief narration of the English rights to the Northern parts of America. 5. Thurl. 81.
1656, Oct. 10.	*8. Car. 2.*	Mr. R. Bennet and Mr. S. Matthew to Secretary Thurloe. 5. Thurl. 482.
1656, Oct. 10.	*8. Car. 2.*	Objections against the Lord Baltimore's patent, and reasons why the government of Maryland should not be put into his hands. 5. Thurl. 482.
1656, Oct. 10.	*8. Car. 2.*	A paper relating to Maryland. 5. Thurl. 483.
1656, Oct. 10.	*8. Car. 2.*	A breviet of the proceedings of the lord Baltimore and his officers and compliers in Maryland against the authority of the parliament of the commonwealth of England and against his highness the lord protector's authority laws and government. 5. Thurl. 486.
1656, Oct. 15.	*8. Car. 2.*	The assembly of Virginia to secretary Thurlow. 5. Thurl. 497.
1657, Apr. 4.	*9. Car. 2.*	The governor of Barbadoes to the protector. 6. Thurl. 169.
1661,	*Car. 2.*	Petition of the general court at Hartford upon Connecticut for a charter. Smith's exam. App. 4.
1662, Ap. 23.	*14. Car. 2.*	Charter of the colony of Connecticut. Smith's examn. App. 6.
1662–3, Mar. 24. Apr. 4.	*15. Car. 2.*	The first charter granted by Charles II. to the proprietaries of Carolina, to wit, to the Earl of Clarendon, Duke of Albemarle, Lord Craven, Lord Berkeley, Lord Ashley, Sir George Carteret, Sir William Berkeley, and Sir John Colleton. 4. mem. Am. 554.
1664, Feb. 10.		The concessions and agreement of the lords proprietors of the province of New Caesa-

rea, or New-Jersey, to and with all and every of the adventurers and all such as shall settle or plant there. Smith's New-Jersey. App. 1.	
A grant of the colony of New-York to the Duke of York.	*1664, Mar. 12. 20. Car. 2.*
A commission to Colonel Nichols and others to settle disputes in New-England. Hutch. Hist. Mass. Bay. App. 537.	*1664, Apr. 26. 16. Car. 2.*
The commission to Sir Robert Carre and others to put the Duke of York in possession of New-York, New-Jersey, and all other lands thereunto appertaining.	*1664, Apr. 26.*
Sir Robert Carre and others proclamation to the inhabitants of New-York, New-Jersey, &c. Smith's N. J. 36.	
Deeds of lease and release of New-Jersey by the Duke of York to Lord Berkeley and Sir George Carteret.	*1664, June 23, 24. 16. C. 2.*
A conveiance of the Delaware counties to William Penn.	
Letters between Stuyvesant and Colonel Nichols on the English right. Smith's N.J. 37–42.	*1664, Aug. 19–29, 20–30, 24. Aug. 25. Sept. 4.*
Treaty between the English and Dutch for the surrender of the New-Netherlands. Sm. N. Jers. 42.	*1664, Aug. 27.*
Nicoll's commission to Sir Robert Carre to reduce the Dutch on Delaware bay. Sm. N. J. 47.	*Sept. 3.*
Instructions to Sir Robert Carre for reducing of Delaware bay and settling the people there under his majesty's obedience. Sm. N. J. 47.	
Articles of capitulation between Sir Robert Carre and the Dutch and Swedes on Delaware bay and Delaware river. Sm. N. J. 49.	*1664, Oct. 1.*
The determination of the commissioners of the boundary between the Duke of York and Connecticut. Sm. Ex. Ap. 9.	*1664, Dec. 1. 16. Car. 2.*

1664.	The New Haven case. Smith's Ex. Ap. 20.
1665, June 13–24. 17. C. 2.	The second charter granted by Charles II. to the same proprietors of Carolina. 4. Mem. Am. 586.
1666, Jan. 26.	Declaration de guerre par la France contre l'Angleterre. 3. Mem. Am. 123.
1666, Feb. 9. 17. Car. 2.	Declaration of war by the king of England against the king of France.
1667, July 31.	The treaty of peace between France and England made at Breda. 7. Corps Dipl. part 1. p. 41. 2. Mem. Am. 32.
1667, July 31.	The treaty of peace and alliance between England and the United Provinces made at Breda. 7. Cor. Dip. p. 1. p. 44. 2. Mem. Am. 40.
1667–8, Feb. 17.	Acte de la cession de l'Acadie au roi de France. 2. Mem. Am. 292.
1668, April 21.	Directions from the governor and council of New York for a better settlement of the government on Delaware. Sm. N. J. 51.
1668.	Lovelace's order for customs at the Hoarkills. Sm. N. J. 55.
16—May 8. 21. Car. 2.	A confirmation of the grant of the northern neck of Virginia to the Earl of St. Alban's, Lord Berkeley, Sir William Moreton and John Tretheway.
1672.	Incorporation of the town of Newcastle or Amstell.
1673, Feb. 25. 25. Car. 2.	A demise of the colony of Virginia to the Earl of Arlington and Lord Culpeper for 31 years. M. S.
1673–4.	Treaty at London between king Charles II. and the Dutch. Article VI.
	Remonstrances against the two grants of Charles II. of Northern and Southern Virginia. Ment[d]. Beverley. 65.
1674, July 13.	Sir George Carteret's instructions to Governor Carteret.
1674, Nov. 9.	Governor Andros's proclamation on taking possession of Newcastle for the Duke of York. Sm. N. J. 78.

A proclamation for prohibiting the importation of commodities of Europe into any of his majesty's plantations in Africa, Asia, or America, which were not laden in England: and for putting all other laws relating to the trade of the plantations in effectual execution.	*1675, Oct. 1.*	*27. Car. 2.*
The concessions and agreements of the proprietors, freeholders and inhabitants of the province of West-New-Jersey in America. Sm. N. J. App. 2.	*1676, Mar. 3.*	
A deed quintipartite for the division of New-Jersey.	*1676, July 1.*	
Letter from the proprietors of New-Jersey to Richard Hartshorne. Sm. N. J. 80.	*1676, Aug. 18.*	
Proprietors instructions to James Wasse and Richard Hartshorne. Sm. N. J. 83.		
The charter of king Charles II. to his subjects of Virginia. M. S.	*1676, Oct. 10.*	*28. Car. 2.*
Cautionary epistle from the trustees of Byllinge's part of New-Jersey. Sm. N. J. 84.	*1676.*	
Indian deed for the lands between Rankokas creek and Timber creek, in New-Jersey.	*1677, Sept. 10.*	
Indian deed for the lands from Oldman's creek to Timber creek, in New-Jersey.	*1677, Sept. 27.*	
Indian deed for the lands from Rankokas creek to Assunpink creek, in New-Jersey.	*1677, Oct. 10.*	
The will of Sir George Carteret, sole proprietor of East-Jersey, ordering the same to be sold.	*1678, Dec. 5.*	
An order of the king in council for the better encouragement of all his majesty's subjects in their trade to his majesty's plantations, and for the better information of all his majesty's loving subjects in these matters. Lond. Gaz No. 1596. Title in Amer. library. 134. 6.	*1680, Feb. 16.*	
Arguments against the customs demanded in New-West-Jersey by the governor of New-York, addressed to the Duke's commissioners. Sm. N. J. 117.	*1680.*	

June 14. 23. 25. *1680, Oct. 16.* *Nov. 4. 8. 11. 18.* *20. 23.* *Dec. 16.* *1680–1, Jan. 15. 22.* *Feb. 24.*	Extracts of proceedings of the committee of trade and plantations; copies of letters, reports, &c. between the board of trade, Mr. Penn, Lord Baltimore and Sir John Werden, in the behalf of the Duke of York and the settlement of the Pennsylvania boundaries by the L. C. J. North. Votes of Repr. Pennsyl. vii.–xiii.
1681, Mar. 4. Car. 2.	A grant of Pennsylvania to William Penn. Votes of Represen. Pennsylv. xviii.
1681, Apr. 2.	The king's declaration to the inhabitants and planters of the province of Pennsylvania. Vo. Rep. Penn. xxiv.
1681, July 11.	Certain conditions or concessions agreed upon by William Penn, proprietary and governor of Pennsylvania, and those who are the adventurers and purchasers in the same province. Votes of Rep. Pennsylv. xxiv.
1681, Nov. 9.	Fundamental laws of the province of West-New-Jersey. Sm. N. J. 126.
1681–2, Jan. 14.	The methods of the commissioners for settling and regulation of lands in New-Jersey. Sm. N. J. 130.
1681–2, Feb. 1. 2.	Indentures of lease and release by the executors of Sir George Carteret to William Penn and 11 others, conveying East-Jersey.
1682, Mar. 14.	The Duke of York's fresh grant of East-New-Jersey to the 24 proprietors.
1682, Apr. 25.	The Frame of the government of the province of Pennsylvania, in America. Votes of Repr. Penn. xxvii.
1682, Aug. 21.	The Duke of York's deed for Pennsylvania. Vo. Repr. Penn. xxxv.
1682, Aug. 24.	The Duke of York's deed of feoffment of Newcastle and twelve miles circle to William Penn. Vo. Repr. Penn.
1682, Aug. 24.	The Duke of York's deed of feoffment of a tract of land 12 miles south from Newcastle to the Whorekills, to William Penn. Vo. Repr. Penn. xxxvii.
1682, Nov. 27. 34. Car. 2.	A commission to Thomas Lord Culpeper to be lieutenant and governor-general of Virginia. M. S.

An act of union for annexing and uniting of the counties of Newcastle, Jones's and Whorekill's alias Deal, to the province of Pennsylvania, and of naturalization of all foreigners in the province and counties aforesaid.	*1682, 10th month, 6th day.*
An act of settlement.	*1682, Dec. 6.*
The frame of the government of the province of Pennsylvania and terrories thereunto annexed in America.	*1683, Apr. 2.*
Proceedings of the committee of trade and plantations in the dispute between Lord Baltimore and Mr. Penn. Vo. R. P. xiii–xviii.	*1683, Apr. 17, 27. May 30. June 12.* *1684, Feb. 12. July 2, 16, 23 Sept. 30. Dec. 9.* *1685, Mar. 17. Aug. 18. 26. Sept. 2. Oct. 8. 17, 31. Nov. 7.*
A commission by the proprietors of East-New-Jersey to Robert Barclay to be governor. Sm. N. J. 166.	*1683, July 17.*
An order of council for issuing a quo warranto against the charter of the colony of the Massachuset's bay in New-England, with his majesty's declaration that in case the said corporation of Masschuset's bay shall before prosecution had upon the same quo warranto make a full submission and entire resignation to his royal pleasure, he will then regulate their charter in such a manner as shall be for his service and the good of that colony. Title in Amer. library. 139. 6.	*1683, July 26. 35. Car. 2.*
A commission to Lord Howard of Effingham to be lieutenant and governor-general of Virginia. M. S.	*1683, Sept. 28. 35. Car. 2.*
The humble address of the chief governor, council and representatives of the island of Nevis, in the West-Indies, presented to his majesty by Colonel Netheway and Captain Jefferson, at Windsor, May 3, 1684. Title in Amer. libr. 142. 3. cites Lond. Gaz. No. 1927.	*1684, May 3.*
A treaty with the Indians at Albany.	*1684, Aug. 2.*

1686, Nov. 16. A treaty of neutrality for America between France and England. 7. Corps. Dipl. part 2. p. 44. 2. Mem. Am. 40.

1687, Jan. 20. By the king, a proclamation for the more effectual reducing and suppressing of pirates and privateers in America, as well on the sea as on the land in great numbers, committing frequent robberies and piracies, which hath occasioned a great prejudice and obstruction to trade and commerce, and given a great scandal and disturbance to our government in those parts. Title Amer. libr. 147. 2. cites Lond. Gaz. No. 2315.

1687, Feb. 12. Constitution of the council of proprietors of West-Jersey. Smith's N. Jersey. 199.

1687, qu. Sept. 27. 4. Jac. 2. A confirmation of the grant of the northern neck of Virginia to Lord Culpeper.

1687, Sept. 5. Governor Coxe's declaration to the council of proprietors of West-Jersey. Sm. N. J. 190.

1687, Dec. 16. Provisional treaty of Whitehall concerning America between France and England. 2. Mem. de l'Am. 89.

Governor Coxe's narrative relating to the division line, directed to the council of proprietors of West-Jersey. Sm. App. N. 4.

The representation of the council of proprietors of West-Jersey to Governor Burnet. Smith. App. No. 5.

The remonstrance and petition of the inhabitants of East-New-Jersey to the king. Sm. App. No. 8.

The memorial of the proprietors of East-New-Jersey to the Lords of trade. Sm. App. No. 9.

1688, Sept. 5. Agreement of the line of partition between East and West-New-Jersey. Sm. N. J. 196.

1691. Conveiance of the government of West-Jersey and territories by Dr. Coxe, to the West-Jersey society.

1691, Oct. 7. A charter granted by King William and Queen Mary to the inhabitants of the province of Massachuset's bay in New-England. 2. Mem. de l'Am. 593.

The frame of government of the province of Pennsylvania and the territories thereunto belonging, passed by Governor Markham. Nov. 7, 1696.	*1696, Nov. 7.*	
The treaty of peace between France and England, made at Ryswick. 7. Corps Dipl. part. 2. p. 399. 2. Mem. Am. 89.	*1697, Sept. 20.*	
The opinion and answer of the lords of trade to the memorial of the proprietors of East-New-Jersey. Sm. App. No. 10.	*1699, July 5.*	
The memorial of the proprietors of East-New-Jersey to the Lords of trade. Sm. App. No. 11.	*1700, Jan. 15.*	
The petition of the proprietors of East and West-New-Jersey to the Lords justices of England. Sm. App. No. 12.		
A confirmation of the boundary between the colonies of New-York and Connecticut, by the crown.	*1700,*	*W. 3.*
The memorial of the proprietors of East and West-Jersey to the king. Sm. App. No. 14.	*1701, Aug. 12.*	
Representation of the lords of trade to the lords justices. Sm. App. No. 13.	*1701, Oct. 2.*	
A treaty with the Indians.	*1701.*	
Report of lords of trade to king William of draughts of a commission and instructions for a governor of New-Jersey. Sm. N. J. 262.	*1701–2, Jan. 6.*	
Surrender from the proprietors of E. and W. N. Jersey of their pretended right of government to her majesty Q. Anne. Sm. N. J. 211.	*1702, Apr. 15.*	
The Queen's acceptance of the surrender of government of East and West-Jersey. Sm. N. J. 219.	*1702, Apr. 17.*	
Instructions to lord Cornbury. Sm. N. J. 230.	*1702, Nov. 16.*	
A commission from Queen Anne to Lord Cornbury, to be captain-general and governor in chief of New-Jersey. Sm. N. J. 220.	*1702, Dec. 5.*	
Recognition by the council of proprietors of the true boundary of the deeds of Sept. 10 and Oct. 10, 1677. (New-Jersey). Sm. N. J. 96.	*1703, June 27.*	

1703.	Indian deed for the lands above the falls of the Delaware in West-Jersey.
	Indian deed for the lands at the head of Rankokus river in West-Jersey.
1704, June 18.	A proclamation by Queen Anne for settling and ascertaining the current rates of foreign coins in America. Sm. N. J. 281.
1705, May 3.	Additional instructions to Lord Cornbury. Sm. N. J. 235.
1707, May 3.	Additional instructions to Lord Cornbury. Sm. N. J. 258.
1707, Nov. 20.	Additional instructions to Lord Cornbury. Sm. N. J. 259.
1707.	An answer by the council of proprietors for the western division of New-Jersey, to questions, proposed to them by Lord Cornbury. Sm. N. J. 285.
1708–9, Feb. 28.	Instructions to the Colonel Vetch in his negociations with the governors of America. Sm. N. J. 364.
1708–9, Feb. 28.	Instructions to the governor of New-Jersey and New-York. Sm. N. J. 361.
1710, Aug.	Earl of Dartmouth's letter to governor Hunter.
1711, Apr. 22.	Premieres propositions de la France. 6. Lamberty, 669. 2. Mem. Am. 341.
1711, Oct. 8.	Réponses de la France aux demandes préliminaires de la Grande-Bretagne. 6. Lamb. 681. 2. Mem. Amer. 344.
1711, Sept. 27. / Oct. 8	Demandes préliminaires plus particulieres de la Grande-Bretagne, avec les réponses. 2. Mem. de l'Am. 346.
1711, Sept. 27. / Oct. 8.	L'acceptation de la part de la Grande-Bretagne. 2. Mem. Am. 356.
1711, Dec. 23.	The queen's instructions to the Bishop of Bristol and Earl of Strafford, her plenipotentiaries, to treat of a general peace. 6. Lamberty, 744. 2. Mem. Am. 358.
1712, May. 24. / June. 10.	A memorial of Mr. St. John to the Marquis de Torci, with regard to North America, to commerce, and to the suspension of arms. 7. Recueil de Lamberty, 161. 2. Mem. de l'Amer. 376.

Réponse du roi de France au memoire de Londres. 7. Lamberty, p. 163. 2. Mem. Am. 380.	*1712, June 10.*	
Traité pour une suspension d'armes entre Louis XIV. roi de France, & Anne, reigne de la Grande-Bretagne, fait à Paris. 8. Corps Diplom. part. 1. p. 308. 2. Mem. d'Am. 104.	*1712, Aug. 19.*	
Offers of France to England, demands of England, and the answers of France. 7. Rec. de Lamb. 491. 2. Mem. Am. 390.	*1712, Sept. 10.*	
Traité de paix & d'amitié entre Louis XIV. roi de France, & Anne, reine de la Grande-Bretagne, fait à Utrecht. 15. Corps Diplomatique de Dumont, 339. id. Latin. 2. Actes & memoires de la pais d'Utrecht, 457. id. Lat. Fr. 2. Mem. Am. 113.	*1713, Mar. 31./Apr. 11.*	
Traité de navigation & de commerce entre Louis XIV. roi de France, & Anne, reine de la Grande-Bretagne. Fait à Utrecht. 8. Corps. Dipl. part. 1. p. 345. 2. Mem. de l'Am. 137.	*1713, Mar. 31./Apr. 11.*	
A treaty with the Indians.	*1726.*	
The petition of the representatives of the province of New-Jersey, to have a distinct governor. Sm. N. J. 421.	*1728, Jan.*	
Deed of release by the government of Connecticut to that of New-York.	*1732,*	*G. 2.*
The charter granted by George II. for Georgia. 4. Mem. de l'Am. 617.	*1732, June 9–20.*	*5. G. 2.*
Petition of Lord Fairfax, that a commission might issue for running and marking the dividing line between his district and the province of Virginia.	*1733.*	
Order of the king in council for Commissioners to survey and settle the said dividing line between the proprietary and royal territory.	*1733, Nov. 29.*	
Report of the lords of trade relating to the separating the government of the province of New-Jersey from New-York. Sm. N. J. 423.	*1736, Aug. 5.*	
Survey and report of the commissioners appointed on the part of the crown to settle the line between the crown and Lord Fairfax.	*1737, Aug. 10.*	

1737, Aug. 11.		Survey and report of the commissioners appointed on the part of Lord Fairfax to settle the line between the crown and him.
1738, Dec. 21.		Order of reference of the surveys between the crown and Lord Fairfax to the council for plantation affairs.
1744, June		Treaty with the Indians of the 6 nations at Lancaster.
1745, Apr. 6.		Report of the council for plantation affairs, fixing the head springs of Rappahanoc and Patowmac, and a commission to extend the line.
1745, Apr. 11.		Order of the king in council confirming the said report of the council for plantation affairs.
1748, Apr. 30.		Articles préliminaires pour parvenir à la paix, signés à Aix-la-Chapelle entre les ministres de France, de la Grande-Bretagne, & des Provinces-Unies des Pays-Bas. 2. Mem. de l'Am. 159.
1748, May 21.		Declaration des ministres de France, de la Grande-Bretagne, & des Provinces-Unies des Pays-Bas, pour rectifier les articles I. & II. des préliminaires. 2. Mem. Am. 165.
1748, Oct. 7–18.	*22. G. 2.*	The general and definitive treaty of peace concluded at Aix-la-Chapelle. Lond. Mag. 1748. 503 French. 2. Mem. Am. 169.
1754.		A treaty with the Indians.
1758, Aug. 7.		A conference between Governor Bernard and Indian nations at Burlington. Sm. N. J. 449.
1758, Oct. 8.		A conference between Governor Denny, Governor Bernard and others, and Indian nations at Easton. Sm. N. J. 455.
1759, July 25.	*33. G. 2.*	The capitulation of Niagara.
175—		The king's proclamation promising lands to souldiers.
1763, Feb. 10.	*3. G. 3.*	The definitive treaty concluded at Paris. Lond. Mag. 1763. 149.
1763, Oct. 7.	*G. 3.*	A proclamation for regulating the cessions made by the last treaty of peace. Guth. Geogr. Gram. 623.

The king's proclamation against settling on any lands on the waters, westward of the Alleghaney.	*1763.*
Deed from the six nations of Indians to William Trent and others for lands betwixt the Ohio and Monongahela. View of the title to Indiana. Phil. Styner and Cist. 1776.	*1768, Nov. 3.*
Deed from the six nations of Indians to the crown for certain lands and settling a boundary. M. S.	*1768, Nov. 5.*

APPENDIX NO. I.

The preceding sheets having been submitted to my friend Mr. Charles Thomson, Secretary of Congress, he has furnished me with the following observations, which have too much merit not to be communicated.

[1.] p. 18. Besides the three channels of communication mentioned between the western waters and the Atlantic, there are two others, to which the Pennsylvanians are turning their attention; one from Presque-isle, on Lake Erie, to Le Boeuf, down the Alleghaney to Kiskiminitas, then up the Kiskiminitas, and from thence, by a small portage, to Juniata, which falls into the Susquehanna: the other from Lake Ontario to the East Branch of the Delaware, and down that to Philadelphia. Both these are said to be very practicable: and, considering the enterprising temper of the Pennsylvanians, and particularly of the merchants of Philadelphia, whose object is concentered in promoting the commerce and trade of one city, it is not improbable but one or both of these communications will be opened and improved.

[2.] p. 21. The reflections I was led into on viewing this passage of the Patowmac through the Blue ridge were, that this country must have suffered some violent convulsion, and that the face of it must have been changed from what it probably was some centuries ago: that the broken and ragged faces of the mountain on each side the river; the tremendous rocks, which are left with one end fixed in the precipice, and the other jutting out, and seemingly ready to fall for want of support; the bed of the river for several miles below obstructed, and filled with the loose stones carried from this mound; in short, every thing on which you cast your eye evidently demonstrates a disrupture and breach in the mountain, and that, before this happened, what is now a fruitful vale, was formerly a great lake or collection of water, which possibly might have here formed a mighty cascade, or had its vent to the ocean by the Susquehanna, where the Blue ridge seems to terminate. Besides this, there are other parts of this country which bear evident traces of a like convulsion. From the best accounts I have been able to obtain, the place where the Delaware now flows through the Kittatinny mountain, which is a continuation of what is called the North ridge, or mountain, was not its original course, but that it passed through what is now called "the Wind-gap," a place several miles to the westward, and above an hundred feet higher than the present bed of the river. This Wind-gap is about a mile broad, and the stones in it such as seem to have been washed for ages by water running over them. Should this have been the case, there must have been a large lake behind that mountain, and by some uncommon swell in the waters, or by some convulsion of nature, the river must have opened its way through a different part of the mountain, and meeting there with less obstruction, carried away with it the opposing mounds of earth, and deluged the country below with the immense collection of waters to which this new passage gave vent. There are still remaining, and daily discovered, innumerable instances of such a deluge on both sides of the river, after it passed the hills above the falls of Trenton, and reached the champaign. On the New-Jersey side, which is flatter than the Pennsylvania side, all the country below Croswick hills seems to have been overflowed to the distance of from ten to fifteen miles back from the river, and to have acquired a new soil by the earth and clay brought down and mixed with the native sand. The spot on which Philadelphia stands evidently appears to be made ground. The different strata through which they pass in digging to water, the acorns, leaves, and sometimes branches, which are found above twenty feet below the surface, all seem to demonstrate this. I am informed that at York town in Virginia, in the bank of York river, there are different strata of shells and earth, one above another, which seem to point out that the country there has undergone several changes; that the sea has, for a succession of ages, occupied the place where dry land now appears; and that the ground has been suddenly raised at various periods. What a change would it make in the country below, should the mountains at Niagara, by any accident, be cleft asunder, and a passage suddenly opened to drain off the waters of Erie and the Upper lakes! While ruminating on these subjects, I have often been hurried away by fancy, and led to imagine, that what is now the bay of Mexico, was once a champaign country; and that from the point or cape of Florida, there was a continued range of mountains through Cuba, Hispaniola, Porto rico, Martinique, Guadaloupe, Barbadoes, and Trinidad, till it reached the coast of America, and formed the shores which bounded the ocean, and guarded the country behind: that, by some convulsion or shock of nature, the sea had broken through these mounds, and deluged that vast plain, till it reached the foot of the Andes; that being there heaped up by the trade-winds, always blowing from one quarter, it had found its way back, as it continues to do, through the gulph between Florida and Cuba, carrying with it the loom and sand it may have scooped from the country it had occupied, part of which it may have deposited on the shores of North America, and with part formed the banks of Newfoundland.—But these are only the visions of fancy.

[3.] p. 39. There is a plant, or weed, called the *James town weed, of a very singular quality. The late Dr. Bond informed me, that he had under his care a patient, a young girl, who had put the seeds of this plant into her eye, which dilated the pupil to such a degree, that she could see in the dark, but in the light was almost blind. The effect that the leaves had when eaten by a ship's crew that arrived at James town, are well known†.

[4.] p. 68. Mons. Buffon has indeed given an afflicting picture of human nature in his description of the man of America. But sure I am there never was a picture more unlike the original. He grants indeed that his stature is the same as that of the man of Europe. He might have admitted, that the Iroquois were larger, and the Lenopi, or Delawares, taller than people in Europe generally are. But he says their organs of generation are smaller and weaker than those of Europeans. Is this a fact? I believe not; at least it is an observation I never heard before.—"They have no beard." Had he known the pains and trouble it costs the men

*Datura pericarpiis erectis ovatis.[1] Linn.

†An instance of temporary imbecility produced by them is mentioned, Beverl. H. of Virg. B. 2. c. 4.[2]

to pluck out by the roots the hair that grows on their faces, he would have seen that nature had not been deficient in that respect. Every nation has its customs. I have seen an Indian beau, with a looking-glass in his hand, examining his face for hours together, and plucking out by the roots every hair he could discover, with a kind of tweezer made of a piece of fine brass wire, that had been twisted round a stick, and which he used with great dexterity.—"They have no ardour for their female." It is true, they do not indulge those excesses, nor discover that fondness which is customary in Europe; but this is not owing to a defect in nature, but to manners. Their soul is wholly bent upon war. This is what procures them glory among the men, and makes them the admiration of the women. To this they are educated from their earliest youth. When they pursue game with ardour, when they bear the fatigues of the chase, when they sustain and suffer patiently hunger and cold; it is not so much for the sake of the game they pursue, as to convince their parents and the council of the nation that they are fit to be enrolled in the number of the warriors. The songs of the women, the dance of the warriors, the sage counsel of the chiefs, the tales of the old, the triumphal entry of the warriors returning with success from battle, and the respect paid to those who distinguish themselves in war and in subduing their enemies; in short, every thing they see or hear tends to inspire them with an ardent desire for military fame. If a young man were to discover a fondness for women before he has been to war, he would become the contempt of the men, and the scorn and ridicule of the women. Or were he to indulge himself with a captive taken in war, and much more were he to offer violence in order to gratify his lust, he would incur indelible disgrace. The seeming frigidity of the men, therefore, is the effect of manners, and not a defect of nature. Besides, a celebrated warrior is oftener courted by the females, than he has occasion to court: and this is a point of honour which the men aim at. Instances similar to that of *Ruth and Boaz are not uncommon among them. For though the women

*When Boaz had eaten and drank, and his heart was merry, he went to lie down at the end of the heap of corn: and Ruth came softly, and uncovered his feet, and laid her down. Ruth iii. 7.

are modest and diffident, and so bashful that they seldom lift up their eyes, and scarce ever look a man full in the face, yet, being brought up in great subjection, custom and manners reconcile them to modes of acting, which, judged of by Europeans, would be deemed inconsistent with the rules of female decorum and propriety. I once saw a young widow, whose husband, a warrior, had died about eight days before, hastening to finish her grief, and who by tearing her hair, beating her breast, and drinking spirits, made the tears flow in great abundance, in order that she might grieve much in a short space of time, and be married that evening to another young warrior. The manner in which this was viewed by the men and women of the tribe, who stood round, silent and solemn spectators of the scene, and the indifference with which they answered my question respecting it, convinced me that it was no unusual custom. I have known men advanced in years, whose wives were old and past child-bearing, take young wives, and have children, though the practice of polygamy is not common. Does this favour of frigidity, or want of ardour for the female? Neither do they seem to be deficient in natural affection. I have seen both fathers and mothers in the deepest affliction, when their children have been dangerously ill; though I believe the affection is stronger in the descending than the ascending scale, and though custom forbids a father to grieve immoderately for a son slain in battle.—"That they are timorous and cowardly," is a character with which there is little reason to charge them, when we recollect the manner in which the Iroquois met Mons. ———,[3] who marched into their country; in which the old men, who scorned to fly, or to survive the capture of their town, braved death, like the old Romans in the time of the Gauls, and in which they soon after revenged themselves by sacking and destroying Montreal. But above all, the unshaken fortitude with which they bear the most excruciating tortures and death when taken prisoners, ought to exempt them from that character. Much less are they to be characterised as a people of no vivacity, and who are excited to action or motion only by the calls of hunger and thirst. Their dances in which they so much delight, and which to a European would be the most severe exercise, fully contradict this, not to mention their fatiguing marches, and the toil they voluntarily and cheerfully undergo in their military expeditions. It is true, that when at home, they do not employ themselves in labour or the culture of the soil: but this again is the effect of customs and manners, which have assigned that to the province of the women. But it is said, they are averse to society and a social life. Can any thing be more inapplicable than this to a people who always live in towns or clans? Or can they be said to have no "republique," who conduct all their affairs in national councils, who pride themselves in their national character, who consider an insult or injury done to an individual by a stranger as done to the whole, and resent it accordingly? In short, this picture is not applicable to any nation of Indians I have ever known or heard of in North America.

[5.] pa. 103. As far as I have been able to learn, the country from the sea coast to the Alleghaney, and from the most southern waters of James river up to Patuxent river, now in the state of Maryland, was occupied by three different nations of Indians, each of which spoke a different language, and were under separate and distinct governments. What the original or real names of those nations were, I have not been able to learn with certainty: but by us they are distinguished by the names of Powhatàns, Mannahòacs, and Mònacans, now commonly called Tuscaròras. The Powhatàns, who occupied the country from the sea shore up to the falls of the rivers, were a powerful nation, and seem to have consisted of seven tribes five on the western and two on the eastern shore. Each of these tribes was subdivided into towns, families, or clans, who lived together. All the nations of Indians in North America lived in the hunter state, and depended for subsistence on hunting, fishing, and the spontaneous fruits of the earth, and a kind of grain which was planted and gathered by the women, and is now known by the name of Indian corn. Long potatoes, pumpkins of various kinds, and squashes, were also found in use among them. They had no flocks, herds, or tamed animals of any kind. Their government is a kind of patriarchal confederacy. Every town or family has a chief, who is distinguished by a particular title, and whom we commonly call "Sachem." The several towns or families that compose a tribe, have a chief who presides over it, and the several tribes composing a nation have a chief who presides over the whole nation. These chiefs are generally men advanced in years, and distinguished by their prudence and abilities in council. The matters which merely regard a town or family are settled by the chief and principal men of the town: those which regard a tribe, such as the appointment of head warriors or captains, and settling differences between different towns and families, are regulated at a meeting or council of the chiefs from the several towns; and those which regard the whole nation, such as the making war, concluding peace, or forming alliances with the neighbouring nations, are deliberated on and determined in a national council composed of the chiefs of the tribe, attended by the head warriors and a number of the chiefs from the towns, who are his counsellors. In every town there is a council house, where the chief and old men of the town assemble, when occasion requires, and consult what is proper to be done. Every tribe has a fixed place for the chiefs of the towns to meet and consult on the business of the tribe: and in every nation there is what they call the central council house, or central council fire, where the chiefs of the several tribes, with the principal warriors, convene to consult and determine on their national affairs. When any matter is proposed in the national council, it is common for the chiefs of the several tribes to consult thereon apart with their counsellors, and, when they have agreed, to deliver the opinion of the tribe at the national council: and, as their government seems to rest wholly on persuasion, they endeavour, by mutual concessions, to obtain unanimity. Such is the government that still subsists among the Indian nations bordering upon the United States. Some historians seem to think, that the dignity of office of Sachem was hereditary. But that opinion does not appear to be well founded. The Sachem or chief of the tribe seems to be by election. And sometimes persons who are strangers, and adopted into the tribe, are promoted to this dignity, on account of their abilities. Thus on the arrival of Capt. Smith, the first founder of the colony of Virginia, Opechàncanough, who was Sachem or chief of the Chickahòminies, one of the tribes of the Powhàtans, is said to have been of another tribe, and even of another nation, so that no certain account could be obtained of his origin or descent. The chiefs of the nation seem to have been by a rotation among the tribes. Thus when Capt. Smith, in the year 1609, questioned Powhatàn (who was the chief of the nation, and whose proper name is said to have been Wahunsonacock) respecting the succession, the old chief informed him, "that he was very old and had seen the death of all his people thrice;* that not one of these generations were then living except himself, that he must soon die and the succession descend in order to his brothers Opichapàn, Opechàncanough, and Catatàugh, and then to his two sisters, and their two daughters." But these were appellations designating the tribes in the confederacy. For the persons named are not his real brothers, but the chiefs of different tribes. Accordingly in 1618, when Powhatan died, he was succeeded by Opichapàn, and after his decease Opechàncanough became chief of the nation. I need only mention another instance to shew that the chiefs of the tribes claimed this kindred with the head of the nation. In 1622, when Raleigh Crashaw was with Japazàw, the Sachem or chief of the Patowmacs, Opechàncanough, who had great power and influence, being the second man in the nation, and next in succession to Opichapan, and who was a bitter but secret enemy to the English, and wanted to engage his nation in a war with them, sent two baskets of beads to the Patowmac chief, and desired him to kill the Englishman that was with him. Japazaw replied, that the English were his friends, and Opichapàn his *brother*, and that therefore there should be no blood shed between them by his means. It is also to be observed, that when the English first came over, in all their conferences with any of the chiefs, they constantly heard him make mention of his *brother*, with whom he must consult,

---

*This is one generation more than the poet ascribes to the life of Nestor.

> τῷ δ' ἤδη δύο μὲν γενεαὶ μερόπων ἀνθρώπων
> ἐφθίαθ', οἵ οἱ πρόσθεν ἅμα τράφεν ἠδ' ἐγένοντο
> ἐν Πύλῳ ἠγαθέῃ, μετὰ δὲ τριτάτοισιν ἄνασσεν.

1 Hom. I. 250

> Two generations now had past away,
> Wife by his rules, and happy by his sway;
> Two ages o'er his native realm he reign'd,
> And now th' example of the third remain'd.

Pope.

or to whom he referred them, meaning thereby either the chief of the nation, or the tribes in confederacy. The Manahòacks are said to have been a confederacy of four tribes, and in alliance with the Monacans, in the war which they were carrying on against the Powhatans.

To the northward of these there was another powerful nation, which occupied the country from the head of the Chesapeak-bay up to the Kittatinney mountain, and as far eastward as Connecticut river, comprehending that part of New-York which lies between the highlands and the ocean, all the state of New-Jersey, that part of Pennsylvania which is watered, below the range of the Kittatinney mountains, by the rivers or streams falling into the Delaware, and the county of Newcastle in the state of Delaware, as far as Duck creek. It is to be observed, that the nations of Indians distinguished their countries one from another by natural boundaries, such as ranges of mountains, or streams of water. But as the heads of rivers frequently interlock, or approach near to each other, as those who live upon a stream claim the country watered by it, they often encroached on each other, and this is a constant source of war between the different nations. The nation occupying the tract of country last described, called themselves Lenopi. The French writers call them Loups; and among the English they are now commonly called Delawares. This nation or confederacy consisted of five tribes, who all spoke one language. 1. The Chihohocki, who dwelt on the West side of the river now called Delaware, a name which it took from Lord De la War, who put into it on his passage from Virginia in the year [1611], but which by the Indians was called Chihohocki. 2. The Wanami, who inhabited the country, called New-Jersey, from the Rariton to the sea. 3. The Munsey, who dwelt on the upper streams of the Delaware, from the Kittatinney mountains down to the Leheigh or western branch of the Delaware. 4. The Wabinga, who are sometimes called River Indians, sometimes Mohickanders, and who had their dwelling between the west branch of Delaware and Hudson's river, from the Kittatinney ridge down to the Rariton: and 5. The Mahiccon, or Mahattan, who occupied Staten island, York island, (which from its being the principal feat of their residence was formerly called Mahatton) Long island, and that part of New-York and Connecticut which lies between Hudson and Connecticut rivers, from the highland, which is a continuation of the Kittatinney ridge down to the sound. This nation had a close alliance with the Shawanese, who lived on the Susquehannah and to the westward of that river, as far as the Alleghaney mountains, and carried on a long war with another powerful nation or confederacy of Indians, which lived to the north of them between the Kittatinney mountains, or highlands, and the lake Ontario, and who call themselves Mingos, and are called by the French writers Iroquois, by the English the Five Nations, and by the Indians to the southward, with whom they were at war, Massawomacs. This war was carrying on, in its greatest fury, when Captain Smith first arrived in Virginia. The Mingo warriors had penetrated down the Susquehanna to the mouth of it. In one of his excursions up the bay, at the mouth of Susquehanna, in 1608, Captain Smith met with six or seven of their canoes full of warriors, who were coming to attack their enemies in the rear. In an excursion which he had made a few weeks before, up the Rappahanock, and in which he had a skirmish with a party of the Manahoacs, and taken a brother of one of their chiefs prisoner, he first heard of this nation. For when he asked the prisoner, why his nation attacked the English? the prisoner said, because his nation had heard that the English came from under the world to take their world from them. Being asked, how many worlds he knew? he said, he knew but one, which was under the sky that covered him, and which consisted of the Powhatàns, the Mànakins, and the Massawòmacs. Being questioned concerning the latter, he said, they dwelt on a great water to the North, that they had many boats, and so many men that they waged war with all the rest of the world. The Mingo confederacy then consisted of five tribes; three who are called the elder, to wit, the Senecas, who live to the West, the Mohawks to the East, and the Onondagas between them; and two who are called the younger tribes, namely, the Cayugas, and Oneidas. All these tribes speak one language, and were then united in a close confederacy, and occupied the tract of country from the East end of lake Erie to lake Champlain, and from the Kittatinney and Highlands to the lake Ontario and the river Cadaraqui, or St. Laurence. They had, some time before that, carried on a war with a nation, who lived beyond the lakes, and were called Adirondacs. In this war they were worsted: but having made a peace with them, through the intercession of the French, who were then settling Canada, they turned their arms against the Lenopi; and as this war was long and doubtful, they, in the course of it, not only exerted their whole force, but put in practice every measure which prudence or policy could devise to bring it to a successful issue. For this purpose they bent their course down the Susquehannah, warring with the Indians in their way, and having penetrated as far as the mouth of it, they, by the terror of their arms, engaged a nation, now known by the name of Nanticocks, Conoys, and Tùteloes, and who lived between Chesapeak and Delaware bays, and bordering on the tribe of Chihohocki, to enter into an alliance with them. They also formed an alliance with the Monacans, and stimulated them to a war with the Lenopi and their confederates. At the same time the Mohawks carried on a furious war down the Hudson against the Mohiccons and River indians, and compelled them to purchase a temporary and precarious peace, by acknowledging them to be their superiors, and paying an annual tribute. The Lenopi being surrounded with enemies, and hard pressed, and having lost many of their warriors, were at last compelled to sue for peace, which was granted to them on the condition that they should put themselves under the protection of the Mingoes, confine themselves to raising corn, hunting for the subsistence of their families, and no longer have the power of making war. This is what the Indians call making them women. And in this condition the Lenopis were when William Penn first arrived and began the settlement of Pennsylvania in 1682.

[6.] Pa. 106. From the figurative language of the Indians, as well as from the practice of those we are still acquainted with, it is evident that it was, and still continues to be, a constant custom among the Indians to gather up the bones of the dead, and deposit them in a particular place. Thus, when they make peace with any nation, with whom they have been at war, after burying the hatchet, they take up the belt of wampum, and say, "We now gather up all the bones of those who have been slain, and bury them, &c." See all the treaties of peace. Besides, it is customary when any of them die at a distance from home, to bury them, and afterwards to come and take up the bones, and carry them home. At a treaty which was held at Lancaster with the six nations, one of them died, and was buried in the woods a little distance from the town. Some time after a party came and took up the body, separated the flesh from the bones by boiling and scraping them clean, and carried them to be deposited in the sepulchres of their ancestors. The operation was so offensive and disagreeable, that nobody could come near them while they were performing it.

[7.] Pa. 113. The Oswegàtchies, Connosedàgos and Cohunnegàgoes, or, as they are commonly called, Caghnewàgos, are of the Mingo or Six-nation Indians, who, by the influence of the French missionaries, have been separated from their nation, and induced to settle there.

I do not know of what nation the Augquàgahs are; but suspect they are a family of the Senecas.

The Nànticocks and Conòies were formerly of a nation that lived at the head of Chesapeak bay, and who, of late years, have been adopted into the Mingo or Iroquois confederacy, and make a seventh nation. The Monacans or Tuscaroras, who were taken into the confederacy in 1712, making the sixth

The Saponies are families of the Wanamies, who removed from New-Jersey, and, with the Mohiccons, Munsies, and Delawares, belong to the Lenopi nation. The Mingos are a war colony from the six nations; so are the Cohunnewagos.

Of the rest of the northern tribes I never have been able to learn any thing certain. But all accounts seem to agree in this, that there is a very powerful nation, distinguished by a variety of names taken from the several towns or families, but commonly called Tàwas or Outawas, who speak one language, and live round and on the waters that fall into the western lakes, and extend from the waters of the Ohio quite to the waters falling into Hudson's bay.

APPENDIX NO. II.

In the Summer of the Year 1783, it was expected, that the ASSEMBLY OF VIRGINIA *would call a* CONVENTION *for the Establishment of a* CONSTITUTION. *The following* DRAUGHT *of a* FUNDAMENTAL CONSTITUTION[4] *for the* COMMONWEALTH OF VIRGINIA *was then prepared, with a Design of being proposed in such Convention, had it taken place.*

To the citizens of the Commonwealth of Virginia, and all others whom it may concern, the Delegates for the said Commonwealth in Convention assembled, send greeting.

It is known to you, and to the world, that the government of Great Britain, with which the American States were not long since connected, assumed over them an authority unwarrantable and oppressive; that they endeavoured to enforce this authority by arms, and that the States of New Hampshire, Massachusets, Rhode island, Connecticut, New York, New Jersey, Pennsylvania, Delaware, Maryland, Virginia, North Carolina, South Carolina, and Georgia, considering resistance, with all its train of horrors, as a lesser evil than abject submission, closed in the appeal to arms. It hath pleased the Sovereign Disposer of all human events to give to this appeal an issue favourable to the rights of the States; to enable them to reject for ever all dependance on a government which had shewn itself so capable of abusing the trusts reposed in it; and to obtain from that government a solemn and explicit acknowledgment that they are free, sovereign, and independant States. During the progress of that war, through which we had to labour for the establishment of our rights, the legislature of the commonwealth of Virginia found it necessary to make a temporary organization of government for preventing anarchy, and pointing our efforts to the two important objects of war against our invaders, and peace and happiness among ourselves. But this, like all other their acts of legislation, being subject to change by subsequent legislatures, possessing equal powers with themselves, it has been thought expedient, that it should receive those amendments which time and trial have suggested, and be rendered permanent by a power superior to that of the ordinary legislature. The general assembly therefore of this state recommend it to the good people thereof, to chuse delegates to meet in general convention, with powers to form a constitution of government for them, and to declare those fundamentals to which all our laws present and future shall be subordinate: and, in compliance with this recommendation, they have thought proper to make choice of us, and to vest us with powers for this purpose.

We therefore, the delegates, chosen by the said good people of this state for the purpose aforesaid, and now assembled in general convention, do, in execution of the authority with which we are invested, establish the following constitution and fundamentals of government for the said state of Virginia.

The said state shall for ever hereafter be governed as a commonwealth.

The powers of government shall be divided into three distinct departments, each of them to be confided to a separate body of magistracy; to wit, those which are legislative to one, those which are judiciary to another, and those which are executive to another. No person, or collection of persons, being of one of these departments, shall exercise any power properly belonging to either of the others, except in the instances hereinafter expressly permitted.

I. Legislature.

The legislature shall consist of two branches, the one to be called the House of Delegates, the other the Senate, and both together the General Assembly. The concurrence of both of these, expressed on three several readings, shall be necessary to the passage of a law.

Election.

Delegates for the general assembly shall be chosen on the last Monday of November in every year. But if an election cannot be concluded on that day, it may be adjourned from day to day till it can be concluded.

Delegates.

The number of delegates which each county may send shall be in proportion to the number of its qualified electors; and the whole number of delegates for the state shall be so proportioned to the whole number of qualified electors in it, that they shall never exceed 300, nor be fewer than 100. Whenever such excess or deficiency shall take place, the House of Delegates so deficient or excessive shall, notwithstanding this, continue in being during its legal term; but they shall, during that term, re-adjust the proportion, so as to bring their number within the limits beforementioned at the ensuing election. If any county be reduced in its qualified electors below the number authorized to send one delegate, let it be annexed to some adjoining county.

Senate.

For the election of senators, let the several counties be allotted by the senate, from time to time, into such and so many districts as they shall find best; and let each county at the time of electing its delegates, chuse senatorial electors, qualified as themselves are, and four in number for each delegate their county is entitled to send, who shall convene, and conduct themselves, in such manner as the legislature shall direct, with the senatorial electors from the other counties of their district, and then chuse, by ballot, one senator for every six delegates which their district is entitled to chuse. Let the senatorial districts be divided into two classes, and let the members elected for one of them be dissolved at the first ensuing general election of delegates, the other at the next, and so on alternately for ever.

Electors.

All free male citizens, of full age, and sane mind, who for one year before shall have been resident in the county, or shall through the whole of that time have possessed therein real property of the value of or shall for the same time have been enrolled in the militia, and no others, shall have a right to vote for delegates for the said county, and for senatorial electors for the district. They shall give their votes personally, and *vivâ voce*.

General assembly.

The general assembly shall meet at the place to which the last adjournment was, on the 42d day after the day of the election of delegates, and thenceforward at any other time or place on their own adjournment, till their office expires, which shall be on the day preceding that appointed for the meeting of the next general assembly. But if they shall at any time adjourn for more than one year, it shall be as if they had adjourned for one year precisely. Neither house, without the concurrence of the other, shall adjourn for more than one week, nor to any other place than the one at which they are sitting. The governor shall also have power, with the advice of the council of state, to call them at any other time to the same place, or to a different one, if that shall have become, since the last adjournment, dangerous from an enemy, or from infection.

Quorum.

A majority of either house shall be a quorum, and shall be requisite for doing business: but any smaller proportion which from time to time shall be thought expedient by the respective houses, shall be sufficient to call for, and to punish, their non-attending members, and to adjourn themselves for any time not exceeding one week.

Privileges.

The members, during their attendance on the general assembly, and for so long a time before and after as shall be necessary for travelling to and from the same, shall be privileged from all personal restraint and assault, and shall have no other privilege whatsoever. They shall receive during the same time, daily wages in gold or silver, equal to the value of two bushels of wheat. This value shall be deemed one dollar by the bushel till the year 1790, in which, and in every tenth year thereafter, the general court, at their first sessions in the year, shall cause a special jury, of the most respectable merchants and farmers, to be summoned, to declare what shall have been the averaged value of wheat during the last ten years; which averaged value shall be the measure of wages for the ten subsequent years.

Exclusions.

Of this general assembly, the treasurer, attorney general, register, ministers of the gospel, officers of the regular armies of this state, or of the United States, persons receiving salaries or emoluments from any power foreign to our confederacy, those who are not resident in the county for which they are chosen delegates, or districts for which they are chosen senators, those who are not qualified as electors, persons who shall have committed treason, felony, or such other crime as would subject them to infamous punishment, or who shall have been convicted by due course of law of bribery or corruption, in endeavouring to procure an election to the said assembly, shall be incapable of being members. All others, not herein elsewhere excluded, who may elect, shall be capable of being elected thereto.

Any member of the said assembly accepting any office of profit under this state, or the United States, or any of them, shall thereby vacate his seat, but shall be capable of being re-elected.

Vacancies.

Vacancies occasioned by such disqualifications, by death, or otherwise, shall be supplied by the electors, on a writ from the speaker of the respective house.

Limits of power.

The general assembly shall not have power to infringe this constitution; to abridge the civil rights of any person on account of his religious belief; to restrain him from professing and supporting that belief, or to compel him to contributions, other than those he shall have personally stipulated, for the support of that or any other; to ordain death for any crime but treason or murder, or military offences; to pardon, or give a power of pardoning persons duly convicted of treason or felony, but instead thereof they may substitute one or two new trials, and no more; to pass laws for punishing actions done before the existence of such laws; to pass any bill of attainder of treason or felony; to prescribe torture in any case whatever; nor to permit the introduction of any more slaves to reside in this state, or the continuance of slavery beyond the generation which shall be living on the thirty-first day of December, one thousand eight hundred: all persons born after that day being hereby declared free.

The general assembly shall have power to sever from this state all or any part of its territory westward of the Ohio, or of the meridian of the mouth of the great Kanhaway, and to cede to Congress one hundred square miles of territory in any other part of this state, exempted from the jurisdiction and government of this state so long as Congress shall hold their sessions therein, or in any territory adjacent thereto, which may be ceded to them by any other state.

They shall have power to appoint the speakers of their respective houses, treasurer, auditors, attorney-general, register, all general officers of the military, their own clerks and serjeants, and no other officers, except where, in other parts of this constitution, such appointment is expressly given them.

II. Executive. Governor.

The executive powers shall be exercised by a *governor*, who shall be chosen by joint ballot of both houses of assembly, and when chosen shall remain in office five years, and be ineligible a second time. During his term he shall hold no other office or emolument under this state, or any other state or power whatsoever. By executive powers, we mean no reference to those powers exercised under our former government by the crown as of its prerogative, nor that these shall be the standard of what may or may not be deemed the rightful powers of the governor. We give him those powers only, which are necessary to execute the laws (and administer the government) and which are not in their nature either legislative or judiciary. The application of this idea must be left to reason. We do however expressly deny him the prerogative powers of erecting courts, offices, boroughs, corporations, fairs, markets, ports, beacons, light-houses, and seamarks; of laying embargoes, of establishing precedence, of retaining within the state or recalling to it any citizen thereof, and of making denizens, except so far as he may be authorised from time to time by the legislature to exercise any of those powers. The powers of declaring war and concluding peace, of contracting alliances, of issuing letters of marque and reprisal, of raising or introducing armed forces, of building armed vessels, forts, or strong holds, of coining money or regulating its value, of regulating weights and measures, we leave to be exercised under the authority of the confederation: but in all cases respecting them which are out of the said confederation, they shall be exercised by the governor, under the regulation of such laws as the legislature may think it expedient to pass.

The whole military of the state, whether regular, or of militia, shall be subject to his directions; but he shall leave the execution of those directions to the general officers appointed by the legislature.

His salary shall be fixed by the legislature at the session of assembly in which he shall be appointed, and before such appointment be made; or if it be not then fixed, it shall be the same which his next predecessor in office was entitled to. In either case he may demand it quarterly out of any money which shall be in the public treasury; and it shall not be in the power of the legislature to give him less or more, either during his continuance in office, or after he shall have gone out of it. The lands, houses, and other things appropriated to the use of the governor, shall remain to his use during his continuance in office.

Council of state.

A *council of state* shall be chosen by joint ballot of both houses of assembly, who shall hold their offices seven years, and be ineligible a second time, and who, while they shall be of the said council, shall hold no other office or emolument, under this state, or any other state or power whatsoever. Their duty shall be to attend and advise the governor when called on by him, and their advice in any case shall be a sanction to him. They shall also have power, and it shall be their duty, to meet at their own will, and to give their advice, though not required by the governor, in cases where they shall think the public good calls for it. Their advice and proceedings shall be entered in books to be kept for that purpose, and shall be signed as approved or disapproved by the members present. These books shall be laid before either house of assembly when called for by them. The said council shall consist of eight members for the present: but their numbers may be increased or reduced by the legislature, whenever they shall think it necessary: provided such reduction be made only as the appointments become vacant by death, resignation, disqualification, or regular deprivation. A majority of their actual number, and not fewer, shall be a quorum. They shall be allowed for the present each by the year, payable quarterly out of money which shall be in the public treasury. Their salary however may be increased or abated from time to time, at the discretion of the legislature; provided such increase or abatement shall not, by any ways or means, be made to affect either then, or at any future time, any one of those then actually in office. At the end of each quarter their salary shall be divided into equal portions by the number of days on which, during that quarter, a council has been held, or required by the governor, or by their own adjournment, and one of those portions shall be withheld from each member for every of the said days which, without cause allowed good by the board, he failed to attend, or departed before adjournment without their leave. If no board should have been held during that quarter, there shall be no deduction.

President.

They shall annually chuse a *president,* who shall preside in council in the absence of the governor, and who, in case of his office becoming vacant by death or otherwise, shall have authority to exercise all his functions, till a new appointment be made, as he shall also in any interval during which the governor shall declare himself unable to attend to the duties of his office.

III. Judiciary.

The *Judiciary* powers shall be exercised by county courts and such other inferior courts as the legislature shall think proper to continue or to erect, by three superior courts, to wit, a Court of Admiralty, a General Court of Common Law, and a High Court of Chancery; and by one supreme court to be called the Court of Appeals.

The judges of the High Court of Chancery, General Court, and Court of Admiralty, shall be four in number each, to be appointed by joint ballot of both houses of assembly, and to hold their offices during good behaviour. While they continue judges, they shall hold no other office or emolument, under this state, or any other state or power whatsoever, except that they may be delegated to Congress, receiving no additional allowance.

These judges, assembled together, shall constitute the Court of Appeals, whose business shall be to receive and determine appeals from the three superior courts, but to receive no original causes, except in the cases expressly permitted herein.

A majority of the members of either of these courts, and not fewer, shall be a quorum. But in the Court of Appeals nine members shall be necessary to do business. Any smaller numbers however may be authorized by the legislature to adjourn their respective courts.

They shall be allowed for the present each by the year, payable quarterly out of any money which shall be in the public treasury. Their salaries however may be increased or abated, from time to time, at the discretion of the legislature, provided such increase or abatement shall not, by any ways or means, be made to affect, either then, or at any future time, any one of those then actually in office. At the end of each quarter their salary shall be divided into equal portions by the number of days on which, during that quarter, their respective courts sat, or should have sat, and one of these portions shall be withheld from each member for every of the said days, which, without cause allowed good by his court, he failed to attend, or departed before adjournment without their leave. If no court should have been held during the quarter, there shall be no deduction.

There shall moreover be a court of *Impeachments* to consist of three members of the council of state, one of each of the superior Courts of Chancery, Common Law, and Admiralty, two members of the House of Delegates and one of the Senate, to be chosen by the body respectively of which they are. Before this court any member of the three branches of government, that is to say, the governor, any member of the council, of the two houses of legislature, or of the superior courts, may be impeached by the governor, the council, or either of the said houses or courts, and by no other, for such misbehaviour in office as would be sufficient to remove him therefrom: and the only sentence they shall have authority to pass shall be that of deprivation and future incapacity of office. Seven members shall be requisite to make a court, and two-thirds of those present must concur in the sentence. The offences cognisable by this court shall be cognisable by no other, and they shall be triers of the fact as well as judges of the law.

The justices or judges of the inferior courts already erected, or hereafter to be erected, shall be appointed by the governor, on advice of the council of state, and shall hold their offices during good behaviour, or the existence of their court. For breach of the good behaviour, they shall be tried according to the laws of the land, before the Court of Appeals, who shall be judges of the fact as well as of the law. The only sentence they shall have authority to pass, shall be that of deprivation and future incapacity of office, and two thirds of the members present must concur in this sentence.

All courts shall appoint their own clerks, who shall hold their offices during good behaviour, or the existence of their court: they shall also appoint all other their attending officers to continue during their pleasure. Clerks appointed by the supreme or the superior courts shall be removeable by their respective courts. Those to be appointed by other courts shall have been previously examined, and certified to be duly qualified, by some two members of the general court, and shall be removeable for breach of the good behaviour by the Court of Appeals only, who shall be judges of the fact as well as of the law. Two-thirds of the members present must concur in the sentence.

The justices or judges of the inferior courts may be members of the legislature.

The judgment of no inferior court shall be final, in any civil case, of greater value than 50 bushels of wheat, as last rated in the general court for settling the allowance to the members of the general assembly, nor in any case of treason, felony, or other crime which would subject the party to infamous punishment.

In all causes depending before any court, other than those of impeachments, of appeals, and military courts, facts put in issue shall be tried by jury, and in all courts whatever witnesses shall give their testimony vivâ voce in open court, wherever their attendance can be procured: and all parties shall be allowed counsel and compulsory process for their witnesses.

Fines, amercements, and terms of imprisonment left indefinite by the law, other than for contempts, shall be fixed by the jury, triers of the offence.

IV. Council of Revision.

The governor, two councellors of state, and a judge from each of the superior Courts of chancery, Common Law, and Admiralty, shall be a council to revise all bills which shall have passed both houses of assembly, in which council the governor, when present, shall preside. Every bill, before it becomes a law, shall be presented to this council, who shall have a right to advise its rejection, returning the bill, with their advice and reasons in writing, to the house in which it originated, who shall proceed to reconsider the said bill. But if after such reconsideration, two thirds of the house shall be of opinion the bill should pass finally, they shall pass and send it, with the advice and written reasons of the said council of revision to the other house, wherein, if two thirds also shall be of opinion it should pass finally, it shall thereupon become law: otherwise it shall not.

If any bill, presented to the said council, be not, within one week (exclusive of the day of presenting it) returned by them, with their advice of rejection and reasons, to the house wherein it originated, or to the clerk of the said house, in case of its adjournment over the expiration of the week, it shall be law from the expiration of the week, and shall then be demandable by the clerk of the House of Delegates, to be filed of record in his office.

The bills which they approve shall become law from the time of such approbation, and shall then be returned to, or demandable by, the clerk of the House of Delegates, to be filed of record in his office.

A bill rejected on advice of the Council of Revision may again be proposed, during the same session of assembly, with such alterations as will render it conformable to their advice.

The members of the said Council of Revision shall be appointed from time to time by the board or court of which they respectively are. Two of the executive and two of the judiciary members shall be requisite to do business: and to prevent the evils of non-attendance, the board and courts may, at any time, name all, or so many as they will, of their members, in the particular order in which they would chuse the duty of attendance to devolve from preceding to subsequent members, the preceding failing to attend. They shall have additionally for their services in this council the same allowance as members of assembly have.

Confederacy.

The Confederation is made a part of this constitution, subject to such future alterations as shall be agreed to by the legislature of this state, and by all the other confederating states.

Delegates to Congress.

The delegates to Congress shall be five in number; any three of whom, and no fewer, may be a representation. They shall be appointed by joint ballot of both houses of assembly for any term not exceeding one year, subject to be recalled, within the term, by joint vote of both the said houses. They may at the same time be members of the legislative or judiciary departments, but not of the executive.

Hab. Corp.

The benefits of the writ of Habeas Corpus shall be extended, by the legislature, to every person within this state, and without fee, and shall be so facilitated that no person may be detained in prison more than ten days after he shall have demanded and been refused such writ by the judge appointed by law, or if none be appointed, then by any judge of a superior court, nor more than ten days after such writ shall have been served on the person detaining him, and no order given, on due examination, for his remandment or discharge.

Military.

The military shall be subordinate to the civil power.

Printing.

Printing-presses shall be subject to no other restraint than liableness to legal prosecution for false facts printed and published.

Convention.

Any two of the three branches of government concurring in opinion, each by the voices of two thirds of their whole existing number, that a convention is necessary for altering this constitution, or correcting breaches of it, they shall be authorized to issue writs to every county for the election of so many delegates as they are authorized to send to the General Assembly, which elections shall be held, and writs returned, as the laws shall have provided in the case of elections of Delegates to assembly, mutatis mutandis, and the said Delegates shall meet at the usual place of holding, assemblies, three months after the date of such writs, and shall be acknowledged to have equal powers with this present convention. The said writs shall be signed by all the members approving the same.

To introduce this government, the following special and temporary provision is made.

This convention being authorized only to amend those laws which constituted the form of government, no general dissolution of the whole system of laws can be supposed to have taken place: but all laws in force at the meeting of this convention, and not inconsistent with this constitution, remain in full force, subject to alterations by the ordinary legislature.

The present General Assembly shall continue till the 42d day after the last Monday of November in this present year. On the said last Monday of November in this present year, the several counties shall, by their electors, qualified as provided by this constitution, elect delegates, which for the present shall be, in number, one for every militia of the said county, according to the latest returns in possession of the governor, and shall also chuse senatorial electors in proportion thereto, which senatorial electors shall meet on the 14th day after the day of their election, at the Court-house of that county of their present district which would stand first in an alphabetical arrangement of their counties, and shall chuse senators in the proportion fixed by this constitution. The elections and returns shall be conducted, in all circumstances not hereby particularly prescribed, by the same persons and under the same forms, as prescribed by the present laws in elections of Senators and Delegates of Assembly. The said Senators and Delegates shall constitute the first General Assembly of the new government, and shall specially apply themselves to the procuring an exact return from every county of the number of its qualified electors, and to the settlement of the number of Delegates to be elected for the ensuing General Assembly.

The present Governor shall continue in office to the end of the term for which he was elected.

All other officers of every kind shall continue in office as they would have done had their appointment been under this constitution, and new ones, where new are hereby called for, shall be appointed by the authority to which such appointment is referred. One of the present judges of the general court, he consenting thereto, shall by joint ballot of both houses of assembly, at their first meeting, be transferred to the High Court of Chancery.

APPENDIX NO. III.

An ACT *for establishing* RELIGIOUS FREEDOM,[5] *passed in the Assembly of Virginia in the beginning of the year 1786.*

Well aware that Almighty God hath created the mind free; that all attempts to influence it by temporal punishments or burthens, or by civil incapacitations, tend only to beget habits of hypocrisy and meanness, and are a departure from the plan of the Holy Author of our religion, who, being Lord both of body and mind, yet chose not to propagate it by coercions on either, as was in his Almighty power to do; that the impious presumption of legislators and rulers, civil as well as ecclesiastical, who, being themselves but fallible and uninspired men have assumed dominion over the faith of others, setting up their own opinions and modes of thinking as the only true and infallible, and as such endeavouring to impose them on others, hath established and maintained false religions over the greatest part of the world, and through all time; That to compel a man to furnish contributions of money for the propagation of opinions which he disbelieves, is sinful and tyrannical; that even the forcing him to support this or that teacher of his own religious persuasion, is depriving him of the comfortable liberty of giving his contributions to the particular pastor whose morals he would make his pattern, and whose powers he feels most persuasive to righteousness, and is withdrawing from the ministry those temporal rewards, which, proceeding from an approbation of their personal conduct, are an additional incitement to earnest and unremitting labours for the instruction of mankind; that our civil rights have no dependence on our religious opinions, more than on our opinions in physics or geometry; that therefore the proscribing any citizen as unworthy the public confidence by laying upon him an incapacity of being called to offices of trust and emolument, unless he profess or renounce this or that religious opinion, is depriving him injuriously of those privileges and advantages to which in common with his fellow citizens he has a natural right; that it tends also to corrupt the principles of that very religion it is meant to encourage, by bribing, with a monopoly of worldly honors and emoluments, those who will externally profess and conform to it; that though indeed these are criminal who do not withstand such temptation, yet neither are those innocent who lay the bait in their way; that to suffer the civil magistrate to intrude his powers into the field of opinion, and to restrain the profession or propagation of principles, on supposition of their ill tendency, is a dangerous fallacy, which at once destroys all religious liberty, because he being of course judge of that tendency, will make his opinions the rule of judgment, and approve or condemn the sentiments of others only as they shall square with or differ from his own; that it is time enough for the rightful purposes of civil government for its officers to interfere when principles break out into overt acts against peace and good order; and finally, that truth is great and will prevail if left to herself, that she is the proper and sufficient antagonist to error, and has nothing to fear from the conflict, unless by human interposition disarmed of her natural weapons, free argument and debate, errors ceasing to be dangerous when it is permitted freely to contradict them.

Be it therefore enacted by the General Assembly, That no man shall be compelled to frequent or support any religious worship, place or ministry whatsoever, nor shall be enforced, restrained, molested, or burthened in his body or goods, nor shall otherwise suffer on account of his religious opinions or belief; but that all men shall be free to profess, and by argument to maintain, their opinions in matters of religion, and that the same shall in no wise diminish, enlarge, or affect their civil capacities.

And though we well know that this Assembly, elected by the people for the ordinary purposes of legislation only, have no power to restrain the acts of succeeding Assemblies, constituted with powers equal to our own, and that therefore to declare this act irrevocable, would be of no effect in law, yet we are free to declare, and do declare, that the rights hereby asserted are of the natural rights of mankind, and that if any act shall be hereafter passed to repeal the present, or to narrow its operation, such act will be an infringement of natural right.

APPENDIX NO. IV.

RELATIVE TO THE MURDER OF LOGAN'S FAMILY[6]

A Letter to Governor Henry,[7] of Maryland.
Philadelphia, December 31st, 1797.

Dear Sir,

Mr. Tazewell[8] has communicated to me the enquiries you have been so kind as to make, relative to a passage in the Notes on Virginia, which has lately excited some newspaper publications. I feel, with great sensibility, the interest you take in this business, and with pleasure, go into explanations with one whose objects I know to be truth and justice alone. Had Mr. Martin thought proper to suggest to me, that doubts might be entertained of the transaction respecting Logan, as stated in the Notes on Virginia, and to enquire on what grounds that statement was founded, I should have felt myself obliged by the enquiry, have informed him candidly of the grounds, and cordially have co-operated in every means of investigating the fact, and correcting whatsoever in it should be found to have been erroneous. But he chose to step at once into the newspapers, and in his publications there and the letters he wrote to me, adopted a style which forbade the respect of an answer. Sensible, however, that no act of his could absolve me from the justice due to others, as soon as I found that the story of Logan could be doubted, I determined to enquire into it as accurately as the testimony remaining, after a lapse of twenty odd years, would permit, and that the result should be made known, either in the first new edition which should be printed of the Notes on Virginia, or by publishing an appendix. I thought that so far as that work had contributed to impeach the memory of Cresap, by handing on an erroneous charge, it was proper it should be made the vehicle of retribution. Not that I was at all the author of the injury. I had only concurred with thousands and thousands of others, in believing a transaction on authority which merited respect. For the story of Logan is only repeated in the Notes on Virginia, precisely as it had been current for more than a dozen years before they were published. When Lord Dunmore returned from the expedition against the Indians, in 1774, he and his officers brought the speech of Logan, and related the circumstances connected with it. These were so affecting, and the speech itself is so fine a morsel of eloquence, that it became the theme of every conversation, in Williamsburgh particularly, and generally, indeed, wheresoever any of the officers resided or resorted. I learned it in Williamsburgh; I believe at Lord Dunmore's; and I find in my pocket-book of that year (1774) an entry of the narrative; as taken from the mouth of some person, whose name, however, is not noted, nor recollected, precisely in the words stated in the Notes on Virginia. The speech was published in the Virginia Gazette of that time (I have it myself in the volume of gazettes of that year) and though in a style by no means elegant, yet it was so admired, that it flew through all the public papers of the continent, and through the magazines and other periodical publications of Great-Britain; and those who were boys at that day will now attest, that the speech of Logan used to be given them as a school exercise for repetition. It was not till about thirteen or fourteen years after the newspaper publications, that the Notes on Virginia were published in America. Combating, in these, the contumelious theory of certain European writers, whose celebrity gave currency and weight to their opinions, that our country, from the combined effects of soil and climate, degenerated animal nature, in the general, and particularly the moral faculties of man, I considered the speech of Logan as an apt proof of the contrary, and used it as such; and I copied, verbatim, the narrative I had taken down in 1774, and the speech as it had been given us in a better translation by lord Dunmore. I knew nothing of the Cresaps, and could not possibly have a motive to do them an injury with design. I repeated what thousands had done before, on as good authority as we have for most of the facts we learn through life, and such as, to this moment, I have seen no reason to doubt. That any body questioned it, was never suspected by me, till I saw the letter of Mr. Martin in the Baltimore paper. I endeavored then to recollect who among my cotemporaries, of the same circle of society, and consequently of the same recollections, might still be alive. Three and twenty years of death and dispersion had left very few. I remembered, however, that general Gibson[9] was still living, and knew that he had been the translator of the speech. I wrote to him immediately. He, in answer, declares to me, that he was the very person sent by lord Dunmore to the Indian town; that, after he had delivered his message there, Logan took him out to a neighboring wood; sat down with him, and rehearsing with tears, the catastrophe of his family, gave him that speech for lord Dunmore; that he carried it to lord Dunmore; translated it for him; has turned to it in the Encyclopedia, as taken from the Notes on Virginia, and finds that it was his translation I had used, with only two or three verbal variations of no importance. These, I suppose, had arisen in the course of successive copies. I cite general Gibson's letter by memory, not having it with me; but I am sure I cite it substantially right. It establishes unquestionably, that the speech of Logan is genuine; and that being established, it is Logan himself who is author of all the important facts. "Colonel Cresap," says he, "in cold blood and unprovoked murdered all the relations of Logan, not sparing even my women and children. There runs not a drop of my blood in the veins of any living creature." The person and the fact, in all its material circumstances are here given by Logan himself. General Gibson, indeed, says, that the title was mistaken; that Cresap was a captain, and not a colonel.—This was Logan's mistake. He also observes, that it was on the Ohio, and not on the Kanhaway itself, that his family was killed. This is an error which has crept into the traditionary account; but surely of little moment in the moral view of the subject. The material question is; was Logan's family murdered, and by whom? That it was murdered has not, I believe, been denied; that it was by one of the Cresaps, Logan affirms. This is a question which concerns the memories of Logan and Cresap; to the issue of which I am as indifferent as if I had never heard the name of either. I have begun and shall continue to enquire into the evidence additional to Logan's, on which the fact was founded. Little, indeed, can now be heard of, and that little dispersed and distant. If it shall appear on enquiry, that Logan has been wrong in charging Cresap with the murder of his family, I will do justice to the memory of Cresap as far as I have contributed to the injury, by believing and repeating what others had believed and repeated before me. If, on the other hand, I find that Logan was right in his charge, I will vindicate, as far as my suffrage may go, the truth of a chief, whose talents and misfortunes have attached to him the respect and commiseration of the world.

I have gone, my dear Sir, into this lengthy detail to satisfy a mind, in the candor and rectitude of which I have the highest confidence. So far as you may incline to use the communication for rectifying the judgments of those who are willing to see things truly as they are, you are free to use it. But I pray that no confidence which you may repose in any one, may induce you to let it go out of your hands, so as to get into a newspaper. Against a contest in that field I am entirely decided. I feel extraordinary gratification, indeed, in addressing this letter to you, with whom shades of difference in political sentiments have not prevented the interchange of good opinion, nor cut off the friendly offices of society and good correspondence. This political tolerance is the more valued by me, who consider social harmony as the first of human felicities, and the happiest moments, those which are given to the effusions of the heart. Accept them sincerely, I pray you, from one who has the honor to be, with sentiments of high respect and attachment,

Dear sir,
Your most obedient
And most humble servant,
THOMAS JEFFERSON.

The Notes on Virginia were written in Virginia, in the years 1781 and 1782, in answer to certain queries proposed to me by Mons. de Marbois, then secretary of the French legation in the United States: and a manuscript copy was delivered to him. A few copies, with some additions, were afterwards, in 1784,[10] printed in Paris, and given to particular friends. In speaking of the animals of America, the theory of M. de Buffon, the Abbe Raynal, and others, presented itself to consideration. They have supposed that there is something in the soil, climate and other circumstances of America, which occasions animal nature to degenerate, not excepting even the man, native or adoptive, physical or moral. This theory, so unfounded and degrading to one third of the globe, was called to the bar of fact and reason. Among other proofs adduced in contradiction of this hypothesis, the speech of Logan an Indian chief, delivered to lord Dunmore in 1774, was produced, as a specimen of the talents of the aboriginals of this country, and particularly of their eloquence; and it was believed that Europe had never produced any thing superior to this morsel of eloquence. In order to make it intelligible to the reader, the transaction, on which it was founded, was stated, as it had been generally related in America at the time, and as I had heard it myself, in the circle of lord Dunmore, and the officers who accompanied him: and the speech itself was given as it had, ten years before the printing of that book, circulated in the newspapers through all the then colonies, through the magazines of Great-Britain, and periodical publications of Europe. For three and twenty years it passed uncontradicted; nor was it ever suspected that it even admitted contradiction. In 1797, however, for the first time, not only the whole transaction respecting Logan was affirmed in the public papers to be false, but the speech itself suggested to be a forgery, and even a forgery of mine, to aid me in proving that the man of America was equal in body and mind, to the man of Europe. But wherefore the forgery? Whether Logan's or mine, it would still have been American. I should indeed consult my own fame if the suggestion, that this speech is mine, were suffered to be believed. He would have a just right to be proud who could with truth claim that composition. But it is none of min; and I yield it to whom it is due.

On seeing then that this transaction was brought into question, I thought it my duty to make particular enquiry into its foundation. It was the more my duty as it was alledged that, by ascribing to an individual therein named, a participation in the murder of Logan's family, I had done an injury to his character which it had not deserved. I had no knowledge personally of that individual. I had no reason to aim an injury at him. I only repeated what I had heard from others, and what thousands had heard and believed as well as myself; and which no one indeed, till then, had been known to question. Twenty three years had now elapsed, since the transaction took place. Many of those acquainted with it were dead, and the living dispersed to very distant parts of the earth. Few of them were even known to me. To those however of whom I knew, I made application by letter; and some others, moved by a regard for truth and justice, were kind enough to come forward, of themselves, with their testimony. These fragments of evidence, the small remains of a mighty mass, which time has consumed, are here presented to the public, in the form of letters, certificates, or affidavits, as they came to me. I have rejected none of these forms, nor required other solemnities from those whose motives and characters were pledges of their truth. Historical transactions are deemed to be well vouched by the simple declarations of those who have borne a part in them; and especially of persons having no interest to falsify or disfigure them. The world will now see whether they, or I, have injured Cresap, by believing Logan's charge against him: and they will decide between Logan and Cresap, whether Cresap was innocent and Logan a calumniator?

In order that the reader may have a clear conception of the transactions, to which the different parts of the following declarations refer, he must take notice that they establish four different murders. 1. Of two Indians, a little above Wheeling. 2. Of others at Grave Creek, among whom were some of Logan's relations. 3. The massacre at Baker's Bottom, on the Ohio opposite the mouth of Yellow Creek, where were other relations of Logan. 4. Of those killed at the same place, coming in their canoes to the relief of their friends. I place the numbers 1, 2, 3, 4, against certain paragraphs of the evidence, to indicate the particular murder to which the paragraph relates, and present also a small sketch or map of the principle scenes of these butcheries, for their more ready comprehension.

Extract of a letter from the honorable judge INNES[11] *of Frankfort in Kentucky to* THOMAS JEFFERSON; *dated Kentucky, near Frankfort, March 2d, 1799.*

I recollect to have seen Logan's speech in 1775, in one of the public prints. That Logan conceived Cresap to be the author of the murder at Yellow Creek, it is in my power to give, perhaps, a more particular information than any other person you can apply to.

In 1774 I lived in Fincastle county, now divided into Washington, Montgomery and part of Wythe. Being intimate in col. Preston's family, I happened in July to be at his house, when an express was sent to him as the County Lieut. requesting a guard of the militia to be ordered out for the protection of the inhabitants residing low down on the north fork of Holston River. The express brought with him a war club, and a note which was left tied to it at the house of one Robertson, whose family were cut off by the Indians, and gave rise for the application to col. Preston, of which the following is a copy, then taken by me in my memorandum book.

"Captain Cresap,
What did you kill my people on Yellow Creek for? The white people killed my kin, at Conestoga, a great while ago; and I thought nothing of that. But you killed my kin again, on Yellow Creek, and took my cousin prisoner. Then I thought I must kill too; and I have been three times to war since; but the Indians are not angry: only myself."

Captain JOHN LOGAN.

July 21st, 1774.
With great respect, I am, Dear Sir,
your most obedient servant,
HARRY INNES.

Allegeney County, ss.
State of Pennsylvania.

Before me the subscriber, a justice of the peace in and for said county, personally appeared John Gibson, Esquire, and associate Judge of the same county, who being duly sworn deposeth and saith that he traded with the Shawnese and other tribes of Indians then settled on the Siota in the year 1773, and in the beginning of the year 1774, and that in the month of April of the same year, he left the same Indian towns, and came to this place, in order to procure some goods and provisions, that he remained here only a few days, and then set out in company with a certain Alexander Blaine and M. Elliot by water to return to the towns on Siota, and that one evening as they were drifting in their canoes near the Long Reach on the Ohio, they were hailed by a number of white men on the South West Shore, who requested them to put ashore, as they had disagreeable news to inform them of; that we then landed on shore; and found amongst the party, a Major Angus M'Donald from West Chester, a Doctor Woods from same place, and a party as they said of 150 men. We then asked the news. They informed us that some of the party who had been taking up, and improving lands near the Big Kanhaway River, had seen another party of white men, who informed them that they and some others had fell in with a party of Shawnese, who had been hunting on the south west side of the Ohio, that they had killed the whole of the Indian party, and that the others had gone across the country to Cheat River with the horses and plunder, the consequence of which they apprehended would be an Indian war, and that they were flying away. On making enquiry of them when this murder should have happened, we found that it must have been some considerable time before we left the Indian towns, and that there was not the smallest foundation for the report, as there was not a single man of the Shawnese tribe, but what returned from hunting long before this should have happened.

We then informed them that if they would agree to remain at the place we then were, one of us would go to Hock Hocking River with some of their party, where we should find some of our people making canoes, and that if we did not find them there, we might conclude that every thing was not right. Doctor Wood and another person then proposed going with me; the rest of the party seemed to agree, but said they would send and consult captain Cresap who was about two miles from that place. They sent off for him, and during the greatest part of the night they behaved in the most disorderly manner, threatening to kill us and saying the damned traders were worse than the Indians and ought to be killed. In the morning captain Michael Cresap came to the camp. I then gave him the information as above related. They then met in council, and after an hour or more captain Cresap returned to me and informed that he could not prevail on them to adopt the proposal I had made to them, that as he had a great regard for captain R. Callender, a brother in law of mine with whom I was connected in trade, he advised me by no means to think of proceeding any further, as he was convinced the present party would fall on and kill every Indian they met on the river, that for his part he should not continue with them, but go right across the country to Red Stone to avoid the consequences. That we then proceeded to Hocking and went up the same to the canoe place, where we found our people at work, and after some days we proceeded to the towns on Siota by land. On our arrival there, we heard of the different murders committed by the party on their way up the Ohio.

This Deponent further saith that in the year 1774, he accompanied lord Dunmore on the expedition against the Shawnese and other Indians on their Siota, that on their arrival within 15 Miles of the towns, they were met by a flag, and a white man of the name of Elliot, who informed lord Dunmore that the chiefs of the Shawnese had sent to request his lordship to halt his army and send in some person, who understood their language; that this deponent, at the request of lord Dunmore and the whole of the officers with him, went in; that on his arrival at the towns, Logan, the Indian, came to where this deponent was sitting with the Corn-Stalk, and the other chiefs of the Shawnese, and asked him to walk out with him; that they went into a copse of wood, where they sat down, when Logan, after shedding abundance of tears, delivered to him the speech, nearly as related by Mr. Jefferson in his notes on the state of Virginia; that he the deponent told him then that it was not Col. Cresap who had murdered his relations, and that although his son captain Michael Cresap was with the party who killed a Shawnese chief and other Indians, yet he was not present when his relations were killed at Baker's, near the mouth of Yellow Creek on the Ohio: that this deponent on his return to camp delivered the speech to lord Dunmore; and that the murders perpetrated as above were considered as ultimately the cause of the war of 1774, commonly called Cresap's war.

Sworn and subscribed the 4th April, 1800, *at Pittsburgh, before me,* } JOHN GIBSON.

JER. BARKER.

Extract of a letter from Col. Ebenezer Zane,[12] *to the honorable* John Brown, *one of the Senators in Congress from Kentucky; dated Wheeling, Feb. 4th, 1800.*

I was myself, with many others, in the practice of making improvements on lands upon the Ohio, for the purpose of acquiring rights to the same. Being on the Ohio at the mouth of Sandy Creek, in company with many others, news circulated that the Indians had robbed some of the land jobbers. This news induced the people generally to ascend the Ohio. I was among the number. [1] On our arrival at the Wheeling, being informed that there were two Indians with some traders near and above Wheeling, a proposition was made by the then captain Michael Cresap to way lay and kill the Indians upon the river. This measure I opposed with much violence, alledging that the killing of those Indians might involve the country in a war. But the opposite party prevailed and proceeded up the Ohio with captain Cresap at their head.

In a short time the party returned, and also the traders, in a canoe; but there were no Indians in the company. I enquired what had become of the Indians, and was informed by the traders and Cresap's party that they had fallen overboard. I examined the canoe, and saw much fresh blood and some bullet holes in the canoe. This fully convinced me that the party had killed the two Indians, and thrown them into the river.

[2] On the afternoon of the day this action happened, a report prevailed that there was a camp, or party of Indians on the Ohio below and near the Wheeling. In consequence of this information, captain Cresap with his party, joined by a number of recruits, proceeded immediately down the Ohio for the purpose, as was then generally understood, of destroying the Indians above mentioned. On the succeeding day, captain Cresap and his party returned to Wheeling, and it was generally reported by the party that they had killed a number of Indians. Of the truth of this report I had no doubt, as one of Cresap's party was badly wounded, and the party had a fresh scalp, and a quantity of property, which they called Indian plunder. At the time of the last mentioned transaction, it was generally reported that the

party of Indians down the Ohio were Logan and his family; but I have reason to believe that this report was unfounded.

[3] Within a few days after the transaction above mentioned, a party of Indians were killed at Yellow Creek. But I must do the memory of captain Cresap the justice to say that I do not believe that he was present at the killing of the Indians at Yellow Creek. But there is not the least doubt in my mind, that the massacre at Yellow Creek was brought on by the two transactions first stated.

All the transactions which I have related happened in the latter end of April 1774: and these can scarcely be a doubt that they were the cause of the war which immediately followed, commonly called Dunmore's war.

I am with much esteem,
Yours, &c.
EBENEZER ZANE.

The Certificate of WILLIAM HUSTON *of Washington county, in the state of Pennsylvania, communicated by* DAVID RIDDICK, *Esquire, Prothonotary of Washington county, Pennsylvania; who in the letter inclosing it says "Mr.* WILLIAM HUSTON *is a man of established reputation in point of integrity."*

I William Huston of Washington county, in the state of Pennsylvania, do hereby certify to whom it may concern, that in the year 1774 I resided at Catfishes camp, on the main path from Wheeling to Red Stone: that Michael Cresap, who resided on or near the Potowmac River, on his way up from the river Ohio, at the head of a party of armed men, lay some time at my cabbin.

[2] I had previously heard the report of Mr. Cresap having killed some Indians, said to be the relations of "Logan" an Indian Chief. In a variety of conversation with several of Cresap's party, they boasted of the deed; and that in the presence of their chief. They acknowledged they had fired first on the Indians. They had with them one man on a litter, who was in the skirmish.

I do further certify that, from what I learned from the party themselves, I then formed the opinion, and have not had any reason to change the opinion since, that the killing, on the part of the [3] whites, was what I deemed the grossest murder. I further certify that some of the party, who afterwards killed some women and other Indians at Baker's Bottom, also lay at my cabin, on their march to the interior parts of the country; they had with them a little girl, whose life had been spared by the interference of some more humane than the rest. If necessary I will make affidavit to the above to be true. Certified at Washington, this 18th day of April, Anno Domini, 1798.

WILLIAM HUSTON.

The certificate of JACOB NEWLAND, *of Shelby county, Kentucky, communicated by the Honorable Judge Innes, of Kentucky.*

In the year 1774, I lived on the waters of Short Creek, a branch of the Ohio, 12 miles above Wheeling. Some time in June or July of that year, capt. Michael Cresap raised a party of men, and came out under col. M'Daniel, of Hampshire county, Virginia, who commanded a detachment against the Wappotommaka towns on the Muskinghum. I met with captain Cresap, at Redstone fort, and entered his company. Being very well acquainted with him, we conversed freely; and he among other conversations, informed me several [2] times of falling in with some Indians on the Ohio some distance below the mouth of Yellow Creek, and killed two or three of them; and that this [3] murder was before that of the Indians by Greathouse and others, at Yellow Creek. I do not recollect the reason which captain Cresap assigned for committing the act, but never understood that the Indians gave any offence. Certified under my hand this 15th day of November, 1799, being an inhabitant of Shelby county, and State of Kentucky.

JACOB NEWLAND.

The certificate of JOHN ANDERSON, *a merchant in Fredericksburg, Virginia; communicated by Mann Page, Esq. of Mansfield, near Fredericksburg, who, in the letter accompanying it, says, "Mr. John Anderson has for many years past been settled in Fredericksburg, in the mercantile line. I have known him in prosperous and adverse situations. He has always shown the greatest degree of equanimity, his honesty and veracity are unimpeachable. These things can be attested by all the respectable part of the town, and neighborhood of Fredericksburg."*

Mr. John Anderson, a merchant in Fredericksburg, says, that in the year 1774, being a trader in the Indian country, he was at Pittsburgh to which place he had a cargo brought up the river in a boat navigated by a Delaware Indian and a white man. That on their return down the river, [1] with a cargo, belonging to Messrs. Butler, Michael Cresap fired on the boat, and killed the Indian, after which two men of the name of [3] Gatewood and others of the name of *Tumblestone, who lived on the opposite side of the river from the Indians, with whom they were on the most friendly terms, invited a party of them to come over and drink with them; and that, when the Indians were drunk, they murdered [4] them to the number of six, among whom was Logan's mother. That five other Indians uneasy at the absence of their friends, came over the river to enquire after them; when they were fired upon, and two were killed, and the others wounded. This was the origin of the war.

I certify the above to be true to the best of my recollection.

JOHN ANDERSON.

Attest.

DAVID BLAIR, *30th June 1798.*

The deposition of JAMES CHAMBERS, *communicated by David Riddick, Esq. Prothonotary of Washington county, Pennsylvania, who in the letter enclosing it shews that he entertains the most perfect confidence in the truth of* MR. CHAMBERS.

Washington county, sc.

Personally came before me Samuel Shannon, Esq. one of the commonwealth justices for the county of Washington in the state of Pennsylvania, James Chambers, who being sworn according to law, deposeth and saith that in the spring of the year 1774, he resided on the frontiers near Baker's bottom on the Ohio: that he had an intimate companion, with whom he sometimes [2] lived, named "Edward King:" That a report reached

---

*The popular pronunciation of Tomlinson, which was the real name.

him that Michael Cresap had killed some Indians near Grave Creek, friends to an Indian [3] known by the name of "Logan:" That other of his friends following down the river, having received intelligence, and fearing to proceed, lest Cresap might fall in with them, encamped near the mouth of Yellow Creek, opposite Baker's bottom; that Daniel Greathouse had determined to kill them: had made the secret known to the deponent's companion, King; that the deponent was earnestly solicited to be of the party, and, as an inducement, was told that they would get a great deal of plunder; and further, that the Indians would be made drunk by Baker, and that little danger would follow the expedition. The deponent refused to have any hand in killing unoffending people. His companion, King, went with Greathouse, with divers others, some of whom had been collected at a considerable distance under an idea that Joshua Baker's family was in danger from the Indians, as war had been commenced between Cresap and them already; that Edward King, as well as others of the party, did not conceal from the deponent the most minute circumstances of this affair; they informed him that Greathouse, concealing his people, went over to the Indian encampments and counted their number, and found that they were too large a party to attack with his strength: that he then requested Joshua Baker, when any of them came to his house, (which they had been in the habit of) to give them what rum they could drink, and to let him know when they were in a proper train, and that he would then fall on them: that accordingly they found several men and two women at Baker's house; that one of these women had cautioned Greathouse, when over in the Indian camp, that he had better return home, as the Indian men were drinking, and that having heard of Cresap's attack on their relations down the river, they were angry, and, in a friendly manner, told him to go home. Greathouse, with his party, fell on them, and killed all except a little girl which the deponent saw with the party after the slaughter; that the Indians in the camp hearing [4] the firing, manned two canoes, supposing their friends at Baker's to be attacked, as was supposed: the party under Greathouse prevented their landing by a well directed fire, which did execution in the canoes; that Edward King shewed the deponent one of the scalps.—The deponent further saith, that the settlements near the river broke up, and he the deponent immediately repaired to Catfish's camp, and lived some time with Mr. William Huston; that not long after his arrival, Cresap, with his party, returned from the Ohio, came to Mr. Huston's and tarried some time: that in various conversations with the party, and [2] in particular with a Mr. Smith, who had one arm only, he was told that the Indians were acknowledged and known to be Logan's friends which they had killed, and that he heard the party say, that Logan would probably avenge their deaths.

They acknowledged that the Indians passed Cresap's encampment on the bank of the river in a peaceable manner, and encamped below him; that they went down and fired on the Indians, and killed several; that the survivors flew to their arms and fired on Cresap, and wounded one man, whom the deponent saw carried on a litter by the [2] party; that the Indians killed by Cresap were [3] not only Logan's relations, but of the women killed at Baker's, one was said and generally believed to be Logan's sister. The deponent further saith, that on the relation of the attack by Cresap on the unoffending Indians, he exclaimed in their hearing, that it was an atrocious murder: on which Mr. Smith threatened the deponent with the tomahawk; so that he was obliged to be cautious, fearing an injury, as the party appeared to have lost, in a great degree, sentiments of humanity as well as the effects of civilization. Sworn and subscribed at Washington, the 20th day of April, anno Domini 1798.

JAMES CHAMBERS.

Before Samuel Shannon.

Washington county, sc.

SEAL. I, DAVID REDDICK, prothonotary of the court of common pleas, for the county of Washington; in the state of Pennsylvania, do certify, that Samuel Shannon, Esq. before whom the within affidavit was made, was, at the time thereof, and still is, a justice of the peace in and for the county of Washington aforesaid; and that full credit is due to all his judicial acts as such as well in courts of justice as thereout.

In testimony whereof I have hereunto set my hand and affixed the seal of my office at Washington, the 26th day of April, anno Dom. 1798.

DAVID REDDICK.

The certificate of CHARLES POLKE, *of Shelby county, in Kentucky, communicated by the hon. judge Innes, of Kentucky, who in the letter inclosing it, together with Newland's certificate, and his own declaration of the information given him by Baker, says, "I am well acquainted with Jacob Newland, he is a man of Integrity. Charles Polke and Joshua Baker both support respectable characters."*

About the latter end of April or beginning of May 1774, I lived on the waters of Cross creek, about 16 miles from Joshua Baker, who lived on the Ohio, opposite the mouth of Yellow creek. A [3] number of persons collected at my house, and proceeded to the said Baker's and murdered several Indians, among whom was a woman said to be the sister of the Indian chief Logan. The principal leader of the party was one Daniel Greathouse. To the best of my recollection the cause which gave rise to the murder was, a general idea that the Indians were meditating an attack on the frontiers. Capt. Michael Cresap was not of the party; but I recollect that some time before the perpetration of the above fact it was currently reported that [2] capt. Cresap had murdered some Indians on the Ohio, one or two, some distance below Wheeling.

Certified by me, an inhabitant of Shelby county and state of Kentucky, this 15th day of November, 1799.

CHARLES POLKE.

The declaration of the honorable JUDGE INNES, *of Frankfort, in Kentucky.*

On the 14th of November, 1799, I accidentally met upon the road Joshua Baker, the person referred to in the certificate signed by Polke, who informed me that the murder [3] of the Indians in 1774, opposite the mouth of Yellow creek, was perpetrated at his house by 32 men, led on by Daniel Greathouse; that 12 were killed and 6 or 8 wounded; among the slain was a sister and other relations of the Indian chief Logan. Baker says captain Michael Cresap was not of the party; that some days preceding the murder at [1] his house, two Indians left him and were on their way home; that they fell in with captain Cresap and a party of land improvers on the Ohio, and were murdered, if not by Cresap himself, with his approbation: he being the leader of the party, and that he had the information from Cresap.

HARRY INNES.

The declaration of WILLIAM ROBINSON.

William Robinson, of Clarksburg, in the county of Harrison, and state of Virginia, subscriber to these presents, declares that he was, in the year 1774, a resident on the west fork of Monongahela River, in the county then called West Augusta, and being in his field on the 12th of July, with two other men, they were surprised by a party of eight Indians, who shot down one of the others and made himself and the remaining one prisoners; this subscriber's wife and four children having been previously conveyed by him for safety to a fort about 24 miles off; that the principal Indian of the party who took them was captain Logan; that Logan spoke English well, and very soon manifested a friendly disposition to this subscriber, and told him to be of good heart, that he would not be killed, but must go with him to his town, where he would probably be adopted in some of their families; but above all things that he must not attempt to run away; that in the course of the journey to the Indian town he generally endeavored to keep close to Logan, who had a great deal of conversation with him, always encouraging him to be cheerful and without fear for that he would not be killed, but should become one of them; and constantly impressing on him not to attempt to run away; that in these conversations he always charged capt. Michael Cresap with the murder of his family: that on his arrival in the town, which was on the 18th of July, he was tied to a stake, and a great debate arose whether he should not be burnt: Logan insisting on having him adopted, while others contended to burn him: that at length Logan prevailed, tied a belt of wampum round him as a mark of adoption, loosed him from the post and carried him to the cabin of an old squaw, where Logan pointed out a person who he said was this subscriber's cousin; and he afterwards understood that the old woman was his aunt, and two others his brothers, and that he now stood in the place of a warrior of the family who had been killed at Yellow creek: that about three days after this Logan brought him a piece of paper, and told him he must write a letter for him, which he meant to carry and leave in some house where he should kill somebody; that he made ink with gunpowder, and the subscriber proceeded to write the letter by his direction, addressing captain Michael Cresap in it and that the purport of it was, to ask "why he had killed his people? That some time before they had killed his people at some place (the name of which the subscriber forgets) which he had forgiven; but since that he had killed his people again at Yellow creek, and taken his cousin, a little girl, prisoner; that therefore he must war against the whites; but that he would exchange the subscriber for his cousin." And signed it with Logan's name, which letter Logan took and set out again to war; and the contents of this letter, as recited by the subscriber, calling to mind that stated by judge Innes, to have been left tied to a war club, in a house where a family was murdered, and that being read to the subscriber, he recognises it, and declares he verily believes it to have been the identical letter which he wrote, and supposes he was mistaken in stating as he had done before from memory, that the offer of the exchange was proposed in the letter; that it is probable it was only promised him by Logan, but not put in the letter; that while he was with the old woman, she repeatedly endeavored to make him sensible that she had [3] been of the party at Yellow Creek, and, by signs, shewed how they decoyed her friends over the river to drink, and when they were reeling and tumbling about, tomahawked them all, and that whenever she entered on this subject she was thrown into the most violent agitations, and that he afterwards understood that, amongst the indians killed at Yellow Creek, was a sister of Logan very big with child, whom they ripped open, and stuck on a pole: that he continued with the Indians till the month of November, when he was released in consequence of the peace made by them with lord Dunmore: that, while he remained with them, the Indians in general were very kind to him; and especially those who were his adopted relations; but above all, the old woman and family in which he lived, who served him with every thing in their power, and never asked, nor even suffered him to do any labor, seeming in truth to consider and respect him, as the friend they had lost. All which several matters and things, so far as they are stated to be of his own knowledge, this subscriber solemnly declares to be true, and so far as they are stated on information from others he believes them to be true. Given and declared under his hand at Philadelphia, this 28th day of February, 1800.

WILLIAM ROBINSON.

The deposition of col. William M'Kee, *of Lincoln county, Kentucky, communicated by the hon.* John Brown, *one of the Senators in Congress from Kentucky.*

Colonel William M'Kee of Lincoln county declareth, that in autumn 1774, he commanded as a captain in the Bottetourt Regiment under col. Andrew Lewis, afterwards gen. Lewis; and fought in the battle at the mouth of Kanhaway, on the 10th of October in that year. That after the battle, col. Lewis marched the militia across the Ohio, and proceeded towards the Shawnee towns on Sciota; but before they reached the towns, Lord Dunmore, who was commander in chief of the army, and had, with a large party thereof, been up the Ohio about Hockhocking, when the battle was fought, overtook the militia, and informed them of his having since the battle concluded a treaty with the Indians; upon which the whole army returned.

And the said William declareth that, on the evening of that day on which the junction of the troops took place, he was in company with Lord Dunmore and several of his officers, and also conversed with several who had been with Lord Dunmore at the treaty; said William, on that evening, heard repeated conversations concerning an extraordinary speech made at the treaty, or sent there by a chieftain of the Indians named Logan, and heard several attempts at a rehearsal of it. The speech as rehearsed excited the particular attention of said William, and the most striking members of it were impressed on his memory.

And he declares that when Thomas Jefferson's Notes on Virginia were published, and he came to peruse the same, he was struck with the speech of Logan as there set forth, as being substantially the same, and accordant with the speech he heard rehearsed in the camp as aforesaid.

Signed,
WILLIAM M'KEE.

DANVILLE, December 18th, 1799. *We certify that col. William M'Kee this day signed the original certificate, of which the foregoing is a true copy, in our presence.*

JAMES SPEED, Jun.
J. H. DEWEES.

The certificate of the honorable STEVENS THOMPSON MASON, one of the senators in Congress from the State of Virginia. "LOGAN'*s speech, delivered at the treaty, after the battle in which col.* LEWIS *was killed in 1774.*"

[Here follows a copy of the speech agreeing verbatim with that printed in Dixon and Hunter's Virginia Gazette of February 4, 1775, under the Williamsburgh head, at the foot is this certificate.]

"The foregoing is a copy taken by me, when a boy, at school, in the year 1775, or at farthest in 1776, and lately found in an old pocketbook, containing papers and manuscripts of that period."

STEVENS THOMPSON MASON.
January 20th, 1798.

A copy of LOGAN'*s speech given by the late general* MERCER, who fell in the battle of Trenton, January, 1776, to LEWIS WILLIS, *Esquire, of Fredericksburgh, in Virginia, upwards of 20 years ago, (from the date of February, 1798,) communicated through* MANN PAGE, *Esquire.*

"The SPEECH of LOGAN, a Shawanese chief, to lord Dunmore."

[Here follows a copy of the speech, agreeing verbatim with that in the Notes on Virginia.]

A copy of LOGAN'S SPEECH from the Notes on Virginia having been sent to captain ANDREW RODGERS of Kentucky, he subjoined the following certificate.

In the year 1774 I went out with the Virginia volunteers, and was in the battle at the mouth of Canhawee, and afterwards proceeded over the Ohio to the Indian towns. I did not hear Logan make the above speech; but, from the unanimous accounts of those in camp, I have reason to think that said speech was delivered to Dunmore. I remember to have heard the very things contained in the above speech, related by some of our people in camp at that time.

ANDREW RODGERS.

The declaration of Mr. JOHN HECKEWELDER,[13] *for several years a missionary from the society of Moravians, among the western Indians.*

In the spring of the year 1774, at a time when the interior part of the Indian country all seemed peace and tranquil, the villagers on the Muskinghum were suddenly alarmed by two runners (Indians,) who reported "that the Big Knife (Virginians) had attacked the Mingoe settlement on the Ohio, and butchered even the women with their children in their arms, and that Logan's family were among the slain." A day or two after this, several Mingoes made their appearance: among whom were one or two wounded, who had in this manner effected their escape. Exasperated to a high degree, after relating the particulars of this transaction, (which for humanity's sake I forbear to mention,) after resting some time on the treachery of the Big Knives, of their barbarity to those who are their friends, they gave a figurative description of the perpetrators; named Cresap as having been at the head of this murderous act. They made mention of nine being killed, and two wounded; and were prone to take revenge on any person of a white color; for which reason the missionaries had to shut themselves up during their stay. From this time terror daily increased. The exasperated friends and relations of these murdered women and children, with the nations to whom they belonged, passed and repassed through the villages of the quiet Delaware towns, in search of white people, making use of the most abusive language to these (the Delawares,) since they would not join in taking revenge. Traders had either to hide themselves, or try to get out of the country the best way they could. And even, at this time, they yet found such true friends among the Indians, who, at the risk of their own lives, conducted them, with the best part of their property, to Pittsburg; although, (shameful to relate!) these benefactors were, on their return from this mission, *waylaid*, and fired upon by whites, while crossing Big Beaver in a canoe, and had one man, a Shawnese, named Silverheels, (a man of note in his nation) wounded in the body. This exasperated the Shawanese so much, that they, or at least a great part of them, immediately took an active part in the cause; and the Mingoes, (nearest connected with the former,) became unbounded in their rage. A Mr. Jones, son to a respectable family of this neighborhood (Bethlehem,) who was then on his passage up Muskinghum, with two other men, was fortunately espied by a friendly Indian woman, at the falls of Muskinghum, who through motives of humanity alone, informed Jones of the nature of the times, and that he was running right in the hands of the enraged; and put him on the way, where he might perhaps escape the vengeance of the strolling parties. One of Jones's men, fatigued by travelling in the woods declared he would rather die than remain longer in this situation; and hitting accidentally on a path, he determined to follow the same. A few hundred yards decided *his* fate. He was met by a party of about fifteen Mingoes, (and as it happened almost within sight of White Eyes Town,) murdered, and cut to pieces; and his limbs and flesh stuck upon the bushes. White Eyes on hearing the Scalp Halloo, ran immediately out with his men, to see what the matter was; and finding the mangled body in this condition, gathered the whole and buried it. But next day when some of the above party found on their return the body interred, they instantly tore up the ground, and endeavored to destroy, or scatter about, the parts at a greater distance. White Eyes, with the Delawares, watching their motions, gathered and interred the same a second time. The war party finding this out, ran furiously into the Delaware village, exclaiming against the conduct of these people, setting forth the cruelty of Cresap towards women and children, and declaring at the same time, that they would, in consequence of this cruelty, serve every white man they should meet with in the same manner. Times grew worse and worse, war parties went out and took scalps and prisoners, and the latter, in hopes it might be of service in saving their lives, exclaimed against the barbarous act which gave rise to these troubles, and against the perpetrators. The name of Greathouse was mentioned as having been an accomplice to Cresap. So detestable became the latter name among the Indians that I have frequently heard them apply it to the worst of things; also in quieting or stilling their children, I have heard them say, Hush! Cresap will fetch you; whereas otherwise, they name the Owl. The warriors having afterwards bent their course more toward the Ohio, and down the same, peace seemed with us already on the return; and this became the case soon after the decided battle fought on the Kanhaway. Traders, returning now into the Indian country again, related the story of the above mentioned massacre, *after the same manner, and with the same words*, we have heard it related hitherto. *So* the report remained and was believed, by all who resided in the Indian country. *So* it was represented numbers of times, in the peaceable Delaware towns, by the enemy. *So* the christian Indians were continually told they would one day be served. With *this* impression, a petty chief hurried all the way from Wabash in 1779 to take his relations (who were living with the peaceable Delawares near Coshachking,) out of the reach of the Big Knives, in whose friendship he never more would place any confidence. And when this man found that his numerous relations, would not break friendship with the Americans, nor be removed, he took two of his relations (women) off by force, saying "The whole crop shall not be destroyed; I will have seed out of it for a new crop:" alluding to, and repeatedly reminding these of the family of Logan, who, he said, had been real friends to the whites, and yet were cruelly murdered by them.

In Detroit, where I arrived the same spring, the report respecting the murder of the Indians on Ohio (amongst whom was Logan's family) was the same as related above; and on my return to the United States in the fall of 1786, and from that time, whenever and wherever in my presence, this subject was the topic of conversation, I found the report still the same; *viz.* that a person bearing the name of Cresap, was the author or perpetrator of this deed.

LOGAN was the second son of SHIKELLEMUS, a celebrated chief of the Cayuga nation. This chief, on account of his attachment to the English government, was of great service to the country, having the confidence of all the Six nations as well as that of the English, he was very useful in settling disputes, &c. &c. He was highly esteemed by Conrad Weisser, Esq. (an officer for government in the Indian department,) with whom he acted conjunctly, and was faithful unto his death. His residence was at Shamokin, where he took great delight in acts of hospitality to such of the white people whose business led them that way.* His name and fame were so high on record, that count Zinzendorf, when in this country in 1742, became desirous of seeing him, and actually visited him at his house in Shamokin.† About the year 1772, Logan was introduced to me, by an Indian friend; as son to the late reputable chief Shikellemus, and as a friend to the white people. In the course of conversation, I thought him a man of superior talents, than Indians generally were. The subject turning on vice and immorality, he confessed his too great share of this, especially his fondness for liquor. He exclaimed against the white people, for imposing liquors upon the Indians; he otherwise admired their ingenuity; spoke of gentlemen, but observed that the Indians unfortunately had but few of these as their neighbors, &c. He spoke of his friendship to the white people, wished always to be a neighbor to them, intended to settle on the Ohio, below Big Beaver; was (to the best of my recollection) then encamped at the mouth of this river, (Beaver,) urged me to pay him a visit, &c. *Note.* I was then living in the Moravian Town on this river, in the neighborhood of Cuskuskee. In April 1773, while on my passage down the Ohio for Muskinghum, I called at Logan's settlement; where I received every civility I could expect from such of the family as were at home.

Indian reports concerning Logan, after the death of his family, ran to this; that he exerted himself during the Shawnee war (then so called) to take all the revenge he could, declaring he had lost

---

*The preceding account of Shikellemus (Logan's father), is copied from manuscripts of the Rev. C. Pyrlooeus,[14] written between the years 1741, and 1748.

†See G. H. Loskiel's[15] history of the Mission of the United Brethren &c. Part II. Chap. II, page 31.

all confidence in the white people. At the time of negociation, he declared his reluctance in laying down the hatchet, not having (in his opinion) yet taken ample satisfaction; yet, for the sake of the nation, he would do it. His expressions, from time to time, denoted a deep melancloly. Life (said he) had become a torment to him: he knew no more what pleasure was: He thought it had been better if he had never existed, &c. &c. Report further states, that he became in some measure delirious, declared he would kill himself, went to Detroit, drank very freely, and did not seem to care what he did, and what became of himself. In this condition he left Detroit, and, on his way between that place and Miami, was murdered. In October, 1781, (while as prisoner on my way to Detroit,) I was shown the spot where this shall have happened. Having had an opportunity since last June of seeing the Rev. David Zeisberger, senior, missionary to the Delaware nation of Indians, who had resided among the same on Muskinghum, at the time when the murder was committed on the family of Logan, I put the following questions to him. 1. Who he understood it was that had committed the murder on Logan's family? And secondly, whether he had any knowledge of a speech sent to lord Dunmore by Logan, in consequence of this affair, &c. To which Mr. Zeisberger's answer was: That he had, from that time when this murder was committed to the present day, firmly believed the common report (which he had never heard contradicted,) *viz.* that one Cresap was the author of the massacre; or that it was committed by his orders: and that he had known Logan as a boy, had frequently seen him from that time and doubted not in the least, that Logan had sent such a speech to lord Dunmore on this occasion, as he understood from me had been published; that expressions of that kind from Indians were familiar to him; that Logan in particular, was a man of quick comprehension, good judgment and talents. Mr. Zeisberger has been a missionary upwards of fifty years; his age is about eighty; speaks both the language of the Onondagoes and the Delawares; resides at present on the Muskinghum, with his Indian congregation; and is beloved and respected by all who are acquainted with him.

JOHN HECKEWELDER.

From this testimony the following historical statement results:

In April or May 1774, a number of people being engaged in looking out for settlements on the Ohio, information was spread among them that the Indians had robbed some of the *land-jobbers*, as those adventurers were called.

1st murder of the two Indians by Cresap.

Alarmed for their safety, they collected together at Wheeling creek. Hearing that there were two Indians and some traders a little above Wheeling, captain Michael Cresap, one of the party, proposed to waylay and kill them. The proposition, though opposed, was adopted. A party went up the river, with Cresap at their head, and killed the two Indians.

2d murder on Grave creek.

The same afternoon it was reported that there was a party of Indians on the Ohio, a little below Wheeling. Cresap and his party immediately proceeded down the river, and encamped on the bank. The Indians passed him peaceably, and encamped at the mouth of Grave creek, a little below. Cresap and his party attacked them, and killed several. The Indians returned the fire, and wounded one of Cresap's party. Among the slain of the Indians were some of Logans family. Colonel Zane indeed expresses a doubt of it; but it is affirmed by Huston and Chambers. Smith, one of the murderers, said they were known and acknowledged to be Logan's friends, and the party themselves generally said so: boasted of it in presence of Cresap; pretended no provocation; and expressed their expectations that Logan would probably avenge their deaths.

Massacre at Baker's Bottom
opposite Yellow creek, by Greathouse.

Pursuing these examples, Daniel Greathouse and one Tomlinson, who lived on the opposite side of the river from the Indians, and were in habits of friendship with them, collected at the house of Polke on Cross creek, about 16 miles from Baker's Bottom a party of 32 men. Their object was to attack a hunting encampment of Indians, consisting of men, women and children, at the mouth of Yellow creek, some distance above Wheeling.—They proceeded, and when arrived near Baker's Bottom, they concealed themselves, and Greathouse crossed the river to the Indian camp. Being among them as a friend, he counted them, and found them too strong for an open attack with his force. While here, he was cautioned by one of the women not to stay, for that the Indian men were drinking, and having heard of Cresap's murder of *their relations* at Grave creek, were angry, and she pressed him, in a friendly manner, to go home; whereupon, after inviting them to come over and drink, he returned to Baker's, which was a tavern, and desired that when any of them should come to his house he would give them as much rum as they would drink. When his plot was ripe and a sufficient number of them were collected at Baker's, and intoxicated, he and his party fell on them and massacred the whole, except a little girl, whom they preserved as a prisoner. Among these was the very woman who had saved his life, by pressing him to retire from the drunken wrath of her friends, when he was spying their camp at Yellow creek. Either she herself, or some other of the murdered women, was the sister of Logan, very big with child, and inhumanly and indecently butchered; and there were others of his relations who fell there.

4th murder by Greathouse.

The party on the other side of the river, alarmed for their friends at Baker's, on hearing the report of the guns, manned two canoes and sent them over. They were received, as they approached the shore, by a well directed fire from Greathouse's party, which killed some, wounded others, and obliged the rest to put back. Baker tells us there were twelve killed, and six or eight wounded.

This commenced the war, of which Logan's war-club and note left in the house of a murdered family, was the notification. In the course of it, during the ensuing summer, great numbers of innocent men, women and children, fell victims to the tomahawk and scalping knife of the Indians, till it was arrested in the autumn following by the battle at Point-Pleasant and as the pacification with Lord Dunmore, at which the speech of Logan was delivered.

Of the genuineness of that speech nothing need be said. It

was known to the camp where it was delivered: it was given out by Lord Dunmore and his officers; it ran through the public papers of these states; was rehearsed as an exercise at schools; published in the papers aud periodical works of Europe; and all this, a dozen years before it was copied into the Notes on Virginia. In fine gen. Gibson concludes the question for ever, by declaring that he received it from Logan's hand, delivered it to Lord Dunmore, translated it for him, and that the copy in the Notes on Virginia is a faithful copy.

The popular account of these transactions, as stated in the Notes on Virginia, appears on collecting exact information, imperfect and erroneous in its details. It was the belief of the day; but how far its errors were to the prejudice of Cresap the reader will now judge. That he and those under him, murdered two Indians above Wheeling: that they murdered a larger number at Grave creek, among whom were a part of the family and relations of Logan, cannot be questioned; and as little that this led to the massacre of the rest of the family at Yellow creek. Logan imputed the whole to Cresap in his war-note and peace-speech; the Indians generally imputed it to Cresap: Lord Dunmore and his officers imputed it to Cresap: the country with one accord imputed it to him: and whether he were innocent let the universal verdict now declare.

I propose that in any future edition of the Notes on Virginia, the passage relating to this subject shall stand in the following form:

"In the spring of the year 1774, a robbery was committed by some Indians on certain land adventurers on the river Ohio. The whites in that quarter, according to their custom, undertook to punish this outrage in a summary way. Captain Michael Cresap, and a certain Daniel Greathouse, leading on these parties, surprized, at different times, travelling and hunting parties of the Indians, having their women and children with them, and murdered many. Among these were unfortunately the family of Logan, a chief celebrated in peace and war, and long distinguished as the friend of the whites. This unworthy return provoked his vengeance. He accordingly signalized himself in the war which ensued. In the autumn of the same year a decisive battle was fought at the mouth of the Great Kanhaway, between the collected forces of the Shawanese, Mingoes and Delawares, and a detachment of the Virginia militia. The Indians were defeated and sued for peace. Logan, however, disdained to be seen among the suppliants. But lest the sincerity of a treaty should be distrusted, from which so distinguished a chief absented himself, he sent, by a messenger, the following speech, to be delivered to Lord Dunmore."[16]

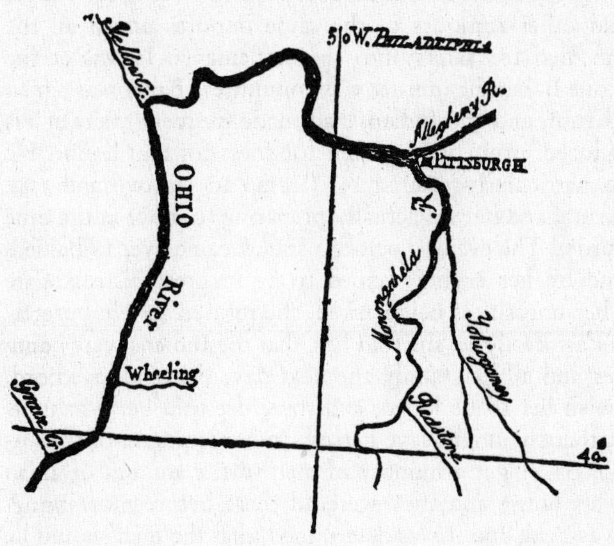

The declaration of JOHN SAPPINGTON, *received after the publication of the preceding Appendix.*

I, JOHN SAPPINGTON, *declare myself to be intimately acquainted with all the circumstances respecting the destruction of Logan's family, and do give in the following narrative a true statement of that affair.*

Logan's family (if it was his family) was not killed by Cresap, nor with his knowledge, nor by his consent, but by the Greathouses and their associates. They were killed 30 miles above Wheeling, near the mouth of Yellow Creek. Logan's camp was on one side of the river Ohio, and the house, where the murder was committed, opposite to it on the other side. They had encamped there only four or five days, and during that time had lived peaceably and neighborly with the whites on the opposite side, until the very day the affair happened. A little before the period alluded to, letters had been received by the inhabitants from a man of great influence in that country, and who was then I believe at Capteener, informing them that war was at hand, and desiring them to be on their guard. In consequence of these letters and other rumours of the same import, almost all the inhabitants fled for safety into the settlements. It was at the house of one Baker the murder was committed. Baker was a man who sold rum, and the Indians had made frequent visits at his house, induced, probably, by their fondness for that liquor. He had been particularly desired by Cresap to remove and take away his rum, and he was actually preparing to move at the time of the murder. The evening before a squaw came over to Baker's house, and by her crying seemed to be in great distress. The cause of her uneasiness being asked, she refused to tell; but getting Baker's wife alone, she told her, that the Indians were going to kill her and all her family the next day, that she loved her, did not wish her to be killed, and therefore told her what was intended, that she might save herself. In consequence of this information, Baker got a number of men to the amount of 21 to come to his house and they were all there before morning. A council was held, and it was determined, that the men should lie concealed in the back apartment; that if the Indians did come and behaved themselves peaceably, they should not be molested; but if not, the men were to shew themselves and act accordingly. Early in the morning 7 Indians, 4 men and 3 squaws, came over.—Logan's brother was one of them. They immediately got rum, and all, except Logan's brother, became very much intoxicated. At this time all the men were concealed, except the man of the house, Baker, and two others who staid out with him. Those Indians came unarmed. After some time Logan's brother took down a coat and hat belonging to Baker's brother-in-law, who lived with him, and put them on, and setting his arms a kimbo began to strut about, till at length coming up to one of the men, he attempted to strike him, saying "white man, son of a bitch." The white man, whom he treated thus, kept out of his way for some time; but growing irritated he jumped to his gun, and shot the Indian as he was making to the door with the coat and hat on him. The men who lay concealed, then rushed out and killed the whole of them, excepting one child, which I believe is yet alive. But before this happened, one with two, the other with five Indians, all naked, painted, and armed completely for war, were discovered to start from the shore on which Logan's camp was. Had it not been for this circumstance, the white men would not have acted as they did; but this confirmed what the squaw had told before. The white men, having killed as aforesaid the Indians in the house, ranged themselves along the bank of the river, to receive the canoes. The canoe with the two Indians came near, being the foremost. Our men fired upon them and killed them both. The other canoe then went back. After this two other canoes started, the one containing 11, the other 7 Indians, painted and armed as the first. They attempted to land below our men; but were fired upon, had one killed, and retreated, at the same time firing back. To the best of my recollection there were three of the Greathouses engaged in this business. This is a true representation of the affair from beginning to end. I was intimately acquainted with Cresap, and know he had no hand in that transaction. He told me himself afterwards at Redstone old fort, that the day before Logan's people were killed, he, with a small party, had an engagement with a party of Indians on Capteener, about 44 miles lower down. Logan's people were killed at the mouth of Yellow creek on the 24th of May, 1774, and on the 23d, the day before Cresap was engaged as already stated. I know likewise that he was generally blamed for it, and believed by all who were not acquainted with the circumstances, to have been the perpetrator of it. I know that he despised and hated the Greathouses ever afterwards on account of it. I was intimately acquainted with general Gibson, and served under him during the late war, I have a discharge from him now lying in the land office at Richmond, to which I refer any person for my character, who might be disposed to scruple my veracity. I was likewise at the treaty held by lord Dunmore with the Indians at Chelicothe. As for the speech said to have been delivered by Logan on that occasion, it might have been, or might not, for any thing I know, as I never heard of it till long afterwards. I do not believe that Logan had any relations killed except his brother. Neither of the Squaws who were killed was his wife. Two of them were old women, and the third, with her child which was saved, I have the best reason in the world to believe was the wife and child of general Gibson. I know he educated the child, and took care of it, as if it had been his own. Whether Logan had a wife or not, I cannot say; but it is probable that as he was a chief, he considered them all as his people. All this I am ready to be qualified to at any time.

JOHN SAPPINGTON.

Attest, SAMUEL M'KEE, Junr.
Madison County, Feb. 13th, 1800.

I do certify further that the above named John Sappington told me, at the same time and place at which he gave me the above narrative, that he himself was the man who shot the brother of Logan in the house as above related, and that he likewise killed one of the Indians in one of the canoes, which came over from the opposite shore.

He likewise told me, that Cresap never said an angry word to him about the matter, although he was frequently in company with Cresap, and indeed had been, and continued to be, in habits of intimacy with that gentleman, and was always befriended by him on every occasion. He further told me, that after they had perpetrated the murder, and were flying into the settlements, he met with Cresap (if I recollect right, at Redstone old fort,) and gave him a scalp, a very large fine one, as he expressed it and adorned with silver. This scalp I think he told me; was the scalp of Logan's brother; though as to this I am not absolutely certain.

Certified by SAMUEL M'KEE, Junr.

FINIS.

LETTERS AND DOCUMENTS

1. QUERIES ORIGINALLY POSED BY FRANÇOIS MARBOIS[1]

1. The Charters of your State.
2. The Present Constitution.
3. An exact description of its limits and boundaries.
4. The Memoirs published in its name in the time of its being a Colony and the pamphlets relating to its interior or exterior affairs present or ancient.
5. The History of the State.
6. A notice of the Counties, Cities, Townships, Villages, Rivers, Rivulets, and how far they are navigable. Cascades, Caverns, Mountains, Productions, Trees, Plants, Fruits, and other natural Riches.
7. The number of its Inhabitants.
8. The different Religions received in that State.
9. The Colleges and public establishments. The Roads, Buildings &c.
10. The Administration of Justice and a description of the Laws.
11. The particular Customs and manners that may happen to be received in that State.
12. The present State of Manufactures, Commerce, interior and exterior Trade.
13. A notice of the best Sea Ports of the State and how big are the vessels they can receive.
14. A notice of the commercial productions particular to that State and of those objects which the Inhabitants are obliged to get from Europe and from other parts of the World.
15. The weight, measures, and the currency of the hard money. Some details relating to the exchange with Europe.
16. The public income and expenses.
17. The measures taken with regard of the Estates and Possessions of the Rebels commonly called Tories.

18. The condition of the Regular Troops and the Militia and their pay.
19. The marine and Navigation.
20. A notice of the Mines and other subterranean riches.
21. Some Samples of these Mines and of the extraordinary Stones. In short a notice of all what can increase the progress of human knowledge.
22. A description of the Indians established in the State before the European Settlements and of those who are still remaining. An indication of the Indian Monuments discovered in that State.

2. JEFFERSON TO THE MARQUIS DE CHASTELLUX,[2] JUNE 7, 1785

Dear Sir,—I have been honored with the receipt of your letter of the 2nd instant, and am to thank you, as I do sincerely, for the partiality with which you receive the copy of the Notes on my country. As I can answer for the facts therein reported on my own observation, and have admitted none on the report of others, which were not supported by evidence sufficient to command my own assent, I am not afraid that you should make any extracts you please for the Journal de Physique, which come within their plan of publication. The strictures on slavery and on the constitution of Virginia, are not of that kind, and they are the parts which I do not wish to have made public, at least, till I know whether their publication would do most harm or good. It is possible, that in my own country, these strictures might produce an irritation, which would indispose the people towards the two great objects I have in view; that is, the emancipation of their slaves, and the settlement of their constitution on a firmer and more permanent basis. If I learn from thence, that they will not produce that effect, I have printed and reserved just copies enough to be able to give one to every young man at the College. It is to them I look, to the rising generation, and not to the one now in power, for these great reformations. The other copy, delivered at your hotel, was for Monsieur de Buffon. I meant to ask the favor of you to have it sent to him, as I was ignorant how to do it. I have one also for Monsieur Daubenton, but being utterly unknown to him, I cannot take the liberty of presenting it, till I can do it through some common acquaintance.

I will beg leave to say here a few words on the general question of the degeneracy of animals in America. 1. As to the degeneracy of the man of Europe transplanted to America, it is no part of Monsieur de Buffon's system. He goes, indeed, within one step of it, but he stops there. The Abbé Raynal alone has taken that step. Your knowledge of America enables you to judge this question, to say, whether the lower class of people in America, are less informed and less susceptible of information, than the lower class in Europe: and whether those in America, who have received such an education as that country can give, are less improved by it than Europeans of the same degree of education. 2. As to the aboriginal man of America, I know of no respectable evidence on which the opinion of his inferiority of genius has been founded, but that of Don Ulloa. As to Robertson,[3] he never was in America, he relates nothing on his own knowledge, he is a compiler only of the relations of others, and a mere translator of the opinions of Monsieur de Buffon. I should as soon, therefore, add the translators of Robertson to the witnesses of this fact, as himself. Paw, the beginner of this charge, was a compiler from the works of others; and of the most unlucky description; for he seems to have read the writings of travellers, only to collect and republish their lies. It is really remarkable, that in three volumes 12mo, of small print, it is scarcely possible to find one truth, and yet, that the author should be able to produce authority for every fact he states, as he says he can. Don Ulloa's testimony is of the most respectable. He wrote of what he saw, but he saw the Indian of South America only, and that, after he had passed through ten generations of slavery. It is very unfair, from this sample, to judge of the natural genius of this race of men; and after supposing that Don Ulloa had not sufficiently calculated the allowance which should be made for this circumstance, we do him no injury in considering the picture he draws of the present Indians of South America, as no picture of what their ancestors were, three hundred years ago. It is in North America we are to seek their original character. And I am safe in affirming, that the proofs of genius given by the Indians of North America, place them on a level with whites in the same uncultivated state. The North of Europe furnishes subjects enough for comparison with them, and for a proof of their equality. I have seen some thousands myself, and conversed much with them, and have found in them a masculine, sound understanding. I have had much information from men who had lived among them, and whose veracity and good sense were so far known to me, as to establish a reliance on their information. They have all agreed in bearing witness in favor of the genius of this people. As to their bodily strength, their manners rendering it disgraceful to labor, those muscles employed in labor will be weaker with them, than with the European laborer; but those which are exerted in the chase, and those faculties which are employed in the tracing an enemy or a wild beast, in contriving ambuscades for him, and in carrying them through their execution, are much stronger than with us, because they are more exercised. I believe the Indian, then, to be, in body and mind, equal to the white man. I have supposed the black man, in his present state, might not be so; but it would be hazardous to affirm, that, equally cultivated for a few generations, he would not become so. 3. As to the inferiority of the other animals of America, without more facts, I can add nothing to what I have said in my Notes.

As to the theory of Monsieur de Buffon, that heat is friendly, and moisture adverse to the production of large animals, I am lately furnished with a fact by Dr. Franklin, which proves the air of London and of Paris to be more humid than that of Philadelphia, and so creates a suspicion that the opinion of the superior humidity of America may, perhaps, have been too hastily adopted. And supposing that fact admitted, I think the physical reasonings urged to show, that in a moist country animals must be small, and that in a hot one they must be large, are not built on the basis of experiment. These questions, however, cannot be decided, ultimately, at this day. More facts must be collected, and more time flow off, before the world will be ripe for decision. In the mean time, doubt is wisdom.

I have been fully sensible of the anxieties of your situation, and that your attentions were wholly consecrated, where alone they were wholly due, to the succour of friendship and worth. However much I prize your society, I wait with patience the moment when I can have it without taking what is due to another. In the mean time, I am solaced with the hope of possessing your friendship, and that it is not ungrateful to you to receive assurances of that with which I have the honor to be, Dear Sir,

your most obedient,
and most humble servant,
TH. JEFFERSON

3. PRESENTATION INSCRIPTION TO LAFAYETTE[4]

Th. Jefferson begs the Marquis de La Fayette's acceptance of a copy of these Notes. The Circumstances under which they were written, and the talents of the writer, will account for their errors and defects. The original was sent to Mr. de Marbois in December 1781.

The desire of a friend to possess some of the details they contained occasioned him to revise them in the subsequent winter. The vices however of their original composition were such as to forbid material amendment. He now has a few copies printed with a design of offering them to some of his friends, and to some estimable characters beyond that line. A copy is presented to the Marquis de La Fayette whose services to the American Union in general, and to that member of it particularly which is the subject of these Notes and in that precise point of time too to which they relate, entitle him to this offering.

To these considerations the writer hopes he may be permitted to add his own personal friendship and esteem for the Marquis. Unwilling to expose these sheets to the public eye, the writer begs the favor of the Marquis to put them into the hands of no person on whose care and fidelity he cannot rely to guard them against publication.

4. DR. RICHARD PRICE[5] *TO JEFFERSON, JULY 2, 1785*

Dear Sir,

This letter will probably be deliver'd to you by *Dr. D'Ivernois*, lately a citizen of Geneva, and the author of an interesting work lately publishe'd and entitled *An Historical and Political view of the constitution and Revolutions of Geneva in the 18th century*. He wishes to be introduced to you; and I doubt not but the respectableness of his character and abilities and the active part he has taken in defending the liberties of a republic once happy but now ruined, will recommend him to your notice and esteem. His habits and principles carry his views to America; and should he remove thither he will make a very valuable addition to the number of virtuous and enlighten'd citizens in the united States.

Accept my best thanks for the account of Virginia which you were so good as to Send me by Mr. Adams. This has been, indeed, a most acceptable present to me, and you may depend on my performing the condition upon which you have honoured me with it. I have read it with Singular pleasure and a warm admiration of your Sentiments and character. How happy would the united States be were all of them under the direction of Such wisdom and liberality as yours?—But this is not the case. I have lately been discouraged by an account which I have received from Mr. Laurens in South-Carolina. Mr. *Grimkey* the Speaker of the House of Representatives, and Mr. *Izard*[6] have agree'd in reprobating my pamphlet on the American Revolution because it recommends measures for preventing too great an inequality of property and for gradually abolishing the Negro trade and Slavery; these being measures which (as the former says in a letter to Mr. Laurens) will never find encouragement in that State: and it appears that Mr. *Grimkey* though himself almost affronted by having the pamphlet presented to him by Mr. Laurens. Should Such a disposition prevail in the other united States, I shall have reason to fear that I have made myself ridiculous by Speaking of the American Revolution in the manner I have done; it will appear that the people who have been struggling so earnestly to save *themselves* from Slavery are very ready to enslave *others*; the friends of liberty and humanity in *Europe* will be mortify'd, and an event which had raised their hopes will prove only an introduction to a new Scene of aristocratic tyranny and human debasement.

I am very happy in the acquaintance of Mr. Adams and Col. Smith.[7] I wish them Success in their mission, but I have reason to fear that this country is still under a cloud with respect to

America which threatens it with farther calamities.—With the greatest respect I am, Sir, Your very obedt: and humble Servant,

RICH. PRICE.

5. BENJAMIN BANNEKER[8] TO JEFFERSON, AUGUST 19, 1791

Sir

I am fully sensible of the greatness of that freedom which I take with you on the present occasion; a liberty which Seemed to me scarcely allowable, when I reflected on that distinguished, and dignifyed station in which you Stand; and the almost general prejudice and prepossession which is so prevailent in the world against those of my complexion.

I suppose it is a truth too well attested to you, to need a proof here, that we are a race of Beings who have long laboured under the abuse and censure of the world, that we have long been looked upon with an eye of contempt, and that we have long been considered rather as brutish than human, and Scarcely capable of mental endowments.

Sir I hope I may Safely admit, in consequence of that report which hath reached me, that you are a man far less inflexible in Sentiments of this nature, than many others, that you are measurably friendly and well disposed toward us, and that you are willing and ready to Lend your aid and assistance to our relief from those many distresses and numerous calamities to which we are reduced.

Now Sir if this is founded in truth, I apprehend you will readily embrace every opportunity to eradicate that train of absurd and false ideas and oppinions which so generally prevails with respect to us, and that your Sentiments are concurrent with mine, which are that one universal Father hath given being to us all, and that he hath not only made us all of one flesh, but that he hath also without partiality afforded us all the Same Sensations, and endued us all with the same faculties, and that however variable we may be in Society or religion, however diversifyed in Situation or colour, we are all of the Same Family, and Stand in the Same relation to him.

Sir, if these are Sentiments of which you are fully persuaded, I hope you cannot but acknowledge, that it is the indispensible duty of those who maintain for themselves the rights of human nature, and who profess the obligations of Christianity, to extend their power and influence to the relief of every part of the human race, from whatever burthen or oppression they may unjustly labour under, and this I apprehend a full conviction of the truth and obligation of these principles should lead all to.

Sir, I have long been convinced, that if your love for your Selves, and for those inesteemable laws which preserve to you the rights of human nature, was founded on Sincerity, you could not but be Solicitous, that every Individual of whatsoever rank or distinction, might with you equally enjoy the blessings thereof, neither could you rest Satisfyed, short of the most active diffusion of your exertions, in order to their promotion from any State of degradation, to which the unjustifyable cruelty and barbarism of men may have reduced them.

Sir I freely and Chearfully acknowledge, that I am of the African race, and in that colour which is natural to them of the deepest dye,* and it is under a Sense of the most profound gratitude to the Supreme Ruler of the universe, that I now confess to you, that I am not under that State of tyrannical thraldom, and inhuman captivity, to which too many of my brethren are doomed; but that I have abundantly tasted of the fruition of those blessings which proceed from that free and unequalled liberty with which you are favoured and which I hope you will willingly allow you have received from the immediate hand of that Being, from whom proceedeth every good and perfect gift.

Sir, Suffer me to recall to your mind that time in which the Arms and tyranny of the British Crown were exerted with every powerful effort in order to reduce you to a State of Servitude, look back I intreat you on the variety of dangers to which you were exposed, reflect on that time in which every human aid appeared unavailable, and in which even hope and fortitude wore the aspect of inability to the Conflict, and you cannot but be led to a Serious and grateful Sense of your miraculous and providential preservation; you cannot but acknowledge, that the

---

*My Father was brought here a S[lav]e from Africa.

present freedom and tranquility which you enjoy you have mercifully received, and that it is the peculiar blessing of Heaven.

This Sir, was a time in which you clearly saw into the injustice of a State of Slavery, and in which you had just apprehensions of the horrors of its condition, it was now Sir, that your abhorrence thereof was so excited, that you publickly held forth this true and invaluable doctrine, which is worthy to be recorded and remember'd in all Succeeding ages. "We hold these truths to be Self evident, that all men are created equal, and that they are endowed by their creator with certain unalienable rights, that among these are life, liberty, and the pursuit of happyness."

Here Sir, was a time in which your tender feelings for your selves had engaged you thus to declare, you were then impressed with proper ideas of the great valuation of liberty, and the free possession of those blessings to which you were entitled by nature; but Sir how pitiable is it to reflect, that altho you were so fully convinced of the benevolence of the Father of mankind, and of his equal and impartial distribution of those rights and privileges which he had conferred upon them, that you should at the Same time counteract his mercies, in detaining by fraud and violence so numerous a part of my brethren under groaning captivity and cruel oppression, that you should at the Same time be found guilty of that most criminal act, which you professedly detested in others, with respect to yourselves.

Sir, I suppose that your knowledge of the situation of my brethren is too extensive to need a recital here; neither shall I presume to prescribe methods by which they may be relieved; otherwise than by recommending to you and all others, to wean yourselves from these narrow prejudices which you have imbibed with respect to them, and as Job proposed to his friends "Put your Souls in their Souls stead," thus shall your hearts be enlarged with kindness and benevolence toward them, and thus shall you need neither the direction of myself or others in what manner to proceed herein.

And now, Sir, altho my Sympathy and affection for my brethren hath caused my enlargement thus far, I ardently hope that your candour and generosity will plead with you in my behalf, when I make known to you, that it was not originally my design; but that having taken up my pen in order to direct to you as a present, a copy of an Almanack which I have calculated for the Succeeding year, I was unexpectedly and unavoidably led thereto.

This calculation, Sir, is the production of my arduous Study in this my advanced Stage of life; for having long had unbounded desires to become acquainted with the Secrets of nature, I have had to gratify my curiosity herein thro my own assiduous application to Astronomical Study, in which I need not to recount to you the many difficulties and disadvantages which I have had to encounter.

And altho I had almost declined to make my calculation for the ensuing year, in consequence of that time which I had allotted therefor being taking up at the Federal Territory by the request of Mr. Andrew Ellicott, yet finding myself under Several engagements to printers of this state to whom I had communicated my design, on my return to my place of residence, I industriously apply'd myself thereto, which I hope I have accomplished with correctness and accuracy, a copy of which I have taken the liberty to direct to you, and which I humbly request you will favourably receive, and altho you may have the opportunity of perusing it after its publication, yet I chose to send it to you in manuscript previous thereto, that thereby you might not only have an earlier inspection, but that you might also view it in my own hand writing.—And now Sir, I shall conclude and Subscribe my Self with the most profound respect your most Obedient humble Servant,

BENJAMIN BANNEKER

6. JEFFERSON TO BENJAMIN BANNEKER, AUGUST 30, 1791[9]

Sir,—I thank you sincerely for your letter of the 19th instant and for the Almanac it contained. No body wishes more than I do to see such proofs as you exhibit, that nature has given to our black brethren, talents equal to those of the other colors of men, and that the appearance of a want of them is owing merely to the degraded condition of their existence, both in Africa & America. I can add with truth, that no body wishes more ardently to see a good system commenced for raising the condition both of their body & mind to what it ought to be, as fast as the imbecility of their present existence, and other circumstances which cannot be neglected, will admit. I have taken the liberty of sending your Almanac to Monsieur de Condorcet, Secretary of the Academy of Sciences at Paris, and member of the Philanthropic society, because I considered it as a document to which your whole colour had a right for their justification against the doubts which have been entertained of them. I am with great esteem, Sir Your most obed^t^ humble serv^t^.

TH. JEFFERSON

7. JEFFERSON TO MARQUIS DE CONDORCET,[10] *AUGUST 30, 1791.*

Dear Sir,

I am to acknoledge the receipt of your favor on the subject of the element of measure adopted by France. Candor obliges me to confess that it is not what I would have approved. It is liable to the inexactitude of mensuration as to that part of the quadrant of the earth which is to be measured, that is to say as to one tenth of the quadrant, and as to the remaining nine tenths they are to be calculated on conjectural data, presuming the figure of the earth which has not yet been proved. It is liable too to the objection that no nation but your own can come at it; because yours is the only nation within which a meridian can be found of such extent crossing the 45th. degree and terminating at both ends in a level. We may certainly say then that this measure is uncatholic, and I would rather have seen you depart from Catholicism in your religion than in your Philosophy.

I am happy to be able to inform you that we have now in the United States a negro, the son of a black man born in Africa, and of a black woman born in the United States, who is a very respectable Mathematician. I procured him to be employed under one of our chief directors in laying out the new federal city on the Patowmac, and in the intervals of his leisure, while on that work, he made an Almanac for the next year, which he sent me in his own handwriting, and which I inclose to you. I have seen very elegant solutions of Geometrical problems by him. Add to this that he is a very worthy and respectable member of society. He is a free man. I shall be delighted to see these instances of moral eminence so multiplied as to prove that the want of talents observed in them is merely the effect of their degraded condition, and not proceeding from any difference in the structure of the parts on which intellect depends.

I am looking ardently to the completion of the glorious work in which your country is engaged. I view the general condition of Europe as hanging on the success or failure of France. Having set such an example of philosophical arrangement within, I hope it will be extended without your limits also, to your dependants and to your friends in every part of the earth.—Present my affectionate respects to Madame de Condorcet, and accept yourself assurance of the sentiments of esteem & attachment with which I have the honour to be Dear Sir Your most obedt & most humble servt,

TH. JEFFERSON

JEFFERSON TO JAMES MONROE[11] *NOVEMBER 24, 1801*

Dear Sir,—I had not been unmindful of your letter of June 15, covering a resolution of the House of Representatives of Virginia, and referred to in yours of the 17th inst. The importance of the subject, and the belief that it gave us time for consideration till the next meeting of the Legislature, have induced me to defer the answer to this date. You will perceive that some circumstances connected with the subject, & necessarily presenting themselves to view, would be improper but for yours' & the legislative ear. Their publication might have an ill effect in more than one quarter. In confidence of attention to this, I shall indulge greater freedom in writing.

Common malefactors, I presume, make no part of the object of that resolution. Neither their numbers, nor the nature of their offences, seem to require any provisions beyond those practised heretofore, & found adequate to the repression of ordinary crimes. Conspiracy, insurgency, treason, rebellion, among that description of persons who brought on us the alarm, and on themselves the tragedy, of 1800,[12] were doubtless within the view of every one; but many perhaps contemplated, and one expression of the resolution might comprehend, a much larger scope.

Respect to both opinions makes it my duty to understand the resolution in all the extent of which it is susceptible.

The idea seems to be to provide for these people by a purchase of lands; and it is asked whether such a purchase can be made of the U S in their western territory? A very great extent of country, north of the Ohio, has been laid off into townships, and is now at market, according to the provisions of the acts of Congress, with which you are acquainted. There is nothing which would restrain the State of Virginia either in the purchase or the application of these lands; but a purchase, by the acre, might perhaps be a more expensive provision than the H of Representatives contemplated. Questions would also arise whether the establishment of such a colony within our limits, and to become a part of our union, would be desirable to the State of Virginia itself, or to the other States—especially those who would be in its vicinity?

Could we procure lands beyond the limits of the U S to form a receptacle for these people? On our northern boundary, the country not occupied by British subjects, is the property of Indian nations, whose title would be to be extinguished, with the consent of Great Britain; & the new settlers would be British subjects. It is hardly to be believed that either Great Britain or the Indian proprietors have so disinterested a regard for us, as to be willing to relieve us, by receiving such a colony themselves; and as much to be doubted whether that race of men could long exist in so rigorous a climate. On our western & southern frontiers, Spain holds an immense country, the occupancy of which, however, is in the Indian natives, except a few insulated spots possessed by Spanish subjects. It is very questionable, indeed, whether the Indians would sell? whether Spain would be willing to receive these people? and nearly certain that she would not alienate the sovereignty. The same question to ourselves would recur here also, as did in the first case: should we be willing to have such a colony in contact with us? However our present interests may restrain us within our own limits, it is impossible not to look forward to distant times, when our rapid multiplication will expand itself beyond those limits, & cover the whole northern, if not the southern continent, with a people speaking the same language, governed in similar forms, & by similar laws;

nor can we contemplate with satisfaction either blot or mixture on that surface. Spain, France, and Portugal hold possessions on the southern continent, as to which I am not well enough informed to say how far they might meet our views. But either there or in the northern continent, should the constituted authorities of Virginia fix their attention, of preference, I will have the dispositions of those powers sounded in the first instance.

The West Indies offer a more probable & practicable retreat for them. Inhabited already by a people of their own race & color; climates congenial with their natural constitution; insulated from the other descriptions of men; nature seems to have formed these islands to become the receptacle of the blacks transplanted into this hemisphere. Whether we could obtain from the European sovereigns of those islands leave to send thither the persons under consideration, I cannot say; but I think it more probable than the former propositions, because of their being already inhabited more or less by the same race. The most promising portion of them is the island of St. Domingo, where the blacks are established into a sovereignty *de facto*, & have organized themselves under regular laws & government. I should conjecture that their present ruler might be willing, on many considerations, to receive even that description which would be exiled for acts deemed criminal by us, but meritorious, perhaps, by him. The possibility that these exiles might stimulate & conduct vindicative or predatory descents on our coasts, & facilitate concert with their brethren remaining here, looks to a state of things between that island & us not probable on a contemplation of our relative strength, and of the disproportion daily growing; and it is overweighed by the humanity of the measures proposed, & the advantages of disembarrassing ourselves of such dangerous characters. Africa would offer a last & undoubted resort, if all others more desirable should fail us. Whenever the Legislature of Virginia shall have brought it's mind to a point, so that I may know exactly what to propose to foreign authorities, I will execute their wishes with fidelity & zeal. I hope, however, they will pardon me for suggesting a single question for their own consideration. When we contemplate the variety of countries & of sovereigns towards which we may direct our views, the vast revolutions & changes of circumstances which are now in a course of progression, the possibilities that arrangements now to be made, with a view to any particular plan, may, at no great distance of time, be totally deranged by a change of sovereignty, of government, or of other circumstances, it will be for the Legislature to consider whether, after they shall have made all those general provisions which may be fixed by legislative authority, it would be reposing too much confidence in their Executive to leave the place of relegation to be decided on by *them*. They could accommodate their arrangements to the actual state of things, in which countries or powers may be found to exist at the day; and may prevent the effect of the law from being defeated by intervening changes. This, however, is for them to decide. Our duty will be to respect their decision.

9. JEFFERSON TO JOEL BARLOW,[13] *OCTOBER 8, 1809*

Dear Sir,—It is long since I ought to have acknowledged the receipt of your most excellent oration on the 4th of July. I was doubting what you could say, equal to your own reputation on so hackneyed a subject; but you have really risen out of it with lustre, and pointed to others a field of great expansion. A day or two after I received your letter to Bishop Gregoire,[14] a copy of his diatribe to you came to hand from France. I had not before heard of it. He must have been eagle-eyed in quest of offence, to have discovered ground for it among the rubbish massed together in the print he animadverts on. You have done right in giving him a sugary answer. But he did not deserve it. For, notwithstanding a compliment to you now and then, he constantly returns to the identification of your sentiments with the extravagances of the Revolutionary zealots. I believe him a very good man, with imagination enough to declaim eloquently, but without judgment to decide. He wrote to me also on the doubts I had expressed five or six and twenty years ago, in the Notes of Virginia, as to the grade of understanding of the negroes, and he sent me his book on the literature of the negroes. His credulity has made him gather up every story he could find of men of color, (without distinguishing whether black, or of what degree of mixture,) however slight the mention, or light the authority on which they are quoted. The whole do not amount, in point of evidence, to what we know ourselves of Banneker. We know he had spherical trigonometry enough to make almanacs, but not without the suspicion of aid from Ellicot, who was his neighbor and friend, and never missed an opportunity of puffing him. I have a long letter from Banneker, which shows him to have had a mind of very common stature indeed. As to Bishop Gregoire, I wrote him, as you have done, a very soft answer. It was impossible for doubt to have been more tenderly or hesitatingly expressed than that was in the Notes of Virginia, and nothing was or is farther from my intentions, than to enlist myself as the champion of a fixed opinion, where I have only expressed a doubt. St. Domingo[15] will, in time, throw light on the question.

I intended, ere this, to have sent you the papers I had promised you. But I have taken up Marshall's fifth volume,[16] and mean to read it carefully, to correct what is wrong in it, and commit to writing such facts and annotations as the reading of that work will bring into my recollection, and which has not yet been put on paper; in this I shall be much aided by my memorandums and letters, and will send you both the old and the new. But I go on very slowly. In truth, during the pleasant season, I am always out of doors, employed, not passing more time at my writing table than will despatch my current business. But when the weather becomes cold, I shall go out but little. I hope, therefore, to get through this volume during the ensuing winter; but should you want the papers sooner, they shall be sent at a moment's warning. The ride from Washington to Monticello in the stage, or in a gig, is so easy that I had hoped you would have taken a flight here during the season of good roads. Whenever Mrs. Barlow is well enough to join you in such a visit, it must be taken more at ease. It will give us real pleasure whenever it may take place. I pray you to present me to her respectfully, and I salute you affectionately.

TH. JEFFERSON

10. JEFFERSON TO JOHN ADAMS, JUNE 11, 1812[17]

Dear Sir,—By our post preceding that which brought your letter of May 21st, I had received one from Mr. Malcolm on the same subject with yours, and by the return of the post had stated to the President my recollections of him. But both your letters were probably too late; as the appointment had been already made, if we may credit the newspapers.

You ask if there is any book that pretends to give any account of the traditions of the Indians, or how one can acquire an idea of them? Some scanty accounts of their traditions, but fuller of their customs and characters, are given us by most of the early travellers among them; these you know were mostly French. Lafitau,[18] among them, and Adair an Englishman, have written on this subject; the former two volumes, the latter one, all in 4to. But unluckily Lafitau had in his head a preconceived theory on the mythology, manners, institutions and government of the ancient nations of Europe, Asia and Africa, and seems to have entered on those of America only to fit them into the same frame, and to draw from them a confirmation of his general theory. He keeps up a perpetual parallel, in all those articles, between the Indians of America and the ancients of the other quarters of the globe. He selects, therefore, all the facts and adopts all the falsehoods which favor his theory, and very gravely retails such absurdities as zeal for a theory could alone swallow. He was a man of much classical and scriptural reading, and has rendered his book not unentertaining. He resided five years among the Northern Indians, as a Missionary, but collects his matter much more from the writings of others, than from his own observation.

Adair[19] too had his kink. He believed all the Indians of America to be descended from the Jews; the same laws, usages, rites and ceremonies, the same sacrifices, priests, prophets, fasts and festivals, almost the same religion, and that they all spoke Hebrew. For, although he writes particularly of the Southern Indians only, the Catawbas, Creeks, Cherokees, Chickasaws and Chocktaws, with whom alone he was personally acquainted, yet he generalizes whatever he found among them, and brings himself to believe that the hundred languages of America, differing fundamentally every one from every other, as much as Greek from Gothic, yet have all one common prototype. He was a trader, a man of learning, a self-taught Hebraist, a strong religionist, and of as sound a mind as Don Quixotte in whatever did not touch his religious chivalry. His book contains a great deal of real instruction on its subject, only requiring the reader to be constantly on his guard against the wonderful obliquities of his theory.

The scope of your inquiry would scarcely, I suppose, take in the three folio volumes of Latin of De Bry.[20] In these, facts and fable are mingled together, without regard to any favorite system. They are less suspicious, therefore, in their complexion, more original and authentic, than those of Lafitau and Adair. This is a work of great curiosity, extremely rare, so as never to be bought in Europe, but on the breaking up and selling some ancient library. On one of these occasions a bookseller procured me a copy, which, unless you have one, is probably the only one in America.

You ask further, if the Indians have any order of priesthood among them, like the Druids, Bards or Minstrels of the Celtic nations? Adair alone, determined to see what he wished to see in every object, metamorphoses their Conjurers into an order of priests, and describes their sorceries as if they were the great religious ceremonies of the nation. Lafitau called them by their proper names, Jongleurs, Devins, Sortileges; De Bry praestigiatores; Adair himself sometimes Magi, Archimagi, cunning men, Seers, rain makers; and the modern Indian interpreters call them conjurers and witches. They are persons pretending to have communications with the devil and other evil spirits, to foretell future events, bring down rain, find stolen goods, raise the dead, destroy some and heal others by enchantment, lay spells, &c. And Adair, without departing from his parallel of the Jews and Indians, might have found their counterpart much more aptly, among the soothsayers, sorcerers and wizards of the Jews, their Gannes and Gambres, their Simon Magus, Witch of Endor, and the young damsel whose sorceries disturbed Paul so much; instead of placing them in a line with their high-priest, their chief priests, and their magnificent hierarchy generally. In the solemn ceremonies of the Indians, the persons who direct or officiate, are their chiefs, elders and warriors, in civil ceremonies or in those of war; it is the head of the cabin in their private or particular feasts or ceremonies; and sometimes the matrons, as in their corn feasts. And even here, Adair might have kept up his parallel, with ennobling his conjurers. For the ancient patriarchs, the Noahs, the Abrahams, Isaacs and Jacobs, and even after the consecration of Aaron, the Samuels and Elijahs, and we may say further, every one for himself offered sacrifices on the altars. The true line of distinction seems to be, that solemn ceremonies, whether public or private, addressed to the Great Spirit, are conducted by the worthies of the nation, men or matrons, while conjurers are resorted to only for the invocation of evil spirits. The present state of the several Indian tribes, without any public order of priests, is proof sufficient that they never had such an order. Their steady habits permit no innovations, not even those which the progress of science offers to increase the comforts, enlarge the understanding, and improve the morality of mankind. Indeed, so little idea have they of a regular order of priests, that they mistake ours for their conjurers, and call them by that name.

So much in answer to your inquiries concerning Indians, a people with whom, in the early part of my life, I was very familiar, and acquired impressions of attachment and commiseration for them which have never been obliterated. Before the revolution, they were in the habit of coming often and in great numbers to the seat of government, where I was very much with them. I knew much the great Outassetè, the warrior and orator of the Cherokees; he was always the guest of my father, on his journeys to and from Williamsburg. I was in his camp when he made his great farewell oration to his people the evening before his departure for England. The moon was in full splendor, and to her he seemed to address himself in his prayers for his own safety on the voyage, and that of his people during his absence; his sounding voice, distinct articulation, animated action, and the solemn silence of his people at their several fires, filled me with awe and veneration, although I did not understand a word he uttered. That nation, consisting now of about 2,000 warriors, and the Creeks of about 3,000 are far advanced in civilization. They have good cabins, enclosed fields, large herds of cattle and hogs, spin and weave their own clothes of cotton, have smiths and other of the most necessary tradesmen, write and read, are on the increase in numbers, and a branch of Cherokees is now instituting a regular representative government. Some other tribes are advancing in the same line. On those who have made any progress, English seductions will have no effect. But the backward will yield, and be thrown further back. Those will relapse into barbarism and misery, lose numbers by war and want, and we shall be obliged to drive them with the beasts of the forest into the stony mountains. They will be conquered, however, in Canada. The possession of that country secures our women and children forever from the tomahawk and scalping knife, by removing those who excite them; and for this possession orders, I presume, are issued by this time; taking for granted that the doors of Congress will re-open with a declaration of war. That this may end in indemnity for the past, security for the future, and complete emancipation from Anglomany, Gallomany, and all the manias of demoralized Europe, and that you may live in health and happiness to see all this, is the sincere prayer of yours affectionately.

TH. JEFFERSON

11. JEFFERSON TO EDWARD COLES,[21] *AUGUST 25, 1814*

Dear Sir,—Your favour of July 31, was duly received, and was read with peculiar pleasure. The sentiments breathed through the whole do honor to both the head and heart of the writer. Mine on the subject of slavery of negroes have long since been in possession of the public, and time has only served to give them stronger root. The love of justice and the love of country plead equally the cause of these people, and it is a moral reproach to us that they should have pleaded it so long in vain, and should have produced not a single effort, nay I fear not much serious willingness to relieve them & ourselves from our present condition of moral & political reprobation. From those of the former generation who were in the fulness of age when I came into public life, which was while our controversy with England was on paper only, I soon saw that nothing was to be hoped. Nursed and educated in the daily habit of seeing the degraded condition, both bodily and mental, of those unfortunate beings, not reflecting that that degradation was very much the work of themselves & their fathers, few minds have yet doubted but that they were as legitimate subjects of property as their horses and cattle. The quiet and monotonous course of colonial life has been disturbed by no alarm, and little reflection on the value of liberty. And when alarm was taken at an enterprize on their own, it was not easy to carry them to the whole length of the principles which they invoked for themselves. In the first or second session of the Legislature after I became a member, I drew to this subject the attention of Col. Bland,[22] one of the oldest, ablest, & most respected members, and he undertook to move for certain moderate extensions of the protection of the laws to these people. I seconded his motion, and, as a younger member, was more spared in the debate; but he was denounced as an enemy of his country, & was treated with the grossest indecorum. From an early stage of our revolution other & more distant duties were assigned to me, so that from that time till my return from Europe in 1789, and I may say till I returned to reside at home in 1809, I had little opportunity of knowing the progress of public sentiment here on this subject. I had always hoped that the younger generation receiving their early impressions after the flame of liberty had been kindled in every breast, & had become as it were the vital spirit of every American, that the generous temperament of youth, analogous to the motion of their blood, and above the suggestions of avarice, would have sympathized with oppression wherever found, and proved their love of liberty beyond their own share of it. But my intercourse with them, since my return has not been sufficient to ascertain that they had made towards this point the progress I had hoped. Your solitary but welcome voice is the first which has brought this sound to my ear; and I have considered the general silence which prevails on this subject as indicating an apathy unfavorable to every hope. Yet the hour of emancipation is advancing, in the march of time. It will come; and whether brought on by the generous energy of our own minds; or by the bloody process of St. Domingo, excited and conducted by the power of our present enemy, if once stationed permanently within our Country, and offering asylum & arms to the oppressed, is a leaf of our history not yet turned over. As to the method by which this difficult work is to be effected, if permitted to be done by ourselves, I have seen no proposition so expedient on the whole, as that as emancipation of those born after a given day, and of their education and expatriation after a given age. This would give time for a gradual extinction of that species of labour & substitution of another, and lessen the severity of the shock which an operation so fundamental cannot fail to produce. For men probably of any color, but of this color we know, brought from their infancy without necessity for thought or forecast, are by their habits rendered as incapable as children of taking care of themselves, and are extinguished promptly whereever industry is necessary for raising young. In the mean time they are pests in society by their idleness, and the depredations to which this leads them. Their amalgamation with the other color produces a degradation to which no lover of his country, no lover of excellence in the human character can innocently consent. I am sensible of the partialities with which you have looked towards me as the person who should undertake this salutary but arduous work. But this, my dear sir, is like bidding old Priam to buckle the armour of Hector "trementibus aevo humeris et inutile ferrum cingitur."[23] No, I have overlived the generation with which mutual labors & perils begat mutual confidence and influence. This enterprise is for the young; for those who can follow it up, and bear it through to its consummation. It shall have all my prayers, & these are the only weapons of an old man. But in the mean time are you right in abandoning this property, and your country with it? I think not. My opinion has ever been that, until more can be done for them, we should endeavor, with those whom fortune has thrown on our hands, to feed and clothe them well, protect them from all ill usage, require such reasonable labor only as is performed voluntarily by freemen, & be led by no repugnancies to abdicate them, and our duties to them. The laws do not permit us to turn them loose, if that were for their good: and to commute them for other property is to commit them to those whose usage of them we cannot control. I hope then, my dear sir, you will reconcile yourself to your country and its unfortunate condition; that you will not lessen its stock of sound disposition by withdrawing your portion from the mass. That, on the contrary you will come forward in the public councils, become the missionary of this doctrine truly christian; insinuate & inculcate it softly but steadily, through the medium of writing and conversation; associate others in your labors, and when the phalanx is formed, bring on and press the proposition perseveringly until its accomplishment. It is an encouraging observation that no good measure was ever proposed, which, if duly pursued, failed to prevail in the end. We have proof of this in the history of the endeavors in the English parliament to suppress that very trade which brought this evil on us. And you will be supported by the religious precept, "be not weary in well-doing." That your success may be as speedy & complete, as it will be of honorable & immortal consolation to yourself, I shall as fervently and sincerely pray as I assure you of my great friendship and respect.

TH. JEFFERSON

EXPLANATORY AND TEXTUAL NOTES

Abbreviations: *TJ* = *Thomas Jefferson.*

Papers = *The Papers of Thomas Jefferson,* Julian P. Boyd, et al., eds. Princeton: Princeton University Press, 1950– . 27 volumes to date.

Ford = *The Writings of Thomas Jefferson,* Paul Leicester Ford, ed. New York: Putnam, 1898. 10 volumes.

INTRODUCTION

1. *D'Anmours: Papers,* 4:168.
2. *his father's "education":* Material in quotation marks in this paragraph is from TJ, *Autobiography,* in *Thomas Jefferson, Writings* (New York: Library of America, 1984), 3–4.
3. *the father of one:* Letter to Thomas Turpin, *Papers,* 1:24.
4. *Twenty years later:* Letter to John Garland Jefferson, *Thomas Jefferson, Writings,* 966–68.
5. *twenty-four years later:* Letter to John Minor, *Ford,* 9:480–81.
6. *James Monroe: Papers,* 6:185.
7. *Herman Melville's Ishmael:* Harrison Hayford and Hershel Parker, eds. *Moby-Dick* (New York: Norton, 1967), 128.
8. *wrote his friend Charles Thomson: Papers,* 6:142.
9. *informed a friend:* Letter to Marquis de Chastellux, *Papers,* 6:467.
10. *proposal of a decimal system:* See *Papers,* 7:150–202, for relevant documents and lengthy note by Julian Boyd.
11. *service on the committee:* For an account of TJ's involvement in developing the Ordinance of 1784, see Peter Onuf, *Statehood and Union: A History of the Northwest Ordinance* (Bloomington: Indiana University Press, 1987), 21–43.
12. *before his departure, he wrote Thomson: Papers,* 7:282.
13. *wrote his friend the Marquis: Papers,* 8:184.
14. *to Madison: Papers,* 8:147.

15. *a useful train of thought:* Letters to James Madison, *Papers*, 9:265; 8:148.

16. *"through my life":* Letter of October 7, 1809, to J. Riley in E. Millicent Sowerby, *Catalogue of the Library of Thomas Jefferson* (Charlottesville: University Press of Virginia, 1983), 4:326; *responding to a Philadelphia publisher:* Letter of December 10, 1814, to John Melish in Sowerby, 4:328.

17. *writing to Marbois: Papers*, 5:58.

18. *The "Rivers" chapter:* For a suggestive discussion of the role of rivers in republican thought, see John Seelye, *Beautiful Machine: Rivers and the Republican Plan, 1755–1825* (New York: Oxford University Press, 1991), esp. pp. 67–70.

19. *Comte de Buffon:* The definitive study of the debate about New World climate and life-forms is by Antonello Gerbi, *The Dispute of the New World: The History of a Polemic, 1750–1900*, trans. Jeremy Moyle (Pittsburgh: University of Pittsburgh Press, 1973). My discussion here largely relies on Gerbi's first chapter, "Buffon and the Inferiority of the Animal Species of America."

20. *"everything languishes":* Buffon, quoted by Gerbi, 7.

21. *"Take from him hunger":* Buffon, quoted by Gerbi, 6, and by TJ in Query VI.

22. *count as "monuments":* Marbois had used the term "monuments" in his original list of queries.

23. *difficult for many readers:* This point of view has been widely expressed in recent years; for one example, see Paul Finkelman, *Slavery and the Founders: Race and Liberty in the Age of Jefferson* (Armonk, N.Y.: M. E. Sharpe, 1995). For more balanced views of Jefferson's attitudes about race and slavery, see Chester E. Miller, *The Wolf by the Ears: Thomas Jefferson and Slavery* (New York: Free Press, 1977), and Robert McColley, *Slavery and Jeffersonian Virginia* (Urbana: University of Illinois Press, 1964).

24. *David Ramsey: Papers*, 9:441.

25. *a fellow member:* Samuel Stanhope Smith, *An Essay on the Causes of the Variety of Complexion and Figure in the Human Species*, Winthrop D. Jordan, ed. (Cambridge: Harvard University Press, 1965), 162.

26. *anonymous Southern reader:* MSS annotation in 1785 edition of *Notes* in the University of Virginia Library.

27. *Walker found:* Quoted from *David Walker's Appeal to the Coloured Citizens of the World*, Charles M. Wiltsie, ed. (New York: Hill and Wang, 1965), 10, 15.

28. *Abraham Lincoln:* "Letter to Henry L. Pierce and Others, April 6, 1859," in *Abraham Lincoln: Speeches and Writings, 1859–1865* (New York: Library of America, 1989), 19.

NOTES ON THE STATE OF VIRGINIA

Ad. *Foreigner of Distinction:* François Barbé de Marbois. This "Advertisement" first appeared in the 1787 London edition of *Notes*.

1. *Mason and Dixon:* Charles Mason (1730–87) and Jeremiah Dixon (d. 1777) were employed by Lord Baltimore and Thomas Penn between 1763 and 1767 to survey the boundary between Maryland and Pennsylvania. Extended, the line also marked the boundary between Virginia and Pennsylvania before the Civil War, and between Pennsylvania and West Virginia after that state separated from Virginia during the war. TJ's description of Virginia's boundaries includes land now part of the states of West Virginia and Kentucky, among others.

2. *Cassini:* Jacques Cassini (1677–1756), director of the Paris Observatory, measured the arc of the meridian between Dunkirk and Perpignan, publishing the results in *De la grandeur et la figure de la terre* (Paris, 1720). This provided an authoritative figure for the measurement of a degree of latitude.

3. *cession:* The Virginia Assembly had offered, in January 1781, to cede its claims to western lands north of the Ohio River, but objections to the terms of the cession on the part of smaller states and of land speculators held up the actual cession until March 1, 1784. Thus, while TJ was writing Queries I and II, Virginia had resolved to cede land in the Northwestern Territory but had not yet done so. For information on the cession, see Peter Onuf, *The Origins of the Federal Republic: Jurisdictional Controversies in the United States, 1775–1787* (Philadelphia, 1983), 75–102; for TJ's involvement in this issue, see Robert Berkhofer, Jr., "Jefferson, the Ordinance of 1784, and the Origins of the American Territorial System," *William and Mary Quarterly* 29 (1972): 231–62.

4. *Cohoes:* Cahokia, one of the Illinois towns captured from the British in a daring raid by by George Rogers Clark in July 1778. Clark (1752–1818), born near Charlottesville and a longtime friend, supplied TJ with information on the western territories.

5. *Acansas:* Arkansas.

6. *treaty of Paris:* Concluded the Revolutionary War in 1783 and established the western boundaries of the U.S. For the Virginia cession of its claims to western land, see note 1 above.

7. *Rio Norte, or North River:* The Rio Grande.

8. *how far this is navigable:* TJ's original manuscript reads "how far this last is navigable."

9. *Capt. Hutchings:* Thomas Hutchins (1730–89), military engineer and first geographer to the United States. TJ owned a copy of Hutchins's *A Topographical Description of Virginia, Pennsylvania, Maryland, and North Carolina,* . . . (London, 1778), and in January of 1784 made a list of errors in Hutchins's map, which he sent to him.

10. *headwaters of James river:* TJ emended this in his printed copy of *Notes* to read "of James and Roanoke rivers."

11. *fixed obstructions (1):* The parenthetical number here refers to the first of Charles Thomson's comments, included in the first Appendix. All further such parenthetical references are to Thomson's appended commentary.

12. *Fry and Jefferson's map:* TJ's father, Peter Jefferson, and Joshua Fry completed a famous map of Virginia in 1751 that was subsequently published in London. TJ used this as a basis for the map which he included with the 1786 French translation of *Notes* and with a few copies of the first edition of 1785.

13. *Evans's analysis:* Lewis Evans (c. 1700–56) discussed his *General Map of the Middle British Colonies in America* in a pamphlet, *Geographical, Historical, Political, Philosophical and Mechanical Essays* . . . (Philadelphia, 1755). TJ ordered a copy of Evans's map from John Stockdale, the London publisher of *Notes*, on July 24, 1786.

14. *passage of the Patowmac through the Blue ridge:* At what is now Harper's Ferry, West Virginia.

15. *the earth itself to its center (2):* TJ annotated his copy, "Herodotus, L.7.c129, after stating that Thessaly is a plain country surrounded by high mountains, from which there is no outlet but the fissure through with the Peneus flows, and that according to antient tradition, it had once been an entire lake, supposes that fissure to have been made by an earthquake rending the mountain asunder."

16. *Peaks of Otter:* In Bedford County, Virginia, not far from TJ's estate at Poplar Forest. Note in this sentence his typical use of "country" here to refer to Virginia, rather than the U.S. as a whole.

17. *of South America:* TJ annotated his copy, "I. Epoq. 434. Mussenbrock § 2312. 2. Epoq. 317.," referring to the Comte de Buffon's *Époques de la Nature* (Paris, 1778), a supplement to his famous *Histoire Naturelle.* See Introduction for Buffon. TJ owned the *Cours de Physique Experimentale et Mathematique* (Paris, 1769) of Pieter van Muschenbroek (1692–1761), a professor of mathematics at Leyden.

18. *the Endless mountains:* TJ annotated his copy, "To what is here said on the height of mountains, subsequent information has enabled me to furnish some additions and corrections.

"Gen. Williams, nephew of Dr. Franklin, on a journey from Richmond by the Warm and red springs to the Allegeny, has estimated by barometrical observations the height of some of our ridges of mountains above the Tidewater as follows:

	Feet
The Eastern base of the Blue ridge subjacent to Rockfish gap	100
Summit of the mountain adjacent to that gap	1822
The valley constituting the Eastern basis of the Warm spring mountain	943
Summit of the Warm spring mountain	2247
The Western valley of the Warm spring mountain, being the Eastern base of the Allegeny	949
Summit of the Allegeny 6 mi. S.W. of the Red springs	2760

"In Nov. 1815 with a Ramsden's theodolite of 3½ I. radius with Nonius divisions to 3 feet and a base of 1¼ mile on the low grounds of Otter River, distant 4. Miles from the summits of the two peaks of Otter, I measured geometrically their heights above the water of the river at it's base and found that of the sharp or S. peak 2946½ [feet, and] that of the flat or N. peak 3103½. As we may with confidence say that the base of the Peaks is at least as high above the Tidewater as that of the Blue ridge at Rockfish gap (being 40 miles farther Westward) and their highest summit of course 3203½ f. above that Tidewater, it follows that the summit of the highest peak is 343½ f. Higher than that of the Alleganey as measured by Genl. Williams.

"The highest of the White mountains in N.H. by barometrical estimate made by Capt. Partridge was found to be 4885 f. from it's base, and the highest of the Catskill mountains in N. York 3105 feet.

"Two observations with an excellent pocket sextant gave a mean of 37° = 28' = 50" for the Lat. of the sharp Peak of Otter.

"Baron Humboldt states that in Lat. 37° (which is nearly over medium parallel) perpetual snow is no where known so low as 1200 toises = 7671 feet above the level of the sea, and in sesquialtoral ratio nearly to the highest peak of Otter."

Jonathan Williams (1750–1815), fellow member of the American Philosophical Society, corresponded extensively with TJ and supplied him with observations on mountains on at least two occasions. Capt. Alden Partridge (1785–1854), professor of mathematics and physics at

West Point, gave these measurements to TJ in 1815. Alexander von Humboldt (1769–1859) met TJ in 1804 and later presented him with a copy of his *Tableaux de la Nature* (Paris, 1808).

19. *deemed Pumice:* TJ annotated, "2. Epoq. 91.112."

20. *in Augusta:* TJ annotated, "Bouguer mentions a cascade of two or three hundred toises height of the Bogota, a considerable river passing by Santa Fé. The caratact is vertical, and is about 15 or 16 leagues below Santa Fé. Bouguer xci. Buffon mentions one of 200 feet at Terni in Italy. I. Epoq. 470." TJ owned Pierre Bouguer's *La Figure de la Terre* (Paris, 1749), an account of scientific observations in Peru made in company with Charles-Marie de La Condamine.

21. *flowing into that valley:* TJ corrected his copy to read "from that valley."

22. *and 130 according:* TJ's original manuscript says 137.

23. *Mr. Zane:* Isaac Zane, owner of the Marlboro Iron Works in Frederick, corresponded with TJ on scientific questions, among other interests, and, while preparing *Notes*, TJ was anxious for him to send "thermometrical trials I asked him to make in his cave." See *Papers*, 7: 288.

24. *hypothesis:* TJ annotated his copy: "See Mussen[broek]. § 2604."

25. *transverse:* TJ revised his copy, replacing this word with "semi-axis which gives it's height."

26. *If the view from the top . . . at the distance each of them of about five miles.* TJ heavily revised this passage in his copy; in his original manuscript, he had made a note for himself: "I write this from memory, after an interval has elapsed of fifteen years since I saw the Bridge. This circumstance must apologize for any error in the description." In his copy of the Stockdale edition he substituted the following language: "This painful sensation is relieved by a short, but pleasing view of the Blue ridge along the fissure downwards, and upwards by that of the Short hills, which with the Purgatory mountain is a divergence from the North ridge; and, descending then to the valley below, the sensation becomes delightful in the extreme. It is impossible for the emotions, arising from the sublime to be felt beyond what they are here: so beautiful an arch, so elevated, so light, and springing, as it were, up to heaven, the rapture of the Spectator is really indiscribable! The fissure continues deep and narrow and, following the margin of the stream upwards about three eights of a mile you arrive at a limestone cavern, less remarkable, however, for height and extent than those before described. It's entrance into the hill is but a few feet above the bed of the stream." He comments on this change: "This description was written after a lapse of several years from the time of my visit to the bridge,

and under an error of recollection which requires apology. For it is from the bridge itself that the mountains are visible both ways, and not from the bottom of the fissure as my impression then was. The statement in the former edition needs the corrections here given to it. Aug. 16. 1817."

27. *"Esta caxa, ó cauce"*: "This cave, or passage is cut in the living rock with such precision that the roughnesses of the entering side correspond to those of the outgoing side, as if that mountain had parted on purpose, with its turns and windings, to give a passage to the waters between the two great walls that form it; they being so matched that if they were joined together, they would mesh without a gap." TJ owned several works by Antonio de Ulloa, Spanish naval officer and scientist who was also a part of the La Condamine expedition to Peru, including his *Noticias Americanas* in both its original Spanish edition (Madrid, 1772) and a French translation (Paris, 1787).

28. *over the Abyss:* TJ added to this note in his own copy: "Another is mentioned by Clavigero, 'The bridge of god, as they call a vast mass of earth which spans the deep Atoyaque river, near the village of Moleaxe, about a hundred miles above Mexico, in the direction of Scirocco, over which carts and carriages pass without difficulty. It might be taken for a fragment of the adjacent mountain, torn from it in times of old by an earthquake.' Storia del Messico. L.I. § 3." TJ owned the four-volume *Storia Antica del Messico* (Cesena, 1780–81) of Francisco Javier Clavijero (1731–87), a Mexican Jesuit who wrote in Bologna, Italy, after the expulsion of the Jesuits from Mexico; Clavijero opposed Buffon's theories about the degeneration of New World life forms. TJ's note quotes Clavijero in Italian.

29. *on Cumberland:* TJ's original manuscript reads thus; printed editions read "in."

30. *marble at Kentucky:* TJ deleted from his original manuscript the comment, "This may or may not be. Those countries have been explored chiefly by people of sanguine complexions of mind, eager to see in every object there whatever is most perfect in nature."

31. *vallies between them:* TJ inserted a large addition that formed an additional paragraph in his own copy of *Notes:* "Adjacent to the vein of Limestone first mentioned, or at least to some parts of it, is a vein of Slate, of greater breadth than that of the limestone, sometimes mixed with it, sometimes a small distance apart from it. The neighborhood of these veins of Limestone and Slate, and of Limestone and Schist between the North mountain and Blue ridge coincides with the following of observations of Bouguer while in Peru. '*Marble* is very frequently found on the banks of several of these rivers: slate rocks are also seen

there, and I have often had occasion to observe the close affinity between these two kinds of rock. I had already made the same remark in the Cordilleras. There slate and marble often touch each other, and I have seen some rocks which were slate at one end and pure marble at the other. Every time a new liquefaction of stone, analogous to slate and cementing its layers, takes place, it makes the whole rock harder and more compact; the rock is no longer slate, but becomes marble. Another rock, called *schist*, is also subject to this transformation. Sometimes the layers are not only cemented together, but one piece of rock joins, as if by chance, another. If the whole is then exposed to the action of gravel and pebbles, rolled by flowing water, and if it receives a kind of rounding off which makes it nearly cylindrical, it assumes full the appearance of the trunk of a tree, and it is sometimes even very difficult to distinguish it from a real tree. I regretted very much not to be able to take with me one of these apparent trees which I had found in a ravine between Guanaca and La Plata, at the foot of a hill called La Subida del Frayle. This was a piece of marble, 20 inches long by 17 or 18 in diameter; you distinguished something like the fibre of the wood, and the surface presented knots of various shapes; even the outline itself was such as to deceive one. There was an indentation on one side, and a projection on the opposite side, about which I was nonplussed as were those who accompanied me. I succeeded finally in making up my mind by noticing other pieces of schist nearby which began to assume the same appearance, but which were not sufficiently changed to deceive one, and which, on the contrary, enlightened me concerning the nature of the piece of marble. It is said that among various kinds of wood the gayac is the one which is most readily petrified. I was assured that I would see below Mompox a cross, the entire upper part of which was still of this wood, while the lower part was actually flint. Several persons assured me they had drawn sparks from it. When I passed that place they confirmed the report but added that six or seven years ago an extraordinary flood had caused the cross to fall into the river.' " TJ quoted Bouguer in French.

32. *above the level of the ocean:* TJ annotated his copy, "On whose authority has it been said? Bouguer, the best witness respecting the Andes, speaking of Peru, says, 'Here one observes no trace of those vast inundations which have left so many marks in all other regions. I made every effort to find some shell, but always in vain. Apparently the mountains of Peru are too high.' Bouguer. Lxv. See 4 Clavigero. Diss. 3. § I. See 2. Epoques. 268. 1 Epoq. 415." Cites Bouguer in French; this note precedes the large addition of note 31, which is written around it in the margins.

33. *to that height only:* TJ annotation, "2 Epoq. 378."

34. *Or without supposing it . . . :* This sentence was added in the 1787 edition.

35. *300 years posterior:* TJ annotated his copy, "Five deluges are enumerated by Xenophon, the author of the tract de Aequivocis. 'There were many inundations. The first, lasting nine months of the earth, took place of old. The second of the Nile, lasting for a month, under the Egyptians Hercules and Prometheus—for two months, however under Attic Ogyges in Achaia. A deluge of three months in Thessaly under Deucalion—A similar of Pharo under Egyptian Proteus during the capture of Helen.' " Quoted passage translated from Latin.

36. *A second opinion has been entertained, . . . :* In some copies of the first edition of 1785, TJ used cancel sheets (pages substituted for the original pages 51–54) to add the text from here to the end of the paragraph and also the next paragraph. The manuscript and early unrevised copies of the 1785 edition read, "Besides the usual process for generating shells by the elaboration of earth and water in animal vessels, may not nature have provided an equivalent operation, by passing the same materials through the pores of calcareous earths and stones? As we see calcareous dropstones generating every day by the percolation of water through limestone, and new marble forming in the quarries from which the old has been taken out, which is said to be the case in the quarries of Italy. Is it more difficult for nature to shoot the calcareous juice into the form of a shell, than other juices into the forms of Chrystals, plants, animals, according to the construction of the vessels through which they pass? There is a wonder somewhere. Is it greatest on this branch of a dilemma, or on that which supposes the creation of such a body of water, and its subsequent annihilation? Have not Naturalists already brought themselves to believe much stranger things? Thus, they seriously concur in the opinion that those immense hills and plains of marble to be found in every quarter of the globe, nay the very foundation of the earth itself, which is of limestone in large tracts of this country, and probably of others, and has been found here to continue solid to the depth of 200 feet, farther than which we have not penetrated, that these, I say, and all other calcareous bodies are animal remains. Monsieur de Voltaire, who seems first to have suspected that shells might grow unconnected with animal bodies, specifies an instance in a particular place in France, which has never yet, as far as I have heard, been disproved or denied." The text as thus originally printed in 1785 follows the manuscript, except that TJ originally wrote that Voltaire suspected "the actual growth of shells" instead of the more specific "that shells might grow unconnected with animal bodies."

37. *(Quest. encyl. Coquilles):* The reference is to the article on shells ("coquilles") in Voltaire's *Questions sur l'Encyclopédie* (Geneva, 1770–72). In June, 1787, while on his journey through southern France, TJ sought further information on this subject by calling on a M. Gentil of Tours, who had corresponded with Voltaire on the subject of fossilized shells and who directed TJ toward better accounts.

38. *Krachininnikow:* Stepan Petrovitch Kracheninnikov (1713–55), Russian explorer, wrote an account of southeastern Siberia, published in France as *Histoire de Kamtchatka et des Contrées Voisines* (1767).

39. *bituminous vapour in so strong a current:* TJ revised this in his annotated copy to read "gaseous stream so strong."

40. *the vapour issuing:* TJ revised this in his copy to "the gas escaping."

41. *If the vapour:* Annotated copy substitutes "gas" for "vapour."

42. *This, with the circumjacent lands:* TJ extensively revised this sentence in his annotated copy to read, "This gaseous fluid is probably inflammable air, the hydrogene of the new chemistry, which we know will kindle on mixing with the oxygenous portion of the atmospheric air, and the application of flame. It may be produced by a decomposition of water or of pyrites, within the body of the hill. The circumjacent lands are the property of General Washington and of General Lewis." This revision and the previous two indicate TJ's interest in the "new chemistry" of Lavoisier and Joseph Priestley, with whom he corresponded between 1800 and 1804, and the dropping of the honorary reference ("Excellency") to Washington reflects his suspicions of antidemocratic influences in American political life after 1790. General Andrew Lewis (1720–81) was a frontiersman and Revolutionary military leader.

43. *General Clarke:* George Rogers Clark.

44. *the mouth of the North Holston:* After this paragraph TJ inserted in his copy of *Notes* an additional paragraph and a diagram: "We are told that during a great storm on the 25th of December, 1798, the Syphon fountain near the end of the North Holston ceased, and a spring broke out 100 feet higher up the hill. Syphon fountains have been explained by supposing the duct which leads from the reservoir to the surface of the earth to be in the form of a syphon, a, b, c, where it is evident that till the water rises in the reservoir to d, the level of the highest point of the syphon, it cannot flow through the duct, and it is known that when once it begins to flow it will draw off the water of the reservoir to the orifice, a, of the syphon. If the duct be larger than the supply of the reservoir, possibly the force of the waters and loosening of the earth by them during the storm above mentioned may have

opened a more direct duct as from e to f horizontally or declining, which issued higher up the hill than the one fed by the syphon. In that case it becomes a common spring. Should this duct be again closed or diminished by any new accident the syphon may begin to play again, and both springs be kept in action from the same reservoir." TJ later annotated this addition, "See Pleasant's Argus. Aug. 16. 99 that this disappeared Dec. 25. 98. On which day a spring out 100 f. higher up the hill." (Samuel Pleasants owned the semiweekly newspaper *The Virginia Argus.*) He also added on a pasted tab the following diagram of the syphon fountain:

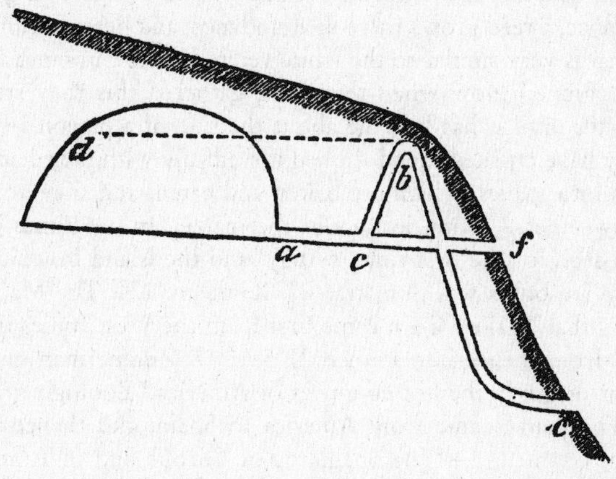

45. *Linnaean:* Referring to the system of botanical classification proposed by Swedish scientist Carolus Linnaeus (1707–78), whose *Systema Naturae, Species Plantarum,* and other works established the first version of the modern system of naming biological forms.

46. *Clayton:* John Clayton (c. 1693–1733), author of the pioneering *Flora Virginica* (Leyden, 1739); TJ seems to have owned the edition of 1762, which was revised in accordance with the Linnaean system of classification.

47. *Linnaeus, Millar, or Clayton:* Philip Miller (1691–1771), English botanist and author of *The Gardeners Kalendar* and *The Gardeners Dictionary;* TJ owned these in the London 1765 and 1768 editions respectively and made continual use of the latter in his own gardening and correspondence about gardens.

48. *Juglans alba:* TJ here uses the Latin descriptive terms for the pecan ("Paccan") of international scientific convention. "*Juglans alba,* lance-shaped leaflets, with sharp points, small egg-shaped fruits in a hard outer covering, closely packed, extracted with difficulty, sweet,

shelled, delicate." He seems to confuse the pecan with the white walnut or butternut, also identified as *Juglans alba* just below this on his list.

49. *Salix. Query species?:* TJ annotated his copy, "*Fluvialis.* Bartr. 393." The reference is to William Bartram (1739–1823) and his *Travels through North and South Carolina, Georgia, East and West Florida* (Philadelphia, 1791). The Latin word *Fluvialis* has to do with growing along rivers.

50. *Maize:* TJ provided a lengthy and learned annotation in his copy of *Notes:* "Qu. If known in Europe before the discovery of America? Ramusio supposes this to be the grain described by Diod[orus] Sic[ulus] L. 2. in his account of the travels of Iambulus, in the following passage: 'For instance, a reed grows there in abundance, and bears a fruit in great plenty that is very similar to the white vetch. (white chick-pea Ital. seed of vetch. Franc.) Now when they have gathered this they steep it in warm water until it has become about the size of a pigeon's egg: then after they have crushed it and rubbed it skillfully with their hands, they mould it into loaves, which are baked and eaten, and they are of surprising sweetness.' Ramusio says of the maize, 'In our times [1550] it has been seen for the first time in Italy' and the island in which it was found by Iambulus was Sumatra.—I. Ramusio. 174. The Maison rustique says that Turkey Corn came first from the West Indies into Turkey, and from thence into France. L. 5. c. 17. Zimmerman says 'They have their origin in the hot countries of America.' Zoologie graphique, p. 24. 'The maize came from America to Spain, and thence to other European countries.'—'The Spaniards in Europe and in America call the maize *maiz*, a word derived from the language of Haiti, now called Hispaniola, or Santo Domingo.' Clavigero. I. 56. 'Maize, a grain granted by Providence to that portion of the globe, instead of the wheat of Europe, the rice of Asia, and the millet of Africa.' 2. Clavig. 218. Acosta classes Indian corn with the plants peculiar to America, observing that it is called 'trigo de las Indias' in Spain and 'Grano de Turquia' in Italy. He says, 'From hence came Indian corn, and why the Italians call this productive grain Turkish grain is more easily asked than answered. Because, in fact, there is no trace of such a plant among the ancients, although the millet, which Pliny says came from India ten years before he wrote, has some resemblance to maize, which he calls a grain that grows in stalks and is covered with leaves, that has at the top a kind of hair, and is remarkably productive—all of which does not apply to mijo, by which they commonly mean millet. After all, the Creator rules all parts of the globe: to one he gave wheat, the principal food of man; to the Indians he gave maize, which next to wheat ranks second as food for man and beast.'—Acosta. 4. 16." In 1788, TJ, in Paris, bought Gio-

vanni Battista Ramusio's (1485–1557) three-volume *Delle Navigationi et Viaggi*, the third volume of which was devoted to America, and a year later from the same bookseller he purchased José de Acosta's (1540–1600) *Historia Natural y Moral de las Indias*. He recommended in 1809 that the Library of Congress acquire Charles Etienne and Jean Liebault's *Maison Rustique, or The Country Farmer*, originally published in French in 1564, and, in a letter written in the same year discussing the origins of the potato, he cited Eberhard August Wilhelm von Zimmerman's (1743–1815) *Zoologie Géographique*. He also owned multiple copies of the Greek historian Diodorus Siculus's *Bibliotheke Historike* as well as the *Historia Naturalis* of the Roman scholar Caius Plinius Secundus the Elder. In this footnote TJ quoted Diodorus in Greek, Ramusio and Clavijero in Italian, Zimmerman in French, and Acosta in Spanish.

51. *Round potatoes:* TJ also annotated this with a quotation in French and one in Italian: " 'Potatoes are indigenous to Guiana.' Zimmerman. Zool. Geogr. 26. 'The *Papa* was brought to Mexico from South America, its native country.' 1 Clavigero. 58."

52. *Gronovius:* Johann Friedrich Gronovius (1690–1760), of Leyden, was one of the most important botanists of the eighteenth century. TJ is mistaken, however, in referring to Clayton as a native of Virginia; although resident there for a great part of his life, he was born in England.

53. *and Indian corn:* Since he had discussed maize, or Indian corn, in his annotation (see note 50), TJ in his copy deleted the reference and inserted an "and" before "broom corn."

54. *Mons. de Buffon:* George Louis Leclerc, Comte de Buffon (1707–88), keeper of the Jardin du Roi and the Royal Museum in Paris, was the foremost naturalist when TJ composed *Notes*. Here begins TJ's refutation of Buffon's contentions about the degeneration of life-forms in the New World because of its supposedly colder and wetter climate.

55. *A delegation of warriors from the Delaware tribe:* These Delaware visitors were probably included in the party from Kaskaskia led by Jean Baptiste Ducoigne that visited Charlottesville in June, 1781. They presented to TJ pictographically illustrated buffalo skins that he promised to "always keep . . . hanging on the walls in remembrance of you and your nation." *Papers*, 6:60. I have found no records of a separate delegation of Delawares, but Shawnees and Delawares did settle in and near Kaskaskia about this time. See Bruce Trigger, ed., *Handbook of North American Indians: Volume 15, Northeast* (Washington, D.C.: Smithsonian, 1978), 600.

56. *Mr. Stanley:* Not identified, although TJ seems to have received

this story from Col. Arthur Campbell, one of the leaders of a military expedition against the Cherokees in Tennessee in 1780 and 1781.

57. *Siberia:* TJ annotated his copy, "Cavigero says, 'I do not remember that any American nation has any tradition of elephants or hippopotami, or other quadrupeds of equal size. I do not know if any of the numerous excavations made in New Spain has brought to light the carcass of a hippopotamus, or even the tooth of an elephant.' 125." TJ quoted Clavijero in Italian.

58. *both hemispheres:* TJ anotated his copy with a reference to Buffon, "2. Epoques. 276. in Mexico; but 1. Epoques. 250. denies the fact as to S. America."

59. *salines last mentioned:* TJ annotated this, "22. Buffon. 233. 2. Epoques. 230."

60. *or river-horse:* TJ annotated this, "2. Epoques. 232. Buffon pronounces it is not the grinder either of the elephant or hippopotamus 'but of a species the first and greatest of all land animals now lost.' " He quoted Buffon in French.

61. *celebrated anotomist:* TJ refers here to John Hunter (1728–93), Scottish-born physiologist and surgeon who founded scientific surgery. Hunter's publications include "Observations on the Bones Commonly Supposed to Be Elephant's Bones, Which Have Been Found Near the River Ohio, in America," *Philosophical Transactions* (Royal Society), 58 (1768), 34–45, and *The Natural History of the Human Teeth* (London, 1778), which TJ owned.

62. *another anatomist:* TJ here refers to Louis Jean Marie Daubenton (1716–99), French naturalist born in the same town as Buffon, who wrote descriptive and anatomical portions of the latter's *Histoire Naturelle* as well as for the *Encyclopédie*. TJ sent copies of the first edition of *Notes* to Buffon and Daubenton.

63. *Buffon has admitted:* TJ annotated this, "XVIII. 178. XXII. 121." in reference to particular volumes of Buffon's *Histoire Naturelle.*

64. *grinding surface flat:* TJ annotated, "qu? see 2 Epoques de Buffon. 231. 234."

65. *limits of habitation for the elephant:* TJ annotated this, "M. de Buffon considers the existence of Elephant bones in Northern regions, where the animal itself is no longer found, as one of the leading facts which support his theory that the earth was once in a liquid state, rendered so by the action of fire, that the process of cooling began at it's poles, and proceeded gradually towards the torrid zone, that with this progress the animals of warm temperature retired towards the equator, and that in the present state of that progress the globe remains of sufficient warmth, for the elephant for instance, in the tropical regions

only, to which therefore they have retired, as their last asylum and where they must become extinct when the degree of warmth shall be reduced below that adapted to their constitution. How does it happen then that no elephants exist at present in the tropical regions of America, to which those of the Ohio must have retired according to his theory."

66. *"La nature vivante":* "Living nature is much less active, much less strong." This is Buffon's central claim to which TJ objects. A marginal note originally cited "Buffon. xviii. 122. ed. Paris, 1764."

67. *The opinion advanced by the Count de Buffon:* Original marginal citation here reads, "xviii. 100—156." TJ later annotated his copy with two quotations from Buffon, here translated: " 'The earth has remained cold, unable to produce the principles necessary for the development of the germs of the largest quadrupeds which require for their growth and propagation all the heat and activity which the sun can give to the loving earth.' xviii. 156. 'The ardor of men and the size of animals depend upon the salubrity and the heat of the air.' ibid. 160."

68. *"en general il paroit":* "In general it seems that countries a bit cold better suit our oxen than hot countries, and they have all the more weight and size as the climate is damper and more abundant in pasturage. The oxen of Denmark, of Podolia, of the Ukraine, and of Tartary where the Kalmuks live are the largest of all." Original marginal citation reads, "viii. 134." Podolia is a region in the western Ukraine. In his personal copy of *Notes*, TJ added quotations from Buffon in French, " 'All that is colossal and grand in nature has been formed in Northern countries.' 1. Epoq. 255. 'It is in our Northern regions that living nature has risen to the largest dimensions.' ibid. 263."

69. *Lievre. Hare:* TJ annotated this, "There exists in the Western and mountainous parts of Pennsylvania, an animal which seems to be nearer the hare than our whabus. The meat is black and an individual weighed 39½ oz. avoird. while the whabus is an animal of white meat and weighs about 29 oz. The fur of the former is white, as is the case with most animals in countries abounding with snow."

70. *the beaver, the otter:* TJ in his copy inserted "the roe" before "the beaver" in this list.

71. *"& cela sans aucune exception":* "& that without any exception."

72. *"dans la forme":* "in *the shape* of this American bear compared to that of Europe."

73. *That the palmated Elk . . . many who have seen them:* Original marginal citation for Kalm reads, "I. 233. Lond. 1772." In his copy, TJ revised this whole passage in several stages to read, "Kalm tells us that the Moose, Original or palmated Elk of America, is as high as a tall horse; and Catesby, that it is about the bigness of a middle sized ox. I

have seen a skeleton 7 feet high, and from good information believe they are often considerably higher. The Elk of Europe is not two-thirds of his height." He later annotated *this* revision by commenting on Catesby's claim, "This is not correct. Kalm considers the Moose as the Elk, and not as the Renne. Musu is the Algonkin name of the Original or Elk." Peter Kalm (1716–79), Swedish botanist and disciple of Linnaeus, published the English translation of his *Travels into North America*, to which TJ here refers, in London, 1770–71. TJ owned this book, as well as the works of two English naturalists Thomas Pennant (1726–98) and Daines Barrington (1727–1800), to whom Gilbert White had addressed *The Natural History of Selborne*. TJ purchased in Paris a first edition of the important work by Mark Catesby (c. 1679–1749), *The Natural History of Carolina, Florida, and the Bahama Islands* (London, 1731), which he drew on when compiling the list of American birds given on pages 72–76.

74. *But Mons. D'Aubenton says:* TJ included a formidable array of marginal references to this passage. He cites Daubenton's work in the *Histoire Naturelle*, XXIV.162 and XV.42; Kalm's *Travels*, I.359, 48, 221, 251, II.52; Catesby's *Natural History*, II.78.

75. *the measures of the Count de Buffon and Mons. D'Aubenton:* Original marginal citation reads, "XXVII. 63. XIV. 119. Harris, II.387. Buffon. Quad. IX. 1." The "Harris" reference is probably to John Harris, *A Compleat Collection of Voyages and Travels* (London, 1705, 2 vols.). "Quad." refers to Buffon and Daubenton's 12-volume *Histoire Naturelle des Quadrupèdes* (Paris, 1753–67), which constituted part of the larger *Histoire Naturelle, Générale et Particulière*.

76. *wolf, roe, glutton:* TJ revised "roe" in his copy to read "the renne." The "glutton" is a wolverine.

77. *mistake the species?:* TJ annotated his copy, "Even Amerigo Vespucci says he saw lions and wild boars in America. Letters. pa. 77. He saw a serpent 8 braccie long, and as thick as his own waist. 111." TJ owned Angelo Maria Bandini's *Vita e lettere di Americo Vespucci* (Florence, 1745), which included Vespucci's first letter from America, the source of this description.

78. *"J'aime autant":* "I love as much a person who corrects me in an error as another who teaches me a truth, because in effect an error corrected is a truth." TJ's marginal note cited Buffon, "Quad.. IX. 158."

79. *"Il n'etoit pas":* "It was not yet fully grown." Marginal notes to this passage read, "XXV.184." "Quad. IX. 132." "XIX.2."

80. *But a subsequent account:* Original marginal note reads, "Quad. IX. 41."

81. *and I could never learn . . . Northern latitudes:* TJ revised this

passage in his copy of *Notes* to read, "the palmated kind is confined to the more Northern latitudes." By "palmated kind" he means the moose; his annotation to the following footnote reads, "See Catesby and Kalm, reason to believe that the Moose is the palmated elk or Original."

82. *Theodat, Denys and La Hontan:* Gabriel Sagard-Théodat (d. 1650), French Recollet missionary, wrote *Le Grand Voyage du Pays du Hurons* (Paris, 1632); Nicolas Denys (c. 1609–86), wrote *Description Geographique et Historique de costes de l'Amerique Septentrionale* (Paris, 1672); Louis Armand de Lom d'Arce, Baron de Lahontan (1666–c. 1713), published his *Voyages du Baron de La Hontan dans l'Amerique Septentrionale* originally in Paris in 1703.

83. *Kalm is of the same opinion:* TJ's original marginal citation was "Kalm II. 340. I. 82."

84. *Thus Monsieur D'Aubenton:* TJ's original marginal citation was "VII. 432."; he also provided a citation for the subsequent reference to Daubenton, "VII. 474."

85. *measured by Mons. D'Aubenton:* Original marginal citation "VIII. 48. 55. 66."

86. *Mons. de Buffon has been sensible:* Original marginal citation "XVIII. 96."

87. *I observe Mons. D'Aubenton:* Original marginal citation "IX. 41."

88. *information of which no one individual is possessed:* TJ annotated his copy, "Dogs in [Hispaniola] have grown so much in number and *in size* as to be the plague of the island. Acosta IV. 33" Quotation originally in Spanish.

89. *Mons. de Buffon supposes:* Original marginal citation is "XXX. 219."

90. *It is the opinion of Mons. de Buffon:* Original marginal citation is "XVIII. 146."

91. *"Quoique le sauvage . . . des animaux":* "Although the savage of the new world is nearly the same height as man in our world, this does not suffice to make him an exception to the general fact of the shrinking of living nature in all of that continent. The savage is weak and small in the organs of generation; he has neither hair nor beard nor any ardor for his female; although he is swifter than the European because he is more accustomed to running, he is, however, less strong in body; he is also less sensitive and yet more fearful and cowardly; he has no vivacity, no emotion; the activity of his body is less an exercise, a voluntary movement, than it is a necessary action caused by need; take away his hunger and thirst, you will destroy at the same time the active principle of all his motions; he will stupidly rest on his haunches or lie down for whole days. There is no need to search far for the cause

of the scattered life of the savages and their distaste for society: the most precious spark of the fire of nature has been refused them; they lack ardor for their females and, by consequence, love for their fellow man; not knowing this attachment, the strongest and tenderest of all, their other feelings are cold and languishing; they love their parents and children weakly; the society the most intimate of all, that of the family itself, has for them only feeble ties; between families there is no tie at all; accordingly they have no community, no commonwealth, no social state. Bodily love makes up their morality; their heart is icy, their society cold, and their rule harsh. They look upon their wives only as laborers or as beasts whom they without consideration load with the burdens from their hunting, and whom they force without mercy, without gratitude, to do work that is often beyond their strength. They have only a few children; they take little care of them. Everywhere they experience the effects of their primary defect; they are indifferent because they have little sexual power, and that indifference to the other sex is the original defect which blights their nature, prevents its development, and by destroying the germs of life, strikes at the roots of society at the same time. Man is here no exception. Nature by refusing him the power of love has treated him worse and diminished him more than any of the animals."

92. *reduced to the same diet and exercise:* TJ annotated his copy, "Amer[igo] Vesp[ucci]. 13. 'Beyond measure lustful,' &c. 108." Quoted phrase originally in Italian.

93. *Sol Rodomonte:* "Rodomont only scorns by any way / To wend, except by what is least secure." These lines are from Lodovico Ariosto (1474–1533), canto 14, stanza 117, *Orlando Furioso*. Translation is by William Stewart Rose (London, 1864).

94. *"Los Indios vencidos . . . lo han estado":* "The conquered Indians are the most cowardly and pusillanimous that can be seen:—they make themselves victims, they humble themselves to contempt, apologize for their inconsiderate boldness, and with supplications and prayers give sure proof of their lack of courage. Either the accounts in the histories of the Conquest about their great deeds are only figures of speech, or the character of these people is not now as it was then. However, there is no doubt that the nations of the northern part live in the same freedom that they have always had, without having been subjugated to any foreign prince, and they live all their lives according to their rules and customs without having had any reason to change their character; in this [timidity] they appear the same as those of Peru or all of South America, enslaved and never enslaved."

95. *"los obrages los aniquilan":* "their hard labor destroys them because of the inhumanity with which they have been treated."

96. *his sensibility is keen:* TJ annotated his copy here, " 'They live a hundred and fifty years.' Amer[igo]. Vesp[ucci]. 111." Quotes Vespucci in Italian.

97. *for games of chance:* In the original manuscript TJ deleted the following passage: "They have less hair on their face and body; they raise fewer children, and leave an unjust portion of labour on their women. In the defect of hair they resemble the blacks. Whether their raising fewer children proceeds from scarcity of food at certain seasons, from the labours and hazards to which their women are exposed, or from a sterility peculiar to their race, seems not well ascertained."

98. *Col. Byrd:* Col. William Byrd III (1728–77) campaigned against the Cherokees in 1760–61 during the Seven Years' War.

99. *prevent conception for a considerable time after:* TJ annotated his copy, "Amer[igo] Vesp[ucci]. 13."

100. *as many children as the white women:* TJ annotated his copy, "Amer[igo] Vesp[ucci]. 13. 'Their women are very fertile.' " Vespucci quoted originally in Italian.

101. *making slaves of the Indians:* TJ added in his copy of *Notes*, "This practice commenced with the Spaniards with the first discovery of America. See Herrera. Amer. Vesp." TJ acquired in France a copy of the *Historia General de los Hechos de los Castellanos en las Islas i Tierra Firme del Mar Oceano* of Antonio Herrera y Tordesillas (1549–1625), appointed by Phillip II as the historiographer of the Indies.

102. *except on the head:* TJ annotated his copy, "Amer. Vesp. 9."

103. *"à peu près de même stature":* "almost the same size as the man of our world."

104. *How has this "combination":* TJ's original marginal note to Buffon reads, "XVIII. 146."

105. *Linn. Syst:* TJ refers to the *Systema Naturae* of Linnaeus for a definition of humans that can include both the people of the Old World and the New.

106. *Logan:* Also known as Tah-gah-jute (c. 1725–80), son of a Cayuga chief, Logan had married a Shawnee and was living in 1774 on Yellow Creek on the north bank of the Ohio. Jefferson's inclusion of this speech and version of the events was later attacked by Federalist opponents, leading to his 1800 addition to *Notes* of what is included here as Appendix No. IV. John Murray, Earl of Dunmore (1730–1809), was the last colonial governor of Virginia; his "war" was a response in 1774 to hostilities by Indians who had been provoked by frontier ex-

pansion from the colonies and incidents such as the massacre described here.

107. *In the spring of the year 1774:* Notice "Appendix No. IV," pp. 260–61, where TJ wishes to revise this passage in editions of *Notes* printed after 1800. Many later editions ignored this request to insert the revised language of the appendix, however, and he did not emend the passage in his own 1787 copy of *Notes.*

108. *Col. Cresap:* Michael Cresap (1742–75), Maryland frontiersman; as the 1800 appendix makes clear, Cresap was not responsible for the death of Logan's family, although he was implicated in another, similar incident.

109. *following speech to be delivered to Lord Dunmore:* TJ in his original manuscript had written "to be delivered verbally to Lord Dunmore."

110. *letters have not yet been introduced among them:* In his copy TJ inserted the marginal annotation, "1. Clavigero. 120."

111. *bewitching language:* TJ in his own copy added further comment, "No writer, equally with M. de Buffon, proves the power of eloquence, and uncertainty of theories. He takes any hypothesis whatever, or it's reverse, and furnishes explanations equally specious and persuasive. Thus in his eighteenth volume wishing to explain why the largest animals are found in the torrid zone, he assumes *heat* as the efficient principle of the animal volume. Speaking of America, he says, 'The earth is *cold*, powerless to produce the active principles to produce the development of the germs of the largest quadrupeds, which require for their growth and propagation all the heat and activity which the sun can give to the loving earth.' pa. 156. 'The Ardor of men and the size of animals depend upon the salubrity and the *heat* of the air.' ib. 160. In his Epochs again when it is become convenient to his theory to consider the bones of the mammoth found in the coldest regions, as the bones of the elephant, and necessary to explain how the elephant there should have been six times as large as that of the torrid zone, it is *cold* which produces animal volume. 'All that is colossal and great in nature has been formed in Northern countries.' 1. Epoques, 255. 'It is in our northern regions that living nature has risen to the largest dimension.' ib. 263." TJ originally quoted Buffon in French.

112. *Abbé Raynal. . . une seule science:* Guillaume Thomas François Raynal (1713–96), French philosophe and historian. TJ owned a 1780 reprint of Raynal's popular *Histoire Philosophique et Politique des Établissements et du Commerce des Européens dans les deux Indes*, which he later characterized as "the effusions of an imagination in deliris." The quotation here from Raynal, "One must be astonished . . . that

America has not yet produced one good poet, one able mathematician, one man of genius in a single art or a single science," cites a different edition, published in the Netherlands in 1774, than the one in the collection TJ later sold to the nation for the Library of Congress.

113. *Mr. Rittenhouse:* David Rittenhouse (1732–96), perhaps the most widely respected American man of science in his day, preceded TJ as president of the American Philosophical Society. His "proof of mechanical genius" was the construction of an orrery, a mechanical model of the solar system in which the various planets and moons were made to move in their elliptical orbits. The English instrument maker George Graham (1673–1751) had priority over Rittenhouse and had named the device after his patron, the Earl of Orrery. Thomas Godfrey (1704–49), a Philadelphia glazier and friend of Benjamin Franklin's, independently invented the nautical quadrant, also developed in England by John Hadley (1682–1744).

114. *An Englishman, only, reads Milton with delight:* In this list of national epic poets, TJ includes with Milton: Torquato Tasso (1544–95), author of *La Gerusalemme Liberata;* François-Marie Arouet de Voltaire (1694–1778), author of *La Henriade*, a poem about Henri IV; and Luis de Camoens (1524–80), whose *Lusiads* is about the explorations of the great Portuguese seafarers of the fifteenth century.

115. *There are various ways:* TJ added in his copy the annotation, "Huyghens gave the first description of an instrument of the former kind [the orrery], under the name of Automatum Planetarium. 2. Montucla. 485." TJ acquired his copy of Jean-Étienne Montucla's (1725–90) *Histoire des Mathématiques* several years after the 1787 publication of *Notes.* Christian Huygens (1629–93), Dutch physicist and astronomer, discovered the rings and fourth satellite of Saturn in 1655.

116. *the Encyclopedists:* Denis Diderot (1713–84) enlisted many of the important French writers of the second half of the eighteenth century to contribute to his *Encyclopédie*, published between 1751 and 1765, particularly Jean le Rond d' Alembert (1717–83), philosophe and mathematician. TJ was particularly interested in this as one of the great products of the French Enlightenment, acquiring the 39-volume reprint done in Lausanne in 1781–82.

117. *An inhabitant of Ireland, Sweden, or Finland:* TJ annotated his copy here, "Amer. Vesp. 115. 'Here the sky and air are seldom darkened by clouds; the days are almost always clear.' " Vespucci was originally quoted in Italian.

118. *Buffon oiseaux:* As part of the argument against Buffon, TJ added the references to the French scientist's *Histoire Naturelle* in the Stockdale edition.

119. *Meleagris Gallopavo:* TJ annotated his copy, "1. Clavigero. 85."

120. *Urogallus minor . . . Pheasant:* TJ annotated his copy, "The Pheasant is rarely or not at all found beyond North Carolina. The grouse is first seen in the upper parts of Maryland, in Pennsylvania and the country North of Ohio, and thence Northwardly. [Capt. Mer. Lewis.]." TJ refers to Meriwether Lewis of Lewis and Clark fame.

121. *Turdus polyglottos:* TJ annotated this: "Clavigero says that in Mexico 'there are renowned nightingales.' " Clavijero quoted in Italian.

122. *Ballcoot:* TJ corrected this in his copy to "Bald-coot" and added as annotation, "The Bald-coot, or Coot is the Fulica of Linnaeus, and the Foulque of the Encyclop. Meth. differing from the description of the latter only in the colour of it's feet and legs, which are olive green, without any circle of red, and that of the bill a faint carnation, brown at the point, and the membrane on the forehead of a very dark purple. It is distinguished from the Gallina chloropis, Poule d'eau, Water-hen, Hydro-gallina, chiefly by the festooned web bordering the toes." The reference here is to the *Encyclopédie Methodique*, begun in 1782 by Charles Joseph Panckoucke (1736–98) as a new, enlarged edition of Diderot's *Encyclopédie*, and to which TJ supplied information on the United States.

123. *Sir Hans Sloane's Jamaica:* Sloane (1660–1753), British physician, wrote *A Natural History of Jamaica* (London, 1707–25), and was successively secretary and president of the Royal Society.

124. *Marcgrave . . . in Brasil:* TJ owned the *Historia Naturalis Brasiliae by* Georg Marcgraf (1610–44) in collaboration with Willem Piso (1611–78), a Dutch physician. TJ annotated this passage in his copy: "See Herrera. Dec. 1. L. 10. c. 8. 'When Yucatan was discovered, an abundance of wax and honey was found.' And ib. c. 9. 'Hornets and bees are found, like those of Castille, although the latter are smaller and sting with more fury.' ib. Dec. 2. 1.3. c.i." Herrera was originally quoted in Spanish.

125. *white settlers:* TJ annotated his copy, "See 1. Clavigero. 107. 'On the borders of Guayaquil are bees which swarm and make honey in the hollows of trees; they are little larger than flies; the wax and honey they make are golden, and although it tastes good, it is not like that of Castile.' 'Herr[era]. 5. 10. 10." Herrera was originally quoted in Spanish.

126. *"Hoc comedunt":* "This they eat in place of things made of sugar." TJ refers to the *Lapponia* (Frankfurt, 1673) of Johann Scheffer (1621–79), which was in his library that was sold to the nation.

127. *Kalm tells us:* The 1787 edition has a marginal reference to Kalm's *Travels*, "I. 126."

128. *where they probably join:* At different times TJ added two annotations in his copy. The first was, "We have it from the Indians also that the common domestic fly is not originally of America, but came with the whites from Europe." Beneath this, "We have the same account from S. America. Condamine in his Voyage de la riviere Amazones, pa. 95 says: 'Various Indians have told us they have seen on the banks of the river Coari, in the upland, open country, flies, and many horned animals, objects which they had not seen before, and which prove that the sources of these rivers water countries adjoining the Spanish colonies of upper Peru.' " Charles-Marie de La Condamine (1701–74), made the first scientific exploration of the Amazon, after he left the French expedition with Bouguer and Ulloa (see page 294) and travelled down the river. TJ owned his *Relation abrégée d'un Voyage fait dans l'Interieur de l'Amerique Méridionale* (Paris, 1745–46). TJ quoted La Condamine in French.

129. *Winds:* TJ annotated his edition by adding further weather notes, apparently having to do with the first frosts and the end of the growing season:

1789	Oct'r 1	Ice	Snow Birds	Spoiled tobacco on the scaffold.
1792	Sep. 21	None	None	Tobacco destroyed totally out of green belt.
1808	Sep. 27	None	None	Tobacco, except in green belt, untouched.
1816	Oct'r 7	thin ice	Snow Birds	Late corn spoiled; all safe in green belt.
1823	Sep. 29	None	None	Green belt unaffected; pumpkin vine frozen.

Also pasted or bound into the volume here is a set of weather observations apparently made in Maine and Washington, D.C., by Henry Dearborn (1751–1829), TJ's secretary of war. It is not clear that they were intended to be included in a revised edition of *Notes*, and they are not included here. They can be found in *Ford*, 3:178.

130. *in thirteen hours:* TJ annotated his copy, "and in a single and most remarkable instance, on the 4th of July, 1793, in Orange county, it fell from 84° to 74° in ten minutes."

131. *Reaumur:* The thermometer devised by René-Antoine Ferchault

de Reaumur (1683–1757) has eighty degrees between the freezing and boiling points.

132. *above boiling water:* TJ included a lengthy annotation pasted into his own copy: "The following observations on heat and cold, as they affect the animal body, may not be unacceptable to those who have not paid particular attention to the subject.

"The living body (not like the dead one, which assumes the temperature of the surrounding atmosphere) maintains within itself a steady heat of about 96°. of Fahrenheit's thermometer, varying little with the ordinary variations of the atmosphere. This heat is principally supplied by respiration. The vital air, or oxygen of the atmospheric fluid inhaled, is separated by the lungs from the azotic and carbonic parts, and is absorbed by them; the caloric is disengaged, diffused thro' the mass of the body, and absorbed from the skin by the external air coming into contact with it. If the external air is of a high temperature, it does not take up the superfluous heat of the body fast enough, and we complain of too much heat: if it is very cold, it absorbs the heat too fast and produces the sensation of cold. To remedy this, we interpose a covering, which acting as a strainer, lets less air come into contact with the body, and checks the escape of the vital heat. As the atmospheric air becomes colder, more or thicker coverings are used, till no more than the requisite portion of heat is conducted from the body. As it would be inconvenient in the day to be burthened with a mass of clothing entirely equivalent to great degrees of cold, we have resort to fire and warm rooms to correct the state of the atmosphere, as a supplement to our clothing. If we have not the opportunity and the cold is excessive, the thinner parts as the ear, the nose, the fingers and toes lose heat till they freeze, and, if the cold be sufficient, the whole body is reduced in heat, till death ensues; as sailors experience who escape from shipwreck, in winter storms, on desert shores, where no fire can be found.

"Of the substances we use for covering, linen seems the openest strainer, for admission of air to the body, and the most copious conductor of heat from it; and it is therefore considered as a cool clothing. Cotton obstructs still more the passage of both fluids; and wool more than cotton: it is called therefore a worse conductor of heat, and warmer clothing. Next to this are the furs, and the most impermeable of all for heat and air, are feathers and down, and especially the down of the Eider duck. (*Anas millissima.*) Hence the insensibility to cold of the beasts with shaggy hair, or fine fur, and of the birds in proportion as they are provided with down and soft feathers, as the swan, goose and duck.

"Among the substances which, as being bad conductors of heat, foment and warm the human body, are the leaves of the Espeletia Frailexon, a plant newly discovered by the great naturalist and traveller Baron Humboldt, on the mountains of S. America, at the height of 2450 toises above the sea. These leaves being furnished abundantly with a soft down, restore immediately to their due warmth the hands, feet, or other members benumbed with cold, and collected as a bed, protect from death the Indian benighted in those regions of extreme cold. The same scientific traveller, by analysis of the air, at different heights on the mountain of Chimborazo, which he ascended to the height of 3036 toises, (546. toises higher than had ever been done by man before, and within 224 toises of it's top) found that the oxygen being specifically heavier than the azotic part of the Atmosphere, it's proportion lessened in that ascent 27. or 28. to 19½ hundredth parts. The same circumstance had been before observed by Saussure, Pini, and Rebout on the high mountains of Europe, and must be among the principal causes of the degree in which the animal body is affected with cold in situations more or less elevated.

"In addition to the the effect of vital air, as the vehicle of animal heat, we may note that it is also the immediate cause, or primum mobile of life. For, entering by respiration into the air-cells of the lungs, divided from those of the blood but by a thin membrane, it infuses thro' that a stimulus into the blood, which, acting on the irritable fibres of the heart, excites mechanically the action and reaction of that muscle. By these the blood is propelled, and received again, in a course of constant circulation, and vital action communicated and maintained thro' all the system. Intercept vital air from the lungs, the action of the heart ceases for want of stimulus, the current of the blood, unaided, yields to the resistance of it's channels, all the vital motions are suspended, and the body becomes an inanimated lump of matter."

133. *6½ degrees above the freezing point:* TJ annotated his copy, "Mussenbrock has seen ice produced at 41°. 2. Muss. 1, 507."

134. *That the dew is very rare:* In his copy TJ revised the final clauses of this sentence to read, "having seldom during that time seen them at Monticello during summer."

135. *the general law of vision, by which they are diminished:* TJ annotated his copy, "Dr. Shaw in his Physical observations on Syria, speaking of the Easterly winds, called by Seamen Levanters, says 'we are likewise to observe further with regard to these strong Easterly winds, that vessels, or any other objects which are seen at a distance, appear to be vastly magnified, or *loom*, according to the mariners expression.' Shaw's travels, 302." TJ owned *Travels, or Observations Relating to Several Parts of Barbary* (Oxford, 1738) by Thomas Shaw

(1694–1751), who, in 1720, became the chaplain at the English factory at Algiers.

136. *a solitary mountain about 40 miles off:* Present-day Willis Mountain.

137. *Census of Inhabitants:* TJ annotated his copy by adding more population figures at the end:

"1756. 173,316 inhabitants
1764. 200,000
1774. 300,000

See Boston *Patriot*, Sept. 16, 09. Pownal's authority quoted in J. Adams's 17th letter." The reference is to Thomas Pownal (1722–1805), colonial governor of Massachusetts in 1757–59. John Adams published a series of letters in the *Boston Patriot* newspaper as one of his periodic efforts to even old political scores and elicit respect for his own accomplishments.

138. *land being abundant:* In his original manuscript TJ wrote here, then crossed out, "but I catch myself wandering from narration to speculation."

139. *a complete emancipation of human nature:* TJ annotated his copy of *Notes*, "The first settlement of Europeans in America was by the Spaniards in St. Domingo in 1493. So early as 1501. we find they had already got into the habit of carrying the negroes there as slaves, and in 1503. they had become so inconvenient, that Ovando, the Governor, put a stop to their importation. Hererra. Dec. 1. B.2. ch. 10. B.4. c. 12. B.5. c. 12. But in 1511, they were again fully in the same habit. The king's instructions at that date were 'that they should look for a way to transport many Guinea negroes, for the work of one negro was worth more than that of four Indians.' Hererra. Dec. 1. L.9. c. 5. Dec. 2. L.2. c. 8. 20." Quotation from Hererra originally in Spanish.

140. *present invasion . . . General Phillips:* General William Phillips's British troops, who had earlier invaded Virginia under the command of Benedict Arnold, led a second invasion of Virginia that began in April 1781, and that eventually drove the Virginia legislature out of Charlottesville and TJ from Monticello. The troubled conclusion of TJ's governorship was one of his most painful and embarrassing experiences as a public figure, and he does not seem to have been willing to come back to this scene of memory after the conclusion of the Revolution in order to revise Queries IX and X on Virginia's military preparedness.

141. *separated into so many little societies:* In the first state of the 1785 edition, this sentence concluded ". . . societies, the principles of their government being so weak as to give this liberty to all its mem-

bers." In some copies TJ inserted cancel sheets for original pp. 167–68 with the long continuation of the paragraph given here; the text so revised was published in the 1787 Stockdale and subsequent editions.

142. *Capt. Smith:* John Smith (1580–1631), one of the leaders of the expedition that founded Jamestown and author of *The Generall Historie of Virginia, New-England, and the Summer Isles* (London, 1624). TJ owned the 1632 edition.

143. *Spirituous liquors:* In his original manuscript TJ originally wrote "which the infecundity of their women" instead of the phrase "which generation."

144. *be found on further search:* In his original manuscript, TJ deleted here the comment, "it is true that these purchases were sometimes made with the price in one hand and the sword in the other."

145. **Smith . . . †Evans:* References are to John Smith and to Lewis Evans (see note 13). The people Evans called the "Erigas" in the text here are the Eries.

146. *infant bones among them:* TJ annotated his copy of *Notes* with, "The custom of burying the dead in barrows was antiently very prevalent. Homer describes the ceremony of raising one by the Greeks.

> *About thee then a matchless sepulchre*
> *The sacred host of the Achaians raised*
> *Upon the Hellespont, where most it seized,*
> *For height and conspicuity, the eyes*
> *Of living men and their posterities.*
>
> *Odys. 24.84.*

And Herodotus 7.117. mentions an instance of the same practice in the army of Xerxes on the death of Artachaeas." TJ originally quoted Homer in Greek, here given in Chapman's translation.

147. *Great question has arisen:* After this sentence TJ annotated his copy, "In the notes on Virginia, the great diversity of languages appearing radically different which are spoken by the red men of America, is supposed to authorize a supposition that their settlement is more remote than that of Asia by it's red inhabitants. But it must be confessed that the mind finds it difficult to conceive that so many tribes have inhabited it from so remote an antiquity as would be necessary to have divided them into languages so radically different. I will therefore hazard a conjecture, as such, and only to be estimated at what it may be worth. We know that the Indians consider it as dishonorable to use any language but their own. Hence in their councils with us, though some of them may have been in situations which from convenience or necessity have obliged them to learn our language well, yet they refuse to

confer in it, and always insist on the intervention of an Interpreter, tho he may understand neither language so well as themselves: and this fact is as general as our knoledge of the tribes of N. America. When therefore a fraction of a tribe from domestic feuds has broken off from it's main body to which it is held by no law or compact, and has gone to another settlement, may it not be the point of honor with them not to use the language of those with whom they have quarreled, but to have one of their own. They have use but for few words and possess but few. It would require but a small effort of the mind to invent these and to acquire the habit of using them. Perhaps this hypothesis presents less difficulty than that of so many radically distinct languages preserved by such handfuls of men from an antiquity so remote that no data we possess will enable us to establish it."

148. *Captain Cook:* James Cook (1728–79) explored the Pacific coast of North America on his third and final voyage (1776–80), although TJ reverses the order of Cook's sailing. Cook went north from California toward the Bering Strait before turning back to Hawaii and his death; afterward, his expedition, under the command of Captain Charles Clerke, visited Kamchatka in a second attempt to discover a northern passage between the Pacific and Atlantic oceans. TJ's library contained several accounts of Cook's exploration of the Pacific Northwest, and he may have been relying here particularly on American-born John Ledyard's *A Journal of Captain Cook's Last Voyage* (Hartford, Conn., 1783).

149. *best proof of the affinity of nations:* TJ crossed out in the original manuscript the following: "so long as a passion for forcing a resemblance between two languages doesn't lead us to those irrational distortions of both which have involved this species of testimony in some degree of ridicule."

150. *the derivation of this part of the human race:* TJ added to this paragraph in his copy, "It will be seen that in several of these vocabularies there is a remarkable resemblance in the numbers when there is not a trace of it in the other parts of the languages. When a tribe has gone farther than it's neighbors in inventing a system of enumeration, the obvious utility of this will occasion it to be immediately adopted by the surrounding tribes with only such modifications of the sounds as may accommodate them to the habitual pronunciation of their own language."

151. *the following remarkable fact:* TJ annotates his copy, "Lettere di Amer. Vesp. 81. ib.II. 12. 4 Clavigero. 21."

152. *But imperfect as is our knowledge . . . of Asia:* TJ added this

entire paragraph to some copies of the 1785 edition by replacing pages 181–84 with cancel sheets.

153. *from four different lists . . . other information:* TJ's authorities on Indian populations include George Croghan (d. 1782), a trader and one of the most important Indian agents of the time; "Colonel Bouquet's printed account" containing the list of the unnamed French trader was in fact written by William Smith (1727–1803) and published in 1765 as *An Historical Account of the Expedition Against the Ohio Indians in 1764;* for Thomas Hutchins, see note 9 to Query II; John Dodge (1751–1800) was an Indian trader at Detroit when the Revolution broke out and returned to Virginia in 1779 to testify against Sir Henry Hamilton, British governor there notorious as "The Hairbuyer." On Jan. 20, 1781, Governor Jefferson ordered George Rogers Clark to inquire into the possibility that Dodge had "been guilty of gross misapplication of what has been confided to him." *Papers*, 4:413–14.

154. *BENNETT . . . CLAIBORNE . . . CURTIS:* These were the commissioners sent to reduce Virginia to obedience to the Cromwellian parliament; by representing their signatures but not those of local Virginia authorities, TJ suggests the one-sided aspect of the assertion of parliamentary authority over Virginians. TJ's text in 1787 used the antique form "ye," which has been replaced here as "the."

155. *there loaded with imposts:* TJ's original manuscript has the crossed-out passage, "But our present object being to give only a general view of our transition from one to another form of government, and of the causes which produced it."

156. *as mere nullities:* The original manuscript has the crossed-out passage, "His first object seems to have been to make peace with his enemies and war with his friends."

157. *ex vi termini:* "By force of the term."

158. *Constitutio dicitur jus quod . . . quod lex":* "A *constitution* is called right because it is made by the ruler." "An *ordinance*, because it is rewritten or ordained by emperors." "A statute is called the same as a law." TJ's reference for the source of his definitions here is to the *Lexicon Iuridicum* by Johannes Calvinus, a seventeenth-century professor of law at the University of Heidelberg; he owned the 1669 Geneva edition.

159. *To* bid, *to* set: L1. is an abbreviation for "Laws." Hlothere and Eadric were kings of Kent; Ine was a West Saxon king; Eadwerd and his son Athelstan were kings of Wessex. TJ was interested in early English legal codes (and in the Anglo-Saxon language) as evidence for a

tradition of liberties and rights that was suppressed by the Norman conquest.

160. *25 Hen. 8. c. 19. §. 1:* Conventional method of referring to English statutes, in this case to a law passed in the twenty-fifth year of the reign of Henry VIII, chapter 19, section 1.

161. *Lord Coke:* Sir Edward Coke (1552–1634), English jurist, lord chief justice, and author of the four-part *Institutes of the Lawes of England*, long a basic text for lawyers in the English common law system. When TJ was studying law in 1762, he wrote a friend, "I wish the Devil had old Coke, for I am sure I never was so tired of an old dull scoundrel in my life." The fourth *Institute*, from which TJ quotes here, deals with the jurisdiction of various courts of law.

162. *"quod leges posteriores priores contrarias abrogant":* "because subsequent laws nullify preceding laws that are contrary."

163. *Lex majoris partis:* "The law of the greater part," or, the law of the majority. TJ's references here are to Sir Robert Brooke (d. 1558), author of *La Graunde Abridgement* (London, 1586), an abstract of the year-books down to his own time; William Hakewell (1574–1655), author of *Modus Tenendi Parliamentum; or, the old Manner of Holding Parliaments in England* (London, 1671).

164. *It is the natural law:* The footnote here refers to Samuel, Freiherr von Pufendorf (1632–94), legal scholar, historian, and natural law theorist, author of *De Officio Hominis et Civis Juxta Legem Naturalem Libri Duo* (Of the Duties of Men and Citizens According to Natural Law, in Two Books). TJ owned the London 1715 edition.

165. *not being able to collect a house:* TJ originally wrote here, "But they might as well have voted that a square inch of linen should be sufficient to make them a shirt, and walk into public view in confidence of being covered by it. Nor would it make the shirt bigger, that they could get no more linen." He deleted this when he was correcting the proof for the 1785 Paris edition of *Notes*.

166. *"Omnia mala exempla . . . fertur":* "All bad examples are derived from good ones; but when power comes to the ignorant or the less good, the new example is transferred from the worthy and fit to the unworthy and unfit."

167. *in June 1781:* TJ annotated his copy, "The delegates were then sitting at Staunton and voted that 40. of their number should make a house. There were between 40. and 50. present when the motion for the dictator was made, and it was rejected by a majority of 6. only." This occurred during the 1781 invasion of Virginia and shortly after TJ's term as governor had expired on June 3, 1781. This story of a dictator was later revived and used against Patrick Henry but was

denied by William Wirt in his *Life of Henry*. See, however, the letter to TJ from Archibald Stuart, dated Sept. 8, 1818, printed in *Ford*, 3:231–32.

168. *bellum omnium in omnia:* "the war of all against all."

169. *Our situation is indeed perilous:* TJ's concern for Virginian constitutional reform was so serious that it formed one reason for his hesitancy in circulating printed copies of *Notes* in 1785–86; he feared it might provoke resistance from persons critical of anything he wrote. For discussion of his constitutional thought, see David N. Mayer, *The Constitutional Thought of Thomas Jefferson* (Charlottesville: University Press of Virginia, 1994).

170. *toss up cross and pile:* In effect, to flip a coin, to decide by chance.

171. *scire facias:* Legal term for a writ requiring a party to come before the court to show cause why some action should not be taken.

172. *The plan of the revisal:* TJ was one of the "three gentlemen" responsible for drafting a revision of the Virginia laws, along with George Wythe (1726–1806) and Edmund Pendleton (1721–1803). See *Papers*, 2:305–657, for the text of the Report of the Revisors, submitted to the Assembly on June 18, 1779, and supporting materials. This Report was never acted on as a whole, although over 50 of the 126 bills proposed had been enacted in one form or another by 1787.

173. *Crawford:* Adair Crawford (1748–95), British physician and member of the Royal Society, author of *Experiments and Observations on Animal Heat, and the Inflammation of Combustible Bodies* (London, 1779). TJ later possessed the second edition of 1788.

174. *A black . . . will be induced by the slightest amusements to sit up till midnight:* TJ's manuscript originally had "sit up by choice" but crossed it out and inserted this wording.

175. *but love seems with them . . . and sensation:* TJ revised his original manuscript reading, "but love is with them only an eager desire, not a tender delicate sentiment, not a delicious feast of the soul" in favor of the present conclusion to this sentence, substituting a more tentative wording for a bare assertion.

176. *Phyllis Whately:* Phillis Wheatley (c. 1753–84), African-born poet whose poems were published in numerous American and British periodicals of the 1770s and 1780s and also in her *Poems on Various Subjects, Religious and Moral* (London, 1773). TJ's misspelling of Wheatley's name suggests that he was not particularly familiar with her work, although her volume was in the library he sold to the nation in 1815.

177. *Dunciad:* Alexander Pope's satiric poem mocking third-rate poets and pedants as disciples of Dullness.

178. *Ignatius Sancho:* Charles Ignatius Sancho (c. 1729–80), born on a slave ship in the Middle Passage, became eventually a protégé of the Duke of Montagu and the friend of notables like Laurence Sterne, author of *Tristram Shandy*, and David Garrick. His correspondence, written in a style that sought to imitate Sterne, was published posthumously as *Letters of the Late Ignatius Sancho* (London, 1782). TJ apparently owned the 1794 Dublin printing that labels itself as "The Third Edition."

179. *This criticism supposes . . . easy investigation:* This sentence is an interlined addition in the original manuscript.

180. *T*ŏς δŏ*l*ŏς: "He stipulated that the male slaves should pay a fixed price to consort with the females." The reference is to the life of Marcus Porcius Cato (234–149 B.C.) as contained in the *Parallel Lives* of Plutarch (c. 46–120), Greek historian and biographer.

181. *Vendat boves vetulos . . . vendat":* The previous sentence provides a translation for this: "Sell the old oxen, old waggons, . . ." The *De Re Rustica* is the only surviving work of Marcus Porcius Cato.

182. *It was the common practice:* The Stockdale edition has a marginal note here, "Suet. Claud. 25," referring to the life of the Emperor Claudius as contained in the *Lives of the First Twelve Caesars* by Gaius Suetonius Tranquillus (75–160).

183. *for having broken a glass:* TJ annotated his copy of *Notes*, "Seneca de ira. L. 3.40. de Clementia. I. 18. Xiphil. Aug. pa. 76." TJ refers here to the philosophical essays "De Ira" ("Of Anger") and "De Clementia" ("Of Mercy") of Lucius Annaeus Seneca (c. 4 B.C.–65 A.D.) and to the account of Augustus in the abridged version of the Greek historian Dio Cassius done in the eleventh century A.D. by Joannes Xiphilinus, a Byzantine monk.

184. *Epictetus, Terence, and Phaedrus:* In his copy TJ inserted the names of Diogenes and Phaedon after that of Epictetus.

185. *a problem which I give to the master to solve:* TJ originally wrote in the manuscript "a problem yet to be solved," and the revision here seems to focus more clearly on slavery as a moral dilemma for the slave owner requiring his response.

186. *Jove fix'd it certain:* TJ here quotes from Alexander Pope's translation of Homer, but gets the line numbers wrong. These are lines 392–93 from Book XVII of the *Odyssey*.

187. *Instead therefore of putting the Bible and Testament:* In the manuscript TJ originally placed this sentence as the third in this long paragraph, but he crossed it out in order to put in this more logically appropriate position.

188. *Mr. Boyle of England:* Robert Boyle (1627–91), Irish-born natural historian and chemist, was the governor of the New England Com-

pany, a group formed to support missionary work among the Indians and which also supported the efforts of John Eliot and others in New England.

189. *The present state of our laws:* The Virginia Declaration of Rights, to which TJ refers, stated, "That religion, or the duty which we owe to our Creator, and the manner of discharging it, can be directed only by reason and conviction, not by force or violence; and therefore all men are equally entitled to the free exercise of religion, according to the dictates of conscience; and that it is the mutual duty of all to practise Christian forbearance, love, and charity towards each other." The "Bill for Establishing Religious Freedom," Bill number 82 of the revisions to Virginia law as proposed by TJ and the committee of revisors, would not be passed until 1786, at which point he included it in *Notes* as the present "Appendix No. III."

190. *1 El. c. 1:* Refers to a law passed in the first year of Queen Elizabeth's reign (1558–59).

191. *De haeretico comburendo:* "For burning a heretic."

192. *Furneaux:* Refers to Philip Furneaux (1726–83), *Letters to the Honourable Mr. Justice Blackstone, concerning his Exposition of the Act of Toleration* (London, 1770); TJ owned the second edition of 1771.

193. *The legitimate powers of government:* TJ annotated his copy here, " 'Nevertheless, it belongs to human right and the power of nature for anyone to worship what he shall think best, *nor does the religion of one man harm or profit another*. Nor is it religious duty to constrain piety, which should be rendered spontaneously and not by force.' Tertullianus and Scapulum cap. I." TJ quotes in Latin from the treatise *Ad Scapulum*, written by the Church Father Tertullian about 212 A.D.

194. *Thus in France:* TJ annotated his copy, "Encyclopedie. Article 'Antimoine' and 'Vomissement,' " referring to articles in Diderot's *Encyclopèdie* on antimony and vomiting.

195. *It is error alone:* TJ annotated his copy, "The parliament of Paris forbade, on pain of death, any doctrine to be taught contrary to Aristotle's. 3. Millot. His. de France. 280." The reference is to *Elèmens de l'Histoire de France*, published in three volumes in Paris, 1767–69, by Claude-François Xavier Millot (1726–85).

196. *communibus annis:* "in a typical year."

197. *rixdollars:* Silver coin in use from the latter part of the sixteenth century to the middle of the nineteenth century in various European countries, including Holland, Austria, Germany, Sweden, and Denmark.

198. *in the form of a table as follows:* TJ had first become involved in the issue of a money unit and coinage for the United States as a

member of Congress in 1776, when he first proposed a decimal coinage, and he returned to the question when he came back to Congress in 1783–84. The issue of a money unit common to all of the states was not resolved when TJ left Congress in 1784 to take up his position as minister in Paris. Many states had their own coinage, and one state's penny did not necessarily have the same value as another's. He drafted a statement which he included as an appendix in the 1785 Paris edition of *Notes* (but not in any later edition) under the title of "Notes on the Establisment [*sic*] of a Money Unit, and of a Coinage for the United States." He also had this printed as a separate text and sent it to Charles Thomson for further circulation. He came back to the subject in 1790 when, as secretary of state, he sent to Congress a "Plan for Establishing Uniformity in the Coinage, Weights, and Measures of the United States." Text for the "Notes on the Establishment of a Money Unit" and a valuable editorial note by Julian Boyd can be found in *Papers*, 7: 175–88; text for the 1790 "Plan" and more notes can be found in *Papers*, 16:602–75. Additionally, TJ included as an annotation in his own copy of *Notes* the following lengthy comment, placed facing the table: "In the states where the Dollar is valued at 6s. the coincidence of their currency with the Greek and Roman monies is so singular as to be worthy notice and to found a suspicion that this object may have had some influence in fixing our monies at this particular point, at a time when the value of Greek and Roman learning was more justly estimated than at this day. The *Penny lawful* is precisely the Roman *as*, which was their unit, 10. of which, equal to *ten Pence lawful*, made the *Attic Drachma*, according to Pliny, 1. 21. c. 33. In the latter ages of their history the monies of these two people were interwoven so as to make parts of the same series, which were in some degree decimal.

The *as* (L. at first *Libralis*, but latterly ½ an ounce of copper and called *Libella*) = 1d. lawful.
10. *as* made the *Denarius* (X.) or *Attic Drachm* = 10d.
100 *denarii* made the *Mina* or *Pondo* = 1000d. or £4.3.4.

The denarius having been divided into fourths of 2½ *as* each the fourth was called

A *Sestertius* or *Nummus* (*LLS.* or *HS.*) = 2d ½.
100 Sesterces made an *Aureus* latterly = 250d = £1.0.10.
1000 Sesterces made the *Sestertium* = £10.8.4.
The *Libra* = 96X. = £4. lawful.
The *Talent of Silver* = 60 Mina = £250.

The *Talent of Gold* was the decuple of the talent of silver at the proportion of £10 for 1. as among the Romans = £2500.

And was the *Miliary* of the *Libra* if valued at 16. for 1. as among moderns = 1000 *Librae* = £4000.

"It is understood that the Attic drachm of pure silver was exactly our *Dram Troy* of 60 grs. The *Denarius* of the Romans was the 7th part of their *Ounce*, which is supposed to have exactly our *Avoirdupois ounce* but this is 437½ grs. Troy, which would make the Roman Denarius 62½ grs. and consequently 24 more than the Attic Drachm, contrary to the testimony of antiquity that the Denarius and Drachm were equal. We may very probably conjecture that our Troy weight is taken from the Grecians, from whom our Physicians derive their science, and in copying their recipes would of course preserve their weights which fix the quantum and proportion of ingredients. We may as probably affirm that our Avoirdupois weight is taken from the Romans, from whom, through their colonies and conquests in France, Spain, Germany, Britain, we derive our Agriculture and Commerce. Accordingly we observe that, while we weigh our physic by the Troy or Grecian weights, we use the Avoirdupois or roman for the productions of agriculture and general articles of Commerce. And since Antiquity affirms that these two series were united by the equality of the Drachm and Denarius, we must conclude that in progress of time, they have become a little separated in use with us, to wit 1/24 part as before noted.

"But the point at which their separation has been arrested and fixed, is a very remarkable one. 1000. ounces avoirdupois make exactly a cubic foot of water. this integral, decimal, and cubical relation induces a presumption that while deciding among the varieties and uncertainties which during the ruder ages of the arts, we know had crept into the weights and measures of England, they had adopted for their standard those which stood so conveniently connected through the medium of a natural element, always at hand to appeal to.

"The ounce avoirdupois being thus fixed at the thousandth part of a cubic foot of water, the Winchester bushel, of 2150.4 cubic inches, filled with water, would weigh 77.7 lb. Avoirdupois, and filled with wheat of statute quality, weighed 64 lb. Amidst the varieties discovered between the standard weights Avoirdupois and Troy in their different depositories, it would be observed that all of them were a little over or under this proportion: and this would suffice to give this proportion the preference, and to fix the standard relation between the Avoirdupois and Troy pounds at that which Nature has established between the weights of water and wheat: and the Troy grain, 5760 of which make the pound Troy, would be so adjusted as that 7000 of them would make the pound Avoirdupois, for 7000 : 5760 :: 77.7 : 64. Exactly the same proportion is known to exist between the dry and liquid measures. For the corn gallon contains 272. cubic inches and the antient liguid gallon of Guildhall 224 cubic inches. So that the system of weights and measures Avoirdupois and Troy, dry and liquid, are found to be in the simple relation of the weights and measures of the two obvious and natural subjects, *water* and *wheat*. That is to say, the *Pound Avoirdupois : Pound Troy ::* the *weight* of *water : weight* of *wheat ::* the *bulk* of the *corn* gallon : the *bulk* of the *liquid* gallon or 7000 : 5760 :: 77.7 : 64 :: 272 : 224.

"These weights and measures seem to have been so combined as to render it immaterial whether a commodity was dealt out by weight or measure. For the dry gallon of wheat, and the liquid one of wine were of the same weight, and the Avoirdupois pound of wheat, and the Troy pound of wine were of the same measure. A more natural, accurate, and curious reconciliation of the two systems of Greece and Rome which happened to be found in use could not have been imagined; and the estension of the connection, from weights and measures, to coins, as is done so integrally by our *Lawful* currency, which makes the penny of 6. grains of silver, as was the Roman *as*, has completed the system.

"It is true, we find no trace either in English or American history, that these were the views which determined the relations existing between our weights and monies. But it is more difficult to conceive that such a series of combinations should have been merely accidental, than that History should have been silent about them.

"I am aware that there are differences of opinion as to the antient weights and coins. Those here stated are taken from Brerewood, Kennet, Ainsworth and the Encyclopedie; and are as likely to have prevailed with our ancestors as the opinions opposed to them."

The authorities cited in the last paragraph are British writers and antiquarians Edward Brerewood (c. 1565–1613), Basil Kennet (1674–1715), and Robert Ainsworth (1660–1743).

199. *& e converso:* "vice versa." A valuable modern guide to the relative value of moneys is John J. McCusker, *Money and Exchange in Europe and America, 1600–1775: A Handbook* (Chapel Hill: University of North Carolina Press, 1978).

200. *So it is of the maintenance of the poor . . . the clergy:* In the 1785 edition this passage originally read, "From these articles if we strike out that of 200,000 dollars for the maintenance of the poor, and 12,000 dollars for its collection, which being merely a matter of charity, cannot be deemed expended in the administration of government; and

the 25,000 dollars for the service of the clergy . . ." This revision first appeared in cancel pages for pp. 315–18 that were substituted in some copies of the first edition.

201. *Query XXIII:* In the 1787 edition this was misnumbered Query XXII.

202. *William Stith:* Stith (1707–55) published *The History of the First Discovery and Settlement of Virginia* in 1747 in Williamsburg.

203. *Beverley:* Robert Beverley (1673–1722), author of *The History and Present State of Virginia* (London, 1705; revised edition, 1722).

204. *Sir William Keith:* Keith (1680–1749), governor of Pennsylvania and Delaware, wrote *The History of the British Plantations in America . . . Part I. Containing the History of Virginia* (London, 1738). Intended as part of a series of colonial histories, this is the only such volume; it was printed by Samuel Richardson for the Society for the Encouragement of Learning.

205. *governor Dinwiddie:* Lieutenant-Governor Robert Dinwiddie (1693–1770) attempted in 1753 to impose on the registering of every land patent a fee of one pistole, a Spanish coin worth 18s 6d in English money, in order to raise funds independently from the Assembly. The ensuing dispute brought forward the question of whether colonial government depended ultimately on the power of the British state to prescribe law for its colonies or on the custom and precedent built up in the colonies.

206. *Mr. Hazard:* Ebenezer Hazard (1744–1817), a New York bookseller, proposed in 1774 a collection of American State Papers, and at that time TJ drew up a list of items to include (see *Papers*, 1:144–49). Hazard's two-volume compilation was not published until 1792–94.

207. *11. H. 7.:* TJ's list of state papers useful for historians of America contains abbreviated references to sources and cites English laws by the customary method of giving the year of a sovereign's reign; for example, as 11. H. 7. = the eleventh year of the reign of Henry VII. Other abbreviations include E. for Edward, El. for Elizabeth, Jac. for James, Car. for Charles, W. for William, and G. for George.

APPENDICES

1. *Datura pericarpiis:* This is the scientific descriptor from Linnaeus: "Jimson weed with erect and ovate pericarps." TJ's note.

2. *An instance:* The reference is to Robert Beverley's *History and Present State of Virginia*. TJ's note.

3. *Mons. ———:* This incident is described by Cadwallader Colden in his *History of the Five Indian Nations* (Ithaca, N.Y., 1951), 17.

4. *Draught of a Fundamental Constitution:* TJ had this printed up in Paris early enough so that it was apparently included with all copies of the first edition. Sensitivity to how his proposed constitution would be received in Virginia contributed to his reluctance to give the first printing of *Notes* wide circulation, but the "Draught of a Fundamental Constitution" appeared as an appendix in the 1787 London and subsequent editions. Not the least of its radical implications was the proposal that all persons born after 1800 would be free.

5. *An ACT for establishing Religious Freedom:* This act, seen through the Virginia Assembly by James Madison, originated as Bill number 82 of TJ's proposed revisions to the Virginia legal code. He saw it as one of his most important accomplishments and included its authorship, along with that of the Declaration of Independence and the founding of the University of Virginia, as acts which he wished to be remembered on his tombstone. For the history and influence of the law, see Merrill D. Peterson and Robert C. Vaughan, eds., *The Virginia Statute for Religious Freedom: Its Evolution and Consequences in American History* (New York: Cambridge University Press, 1988).

6. *Relative to the Murder of Logan's Family.* TJ drew up this appendix after being attacked in print by Luther Martin (1748–1826), a Maryland lawyer and politician who had married Michael Cresap's oldest daughter in 1783. Martin, initially an antifederalist opponent of the constitution, later threw in with the Federalists because of his lifelong enmity toward TJ. This appendix was first printed in a separate edition in Philadelphia in 1800, and in the same year it was included as the fourth appendix to the edition of *Notes* published in Baltimore by W. Pechin. The Baltimore printing included for the first time the final two comments from John Sappington and Samuel McKee, Jr., and is followed here. This appendix continued to be printed in editions of *Notes* in the nineteenth century, and it continued to be controversial. See Brantz Mayer, *Tah-Gah-Jute; or Logan and Cresap, an Historical Essay* (Albany, 1867). For a judicious summary of the facts and of Martin's accusations, see Merrill Peterson, *Thomas Jefferson and the New Nation* (New York: Oxford University Press, 1970), 581–86.

7. *Governor Henry:* John Henry (1750–98), Maryland delegate to Congress, senator, governor in 1797–98.

8. *Mr. Tazewell:* Henry Tazewell (1753–99), friend of TJ and Virginia senator from 1794–99. Both Tazewell and Governor Henry died before the publication of this appendix.

9. *general Gibson:* John Gibson (1740–1822), frontier soldier, was captured by Indians in 1763 near the mouth of Big Beaver Creek in Ohio and spent a year with them. He is said to have married Logan's

sister or sister-in-law, who later was killed at Yellow Creek. TJ later appointed him as secretary of the Indiana territory.

10. *A few copies . . . in 1784:* TJ misremembers; the first copies were printed in 1785.

11. *judge Innes:* Harry Innes (1752–1816), federal district judge in Kentucky.

12. *Ebenezer Zane:* Zane (1747–1812), a pioneer and land speculator, was a colonel and disbursing agent for the Virginia militia in Lord Dunmore's War.

13. *John Heckewelder:* Heckewelder (1743–1823) lived among the Delaware and other Indians in Ohio in the 1770s and later as a Moravian missionary associated with David Zeisberger and Christian Post. He published important accounts about the Indians later in his life, notably *History, Manners, and Customs of the Indian Nations Who Once Inhabited Pennsylvania* (Philadelphia, 1818).

14. *Pyrlooeus:* John Christoph Pyrlaeus (1713–79), a German missionary to the Indians in Pennsylvania, left in manuscript several philological studies of the Mohawk and Mohican languages. Heckewelder was able to consult them in Bethlehem, Pennsylvania, where he lived in 1800.

15. *Loskiel's:* George Henry Loskiel (1740–1814), bishop of the Moravian denomination in America, published an English version of an earlier German-language text as *The History of the Mission of the United Brethren among the Indians in North America* in London, 1794.

16. *to be delivered to Lord Dunmore:* At this point in the 1800 separate printing of *Appendix . . . Relative to the Murder of Logan's Family*, TJ printed Logan's speech as it appears on pp. 67–68. The 1800 Baltimore printing followed the text of the separately printed appendix but did not revise the material about Logan in the main body of the text as requested by Jefferson, following the Stockdale text instead. Since the version of Logan's speech printed here in 1800 merely repeats that given in Query VI, it has not been included in this edition. Editions of *Notes* beginning with the one published in 1801 in Philadelphia by R. T. Rawle follow TJ's wishes and revise the text in Query VI.

LETTERS AND DOCUMENTS

1. *Queries:* TJ received this list of queries sometime before November 1780. Joseph Jones apparently copied the topics on which Marbois sought information, since the manuscript in the Library of Congress is in his hand. Notice that TJ reordered the queries and rearranged them into twenty-three separate queries.

2. *Chastellux:* François-Jean, Marquis de Chastellux (1734–88), soldier and philosopher, published *De la Fèlicitè Publique* in Amsterdam in 1772. He came to America with the French military forces supporting the Revolution, became friendly with TJ, and visited him at Monticello. A copy of this letter is in the Jefferson papers at the Library of Congress; it was first printed in the collection edited by TJ's grandson, Thomas Jefferson Randolph, in 1829: *The Memoirs, Correspondence and Private Papers of Thomas Jefferson* (Charlottesville), I:228–31.

3. *Robertson:* William Robertson (1721–93), Scottish historian whose *History of America* first appeared in London in 1777.

4. *Lafayette:* This presentation to the Marquis de Lafayette is typical of many such inscriptions by Jefferson for friends and scholars. It differs mostly in the more fervent expressions of friendship; TJ had known Lafayette in Virginia and saw him and members of his family frequently while he was in Paris. This copy of the 1785 Paris edition of *Notes* is in the University of Virginia Library.

5. *Richard Price:* Price (1723–91), a dissenting preacher, wrote on moral philosophy, economics, and politics. His *Observations on Civil Liberty and the War with America* (1776) brought him an invitation from Congress to assist in regulating finances. The original of this letter is in the Library of Congress's Jefferson papers.

6. *Mr. Laurens . . . Mr. Grimkey . . . and Mr. Izard:* Henry Laurens (1724–92) was a planter, merchant, and diplomat. Enroute to Holland to negotiate an alliance in 1779, he was captured by the British and imprisoned in the Tower of London. John Faucheraud Grimkè (1752–1819) was speaker of the South Carolina House of Representatives in 1785–86; his daughters Sarah and Angelina became eminent campaigners for abolition of slavery and for women's rights. Ralph Izard (1742–1804), a wealthy planter, had been sent to Europe as an emissary to Tuscany; he was a member of the South Carolina legislature in 1783–88.

7. *Col. Smith:* William Smith (1755–1816) accompanied John Adams on his diplomatic mission to Britain, and later married his daughter Abigail.

8. *Benjamin Banneker:* Banneker (1731–1806) was a member of Maryland's free-black community had a lifelong interest in mathematics and technology. His reputation as a mathematician and surveyor was sufficiently well known by 1791 for him to join his neighbor Andrew Ellicott in surveying the boundaries of the new national capital. He published his first almanac in 1791 (for the year 1792) and brought out a new edition every year until his death. Calculating the astronomical data for an almanac took more than the usual amount of mathematical

skill, and Banneker's presentation of his almanac to TJ is clearly intended to counter Jefferson's comments about blacks in Query XIV. Banneker and his Quaker supporters arranged for the publication in 1792 of this letter and TJ's reply; in the election of 1800 the exchange was used by Jefferson's enemies who tried to argue that he favored abolition. The original of this letter is in the Massachusetts Historical Society.

9. *Banneker, August 30, 1791:* From *Ford*, 5:377–78.

10. *Condorcet:* Marie-Jean-Antoine-Nicolas Caritat, Marquis de Condorcet (1743–94), became a close friend of TJ during the latter's tour as minister to France. Condorcet was a distinguished mathematician, a contributor to the *Encyclopédie*, and fervent supporter of the French Revolution. His *Progrès de l'esprit humain* (1794) argued for the perfectibility of the human race and the justice of universal civic and political equality, including between men and women. A copy of this letter is in the Library of Congress.

11. *Monroe:* TJ's neighbor and friend, James Monroe (1758–1831) was governor of Virginia at the time of this letter. A copy is in the Library of Congress, and it has been printed in *Ford*, 8:88–92.

12. *the tragedy, of 1800:* TJ refers to Gabriel's Rebellion. See Douglas R. Egerton, *Gabriel's Rebellion: The Virginia Slave Conspiracies of 1800 and 1802* (Chapel Hill: University of North Carolina Press, 1993) for a full account.

13. *Barlow:* Joel Barlow (1754–1812), author of *The Columbiad* (1807), had spent considerable time in France as a sympathizer with the French Revolution. This letter is printed in *Ford*, 9:261–64.

14. *Gregoire:* Henri Grégoire (1750–1831), a Jesuit who embraced the French Revolution and became the "constitutional" bishop of Loir-et-Cher. TJ refers to his *De la littérature des nègres* (1808), which later was translated into English as *An Enquiry Concerning the Intellectual and Moral Faculties, and Literature of Negroes*. The dedication "To all those men who have had the courage to plead the cause of the unhappy blacks and mulattoes" included Jefferson in its long list of opponents of slavery.

15. *St. Domingo:* Refers to Haiti, which had been established as an independent state by black revolutionaries there.

16. *Marshall's fifth volume:* The reference is to John Marshall's five-volume *Life of George Washington* (1804–1807), which TJ criticized for its federalist ideology.

17. *Adams, June 11, 1812:* This letter has been printed in *Ford*, 9: 355–59.

18. *Lafitau:* Joseph-François Lafitau (1681–1746), author of *Moeurs*

des Sauvages Ameriquains, comparées aux Moeurs des Premiers Temps (Paris, 1724), hoped to prove the Indians were related to the Tartars.

19. *Adair:* James Adair (c. 1709–c. 1783), Irish-born trader among the Catawbas, Cherokees, and Chickasaws, published his *History of the American Indians* in 1775.

20. *De Bry:* Theodore De Bry (1528–98), German engraver and publisher whose collections of early voyages to America were at the end of the sixteenth century an important source of information about the New World.

21. *Coles:* Edward Coles (1786–1868), born in Albemarle County, Virginia, was private secretary to President James Madison. In 1819 he moved to Illinois and emancipated his slaves; he was elected governor in 1822 with antislavery support. This letter is published in *Ford*, 9:477–79.

22. *Col. Bland:* Richard Bland (1710–76) was an early advocate of the right of colonists to conduct their own affairs. A longtime member of and leader in the House of Burgesses, he was a representative to Congress in 1774–75.

23. *"trementibus aevo humeris et inutile ferrum cingitur":* "on aged trembling shoulders he girds his useless sword." TJ quotes phrases here from Virgil's *Aeneid*, II: 509–11, where the death of Priam is described. In the Ford edition this passage is misquoted.

FOR THE BEST IN PAPERBACKS, LOOK FOR THE